EC Merger Control:
A Major Reform in Progress

Published by:

Richmond Law & Tax Ltd.
12-14 Hill Rise
Richmond TW10 6UA
United Kingdom
Tel. +44 (0) 20 8614 7650
Fax +44 (0) 20 8614 7651
info@richmondlawtax.com
www.richmondlawtax.com

International Bar Association
271 Regent Street
London W1B 2AQ
United Kingdom
Tel. +44 (0) 20 7629 1206
Fax +44 (0) 20 7409 0456
publications@int-bar.org
www.ibanet.org

ISBN 1-904501-07-9

British Library Cataloguing in Publication Data
A catalogue record for this book is available from the British Library

Cover design by Metaphors. Typeset by Data Standards. Printed and bound by Antony Rowe.

EC Merger Control: A Major Reform in Progress

Papers from the EC Merger Control Conference held in Brussels in November 2002 under the auspices of the European Commission Directorate General for Competition and the International Bar Association

Including a Foreword and Keynote Address by Mario Monti, the Commissioner for Competition at the European Commission

RICHMOND

INTERNATIONAL BAR ASSOCIATION
the global voice of the legal profession

Contents

About the International Bar Association the global voice of the legal profession

In its role as a dual membership organisation, comprising 16,000 individual lawyers and 190 Bar Associations and Law Societies, the International Bar Association (IBA) influences the development of international law reform and helps shape the future of the legal profession. Its Member Organisations cover all continents and include the American Bar Association, the German Federal Bar, the Japan Federation of Bar Associations, the Law Society of Zimbabwe and the Mexican Bar Association.

Grouped into three Sections – Business Law, Legal Practice, and Energy & Natural Resources Law – more than 60 specialist Committees provide members with access to leading experts and up to date information as well as top-level professional development and network-building opportunities through high quality publications and world-class Conferences. The IBA's Human Rights Institute works across the Association, helping to promote, protect and enforce human rights under a just rule of law, and to preserve the independence of the judiciary and the legal profession worldwide.

As the world's leading organisation of lawyers, the IBA is ideally placed to facilitate discussion on issues such as global merger control. For many years, competition law has been high on the agenda of the IBA's Section on Business Law (SBL). This is clearly demonstrated through the work of the SBL's specialist Committee devoted to Antitrust and Trade Law (Committee C). Committee C also works alongside the World Bank under the aegis of the Global Forum for Competition and Trade Policy – a group of experts who are committed to expanding the global discussion of the ramifications of competition policy for global trade and investment.

For further information on the IBA, SBL and Committee C or the Global Forum for Competition and Trade Policy, visit the IBA website at www.ibanet.org, telephone +44 (0)20 7629 1206 or email: member@int-bar.org.

Foreword

Mario Monti

Commissioner for Competition, European Commission, Brussels

The merger review process is now well under way. In December 2002, the Commission presented a comprehensive package of reform, including a proposal to the Council to amend the Merger Regulation, a Draft Notice on the assessment of horizontal mergers and draft guidelines on best practices in merger procedures. The first one is presently being discussed at the Council while the remaining two documents were submitted for public consultation. We aim to have the full reform package in force in May 2004, coinciding with the enlargement of the European Union.

With hindsight it becomes apparent that the Second EC Merger Control Conference could not have taken place at a better time. It was held briefly before the final merger review proposals were submitted for the approval of the Commission. The two days of intense debates on the different aspects of the reform, both substantive and procedural, represented, therefore, a highly valuable contribution to the quality of the final proposals.

When eminent specialists in the field of mergers – lawyers, economists, as well as distinguished representatives of the European Parliament, the Court of First Instance and several competition authorities – meet officials of the Commission to exchange well-informed views on possible reforms, they can only enrich the debate and help to formulate a better merger control system in the interests of all involved in its application.

I would like to take this opportunity to thank warmly all the speakers who intervened at the Conference. I would also thank the IBA which, along with the staff in the Merger Task Force of DG Competition, was of enormous help in organising this event at such a timely moment.

Looking back on the first EC Merger Control Conference – a celebration of the then tenth anniversary of the EC Merger Regulation – it becomes apparent that we have come a long way in two years. While the first Conference focused on achievements within the first ten years of merger control, and opened the debate about the need to reform our merger control instruments and procedures, last year's Conference looked to the future, and laid the building blocks for a wide-reaching reform that should lead to a largely improved merger control system equipping us to face the challenges ahead.

The Conference discussed several proposals to make the Commission's decision-making process more transparent, accountable, and based on solid evidence and advice. The decisions taken by the CFI before the Conference to annul three prohibition decisions had strengthened our conviction to bring reforms to this area. The discussions proved that, even though lessons needed to be drawn from these setbacks, they did not question the pillars of our practice but hold us rather to an even higher standard of proof. While we are willing to improve our procedures, we must exercise caution in preserving the essential and positive features of the existing system. We should not 'throw the baby out with bath water', as several speakers expressively put it.

In the course of the Conference we also addressed important substantive issues. It was clear from the debates that we have a duty to ensure that the words used by our legislative instruments make clear what they stand for. The proposal eventually made by the Commission with regard to the modification of the test tries to clarify, in this regard, that there should not be a gap between a dominance test interpreted from an economic perspective and the substantial lessening of competition (SLC) test. This economic approach was also applied in describing how the Commission would take efficiencies into account in the text of the Draft Notice on the assessment of horizontal mergers.

These far-reaching reforms can only be successfully decided on and implemented after an open, honest debate on the contentious issues. The Conference provided the framework for such a debate. The comprehensive reform package the Commission proposed in December benefited from it. I am convinced that it will significantly help to increase both the efficiency of EC merger control and legal certainty for merging parties, and ensure that the EC merger control system remains a key instrument in fostering Europe's economic success in the years ahead.

This publication is an extensive collection of papers and speeches provided by the majority of speakers and moderators who outlined their views at the Conference. I wish you an enjoyable read and hope that it provides valuable insight into all those subjects that are currently the object of debate in relation to merger control in Europe.

Introduction

Commissioner Monti – Architect of Reform

Michael Reynolds

Allen & Overy, Brussels

The International Bar Association's EC Merger Control Conference, held on 7 and 8 November 2002, took place at a time of great change for all those involved in merger regulation in the European Union. The Commission is set to adopt a comprehensive package of reforms to the EU merger control regime in time for the accession of the new Member states, the culmination of a review process dating back as far as June 2000.

This exercise will be the first radical reform of the EU merger control regime since the current merger Regulation was adopted in 1989 and is likely to prove to be more extensive than that envisaged by the Green Paper, published in December 2001, since it has now become apparent that the proposals made in that paper are simply not sufficient to answer the criticisms that have been levelled at the Commission by the European Court of First Instance (CFI) in recent months.

The last year has proved a far more controversial and challenging time for the Commission than the years that preceded it. The CFI's unprecedented quashing of the Commission's decisions in *Airtours*,[1] *Schneider/Legrand*[2] and *Sidel/Tetra Laval*,[3] and the stinging judgments that it delivered, have raised significant questions about the way in which the Commission treats major merger evaluations, both in terms of the standard of proof that the Commission uses to justify its decisions and the level of economic analysis which underlies the Commission's decisions. In the light of such pressure on the Commission the joint Conference gave the attendees, including competition officials, lawyers, policy makers and economists, a timely opportunity to influence the extent and shape of the reforms to be adopted by the Commission.

Throughout the period, Commissioner Monti has maintained his course and has shown leadership in these troubled times. Indeed, he came into his job four years ago in the knowledge that he would be asked to steer through some major controversial cases which had been put in the pipeline by his predecessor, Karel van Miert. He showed his mettle throughout what we now know to have been the end of the merger boom and led DGCOMP through controversy with political skill. The Commissioner took up the challenge of reform and did not at any time attempt to downplay the difficulties he faced. He has pointed out on many occasions that the reform process had already been put in motion long before the negative judgments of the CFI and flows from political as well policy considerations. He is not only steering the merger package through but has also been responsible for the adoption of the Modernisation

1 Case T-342/99.

2 Case No COMP/M.2283.

3 Case No COMP/M.2416.

Regulation which will entirely change the way antitrust law is enforced across the 25 Member States as from May 2004.

It is to be noted that DG COMP has had a particularly tight schedule in which to implement all of the reforms since the Copenhagen summit in December 2002 set the target date for accession of new Member States to be 1 May 2004.

Indeed, it was with enlargement in mind that in his closing address to the IBA's last conference organised jointly with the Commission to celebrate the 10th Anniversary of the Merger Task Force in September 2000, Commissioner Monti stated that:

> 'it appears that a significant number of operations with cross-border effects continue to fall outside the scope of the Regulation. From the Commission's viewpoint, this raises the question of whether such transactions involve a Community interest, and if so, whether this interest is adequately preserved. From an industry viewpoint, this raises concerns relating to having to deal with multiple notifications, which increase legal uncertainty as well as effort and cost.'[4]

Since the Green Paper on Merger Review was launched, it has become increasingly clear that industry in particular is generally very supportive of a 'one-stop shop' system of merger control but that there is a fundamental need for a more practical referral system.

As an eminent economist, Commissioner Monti has been at the forefront not only of administrative and procedural reform enabling DG COMP to have the tools for better economic analysis of merger cases but also he has had a great influence on the substantive debate surrounding the merger review.

The Commissioner has made several incisive speeches about the continuing debate on the dominance test as opposed to the SLC test (Substantial Lessening of Competition) used in the US and other jurisdictions and has not shunned the question of the extent to which the dominance test is an appropriate mechanism for the analysis of oligopolistic markets which in particular was brought to the fore in the *Airtours* case. The Commission's decision to prohibit the proposed merger on the grounds of collective dominance was overturned and criticised by the CFI for containing inadequate factual and substantive analysis. Greater guidance on the assessment criteria for collective dominance can be expected in the forthcoming draft Regulation.

The Green Paper invited views as to the proposed role and scope of efficiency considerations in mitigating a finding of dominance. Commissioner Monti has given some indication of how the Commission is considering tackling this matter. In June of this year he noted that:

> 'In my view it is appropriate to maintain a touch of "healthy scepticism" with regard to efficiency claims, particularly in relation to transactions which appear to present competition problems. But it is important to provide as much clarity as possible ... this will be done in forthcoming guidelines.'[5]

Finally, we have seen over the last years the commitment Commissioner Monti has shown to modernising his Services. He has been willing to take account of the need for

4 See *EC Merger Control: Ten Years On,* (International Bar Association), 2000, page 433.

5 See Mario Monti's speech: 'Roadmap for the reform project' to the Conference on Reform of European Merger Control at the British Chamber of Commerce. (Speech/02/252, 4 June 2002.)

a more flexible administration as well as increasing the right of undertakings to more transparency and to a better protection of their rights of defence.

To this end, he has pushed through a major reform in the organisation of the Directorate General as well as giving the Hearing Officer an increased role. The introduction of the Chief Economist and the Peer Review Panels will surely give the Commission what Commissioner Monti hopes will be a 'Fresh Pair of Eyes'.

It is to be hoped that Commissioner Monti will not go down in history as some in the Press would have it, as the Commissioner who oversaw the demise of the MTF but as the architect of a reform enabling the Commission better to understand the global economic environment in which it enforces competition. He has long advocated a more global vision of what enforcement should be. His influence has been crucial in this matter as is evidenced by his leading role in the International Competition Network (http://www.internationalcompetitionnetwork.org/index.html), a body that he was instrumental in creating.

Keynote Address: Merger Control in the European Union – a Radical Reform

Mario Monti

European Commissioner for Competition, European Commission, Brussels

1. Introduction

Just over two years ago, we celebrated the tenth anniversary of the entry into force of the EC Merger Regulation. It was a remarkable event; an occasion to review extensively the first decade of application of European merger control. Today, I have the honour of opening a similar conference to reflect on the challenges facing our merger control regime in the years ahead and discussing the reforms that we will propose to meet these challenges.

As you know, I took the firm commitment to submit a reform package to the Commission before the end of this year. It will be the most far-reaching reform of European merger control since the adoption of the EC Merger Regulation in December 1989. Our proposals are the result of a long period of review, which commenced in July 2000 with the submission of a Report to the Council on the functioning of the Merger Regulation, and continued with the adoption of a Green Paper by the Commission in December of last year. The more than 120 submissions that were received in reply to the Green Paper, presenting various options for reform, have been crucial for our reflection. I would like to thank warmly all those who replied or contributed, one way or another, to our discussions.

2. A comment on the recent judgments

Before describing our proposed reforms, let me briefly turn to matters which have been drawing a lot of my attention in recent weeks, and no doubt have caught many of your eyes too. The Commission, as you know, has faced unprecedented criticism in the wake of three judgments of the Court of First Instance overturning on appeal the prohibition decisions we had taken in *Airtours/First Choice*, *Schneider/Legrand* and *Tetra Laval/Sidel*. Two of those judgments were rendered just a fortnight ago, and we are still studying them carefully before deciding whether or not to lodge an appeal to the European Court of Justice in either or both cases.

I believe that, in a certain time, with more hindsight, we will say that these judgments, no matter how painful, came at a right moment. Indeed, there are no doubt lessons to be drawn from the judgments: in particular, it is clear that the CFI is now holding us to a very high standard of proof, and this has clear implications for the way in which we conduct our investigations and draft our decisions. We have taken very seriously into account the shortcomings in our process highlighted in the judgments by strengthening our reforms even further.

While the judgments were sharply critical of the Commission in some respects, they also confirmed some of our views. In *Schneider/Legrand*, the Commission's decision was overturned on account of what the CFI saw as a procedural error by the Commission. The Court did, however, confirm that the operation would have engendered serious competition problems in France. And in *Tetra Laval/Sidel*, the Court upheld the principle that conglomerate mergers could, under certain circumstances, fall under the Merger Regulation.

In any case, we should not allow these setbacks to distort our view of the Community's merger control policy. We should transform them into an opportunity for even deeper reform than originally envisaged. At the same time, let me reassure you that if the Commission reaches the conclusion that a merger is likely to give rise to serious competition concerns, it has a duty to intervene and will continue to do so. Let us not lose sight of the crucially important job that the Commission is doing here – we are seeking to ensure that markets function properly and, ultimately, that our consumers do not suffer as a result of having to pay higher prices or being offered poor choice.

3. Objectives of the reform

Let me turn now to discuss briefly the aim of our reforms. It has been our objective, throughout our review period, to substantially improve the EU merger control system, but without losing sight of the merits inherent in that system.

There are, indeed, important merits to preserve. The Merger Regulation, far from standing in the way of industrial restructuring in Europe, has facilitated it, while ensuring that it did not result in damage to competition. It has provided a 'one-stop shop' for the scrutiny of large cross-border mergers, dispensing with the need for companies to file in a multiplicity of national jurisdictions here in the European Union. It has guaranteed that merger investigations are completed within tight, predeterminable deadlines; a remarkable degree of transparency has been maintained in the rendering of decisions – each and every merger notified to the Commission results in the communication and publication of a reasoned decision. Above all, we have put in place a merger control system that is characterised by the complete independence of the decision-maker, the Commission, and by the certainty that mergers will be exclusively assessed for their impact on competition.

Merger activity has increased beyond most expectations since the introduction of the Merger Regulation. The number of concentrations notified to the Commission increased spectacularly during the 1990s, to the point where the Commission now annually reviews more than five times as many cases as in the early years, even if we noticed a slowdown in the last year. Only a very limited proportion of all these notified transactions, though, has required intervention by the Commission. Outright prohibitions are rare: the total of 18 such prohibitions since 1990 represents just under one per cent of all notified transactions. During the same period, a further six per cent or so of notifications resulted in clearances conditional on the acceptance of remedies. All the remaining cases were cleared, mostly in a period of one month after notification.

It has to be acknowledged, however, that while the current EU merger control system has performed well, it has shown some strains. Through our reform, we should resolve the shortcomings that have been appearing these years and ensure that the original goals and merits of EU merger control are preserved, in the legal framework as well as in the behaviour and attitudes of the staff that applies it. Allow me, at the same time, to underline publicly my appreciation for the professionalism of the members of the Merger Task Force and of its Director, Götz Drauz, and in particular the hard work and devotion to public service, even under sometimes very difficult circumstances.

4. Reform package

I will describe now the reforms that I will be proposing to the Commission. I will start by dealing with the substantive issues covered by the reform, before turning to matters of procedure and to the improvements to the Commission's decision-making system. I will also say a few words about judicial review and finish by briefly outlining the jurisdictional changes I have in mind.

4.1 Substantive issues

4.1.1 The substantive test

First, issues of substance. As you know, the Commission's Green Paper launched a reflection on the merits of the substantive test enshrined in Article 2 of the Merger Regulation. In particular, it invited comment on how the effectiveness of this test compares with the 'substantial lessening of competition' (SLC) test used in several other jurisdictions (and notably in the United States). The consultation spawned a wide range of commentary pleading both for and against change. The main thrust of the arguments for a change to SLC is that such a test would be inherently better-suited to dealing with the full range and complexity of competition problems that mergers can give rise to, and in particular that there may be a 'gap' or gaps in the scope of our current test. In addition, there is a fear that a broadening of the concept of dominance in Article 2 of the Merger Regulation in merger cases is at the same time broadening the category of companies to whom the 'special' rules in Article 82 EC Treaty apply, thereby potentially curtailing their ability to engage in certain types of commercial conduct.

Based on our experience to date, however, these potential drawbacks to retention of the dominance test should not be over emphasised. What matters even more than the precise wording of the test itself is, in my view, the way in which it is applied. The dominance and SLC standards have produced broadly convergent outcomes, especially in the European Union and United States in recent years, and the dominance test is proving to be an instrument capable of being adapted to a wide variety of situations. In particular, it is worth noting that the test has been successfully used to assess the dynamic impact of mergers, and has not confined the Commission to making static market analyses. Indeed, I believe that the dominance test, if properly interpreted, is capable of dealing with the full range of anti-competitive scenarios which mergers may engender. Not changing it has the additional advantage of preserving the jurisprudence that the courts have developed all these years in interpreting its meaning and, therefore, in maintaining a high degree of legal certainty.

However, with a view to enhancing transparency regarding the scope of our current test, I will be proposing a clarification of the notion of dominance contained in the current substantive test (by the addition of a paragraph in Article 2 and of further preambles to the Regulation), so as to make it clear that the test also applies where a merger results in so-called 'unilateral effects' in situations of oligopoly, a potential 'gap' to which some commentators have pointed. The clarification which I will be proposing is consistent with how the ECJ has defined dominance in merger cases, but the approach has – I think – the advantage of not linking the definition of dominance under the Merger Regulation to any future interpretations given by the ECJ to the concept of dominance under Article 82 of the Treaty.

4.1.2 Draft Notice on horizontal mergers

We should not, in my view, however, exaggerate the importance of this (undoubtedly intellectually fascinating) dominance versus SLC debate. After all, what matters most surely is the reasoning underlying our analytical approach to merger analysis. What is in my view, therefore, of considerably more importance is the fact that the Commission now intends to articulate clearly and comprehensively the substance of its merger policy. Accordingly, it is my intention to submit to the Commission a draft Notice on the assessment of dominance in 'horizontal' mergers as part of the reform package, thereby providing transparency and predictability regarding the Commission's thinking, and consequently greater legal certainty for all concerned. It is also my intention that the Commission should adopt, at a later stage, further guidance on its approach to the assessment of 'vertical' and 'conglomerate' mergers.

The first set of guidelines will be drafted with a view to setting out a sound economic framework for the assessment of concentrations where the undertakings concerned are active sellers on the same relevant market or potential competitors on that market. In doing so, it will deal with how the effect of a merger on competition in a market should be analysed, providing clarity, among other issues, about how the Commission will apply the notion of collective dominance.

The guidelines will deal as well with particular factors that could mitigate against an initial finding of likely harm to competition – factors such as buyer power, ease of market entry, and efficiencies. I consider this last point as particularly relevant.

4.1.3 Treatment of efficiencies

We are of the opinion that an explicit recognition of merger-specific efficiencies is possible without changing the present wording of the substantive test in the Merger Regulation. Article 2(1)(b) of the Merger Regulation provides a clear legal basis in that respect by stating that the Commission shall take account, *inter alia,* of 'the development of technical and economic progress provided it is to consumers' advantage and does not form an obstacle to competition'.

The guidelines should say that the Commission intends to carefully consider any efficiency claim in the overall assessment of the merger, and may ultimately decide that, as a consequence of the efficiencies the merger brings about, the merger does not create or strengthen a dominant position as a result of which effective competition would be significantly impeded.

A note of caution, however: efficiency claims should only be accepted when the Commission is in a position to conclude with sufficient confidence that the efficiencies generated by the merger will enhance the incentive of the merged entity to act pro-competitively for the benefit of consumers, because the efficiencies generated by the merger will either outweigh any adverse effects on consumers or make these effects unlikely. For the Commission to reach such a conclusion, the efficiencies would have to be of direct benefit to consumers, as well as being merger-specific, substantial, timely, and verifiable. The burden of proof should moreover clearly rest on the parties, including the burden of demonstrating that the efficiencies are of such a magnitude as to outweigh the negative effects of the merger on competition. The draft guidelines will also indicate that it is very unlikely that efficiencies could be accepted as sufficient to permit a merger leading to monopoly or quasi-monopoly to be cleared.

4.2 Decision-making process

Now let me turn to the decision-making process. The Green Paper already opened a debate on this issue and the consultation process, as well as the subsequent developments, have demonstrated that this issue is central to the success of our reform. We will adopt changes, as radical as necessary, to ensure that our merger investigations are conducted in a manner which is more thorough and more firmly grounded in economic reasoning and to further strengthen the due process guarantees built into our merger proceedings.

Let me begin with some of the most relevant changes that we seek to introduce to our decision-making process, but that do not require a change of the Regulation, only important internal changes in our organisation.

4.2.1 Enhancing the Competition DG's economic capabilities

First of all, in view of the increasing complexity and global scale of merger cases, it is clear that there is a need to improve the economic capabilities of the Competition Directorate-General. Accordingly, I will be proposing that a new position of Chief Competition Economist be created within the Competition DG, with the staff necessary to provide an independent economic viewpoint to decision-makers at all levels, as well as guidance throughout the investigative process. He or she should be an eminent economist, on temporary secondment to the Commission, thus ensuring that the holder of this post is someone with very sound knowledge of industrial economics. He or she will be directly attached to the Director General. It goes without saying that the role of the Chief Competition Economist would not be limited to his/her involvement in merger control, but would also extend to competition law enforcement generally, including the control of state aids.

I also intend to accelerate the Competition DG's recruitment of industrial economists, something that has already been a priority for some time, and that greater use be made of outside economic expertise. In particular, I envisage that we will more frequently be commissioning our own independent econometric studies in Phase II merger investigations.

4.2.2 Panel review

I intend to introduce systematic use of a peer review 'Panel' system in Phase II merger cases. A Panel, independent from the Merger Task Force, composed of experienced officials, would be appointed for all in-depth investigations, and would have the task of scrutinising the case team's conclusions with a 'fresh pair of eyes' at key points of the enquiry. This will prevent the natural tendency of all human beings of being convinced by their own arguments from determining the outcome of our investigations.

Those serving on the Panel would be chosen from throughout the Directorate-General. Officials from other relevant services of the Commission will be, when appropriate, invited to contribute to the discussions. To this end, I have charged my Director-General, Philip Lowe, with overseeing the creation of a new Unit providing the necessary support and structure to allow these Panels to become a real and effective internal check on the soundness of the investigators' preliminary conclusions. Indeed, it is my intention that this Panel system should be deployed throughout the Directorate-General: I see no reason why our decision-making in the antitrust and state aid areas would not benefit equally from such an approach.

4.2.3 Enhancing the parties' ability to defend their points of view

The Commission's decision-making process has also sometimes been criticised for being too prone to capture by the competitors of the merging parties, who, the critics say, are able to influence excessively the investigation. While I believe this criticism is exaggerated, and that it is in the interest of the Commission to listen to all – merging parties, consumers and competitors – I also consider that the merging parties should be given ample opportunity to defend their points of view during the procedure and confront the concerns of third parties at the earliest stages of the investigation.

To this purpose, I intend to allow an earlier access to the Commission's file than is currently foreseen. First, the merging parties will be granted full access to the file shortly after the opening of an in-depth investigation (ie following the issuance of a 6(1)(c) decision). Secondly, I intend to ensure that merging parties are given ad hoc access throughout the investigation to the main third party submissions running counter to the merging parties' views – respecting, of course, legitimate claims to the protection of confidential information. This will enhance even further the transparency of our procedures and allow the parties to contest these submissions at early stages of the investigation and not, as presently, only once the Statement of Objections is issued.

An opportunity should, in my view, furthermore be provided for the parties to confront 'complaining' third parties in a meeting which should ideally be held in good time before the issuing of a Statement of Objections. This should enable some arguments against the proposed merger to be given an earlier 'hearing' and, if appropriate, to be thrashed out informally before a Statement is issued.

I also intend to introduce some further discipline and transparency in the conduct of investigations, by offering merging companies the possibility to attend so-called 'State-of-Play' meetings with the Commission at decisive points in the procedure. This should guarantee that the merging parties are kept constantly updated on progress in the investigation, and that they are given an ongoing opportunity to discuss the case with senior Commission management.

4.2.4 Strengthening the Hearing Officers

A further strengthening of the Hearing Officers will also be part of our reforms. They already perform an indispensable role in guaranteeing protection of the merging parties' rights of defence and the appropriate conduct of our procedures. I intend to see to it that the Hearing Officers are equipped with resources, including A grade officials, sufficient to enable them to fully discharge their responsibilities.

4.2.5 Consumer participation

We also plan to enhance consumer involvement in our proceedings. Even if our ultimate goal is the protection of consumer welfare, consumers rarely express their views to us about the likely impact of specific mergers. We will be taking measures designed to change this situation. In particular, I will propose the creation of a Consumer Liaison function within our Directorate General, to encourage and facilitate the involvement of consumer associations which are often poorly resourced bodies.

4.2.6 Time frame for investigation

Unlike those mentioned so far, other key improvements to the decision-making process that I will be proposing will require an amendment to the Regulation. First, timing issues.

While I am firmly opposed to a general erosion of the tight timetable inherent in the current regime under the Merger Regulation, I consider it important to introduce a degree of flexibility with regard to the time frame for merger investigations, in particular in complex Phase II cases. To that end, I will propose a number of significant changes. First, I would like to allow the parties to request an additional three weeks being added to Phase II following the submission of a remedy offer, thereby allowing more time for the proper consideration of remedies, including the consultation of the Member States.

Secondly, I will also be proposing that more time (up to four weeks) could be added to Phase II for the purpose of ensuring a thorough investigation in complex cases, particularly in view of the high evidentiary burden that is incumbent on the Commission in cases where it proposes to intervene. This extra time could be added at the request of the merging parties, or at the request of the Commission, but with the agreement of the merging parties, where the Commission is convinced that additional investigation time is warranted.

4.2.7 Flexibility in timing of notification

I have also decided that more flexibility is merited as regards when merging companies can present a notification to the Commission. I propose to make it possible to notify prior to the conclusion of a binding agreement, and would, provided no steps are taken towards its implementation, also remove the current deadline for notification of one week after such an agreement has been reached. The more flexible rules should allow companies to organise their transactions more effectively without having to fit their planning around unnecessary regulatory rigidities, and would at the same time facilitate international cooperation on merger cases (particularly when it comes to synchronising the timing of investigations by different agencies).

4.2.8 Fact-finding powers

I will also propose to amend the Merger Regulation's provisions on enforcement powers (fact-finding and fining powers) to align them with those being proposed in the new draft implementing Regulation for Articles 81 and 82. I would like, in particular, to underline the importance of enhancing the effectiveness of our fact-finding powers in merger control, particularly given the very tight time constraints that we are working with. However, as I already announced some months ago, I will not be proposing that the Merger Regulation include the power to conduct home searches. That is a power which is specifically required for the detection of secret cartels: I am not convinced that it is necessary for the effective enforcement of the Merger Regulation.

4.2.9 Improving case management and investigation

Finally, I intend to see that important practical management measures are taken to improve the way our investigations are conducted. To this purpose, a post of Deputy Director General for Mergers was recently established by the Commission. For the time being, I have requested Philip Lowe, our new Director General, to take up these functions directly.

Let me underline some of these necessary improvements. We will have to ensure that there is sufficient management oversight to deal with the Commission's full merger case-load, that case teams are sufficiently large, and that they are equipped with the expertise necessary to cope with in-depth investigations. We must also see to it that due attention is paid to the quality of evidence, and to ensuring that decisions reference such evidence clearly and comprehensively. Ensuring that the staff resources of the entire Directorate-General are deployed to maximum benefit, including via increased flexibility of staff tasks, will be an immediate priority to achieve these goals.

4.3 Judicial review

Our reflection on how to improve EU merger control has also focused on judicial review. I am acutely conscious of the fact that, as with any administrative system, effective judicial review is the ultimate guarantor of accountability. That is as it should be, and the CFI's recent judgments have demonstrated beyond any doubt that the European courts provide meticulous and stringent review of the substance of the Commission's analysis in merger cases. Moreover, the CFI has for all practical purposes become a specialised competition court, exerting constant pressure on the Commission continuously to improve its level of expertise.

However, due process requires that judicial review should not only be effective in terms of substance – it must also be timely. There is clearly still some scope for improvement in the speed with which judgments are delivered, particularly in cases where the merging parties are keen to 'keep the deal alive' pending the outcome of the appellate process.

To that end, the introduction by the CFI of a fast-track procedure represents an important step forward, demonstrating that judicial review can be delivered with relative speed: the efficiency with which the CFI disposed of the appeals in *Schneider/Legrand* and *Tetra Laval/Sidel* represents real progress. It would be desirable, however, to shorten further the time it takes for merger appeals to be dealt with. And let me once again stress what I have said on several occasions before: to the extent that the Commission can assist, I am ready to advocate strongly for the additional resources that would no doubt be required by the CFI for such further improvements.

There may, however, be additional ways of further improving the timeliness of the judicial review process, and the merits of any proposal to that effect deserve careful examination. It may, for example, be appropriate to consider introducing improvements in the field of the interim measures procedure. Already now, the Treaty allows parties to claim interim relief. However, we should explore whether this procedure can be adapted to better serve the needs of merger proceedings.

It would also be useful to examine whether, for the purposes of speeding up the judicial review process, it might be appropriate to create specialised 'judicial panels' (an option available once the Treaty of Nice enters into force) to deal with certain categories of cases at first instance or to create a specialised merger chamber within the CFI.

As regards the creation of judicial panels, one option would be to create a competition judicial panel acting as the first instance court. Another option would be to transfer other categories of cases to judicial panels, thereby liberating resources within the CFI, which could then be allocated to dealing with competition cases. Staff cases, which currently make up a significant part of the case-load of the CFI, could be obvious candidates.

The creation of a special merger chamber within the CFI would also be an alternative to consider, but it seems evident that this would contribute to speed up the review process only when the CFI obtains new resources.

As you can see, there are a number of options that could speed up the rendering of judgments on appeal. We have already started a discussion with the CFI on these issues and I also plan shortly to consult Member States on their views. As you know, the Commission might play a role in advocating, or proposing, any such changes, and we will be considering doing this in due time, but it does not correspond to it to take the final decision.

4.4 Jurisdiction

And now, to conclude, a few words on jurisdiction. One of the objectives of the review is to optimise the allocation of merger cases between the Commission and national competition authorities in the light of the principle of subsidiarity, while at same time tackling the persistent phenomenon of 'multiple filing' (ie notification to various competition authorities within the European Union). It should also be recalled that, unlike in 1989, all of our Member States (with the exception of Luxembourg) now have merger control systems, as do the ten candidate countries for early accession to the Union, hopefully in 2004, many of whom I am glad to see are represented here today.

The core of our jurisdictional reform will be centred on a proposal to simplify and render more flexible the Merger Regulation's provisions concerning referral of cases from the Commission to Member States and vice versa.

So what would we like to change? First, we will be proposing a simplification of the criteria for such referral, including a closer 'mirroring' of the criteria for referral in both directions. Secondly, we would propose that referral be made applicable at the pre-notification stage. Notifying parties would make a reasoned request for a pre-notification referral of the case in either direction. The request would have to be acceded to by both the Commission and the national competition authorities concerned. Thirdly, we would propose that, if a minimum number of Member States agree to a case being referred to the Commission, the case should be deemed to fall under exclusive Community jurisdiction. Fourthly, we would propose to make it possible for the Commission to invite Member States to make referrals, and for the Commission to invite Member States to request the Commission to refer cases to them; currently the Commission has no such 'right of initiative'. The amendments to the Merger Regulation would be complemented by a set of guiding principles on which referral decisions should be based.

4.5 The package form

Wrapping up, then, let me spell out what form the reform package that I will submit to the Commission in December will take. It will consist of:

1. A draft proposal for a new Council Regulation (the new EC Merger Regulation) – with the agreement of the Commission, this proposal would be subsequently submitted to the Council for adoption.
2. A draft Commission Notice containing comprehensive guidelines on the assessment of dominance in horizontal mergers. The draft would be agreed on by the Commission with a view to publishing it for wider public consultation.
3. A draft set of best practice guidelines on the conduct of merger investigations, to be discussed with the legal and business community. They will outline the reforms that I have already advanced on the day-to-day handling of merger cases by DG Competition, in particular the Commission's relationship with the merging parties and interested third parties as well as the timing of meetings, transparency, and due process in merger proceedings.
4. Finally, we will also adopt a number of proposed measures relating to the staffing and resources of DG Competition, as well as to the management and investigation of merger cases within the Directorate-General.

4.6 Conclusion

Let me now, at the end of my presentation, take a broader perspective. European merger control policy, by facilitating restructuring but at the same time ensuring that markets remain competitive and eliminating barriers to cross border consolidation, has contributed decisively to foster structural and economic reform in Europe. This is one of the major long-term benefits provided by a vigorous enforcement of competition policy instruments – not only merger control, but also the fight against cartels, liberalisation measures and, above all, control of public subsidies to companies. By reforming the present merger control system as radically as needed, therefore, I am determined to ensure that it remains a key instrument to foster Europe's economic success in the years ahead.

Session 1

Optimising Case Allocation in the European Union and Dealing with Multijurisdictional Filings

1
Merger Review – Jurisdictional Issues

Götz Drauz*

Director, Merger Task Force, Directorate-General for Competition, European Commission, Brussels

1. Introduction

In its Green Paper on the Review of Council Regulation (EEC) No 4064/89,[1] the Commission invited comments, among others, on the issue of jurisdiction, ie the allocation of cases between the Commission and the Member States ('who does what?'). As set out in the Summary of the replies received,[2] a series of detailed submissions from Member States as well as the business and legal communities have been received.

This paper is prepared for the purposes of widening the discussion on the review of the case allocation system of the Merger Regulation. It attempts to summarise the strengths and weaknesses of the main alternatives for amendment.

2. Main objectives

One of the aims of the merger review exercise, as set out in the Commission's Green Paper, is an optimisation of the allocation of merger cases between the Commission and national competition authorities ('who does what?'), in line with the principle of subsidiarity.

In this context, it is DG Competition's stated objective to ensure that the Commission can deal with cases having a significant cross-border impact, but which are not currently caught by the turnover thresholds of Articles 1(2) and 1(3) of the Merger Regulation, while ensuring that Member States deal with cases whose impact is mainly national or local.

In line with the principle of subsidiarity, and in order to preserve administrative efficiency and the 'one-stop shop' concept – one of the main assets of the current system – the Community legislator should at the same time adopt a solution which helps to reduce the significant number of multiple filings, ie mergers requiring notifications in several Member States.

* All views and opinions expressed in this paper are personal and do not necessarily represent those of the European Commission.

1 COM (2001) 745 final, dated 11 December 2001.

2 Available on DG Competition's website: http://europa.eu.int/comm/competition/mergers/review/comments/summary_publication.pdf.

3. Solutions discussed in the Green Paper

3.1 Background[3]

Among the main findings of the Green Paper was the conclusion that the thresholds in Article 1(2), including the 2/3 rule, continue to function effectively as proxies for those cases that are most appropriately dealt with at Community level. During the consultation, respondents have broadly confirmed these findings. However, the Green Paper concluded that Article 1(3) has fallen short of achieving its underlying objective, ie to confer Commission competence over cases that affect three or more Member States.[4]

Given these findings, the Green Paper looked at various alternatives aimed at improving the functioning of Article 1(3). The main alternatives set out in the Green Paper were:

1. amending the current thresholds of Article 1(3);
2. modifications to the Article 22 system;
3. a system whereby automatic Community competence would be established over mergers that are notifiable in three or more Member States (the so-called 'mandatory 3+ system').

Before analysing each of the above proposals in greater detail, it is worth noting some general principles emerging from the responses received on jurisdictional issues. In summary, the consultation on the Green Paper has provided the following results as regards multiple filings in general:

- Very strong support for application of the notion of subsidiarity in merger control, and thus that the Commission should deal with concentrations having significant cross-border impact, eg where the merging parties are active on markets that are, or that are in the process of becoming, wider than national. Conversely, the relevant national authority should deal with purely national cases.
- Broad support for basing the jurisdictional rules on objective and transparent criteria, such as turnover thresholds, and for refraining from direct or indirect introduction of more subjective mechanisms such as market shares or the discretion of national authorities.
- Large agreement that Article 1(3) in its current form has failed to create a system of division of jurisdiction fully in line with subsidiarity, and that the need to address this issue is strong in view of enlargement and the internationalisation of markets.
- Support for at least some harmonisation of merger control rules at national level, particularly relating to methods for the establishment of jurisdictional nexus (definition of a concentration, as well as sufficient connection to the national economy), procedural rules on triggering events for notification and on

3 See Green Paper, para 21-68, and Summary on the Green Paper feedback.

4 As set out in the Green Paper, in 2000, only about one in five cases known to be subject to multiple notifications to three or more Member States were caught by the provision. In addition, a trend was observed according to which multiple notifications involving three or more Member States are steadily increasing, and the approaching enlargement of the Community to up to 25 Member States as from 2004 is likely to accentuate further the negative effects of multiple filings involving a significant number of Member States.

review periods. It should be noted that the European Parliament is particularly supportive of harmonisation.

3.2 Green Paper proposals should not be pursued in their original form

3.2.1 Amending the Article 1(3) thresholds

The first such option that was assessed would have consisted of making alterations to the five constituting criteria of Article 1(3). The Green Paper, however, concluded that no such modifications were likely to provide the envisaged results, as they would not sufficiently impact on multiple filings in three or more Member States. In addition, such modifications might have the unwanted effect of conferring Commission jurisdiction over a number of cases that are not subject to such multiple filings (see Green Paper, para 51). The consultation largely provided support for these findings. Most respondents to the Green Paper felt that alterations to the five constituting criteria of Article 1(3) were unlikely to be targeted at cases with cross-border effects, or indeed to 'catch' multiple filings in three or more Member States. Some respondents also referred to the unwanted effect of conferring Commission jurisdiction over a number of cases that are not subject to multiple filing requirements. In conclusion, the consultation confirmed that improvements to the case allocation system should be sought through means other than a complex multi-levelled threshold approach.

3.2.2 Modifications to the Article 22 system

The second alternative considered by the Green Paper would consist in making modifications to the referral provision in Article 22, with the aim of addressing the multiple filing problem. The Green Paper concluded (paras 52-53) that the possibilities for making Article 22 a useful measure of general application to multiple notification cases appeared to be limited unless significant modifications were made. The results of the consultation broadly support this conclusion. A significantly modified system based on Articles 9 and 22 referrals at the pre-notification stage would, however, involve a number of advantages. This is outlined further under 'How a system of streamlined referrals could improve the jurisdictional system' below.

3.2.3 Mandatory 3+ system

The Green Paper developed, as its main proposal for amending Article 1(3), a system whereby automatic Community competence would be established over mergers that are notifiable in three or more Member States (the 'mandatory 3+ system').

As presented, the system would have included the following steps: in cases not fulfilling the thresholds of Article 1(2), the parties would look at national merger laws in order to determine whether their transaction would be notifiable in three or more Member States. If that were the case, the transaction would automatically have Community dimension and would be subject to mandatory notification to the Commission under the Merger Regulation.

The advantages of this mandatory 3+ system would, at first sight, have been its simplicity and clarity, as it would have conferred automatically Community dimension on the basis of clearly established national laws. The system would quite evidently also have eliminated the multiple filings problem as all transactions notifiable in three or more Member States would automatically benefit from the 'one-stop shop' principle.

However, the consultation revealed a number of serious misgivings which in combination pointed clearly against pursuing the 3+ system in its original format:

- *3+ system would not catch the right type of cross-border interest cases.* While many respondents felt that such a rule, in principle, would strike a more reasonable balance than the current Article 1(3) between those cases that are of a cross-border nature and those that are not, a general criticism that has been expressed by some respondents is that the requirement to notify in three or more Member States is not a sufficient indication of the existence of a Community interest.

  The main reason for this is that national notification rules may rely on low triggering levels or may even lack reference to a specific national jurisdictional nexus. Although this has been raised in relation to certain current Member States,[5] some have identified the problem as being worse in applicant countries. Low national thresholds could result in a case having Community dimension simply because it was technically notifiable in three Member States with low jurisdictional tests. Such a case might lack significant cross-border impact altogether.

  Indeed, several industry representatives have warned that a 'mandatory 3+ system' could have significantly wider applicability than could be estimated on the basis of current statistics on multiple notifications to Member States. The reason for this is that, currently, even though a transaction may be technically notifiable in a particular national jurisdiction, the parties may decide to 'take the risk' and not notify there, if the transaction is unlikely to have any substantial material impact in that jurisdiction. According to the same respondents, such a 'pragmatic' approach would not be possible with a mandatory notification to the Commission under the 3+ system. Indeed, notifying parties would need to satisfy themselves that their deal was not notifiable in three or more Member States by checking the tests of each EU jurisdiction (soon likely to be some 25 jurisdictions), at the risk of the transaction being declared null and void for failure to notify the case to the Commission. Although none of these commentators has provided any quantification, this could imply that the potential number of cases that would be caught by the proposed system would be higher than foreseen in the Green Paper, in particular after an enlargement of the European Union.
- *3+ system would introduce unacceptable legal uncertainty due to problems with national jurisdictional tests.* Many respondents criticised the '3+ system' for incorporating existing legal uncertainty in national merger control rules into the Merger Regulation. This criticism relates primarily to those systems that base their notification requirements on market share thresholds (currently, Greece, Spain and Portugal, as well as the UK concept of 'share of supply'). Several applicant countries also apply notification requirements involving market share tests.[6]

5 Some jurisdictions have been more frequently referred to than others in this respect. Among current Member States, many respondents feel that the national rules in Austria, Finland, Germany, Ireland, Italy and the UK frequently catch cases that have minimal impact in those countries.

6 Bulgaria, Latvia, Poland, Slovak Republic, Slovenia and Turkey.

In relation to the mandatory '3+ system', such market share tests are seen as a problem, primarily as they increase the scope for time-consuming disagreement on market definition before jurisdiction can be established. As such, it is felt inappropriate to base Community jurisdiction on criteria about which the merging parties, the relevant Member State and, possibly, the Commission could adopt differing views.

Several respondents have submitted that the legislation in several Member States applies definitions of a concentration which vary from that in the Merger Regulation. Some have suggested that this could be resolved by applying the '3+ system' only to cases meeting both the definition in the Merger Regulation and in the relevant Member States.

Even though these weaknesses emanate from national law, several respondents have argued forcefully that the associated legal uncertainty would be more unacceptable under EU law. The reason for this is that any negative consequences, such as potential nullity or any risk of subsequent action against the parties for making a wrong assumption would relate to the whole (soon to be enlarged) EU territory, whereas currently the potential effects of any such mistake are limited to the individual Member States.

3.2.4 Amendments to the 3+ system would not eliminate the identified disadvantages

As explained in the preceding subsection, the 'mandatory 3+ system' proposed in the Green Paper attracted a fair amount of criticism for two main, but interlinked reasons. First, the test is simple, but also somewhat crude in its ability to target cross-border cases (some 3+ cases might not have any significant cross-border impact while others may have cross-border effects, but not meet the 3+ test). Secondly, several difficulties exist with regard to national jurisdictional tests (market share thresholds, extremely low thresholds, differences in notion of concentration, etc).

Many respondents who were generally supportive of the proposal suggested improvements to the original 3+ system. On closer examination, however, it seems that no amendment to a '3+ system' that remained *mandatory* could cure the main problem of legal uncertainty raised by many respondents. That is, as long as a 3+ system would remain mandatory, any mistake by the parties on the potential applicability of a national law could involve a risk of nullity in the whole of the EEA.

3.3.5 Optional 3+ system

Many respondents advocated in favour of an optional '3+ system'. Under such a system the 3+ rule would remain intact, that is the test would be whether a transaction below the Articles 1(2) and 1(3) thresholds was notifiable in three or more Member States.[7] The parties would first check whether the 3+ rule was met. If this were the case, the parties would have a choice: either notify in the national jurisdictions or

7 Some suggested that an additional turnover test could be added to exclude Community dimension for 'small' cases satisfying low national thresholds. Under this additional test, a transaction below the Article 1(2) thresholds, would still have a Community dimension if it fulfilled two cumulative criteria: (a) the parties had a Community-wide turnover of at least €100 million; and (b) the transaction would be notifiable in three or more Member States. Thanks to the additional €100 million threshold, this system could go some way to minimising the problem of the original 3+ system catching too many 'small', non-cross-border transactions.

make a request that the case ought to be deemed to have Community dimension and hence notified to the Commission.

One possibility in such a system might be to introduce a verification process whereby the parties' request would be circulated to all national authorities which would have a set period to verify (through a non-opposition procedure) that the transaction was indeed caught by national law. The verification would be necessary to avoid disagreement with the parties as to the correct application of national law. The national authorities and the Commission could also have a right of refusing the transfer of jurisdiction, for example by exercising a 'veto' within a set period of time following the request. The veto would be based on criteria defined in guidelines, for example on the existence or absence of a significant cross-border impact (ie where it was deemed that the case had no such significant cross-border impact, national authorities or the Commission would refuse the transfer).

The advantage of such an optional 3+ system would be that it would reduce the burdens placed on companies that currently have to seek regulatory clearance from several Member States appraising the same transaction. In addition, as submitted by many respondents, an optional '3+ system' would limit any increased legal uncertainty to cases where the parties would feel that the case was suited for treatment by the Commission; in cases where they would choose not to trigger the optional '3+ system', the current situation would remain unchanged. Indeed, by being optional, the system would relieve notifying parties of the need to verify whether their deal was notifiable in 3+ jurisdictions in each and every case, including those with no evident cross-border impact of any significance.

However, even such an improved optional 3+ system would retain many of the disadvantages raised in relation to the original 3+ proposal while also being more complex. First, an optional 3+ system would remain a relatively crude test for 'catching' or 'missing' cross-border cases. As expressed in several responses to the Green Paper, the fact that a transaction would be notifiable in three or more Member States would not necessarily mean that the transaction had significant cross-border effects. Vice versa, some cases notifiable in only one or two Member States might have significant cross-border effects and would not be caught. Secondly, by giving the parties the right to choose where to notify and hence the right to determine jurisdiction, there would be a risk of forum shopping (or at the very least a perception thereof). Exercise of veto would not necessarily eliminate this risk, and would at least create delays in those cases where corrective measures under Articles 9 and 22 would need to be contemplated. The need to have a safety measure against forum shopping could also in itself create legal uncertainty. Thirdly, an optional 3+ system could also increase burdens on parties by cumulating two tests: the parties would have to assess the notifiability of a given transaction according to national laws and also face the likelihood of a subsequent exercise of veto.

4. How could a system of streamlined referrals rebalance case allocation?

In the light of the above and taking into account the results of the public consultation, the most effective way of optimising case allocation seems to be through a more streamlined system of referrals. Such a system would be based on an enhanced recourse to the Merger Regulation's referral mechanisms under Articles 9 and 22, including their improvement and use at a pre-notification stage.

The main elements of the system would be the following:

- improvement of the criteria for referrals, including a closer 'mirroring' of the criteria for referral in both directions;
- applicability of Articles 9 and 22 at the pre-notification stage at the request of the parties. Notifying parties could make a reasoned request for a pre-notification referral of the case in either direction. The request would have to be acceded to by both the Commission and the national competition authorities concerned. The relevant authorities would be organised in an informal 'network' so as to enhance the efficiency and effectiveness of the process;
- conferring exclusive jurisdiction to the Commission if a minimum number of Member States (eg three) agree to a case being referred under Article 22;
- possibility for the Commission to invite Member States to make referrals under Article 22, and for the Commission to invite Member States to request the Commission to refer cases to them under Article 9; currently the Commission has no such formal 'right of initiative'.

4.1 Improvement of the substantive criteria in Articles 9 and 22

First of all, the substantive criteria for the application of both provisions should be simplified and improved.[8] As regards Article 9, the current wording of paragraph 2(a) requires Member States to assess whether or not the proposed concentration threatens to create or strengthen a dominant position. As set out in the Green Paper, this wording could be relaxed, so as to allow referral requests on the basis that competition would be significantly affected on a distinct market within a given Member State. National authorities would thus not be obliged to present elaborate preliminary conclusions with regard to the competitive assessment of the case. This would facilitate a speedier use of Article 9, in particular at a pre-notification stage. It should also serve to make such decisions somewhat less controversial for all parties involved.

Conversely, Article 22 would be applied mainly in those cases which have a significant impact on competition beyond single Member States. Nevertheless, the possibility for a single Member State to refer cases to the Commission should not be completely excluded in the wording of Article 22. Indeed, the initial function of Article 22 has been to provide a possibility for Member States that are unable to deal with a merger under their national legislation to refer cases with an impact on trade between Member States to the Commission.

4.2 Application of Articles 9 and 22 at a pre-notification stage at the request of the parties

The simplifications and improvements set out above would, however, not be sufficient to make the referral mechanism provided by Articles 9 and 22 an effective tool for fine-tuning the case allocation resulting from the turnover thresholds (Articles 1(2) and 1(3) of the Merger Regulation). Indeed, the current referral provisions can only be used

8 In part, this issue had already been set out in the Commission's Green Paper.

after a merger has been notified to either the Commission or the national competition authorities, as the case may be. This inevitably brings about a significant loss of time and administrative efficiency and imposes unnecessary costs and burdens on the merging companies. Practical experience shows that the delay can easily amount to several months in Article 22 cases.

In order to address these drawbacks, Articles 9 and 22 could be rendered applicable at a pre-notification stage, at the request of the merging parties. The merging parties will clearly be best placed to identify cases that may merit referral at an early stage. They should therefore be given exclusive rights to initiate the procedure.

As regards cases fulfilling the turnover thresholds of Articles 1(2) or 1(3), it could then be determined at an early stage whether a transaction could be better dealt with at Member State level. Conversely, in early application of Article 22, cases remaining below the turnover thresholds of Articles 1(2) and 1(3) of the Merger Regulation but which are likely to have a significant cross-border impact could be referred to the Commission prior to any national notification.

Such referrals would be made on the basis of a request and information provided by the merging parties. As is generally the case with referrals under Articles 9 and 22 of the Merger Regulation, all competition authorities involved would retain some discretion as to whether or not to request, grant or accept a referral. Importantly, the system should provide for short and legally certain deadlines for any involved competition agency, so as to exclude any risk of deadlock. The system should also be made fully transparent through the issuing of guiding principles.

4.3 Exclusive Community jurisdiction under Article 22 where three or more Member States make a request

Experience has shown the need to amend Article 22 in order to make it an efficient mechanism for the review of cases with significant cross-border effects, and to reduce legal uncertainty. Thus, where three or more Member States decide to refer a case to the Commission, it should be qualified as having a Community dimension for which the Commission should acquire exclusive jurisdiction throughout the EEA.

A number of the procedural rules relating to joint referrals under Article 22 should also be amended in light of the experience gained in the *Promatech/Sulzer* and *GEES/Unison* cases.

4.4 Guiding principles for the use of the referral mechanism

Ideally, notification thresholds should be based on objectively verifiable criteria,[9] such as those set out in Articles 1(2) and 1(3) of the Merger Regulation. It should, however, be underlined that the current ideas for improving case allocation within the Community go beyond normal jurisdictional thresholds. In other words, it is already clear that these mergers have to be notified in Europe, the only relevant questions are where they should be notified, and how this can be identified most expeditiously.

Having said this it should nevertheless be recognised that there is a particular need to make the referral mechanism sufficiently predictable and transparent. This could be

9 See for example the ICN 'Recommended Practices for Merger Control', available at www.internationalcompetitionnetwork.org.

achieved through a set of guiding principles to which both the Commission and Member States would adhere. Such principles may include:

- at the pre-notification stage, a '*prima facie* test' should be used for case allocation;
- cases involving worldwide, EEA-wide and/or other clearly definable geographical markets which are wider than national should be reviewed by the Commission;
- cases involving local markets or distinct national markets in not more than two Member States should, as a general rule, be reviewed by the national competition authorities;
- if parties invoke pre-notification referrals in cases that do not clearly fall into either of the two preceding categories, decisions would have to be made on an ad hoc basis. In such scenarios, the Commission would be guided by a general principle of Community interest;
- in the absence of mutual consent, the original allocation of cases provided by the turnover thresholds of Article 1 of the Merger Regulation will prevail.

4.5 Referrals at the request of the Commission

For both Articles 9 and Article 22 of the Merger Regulation, it would make sense to expressly provide for the possibility that the Commission would invite Member States to make a referral request. At a pre-notification stage, however, this possibility should be conditional on the existence of a request of the merging parties. Such invitations would at least partly grant similar right to the Commission as those currently held by Member States. It would therefore improve the mirror image and facilitate a more expeditious network-based approach to case allocation.

4.6 Conclusions

The main advantage of a system of streamlined referrals would be its precision. Unlike the relatively crude multi-layer turnover test or '3+' type tests, such a system would ensure that only cases with significant cross-border impact would be dealt with at the Community level, and that cases without impact beyond national borders would not. The system would also have the advantage of striking a balance between Community and national interests by providing a 'two-way approach': it would allow for streamlined referrals both from and to the Commission. Last but not least, this system would also deal with the issue of jurisdiction in a short time frame if triggered by the parties at the pre-notification stage. A transaction would be notified to the 'right' authority from the start reducing legal uncertainty and cost for the merging parties.

The streamlined referral system would ensure that the authority competent to deal with a given case is identifiable on the basis of clear-cut criteria.[10] The system should ensure that deadlock situations would not be possible, by reverting to the original allocation of Article 1 in case no mutual agreement has been reached within a short and defined period. In case the referral mechanism, triggered by a request of the

10 Complex criteria, such as market shares, should be avoided in the proposed guiding principles. Compared to the current situation under Articles 9 and 22, this system would provide further explanations and would thus contribute to legal certainty.

parties, would not be accepted by the relevant agencies, the normal turnover thresholds laid down in Articles 1(2) and 1(3) of the Merger Regulation should therefore remain applicable for the allocation of jurisdiction.

It must be stressed that the functioning of the streamlined referral system will require both the Commission and Member States to actively cooperate within a network of competition authorities and to make active and appropriate use of the referral mechanism. Member States have already acquired some experience in this regard as confirmed by the recent practice (eg in the Article 22 referral cases *GEES/Unison* and *Promatech/Sulzer*) and by the proposals on Article 22 made by Member States within the network of European Competition Authorities (ECA).

It should also be noted that, in order to be effective, especially at the pre-notification stage, the system ought to be coupled with an amendment to Article 22 in line with the proposal discussed above. In line with the one-stop shop principle, this should grant the Commission exclusive Community-wide jurisdiction over a case if a minimum number of Member States have agreed to its referral.

As regards the business and legal communities, it must be acknowledged that they have expressed some scepticism about a more extensive use of the referral mechanism. Their criticism, however, relates to the fact that the prospect of referrals *after* notification of a case to a given authority creates additional costs and legal uncertainties for the parties as their case will be dealt with by an authority different from the one to whom they have initially turned. The proposed amendments to the referral provisions, in particular their applicability at a pre-notification stage and the right of initiative granted to the merging parties, should therefore address most of the scepticism voiced by the business and legal communities with regard to referrals.

The EC Merger Regulation is based on the concept of exclusive jurisdiction, that is to say, a merger is to be reviewed either at the Community level or at the national level. A parallelism of jurisdiction does not exist (see Article 21(1) and (2) of the Merger Regulation and recital 29).

Moreover, the Commission and national competition authorities do not apply the same substantive and procedural rules. While the Commission reviews mergers falling within its own jurisdiction on the basis of the Merger Regulation, the national competition authorities apply their respective national legislation to mergers falling within their jurisdiction; they do not apply the Merger Regulation (see Article 21(1) and (2) of the Merger Regulation). The same basic rule also applies in a referral scenario: referrals under Article 9 of the Merger Regulation are made with a view to the application of the national competition law of the Member State concerned, while cases referred to the Commission under Article 22 are reviewed on the basis of the Merger Regulation.

Given that a given case does not qualify, *a priori*, for review by both the Commission and national authorities, and given that the Commission and national authorities do not apply the same substantive rules, the proposed system does not require legal mechanisms ensuring the uniform application of competition law.

In conclusion, the system of streamlined referrals discussed in this paper should bring about the following positive results:

- It would lead to a better fine-tuning of allocation of merger cases among competition authorities in Europe, in accordance with the principle of subsidiarity. This should also limit the incidence of multiple filings, especially seen in the context of enlargement.

- It would bring more frequent and improved contacts between competition authorities in Europe, thereby ultimately strengthening the protection of competition.
- It would allow the merging parties a more direct role in the procedure leading to a referral of their case, and in so doing create more transparency in such procedures.
- By allowing for referral decisions to be taken earlier in the procedure, it would contribute to minimising the costs involved for both the merging parties and the competition authorities involved.

2

The Green Paper on the Review of Council Regulation 4064/89: Some Comments on the Jurisdictional Issues

Alberto Heimler*

Director, Research and Institutional Relations, Italian Competition Authority, Rome

1. Introduction

The objective of the review is to assess whether in the current system a significant number of mergers with a cross-border dimension do not fall within the scope of the Regulation. On this matter, valuable work has been conducted by the Commission and is set forth in Annex I of the Green Paper. However, the picture is still unclear, nor is the evidence collected in this process unequivocal. In particular, the technical report on multiple filings does not provide conclusive evidence that mergers that have been the object of multiple filings are indeed mergers of Community interest. This is due to a number of reasons.

First, the sample used in the study is quite small in statistical terms and thus not sufficiently illustrative of the real situation. Moreover, the investigation does not contain any qualitative analysis of the actual transactions being examined. As a consequence, it remains unclear whether these multiple filings constitute cases involving a Community interest with regard to the impact of the operation on markets wider than national.

Indeed, the alleged one-to-one correspondence between multiple filings and mergers of Community interest is simplistic. The fact that a transaction is notified to more than one Member State does not automatically imply that it becomes of Community interest. Indeed a number of Member States have introduced very low thresholds above which a notification is mandatory. Other Member States have a worldwide turnover threshold, irrespective of domestic relevance. Accordingly, the filing requirement could depend on the extensive scope of some merger national provisions, rather than on the genuinely cross-border nature of a given transaction. Furthermore, it appears from the Commission statistics that most multiple filings which are not notifiable under the Merger Regulation involve only two EU countries. In such cases it may be reasonable to assume that bilateral cooperation between the two EU countries concerned could adequately address the problems.

In any case, irrespective of the statistical results, the current set of jurisdictional rules, including the referral procedures, contains some objective inconsistencies that it would be worth amending.

* This paper draws heavily on the Italian Competition Authority submission to the Commission as a comment to the Green Paper.

Moreover, the problem of multiple filings, which to date may well be overstated, in a mid-term perspective could eventually become a sensitive political problem. In particular, there is little doubt that with the enlargement of the Union the number of multiple filings involving EU countries will significantly increase. This in turn could cause the business community to complain about a system which requires companies to bear the unjustified burden to notify a transaction to say three, four or more EU jurisdictions, despite the existence of the one-stop shop provided by the Commission in the context of the Merger Regulation.

This is why it is best to leave aside the discussion over the statistical study and focus on possible improvements to the current system. The amendments introduced should be inspired by the principle of subsidiarity which is at the core of the current process of reform of EC competition policy. The reform, however, should never frustrate those principles which have made EC merger control so successful, namely (1) the one-stop shop and (2) the expeditious and effective scrutiny of cases subject to the European Commission Merger Regulation.

2. Changes in the level of turnover thresholds

It has always puzzled me why we need a worldwide turnover threshold for assessing European jurisdiction in merger control. All that should matter is that the merger affects EU markets, so a European turnover threshold should be enough. The introduction of a worldwide turnover has been justified by arguing that the European Commission should deal only with mergers of a certain size, but what should have mattered is the European size, not the worldwide one. It is probably the case, however, that companies with a turnover of at least €250 million in the Community have also five billion euros worldwide. So an elimination of the reference to worldwide turnover might not change much in terms of actual coverage. In any case it would be an important sign for adhering to the principle of local nexus in merger notifications.

A major amendment consisting of a threshold lowering in Article 1(2) would not be justified, as such interventions could have negative side effects in terms of the allocation of cases. In particular, there is a serious risk that, as a result of lower thresholds, many genuinely national mergers would unduly fall under Community jurisdiction.

There have been objective difficulties in the implementation of Article 1(3) thresholds to multiple filing cases. The major shortfall of the system has been that many mergers did not fall under Article 1(3) because the third country involved was relatively small and for that country the parties' turnover was below the thresholds. In order to find a solution the Commission has reverted to a proposal which was discussed thoroughly in 1998 but at that time was not considered efficient, that is establishing EC jurisdiction whenever a merger is notified in more than three Member States. The reasons why the EC proposal would create more problems than it solved are:

1. many Member States require a notification based on worldwide turnover, so that a merger would be notified irrespective of the fact that the companies show some turnover in that country;
2. domestic turnover thresholds are not homogenous across countries, hence the Community or national dimension of individual mergers across Europe would vary depending on the merger notification regime of the jurisdictions involved;

3. in some countries the obligation to notify is based on market share thresholds, not an easily verifiable concept;
4. the general appeal of European law is its clarity, that is the fact that the law is self-contained in EU laws and regulations. Should the Commission's proposal be approved, EC jurisdiction would be based on 15 different domestic laws;
5. the Commission would not be able to ascertain jurisdiction for a merger since it should rely on the cooperation of national authorities, but under which law would the decision of a national authority declaring EC jurisdiction be challenged and what would happen in case jurisdictional problems were to arise at the end of a proceeding?

These same objections have already been raised in the Council Working Group with respect to the original 1998 EC proposal. At that time, the Italian approach was eventually approved and, with minor refinements, became Article 1(3). At this stage I do not see reasons for a radical change.

There are, however, possible improvements to Article 1(3) that could eliminate some of its shortfalls. For example, especially on the occasion of the new countries accessing the European Union, it would be advisable to take into account the fact that EU member countries are of different sizes. This would imply providing in Article 1(3) for different turnover thresholds, to be set for each country, for example in proportion to their GNP (thresholds could be defined as turnover per billion of GNP). In this way many of the concerns the Commission raises in the Green Paper with respect to multiple filing would be adequately addressed.

Furthermore, the 2/3 rule is inconsistent with Article 1(3) thresholds because, if conditions (a), (b), (c) and (d) are fulfilled, then the merger, should it not be notified to the Commission because of the 2/3 rule, would lead to multiple notifications anyway. For reasons of logic, the 2/3 rule should be eliminated from Article 1(3). However, considering the pros and cons, it is better to maintain it so as to make the whole system more user-friendly. When checking whether a merger has to be notified to the Commission or not, enterprises know that if the 2/3 rule is met (according to both Articles 1(2) and 1(3)), the case goes to national authorities. Otherwise, should the 2/3 rule be eliminated from Article 1(3), every time the 2/3 rule applies for Article 1(2) cases, then the merging parties should verify that the conditions in 1(3) do not apply. Perhaps this is too cumbersome a system. This is why for practical reasons it is probably better to keep the 2/3 rule in Article 1(3).

3. Article 9 – possible amendments

For Article 9 there are a number of changes proposed in the Green Paper. A first simple reform is to remove the reference contained in Article 9(2)(b) to the non-substantial part of the Common Market. In fact the existing provision was never used because the acknowledgment that a market does not represent a substantial part of the Common Market would stand as a precedent whereby the Commission would declare its lack of jurisdiction, thus causing a sort of shrinking effect of the Commission jurisdiction under the Merger Regulation. Once the *de minimis* requirement were removed, the Commission would be able to refer mergers without the risk of losing jurisdiction over such markets. At the same time, the burden of proof for Member States to request a referral would be softened as it would suffice to show that competition is affected as a result of a given transaction. This would also imply the abrogation of Article 9(2)(a), which would be absorbed by Article 9(2)(b), eliminating another difficulty in the application of Article 9, that is the duty on the part of the Member State asking for referral to prove in only three weeks' time the threat of dominance.

The Green Paper also refers to the possibility of obliging Member States, in case of a referral, to follow the EC regulation procedure or to adopt the EC time frame. If the proposal were to be accepted, a Member State would follow domestic procedures for all domestic mergers, including those falling under domestic law because of the 2/3 rule, and then adopt EC procedures or time frames for Article 9 referrals only, a solution which would not create a level playing field.

Article 9 referrals (and the same can be argued for Article 22 referrals) are the exception not the rule and it is impossible to eliminate all time delays and additional filing costs. Each referral request by a Member State triggers an extension of deadlines that can be shortened, but cannot be reduced to zero. Moreover, a referral implies by definition that the parties to the transaction first have to file before the Commission, and then before the relevant national competition authority.

A system of automatic referral could be preferable, but only in principle. In fact an automatic system of referral is so difficult to implement as to become unfeasible. The objective of an automatic referral system is to guarantee that national competition authorities have immediate jurisdiction over those cases where competition is affected on a market within one and the same Member State, which presents all the characteristics of a distinct market. This implies that the merging parties, when the market affected is national, would notify the Member State. The Commission could then exercise its advocacy function, when the case is of Community interest.

However, such a solution would not be very sound since the definition of the relevant market is one of the most controversial issues in the context of merger review, leading to discussions that continue until the end of the procedure. Furthermore, the notifying parties, based on their own market definition, would be in a position to determine which authority rules on the case which could, in turn, give rise to forum shopping and legal controversies.

Summing up, leaving the actual system in place with some refinements to Article 9 seems the best option available.

4. Article 22 – possible amendments

As the Green Paper correctly argues, the main impediment to Article 22 working properly has been the lack of coordination between national competition authorities, which is in turn due to the different procedural regimes applicable in each country as regards deadlines and obligation to notify. Another problem is the lack of incentives for Member States to trigger the referral procedure.

Against this background, the first option would aim at ensuring a minimum level of coordination among Member States, a task beyond the scope of the Regulation. In this respect, it is worth noting that Member States' national competition authorities have recently formed an association of European Competition Authorities (ECA) in order to promote horizontal coordination among them. Its simple existence and the facilities it provides for coordination have made it possible for ECA to become a forum within which Member States engage in timely consultation over multiple filings. Coordination within ECA has made it possible for the first time to apply the joint referral procedure of Article 22 in two cases (*Promatech/Sulzer* and *GE/Unison*), quite an accomplishment after only one year of existence. Much of the pessimism of the Green Paper with respect to the possibilities of Article 22 has to be reconsidered after its recent extensive use.

The recent experience with Article 22 referrals has made it clear that some changes to Article 22 would make the procedure more efficient. In particular the referral should also be triggered on a formal request to national authorities by the Commission. This amendment would introduce in Article 22 a system of incentives similar to the one currently in force under Article 9, expanding the existing formulation of Article 22 that had the objective of referring to the Commission mergers that would not be analysed by Member States without a domestic merger control system (the so-called Dutch Clause), a case where the Member State has a clear incentive to refer the case. Giving the Commission the power to ask for a referral would also avoid partial referrals which frustrate the logic of Article 22.

These refinements of the current system would leave unresolved other obstacles to the effective functioning of Article 22. In particular, national merger control procedures remain highly diverse as regards mandatory notification and deadlines within which to evaluate the operation. This leaves coordination between Member States very difficult. Nor does the harmonisation of national procedures seem a realistic option, having regard to the difficulty of obtaining legislative amendments at the national level. In addition, the whole referral procedure would still entail substantial delays and costs for the companies involved, as any transaction eligible for referral would need to be filed before all the competent national authorities; only then would the latter be in a position to coordinate among themselves and possibly refer the case to the Commission. This implies that, besides coordination problems and timing inconsistencies, referral to the Commission would in any event remain a lengthy and costly procedure for undertakings.

It is true that the latter point can be regarded as a minor issue, as long as Article 22 remains an exceptional tool designed to operate for a small number of problematic cross-border transactions accidentally falling outside the scope of the Regulation. Recent experience shows that there are grounds for optimism in this respect, especially if the Commission is given the power to ask for a referral and exclude the possibility of partial referrals.

A more radical reform could entail the introduction of some elements of automatism but, as with Article 9, the complexities of an automatic referral mechanism would make it unfeasible. In fact, since jurisdiction would be asserted on the basis of a preliminary definition of the relevant market, the complexity of the matter and the legal controversies that it would entail would make such a solution impractical.

5. Minority shareholdings and the definition of a merger

An acquisition falls under the Merger Regulation when the investing companies(y) acquire(s) control of a target company. The Merger Regulation defines 'control' as the possibility of exercising a decisive influence over the activity of an undertaking, implying that under the Merger Regulation control is something wider than simple majority control. In practice, decisive influence has been interpreted narrowly, and minority shareholding only becomes relevant when it gives rise to sole or, more often, joint control.

Throughout the European Union, only German law explicitly provides that the acquisition of 25 per cent of shares or voting rights constitutes by itself a merger and is subject to a prior notification obligation. In all other countries, a decisive influence needs to be exercised for a minority acquisition to qualify as a merger. As for the United States, section 7 of the Clayton Act, which has the objective of preventing a merger from substantially lessening competition, also applies to minority shareholding acquisitions. Only pure (passive) financial investment is excluded from merger control.

In some sense the German and US systems address a real issue, even though Areeda and Turner (1980)[1] in their antitrust manual concluded that 'a non-controlling acquisition has no intrinsic threat to competition at all'. Indeed Areeda and Turner's conclusions are not always correct. In fact, as Gilo (1996)[2] explains, from a competition viewpoint a minority shareholding acquisition is not neutral with respect to the effective behaviour of the companies involved in a number of circumstances, such as, for example:

1. a minority shareholding acquisition may strongly reduce the incentive for two enterprises to compete aggressively against each other, leading to a less competitive market equilibrium;
2. the probability of collusion increases if a firm more willing to play the maverick role holds a minority shareholding position in the capital of a competitor.

This implies that minority shareholdings can entail a structural modification of market incentives and the need for a case-by-case analysis similar to that used for merger control. Under a legal perspective, the solution requires an identification of the proper tools for addressing the competition-dampening effect originating from minority shareholdings.

As mentioned before, only in the United States, where the prior notification obligation is based on the value of the assets being acquired (and not as in Europe on turnover thresholds), minority shareholding qualifies unconditionally (with the only exception of pure financial investment) for merger control. In fact the 25 per cent German threshold, which at first sight might look very similar to the US system, is easily overcome by minority shareholding acquisitions running just slightly short of the 25 per cent limit. Furthermore, the 25 per cent threshold would never be reached with companies, like public utilities, where ownership is very widespread. On the other hand, it would be in precisely those companies, should they operate in liberalised markets, where the competition problems of minority shareholding would be most probable.

Without the introduction of a system of notification, minority shareholding acquisitions could at best be characterised as a restrictive practice. In the European Union, in *Warner-Lambert/Gilette and others* and in *Bic/Gilette* the Commission found

1 Phillip Areeda and Donald F Turner, *Antitrust law: An analysis of antitrust principles and their applications* (Boston: Little Brown and Company, 1980).

2 David Gilo, 1996, 'The anticompetitive effects of passive investment' (2000) *Michigan Law Review* n 99, pp 1-47.

that a minority shareholding acquisition by a dominant firm was a violation of Article 82. The problem is that in order for an acquisition to fall under Article 82, the minority shareholder has to be a dominant firm.

Another possibility for addressing the restrictive nature of minority shareholding is to apply Article 81. However, in order for it to qualify as an agreement, a minority shareholding acquisition has to be accompanied by other convergent factors. This approach has been followed in Italy in the *Parmalat/Consorzio Emiliano Romagnolo Produttori Latte* case, originated by the proposed acquisition by Parmalat of ten per cent of the equity of Granarolo Felsinea SpA (a subsidiary of Consorzio Emiliano), a competitor of the former in the dairy and cheese markets. Indeed the Italian authority found that the minority shareholding acquisition would be accompanied by the right given to Parmalat to appoint its own representative to the board of directors of Granarolo and in a later phase would lead to closer cooperation agreements, leading to the joint setting up of all commercial policies. Parmalat and Granarolo account for a very substantial share of the relevant market and the authority ruled the proposed minority acquisition to be in violation of the national rules against restrictive agreements.

The problem with Article 81 is that pure unilateral minority shareholding acquisitions would not qualify and other conditions should be present (interlocking directorates and plans for achieving a greater degree of cooperation), as was the case in the *Parmalat/Consorzio Emiliano Romagnolo Produttori Latte* case.

On the other hand, minority shareholding acquisitions can be an important facilitating practice, for example because of the related opening up of informal communications channels associated with the appointment of directors in the board of the target company, for achieving a non-cooperative collusive equilibrium in an oligopolistic setting. Indeed the Commission, both in the *Kali und Saltz* and in the *Gencor/Lonhro* decisions, pointed out that minority shareholdings were an important facilitating practice, together with other structural market characteristics, for achieving a collusive market equilibrium.

Now, if collective dominance is a way of prohibiting mergers that are likely to result in a collusive market equilibrium, irrespective of whether the collusion is tacit or explicit, then the same should hold for any structural facilitating practice that, short of a merger, would lead a tight oligopoly to the same collusive equilibrium. In fact, for example, if in a tight and stable oligopoly a potential maverick were to acquire a minority interest in one of its competitors, this acquisition, which could strongly reduce competition in the relevant market, should be analysed as a merger. In fact such a minority acquisition cannot by itself be considered a violation of Article 81 because it effectively originates from unilateral action, not from an agreement. At the same time, it cannot be considered a violation of Article 82 because there is no dominance.

In the current legal system there are no other viable solutions than making a minority shareholding acquisition subject to prior control, ie treating it like a merger. Indeed if divesting a minority interest in a competitor can be a viable remedy for a merger otherwise leading to joint dominance, then it is necessary to complete the picture and also consider the possibility that a minority shareholding acquisition might lead by itself to joint dominance.

Of course such a move would require a change in the notification criteria and the introduction of an additional asset or capital share-based threshold disjoined from the acquisition of a decisive influence. With such an addition, all structural modifications could be analysed under the Merger Regulation with common procedures and instruments. However, unlike traditional mergers, the analysis of partial ownership requires an assessment of the influence partial owners have over the corporation and also, as Salop and O'Brien (1999)[3] indicate, 'how this influence translates into competitive effects'.

Changing the notification system by adding an asset-based dimension is a major change, however, and is probably a bit premature at this stage. As an initial way of addressing the issue, a German-type approach, with a specified share of control to be added to the definition of a concentration in Article 3, could certainly be considered.

3 Daniel P O'Brien and Steven C Salop, 1999, 'Competitive effects of partial ownership: Financial interest and corporate control' (2000) 67 *Antitrust Law Journal* 559-614.

3
Optimising Case Allocation in the European Union and Dealing with Multijurisdictional Filings

Kurt Stockmann

Vice-President, Bundeskartellamt, Bonn

1. Multijurisdictional filings

The principle ultimately deciding on the delimitation of jurisdiction between the Commission and Member States is the principle of subsidiarity as laid down in Article 5 of the Treaty. Article 5 rules that the Commission may act only as far as the aim of protecting effective competition in the European Union cannot satisfactorily be attained at the level of Member States. This general principle has been taken into account in the Merger Regulation. According to Article 1(1) of the Merger Regulation, exclusive jurisdiction of the Commission in merger cases is established only if the case has a 'Community dimension'. As Article 1(1) of the Merger Regulation itself does not define the notion of 'Community dimension', Article 1(2) and (3) introduce turnover thresholds at which a Community dimension is presumed to exist. The Bundeskartellamt agrees with the Commission that the two-thirds rule in Article 1(2)(b) of the Merger Regulation is both effective and in conformity with the principle of subsidiarity. Accordingly, it should be retained as it stands. The thresholds, however, should be reviewed from time to time to take account of both the growth of national products and inflation as both lead to a factual lowering of thresholds. Such adaptation of thresholds would also prevent a further increase of the already tremendous workload of the Commission. This consideration may become the more important as recent decisions of the Court of First Instance seem to indicate, that individual merger cases may require more input in terms of the Commission's resources than previously thought.

A permanent subject of discussion and controversy between the Commission and Member States is Article 1(3) of the Merger Regulation. In its Green Paper,[1] the Commission stated that this rule has failed to meet its purpose, which the Commission held was to prevent multijurisdictional filings and to establish Community jurisdiction in all cases in which filing under national law would be required in at least three Member States. In general, the Commission argued, such cases by their very nature had a Community dimension. At the same time, it appeared necessary in view of the enlargement of the European Union to reduce the administrative burden of enterprises engaged in mergers. In this context, the Commission took up a proposal

1 Green Paper on the Review of Council Regulation (EEC) No 4064/89, 11 December 2001, COM (2201) 745/6 final.

from its 1996 Green Book to substitute Article 1(3) of the Merger Regulation in its present form by a rule establishing automatic and exclusive jurisdiction of the Commission in all cases in which a merger project would have to be filed in at least three Member States. In this sense, the rule would have established a Community dimension of such cases independent from turnover thresholds.

The Bundeskartellamt – and others[2] – disagreed with this proposal for a number of reasons. There is no point now in returning to these objections in detail as the Commission has in the meantime abandoned its proposal. As the main considerations may possibly be relevant in future discussions, they shall be briefly mentioned. First, in view of the Office, filing requirements in at least three Member States in light of the principle of subsidiarity are not a meaningful criterion to establish a Community dimension of a merger. The purpose of national merger control is generally to protect competitive structures within the Member States concerned and therefore to establish control criteria at a reasonably low level. Accordingly, the fact alone that a merger project meets filing requirements in three Member States does not allow an assumption that it would necessarily produce substantial cross-border effects. Furthermore, such rule would not alleviate the administrative burden of enterprises involved in the project. On the contrary: in addition to the information requirements under Form CO, enterprises would have to submit information on difficult criteria such as market shares, and why and where filing requirements existed under which national laws before Community jurisdiction would be finally established. In the end, there would have been increased legal uncertainty over jurisdiction. Another suggestion to be mentioned in this context is the introduction of an optional 'three-country rule'. This appeared likewise unacceptable, and was rightly rejected by the Commission, as it would have allowed participating enterprises to choose between control by the Community and by the countries in which there were filing requirements. Such open invitation to forum shopping would have become even more attractive after the enlargement of the European Union.

For these and other reasons, the Bundeskartellamt welcomes the abandonment of the original proposal to substitute Article 1(3) of the Merger Regulation by a 'three-country rule'. The question remains of how to solve the problems rightly associated with this provision and those connected with multijurisdictional filings, problems which, although sometimes overstated, cannot be denied. One of the options discussed at present and proposed by the Commission is to retain Article 1(3) of the Merger Regulation in its original form and to simplify at the same time rules on referral to Member States and to the Commission in Articles 9 and 22 of the Merger Regulation. The Bundeskartellamt agrees with the Commission that both Articles 9 and 22 of the Merger Regulation should be modified in order to allow for a finer tuning in the allocation of merger case jurisdiction under procedures providing predictability and legal certainty. In line with the principle of subsidiarity, jurisdiction should be with the authority best suited and equipped to handle the case.

2 See, eg Duncan Sinclair, 'Reflections on the European Commission's Proposal to Amend the Jurisdictional Test in the Merger Regulation: A Hall of Mirrors?' [2002] ECLR 326, and Morten Broberg, 'Muddying the Clear Waters: On the Commission's Proposal for a New Delimitation of Jurisdiction in the Field of Merger Control' [2002] ECLR 429.

2. Referral to Member States

Article 9(2) of the Merger Regulation contains two different rules according to which the Commission may refer a merger to the competent competition authority of a Member State. First, Article 9(2)(b) of the Merger Regulation introduced in 1998 provides for a referral to a Member State if the merger affects competition in this Member State on a distinct market which does not constitute a substantial part of the Common Market. This new rule has had no practical impact so far, probably in the first place because of the extremely wide interpretation of 'substantial part of the Common Market' by the Commission.[3] Of greater practical importance have been referrals according to Article 9(2)(a) of the Merger Regulation, although this rule has also been applied very cautiously by the Commission. This provision allows for referrals where a merger threatens to create or strengthen a dominant position as a result of which effective competition would be substantially impeded in a Member State on a distinct market constituting a substantial part of the Common Market. In most of the cases in which the Commission has applied this rule, markets affected were regional or even local, so that Article 9(2)(b) of the Merger Regulation would have been a more appropriate basis for referral.

The Bundeskartellamt welcomes the Commission's intention to reform Article 9 of the Merger Regulation, which, in our view, has been too narrowly construed by the Commission and too reluctantly applied in the past, but also, by the way, too reluctantly invoked by Member States. One major difficulty of Member States had been, for instance, to show within a very short time the threat of the creation or strengthening of a dominant position. The Commission's proposal to alleviate the burden of proof in this regard and to require only a showing of substantial effects on a distinct market within the Member State concerned certainly goes in the right direction. This and further modifications could help to make out of Article 9 of the Merger Regulation a genuine instrument of case allocation in line with the principle of subsidiarity and of a genuine decentralisation safeguarding that cases of only limited geographical or even local significance within Member States are dealt with at that level.[4]

3. Referral to the Commission

Referrals under Article 22 of the Merger Regulation were initially introduced in order to allow Member States having no merger control of their own to refer merger cases affecting national markets to the Commission. In 1998, Article 22 of the Merger Regulation was amended in order to allow Member States also to jointly refer a case to the Commission. Such an option seemed particularly appropriate in multinational cases for which only a uniform solution appeared acceptable and where, accordingly

3 According to Article 2(3) of the Merger Regulation only such mergers may be declared incompatible with the Common Market which affect competition in the Common Market or a substantial part thereof. In regard to mergers affecting only markets not falling under these qualifications, the Commission has no such powers.

4 See Sinclair, n 2 above, at 330.

conditions and obligations also have to be uniform. Unfortunately, the revised law so far has not had the necessary corrective impact.[5] Failing to accomplish this purpose seems to be mainly the consequence of unclear terms in the law. On the other hand, goodwill on all sides and the determination to improve case allocation between the Commission and Member States, assisted by the network of European Competition Authorities (ECA), may already lead to satisfactory results. This still modest optimism is supported by the first referral cases, both less than a year ago, of *Promatech/Sulzer*[6] (involving seven Member States) and *GEES/Unison*[7] under Article 22 of the Merger Regulation.

One of the options proposed by the Commission would provide its automatic jurisdiction for entire merger projects if referral requests have been submitted by at least three Member States (the 'three requests rule'). In the view of the Bundeskartellamt, this idea merits consideration. One substantial advantage would be to clarify swiftly the question of jurisdiction. A risk involved in a purely 'mechanical' referral rule of this kind would be, however, that cases referred under it are not of a Community dimension. In fact, it could lead, under certain circumstances, to paradox results.[8] Thus, eg, a minority of three out of 15, perhaps soon 25, Member States could establish Community jurisdiction although a majority of (even of affected) Member States finds the conditions for a referral are not met and objects. Also, referrals could be effected in cases where the main competitive impact is in a Member States disagreeing with the referral. Obviously, in such a case the three Member States could establish exclusive Community jurisdiction and thereby cause the Member State mainly affected to require referral under Article 9 of the Merger Regulation. Besides the arbitrariness of such procedure, the inevitable delays it would cause advocate for less mechanical procedures. In particular, the new rule should define more clearly under which substantive circumstances such jurisdiction should exist. In my view, one indispensable amendment would be to make sure that the Member State (or States) economically and competitively most affected are among those referring a case to the Commission. One criterion possibly to be used in this context is the tested and functioning two-thirds rule of Article 1(2) of the Merger Regulation. That would mean that a joint referral would only establish an exclusive jurisdiction of the Commission if the referring Member States account for at least two-thirds of the participating enterprises aggregated Community-wide turnover. Another solution worthwhile considering could be to use a percentage criterion relating to the Community-wide turnover of participating enterprises in the referring Member States.

A further modification contemplated by the Commission[9] in this context would introduce a provision to Article 22 of the Merger Regulation allowing the Commission to invite Member States to refer a case. If the Member State concerned does not within a certain period of time oppose this invitation, this non-opposition should be treated as

5 A certain scepticism regarding the sufficiency of Article 22(3) of the Merger Regulation as it currently stands to deal satisfactorily with multijurisdictional merger cases is insofar quite understandable, see Sinclair, n 2 above, at 327 *et seq.*
6 Case COMP/M.2698, OJ 2002 C 61/04.
7 Case COMP/M.2738, OJ 2002 C 72/04.
8 Substantial objections have also been raised by Denmark, Finland, France, Spain and the United Kingdom.
9 Green Paper, para 60.

a referral. I don't think that this is an acceptable solution. A deviation from the regular lines delimiting jurisdiction between Member States and the Commission requires an explicit will of the Member State concerned. Thus, the only acceptable interpretation of the non-reaction of a Member State would be to treat it as a refusal to submit a request for referral, thereby confirming regular jurisdiction.

4. Referral on the initiative of enterprises

Another modification contemplated with the aim to determine swiftly and without bureaucracy which authority should have jurisdiction in a merger case would introduce a provision allowing enterprises to initiate referrals in the pre-notification phase both in Articles 9 and 22 of the Merger Regulation. Such a possibility is not completely unacceptable, and has obvious advantages, ie to involve the undertakings participating in the merger at an early stage in the search for the most adequate and efficient forum. On the other hand, it obviously also implies certain risks. The most important one appears to be forum shopping. To some extent this risk would be reduced if the initiative of enterprises to initiate referrals would be limited to the phase before the first filing of the merger project in one of the Member States having jurisdiction, thereby preventing enterprises from sounding out the position of the authority addressed and, if it is negative, instead of continuing the filings initiate a referral to the Commission. Another difficulty connected with this suggestion derives from the fact that any decision on a referral in this early phase will have to be based primarily on the facts submitted by participating enterprises. For all these reasons, the suggestion merits contemplation but also requires further in-depth examination.

5. Cooperation within the network of ECA

A device explicitly to be mentioned in this context is the network of European Competition Authorities (ECA) established in April 2001 by the competition authorities of the European Economic Area, the European Commission and the EFTA Surveillance Authority. The purpose of this network is to intensify and facilitate cooperation between the authorities involved. In the field of merger control, the network has, among others, introduced an information system in which national authorities inform each other about cases requiring multijurisdictional filings. Based on the experience of the first year, the network adopted a Procedures Guide in April 2002. On the whole, it may be stated already now that the network has substantially enforced and intensified cooperation between the authorities involved, a fact that is illustrated by the joint referral requests in the cases *Promatech/Sulzer* and *GEES/Unison.*[10] I think there is reason to be optimistic as to the role this network will play in the future in optimising merger case allocation in Europe and alleviating problems connected with multijurisdictional issues.

6. Summary

The Bundeskartellamt follows with great sympathy the Commission's efforts to improve merger case allocation and to better deal with multiple filings of merger

10 See nn 3 and 4.

projects. We think that the risks of some of the measures presently discussed can be adequately dealt with and that a workable mechanism acceptable under the principle of subsidiarity can be established, allowing mergers to be handled at the most appropriate level in an effective, efficient, fair and transparent manner.

4
Dealing with Multijurisdictional Merger Filings

Hans Peter Frick

Senior Vice-President and Group General Counsel, Nestlé, Vevey

Felix Kühlmann*

Legal Counsel, Nestlé, Vevey

1. Introduction

It is well known that multinational companies often have to notify an acquisition in many jurisdictions. Some of these notifications lead to different results in high-profile cases on either side of the Atlantic, as was the case with the *GE/Honeywell* decision, and are followed by a wave of publications discussing the implications for future cases. The resulting difficulties are obvious and will not be dealt with here. In most cases, however, companies face high costs in terms of external spending and management time even where there are no competition concerns. We will describe the practical difficulties a multinational company now faces and propose some solutions that would ease the company's burden without leading to less scrutiny on substantive issues.

2. First steps – collecting data

The increasing number of jurisdictions with pre-merger notification systems leads to an ever-increasing amount of data that needs to be collected before decisions on M&A projects can be made. Multinational companies have to collect turnover figures per country of the target, market shares and information on subsidiaries and physical presence to decide whether notifications will be necessary and to determine the chances of success.

In information memoranda the information is usually limited to the most important countries and countries with subsidiaries. Detailed information is not made available due to confidentiality and sometimes because the target does not even have such data. Obtaining the necessary information is particularly time consuming if the target is using third party importers for some countries.

Additional problems arise when the target is using several channels to sell its products in a given country for different products, eg a third-party distributor and a subsidiary or sales offices. The result of this exercise is typically a list of countries where further investigation is necessary.

* Both authors express their personal views.

3. Second step – filing?

The second step couples the practical difficulties with additional legal ones for the countries that base an obligation to notify on market share tests or that have broad thresholds that do not require a significant impact on the local market to trigger a notification.

For these countries relevant markets have to be defined and the impact has to be assessed, without access to local business people – due to confidentiality obligations – who know the situation best.

As relevant markets are often not in line with business reporting systems, estimates have to be obtained to understand whether the joint market share is close to the threshold. If market shares are close to the threshold, a detailed analysis might be necessary even before or immediately after signing the deal. The exercise is similar to a merger notification but unfortunately with less enthusiastic support from business people.

If market shares are low, an assessment of the potential local effects of a transaction is necessary. The local effects test is used by most antitrust authorities to determine whether they have jurisdiction in cases that occur abroad.

In some countries the national laws include a provision explicitly requiring local effects, in other countries it can be inferred from provisions of the law or from the practice of the authorities. To indicate the wide array here are some examples:

- in Germany an explicit provision in the law requires local effects;
- in Finland the law requires that the parties be engaged in business;
- in the Czech Republic it can be inferred from the practice and publications from the authorities that a physical presence of both parties and a combined market share in excess of ten per cent is required;
- some authorities simply refuse to take this criterion into account; for example, the European Commission requires a notification whenever the turnover thresholds are met without reference to any other criterion.[1]

As the local effects test originates in public international law it is far from clear where the limits are. Discussing the question with the authorities does not help as it leads to the request for a notification. For practical purposes a risk assessment is therefore what is usually needed and therefore made, based on local commercial activity and the visibility of the acquisition.

The result of this exercise and additional discussions with local lawyers for borderline cases lead to a list of countries where filing is necessary.

4. Costs are often not linked to competitive issues

The prohibition of mergers that are impeding competition in the market is a justified aim but the costs of the system have to be taken into account. Over-deterrence and under-enforcement need to be balanced against transaction costs. Avoidable bureau-

1 One might have second thoughts about the compatibility with international law as interpreted by the Court of First Instance in *Gencor/Lonrho* (Case T-102/96, [1999] ECR II-00753, § 90) where the Court required an immediate and substantial effect within the European Union and accordingly whether this decision is legal in cases of joint ventures that are contractually limited to a territory outside the European Economic Area for parties that do not and will not export any products to the EEA.

cracy should therefore be avoided to ensure efficient allocation of resources by the authorities and to avoid burdening companies unnecessarily. This is not only a sound policy option but also a legal requirement as it has to be borne in mind that companies are free to merge as this is protected by the parties' freedom to use their property as they wish.[2] This freedom is of course limited by a sound antitrust policy, and serious problems for the structure of a market justify such a far-reaching limitation as a blocking of a merger. Nevertheless, any such limitation has to be proportional to the target and this requires not only that blocking decisions be well founded but also that the process is structured in such a way as to limit the burden to a minimum.

In many instances this is not the case. Some of the most evident but costly difficulties that arise in unproblematic merger cases will be explained below.

4.1 Filing requirements

In view of the aims of competition policy, a notification requirement should be limited to situations that are likely to require closer scrutiny. In addition, the threshold should be easy to assess and ensure that a merger is dealt with in the countries with potential issues. Unfortunately, that is often not the case. Many countries extend their jurisdictions as far as possible.

As a result, a filing is often not necessary in the country where both companies have a significant[3] presence, but in several other countries. Thresholds that are unsuited to meet the described test are not limited to countries with new merger regimes – within the EU/EC, Austria, Denmark, Finland, Germany, Ireland, Italy and Portugal do not meet the described test as they do not require a significant turnover of both companies (target and buyer) in the territory. The same applies to some candidate countries/future member states like the Czech Republic, Malta, the Slovak Republic and Slovenia.

The situation is worse for joint ventures, as the turnover that is taken into account is usually the group turnover. Notification requirements can therefore be triggered even for jurisdictions that require a minimum turnover in the territory for all companies involved in cases that have strictly no effect in the territory if (at least) two founding companies meet the turnover threshold irrespective of the activities of the joint venture.

Under the EC merger regime, a joint venture that is created by two companies that meet the thresholds themselves triggers a notification, even if there is no turnover in the territory and the territory is explicitly excluded from the scope of the joint venture. Theoretically, the formation of a joint staff canteen in Guatemala between two multinational companies needs to be notified in Brussels.[4] Experience shows that the practice is not too far from this theoretical situation, as the European Commission requests a notification even if the territory is explicitly excluded or in cases of start-up businesses that are new for both founders. The difficulties created by this interpretation are exacerbated by the reluctance of case handlers in the European Commission to grant waivers from information requirements.

2 *Cf* Articles 6, 15, 16, and 17 of the Charter of Fundamental Rights of the European Union, OJ 2000 C 364/1.

3 This does not mean that there is an issue. It is only meant that both companies ship more then one container of goods per year to that country.

4 If it is considered as a full function joint venture.

This extensive interpretation is taken up by other (European) jurisdictions that follow the European Commission's example. Some competition authorities interpret the provision in their laws in such a way as to be able to catch the same cases even though these laws are better suited to catch the relevant cases.

The Swiss merger ordinance, for example, requires that existing activities of at least one of the founding companies be brought into the joint venture. The Competition Commission has interpreted the provision in such a way that it is hardly noticeable to be in line with the EC approach. This is most unfortunate as the Swiss provision seems to be well suited to catch joint ventures that are potentially anti-competitive and only those, as an increase of market power seems to be only possible in cases where at least one of the companies was active in a relevant market. Otherwise the joint venture enters a new market and creates additional competition and one would usually interpret this as a positive effect. An anti-competitive effect is hard to imagine and would probably result from the effect on the behaviour of the parents that is governed by general antitrust provisions.

4.2 Unnecessary formalities in a notification process

Ideally, formalities should be kept to a minimum and information and document production be limited to the strictly necessary to understand the competitive situation. This is unfortunately rarely the case. The most flagrant (and most costly) example is the United States with vast requests for document production.[5] But there are examples in Europe as well, especially in countries with relatively new antitrust authorities. Typical problems are translation of documents not containing market-related information, legalisation/notarisation of documents and excerpts from company registers.

4.3 Broad information requests

In many instances, information requests and notification forms include data that are not necessary for the purpose at hand. Flexibility in this respect could ease the burden significantly and correct the over-deterrence due to unsuitable notification thresholds to a certain extent. If the authorities would not require a formal notification based on a lengthy form (like Form C/O) in every case, the burden of companies could be eased. Unfortunately, many authorities such as the European Commission require a full set of data even if it is clear that the case is not problematic. Some notable exceptions exist of course, like the Federal Cartel Office (Bundeskartellamt) in Germany.

4.4 Unreasonable questions

Unfortunately, many authorities do not limit themselves to asking questions that are linked to market conditions or request more information than necessary even in cases which are not problematic. Obviously, antitrust authorities need information to decide a case and this information has to be correct. It is also obvious that the authorities need detailed information on the relevant/affected markets in critical cases.

5 The FTC announced changes to the process on 11 December 2002. It remains to be seen what the practical results will be.

The notification process seems often to be used as a 'fishing expedition'. Some of the questions that are not related to competitive conditions on the market are contained in national notification forms, others are asked during the procedure. Practical examples are questions relating to products such as soups, seasonings and coffee in an acquisition where the parties had no overlapping activities, the markets were national and the target only sold frozen food and ice cream, or questions on the impact of an acquisition on local production and workforce or on imports and exports for product categories that are not affected by the merger.

All of these questions add to the workload of the parties, but in addition they undermine the credibility of the authorities as the lawyers and business people involved second-guess the reasons for these questions.

5. Compliance cost could be significantly reduced

The compliance cost for companies could be significantly reduced by applying the principle of proportionality and limiting notifications and information requests to those strictly necessary for the enforcement of competition laws.

5.1 By using appropriate thresholds

Turnover thresholds should always include a national component for at least two parties to a transaction – no joint national turnover. Theoretically this could (and probably should) be the only threshold, as worldwide turnover does not indicate market power in the jurisdiction at hand.

With respect to joint ventures, it should be possible to limit merger notifications by including territorial restrictions in a joint venture contract. In addition, notification requirements should not necessarily be triggered by a global agreement, if national implementation agreements will follow. Companies should have the possibility to notify only if and when they want to start cooperating in a jurisdiction. Otherwise parties have to notify agreements that might not be implemented if a test phase showed that the commercial success was not as expected.

A dominant position in a relevant market should not trigger full notifications for all acquisitions in a jurisdiction, if there is no link to the relevant market where the company holds the dominant position. Practical experience shows that authorities tend to be reluctant to grant a waiver from the notification requirement – even if there is clearly no link, for example, between a dominant position in a noodles market and an acquisition of a pet food company. Notification requirements should be limited to acquisitions in neighbouring or closely related markets if such a provision is considered necessary – typically a turnover threshold will catch the relevant cases.

5.2 By limiting information requests and formalities to a minimum

Whether a notification is expensive and time consuming depends heavily on the amount of data requested. Therefore, simplified procedures should be introduced and used as far as possible.

Unfortunately, authorities use them to ease their own burden and not that of the companies. The European Commission, for example, is in a simplified procedure often not willing to limit the information to be provided accordingly. The only difference to a normal procedure for the parties is therefore often a shorter decision.

Standard forms are useful for companies and for the authorities as they help to prepare a notification and to structure the process if they are used in a flexible way. Unfortunately this is not always the case. The European Commission, for example, does not usually use Form C/O in a flexible way, as many case handlers do not know the relevant markets sufficiently to limit themselves to relevant questions. The result is that the companies often have to provide information of which only a very limited amount is used.

The practice of the European Commission creates additional problems in other jurisdictions, as many other authorities automatically request the same information as was presented to the European Commission. In cases where the relevant markets are national and the competitive situation (eg significantly lower market shares) is different, this is often neither efficient nor appropriate. In addition, it is often difficult to provide the requested information for countries that are of lower importance to the parties themselves, as they have less information. Parties are therefore often reluctant to grant the right to exchange information with other authorities for fear of being asked questions that are of no relevance in the jurisdiction (eg because there are no overlaps and the parties do not have high market shares in national markets).

5.3 By keeping a one-stop shop in the EC/EU for as many mergers as possible

For a multinational company it is preferable if it has to deal only with one set of rules and the one-stop shop principle is therefore very valuable. It is easier to monitor and understand the way the authority works, notifications can be prepared in a language that is spoken in the company and the company does not have to rely on translations without being able to check them. In addition, it is of course much cheaper to notify only once.

This is not necessarily linked to the competence of the European Commission for a decision. It simply means that there should only be one authority competent for a case within the European Economic Area and it should always be the same procedure that is used in line with a possibility to notify at least in English.

The European Merger Regulation contains some provisions that allow a referral from one or more national authorities to the European Commission or vice versa. This can be used to allocate the case to the authority which is best suited for the particular case without burdening companies significantly, provided that the decision is taken fast, that there is only *one* authority competent, that the referral does not result in a requirement of submitting a notification in a different language and that it is made for the complete notification. As these conditions are not currently met, referrals should be used rarely, if at all.

5

Optimising Case Allocation in the European Union and Dealing with Multijurisdictional Filings

Gerwin van Gerven*

Partner, Linklaters, Brussels

1. Introduction

Case allocation between the European Commission (the 'Commission') and national competition authorities (NCAs) has been a key issue in the 1993, 1996-1997 and 2001-2003 reviews of the Merger Regulation (ECMR). The current Green Paper on the Review of the Merger Regulation[1] contains the most elaborate proposals to date for reform in this respect. The proposals are most timely because the European merger control scene has changed dramatically since the adoption of the ECMR. With some 25 national merger control regimes soon in the European Economic Area, the time has come to improve case allocation between the Commission and the NCAs in order to create a more efficient and less burdensome regulatory structure.

The Commission's efforts towards improving case allocation occur within a wider context. The rapid growth in merger control laws worldwide has created a patchwork of filing requirements – also beyond the borders of Europe – that has resulted in a significant cost for business. In particular, many of these merger control laws assume jurisdiction based on criteria that postulate a low nexus or whose application to a particular transaction may be difficult to ascertain. This has led to calls from many corners to seek convergence towards sensible notification thresholds. The International Competition Network (ICN)[2] has emerged as the forum where the tools for such convergence are developed. The first recommended practices were recently adopted by ICN members which, if implemented, will also have an impact on case allocation in Europe.

In this paper, I will discuss the case allocation proposals in the Commission's Green Paper and the ICN-recommended practices on jurisdiction. This paper deals extensively with *both* Green Paper proposals with regard to case allocation: (1) the proposal to give the Commission jurisdiction if a concentration not having a Community dimension is notifiable in three or more national jurisdictions – the so-called '3+ proposal' – and (2) the proposal to make referrals between the Commission and NCAs more easy.

* I wish to thank Peter Citron and Thomas Franchoo who have assisted me in preparing this paper.

1 Green Paper on the Review of Council Regulation (EEC) No 4064/89, COM (2001) 745/6 final, issued on 11 December 2001. The text of the Green Paper is available at http://europa.eu.int/comm/competition/mergers/review/.

2 For additional details on the ICN, see: http://www.internationalcompetitionnetwork.org.

At the time of writing, in September 2002, the Commission had not yet announced that it would not pursue the 3+ proposal but instead rely on referrals 'down' and 'up' in order to ensure that cases are dealt with at the level that is best placed to review a concentration. When reviewing the manuscript in December 2002, I have decided not to remove the comments dealing with the 3+ proposal because I believe that many arguments used against this proposal are, on a closer look, not valid and the proposal was 'rejected' for the wrong reasons (although the real reasons may have been opposition from certain NCAs). There remains some merit in advocating the wisdom of a 3+ proposal, although for the time being the proposal is off the table. Going forward, it is likely that case allocation will be based on vague criteria that are in urgent need of further definition, as this paper will show, if this case allocation mechanism is not to fall foul of ICN recommended practices that the Commission itself has subscribed too.

2. Setting the scene: an overview of merger control regimes in Europe

Below is a list of all the countries in Europe (defined to include the EEA member states, all 13 candidate accession countries and Switzerland) that have pre-merger filing laws (M = mandatory; V = voluntary). Today there are no less than 31 merger control regimes in Europe. When the ten new Member States join the European Union and the EEA on 1 May 2004, at that time all of the 28 EEA member states, except Luxembourg and Liechtenstein, will have a pre-merger filing law.

European countries with merger control laws[3]

Austria (M)	Belgium (M)	Bulgaria (M)
Cyprus (M)	Czech Republic (M)	Denmark (M)
Estonia (M)	EEA (M)	EU (M)
Finland (M)	France (M)	Germany (M)
Greece (M)	Hungary (M)	Iceland (M)
Ireland (M)	Italy (M)	Latvia (M)
Lithuania (M)	Netherlands (M)	Norway (V)
Poland (M)	Portugal (M)	Romania (M)
Slovak Republic (M)	Slovenia (M)	Spain (M)
Sweden (M)	Switzerland (M)	Turkey (M)
United Kingdom (V)		

3 Malta is expected to adopt a pre-merger filing law in the near future.

Of the 31 merger control regimes in Europe, only nine require that each of at least two parties have sales above a minimum threshold in the jurisdiction concerned.[4] In no less than 20 countries, a pre-merger filing may be required even if one of the parties has only *de minimis* sales in the country concerned.[5]

In nine jurisdictions, a filing may be required based on the parties meeting, on a combined basis or on their own, a market share threshold.[6] In two more countries, a filing is voluntary but a market share threshold is used to define the scope of the law.[7] The difficulties with market share thresholds are by now familiar. In short, they require the notifying parties to make a substantive analysis in order to determine whether a filing is required. Deciding what the relevant market is may be data-intensive and time-consuming, and even such considerable efforts may not produce unequivocal results. Moreover, market share information is not always readily available. The parties will know their sales but may not know those of others.

3. A LITTLE BIT OF HISTORY

Case allocation between the European Commission and EU NCAs has been a point of discussion since the start of the Merger Regulation – indeed since long before its adoption.[8] The thresholds in Article 1(2) of the ECMR were a political compromise and Article 1(3) initially provided that the thresholds would be reviewed before the end of 1993. At the time of the adoption of the ECMR, the Commission officially declared that turnover thresholds should be reduced as soon as possible: the worldwide turnover

4 Belgium; EEA (EFTA Surveillance Authority); EU (European Commission); France; Iceland, Lithuania; Netherlands; Sweden and Switzerland.

5 Austria; Bulgaria; Cyprus (but the target has to conduct business in Cyprus); Czech Republic; Denmark; Estonia (but the target has to conduct business in Estonia); Finland (but the target has to conduct business in Finland); Germany; Greece (but a market share test must then be satisfied); Hungary (but the target needs to achieve minimum sales in Hungary); Ireland (but both parties need to carry out business in Ireland); Italy; Latvia (but a market share test must then be satisfied); Poland (but there is an additional target sales test or market share test); Portugal; Romania; Slovenia; Spain (but a market share test must then be satisfied); Slovakia; and Turkey.

6 Bulgaria, Greece, Latvia (in addition to a sales threshold), Poland (in addition to a sales threshold), Portugal, Slovakia, Slovenia, Spain, Turkey. In recent years, Belgium and France have abolished market share thresholds. Both have incorporated the 'each of at least two parties' nexus requirement modelled on the EC Merger Regulation. The Czech Republic moved away from a market share threshold in 2001. We understand that Portugal is in the process of reviewing its merger control laws and may move away from a market threshold. The Greek Antitrust Authority has also come out in favour of abolishing the market share threshold. Likewise, in Bulgaria, a proposal is pending to abolish the market share threshold.

7 Norway (based on guidelines issued by the NCA about which concentrations it will as a rule investigate), the United Kingdom (using 'share of supply', a concept akin to market share).

8 See, eg William Elland, 'The Merger Control Regulation (EEC) No 4064/89' [1990] ECLR 111.

threshold from €5 billion to €2 billion and the Community-wide turnover threshold from €250 million to €100 million.[9]

In its 1993 Report on the Implementation of the Merger Regulation,[10] the Commission did not propose a threshold reduction because insufficient experience had been gained with the application of the thresholds. Politically more relevant was that there was almost unanimous support from the business community for such a reduction but opposition from many NCAs. Faced with this opposition, the Commission proposed revisiting the issue of threshold reduction by the end of 1996.

In 1996, the Commission issued a Green Paper, organising for the first time a wide-ranging consultation.[11] This time, the Commission advocated a threshold reduction: to €2 billion and €100 million. At the same time, it proposed a fall-back alternative should these lower thresholds not be adopted. Concentrations that would otherwise fall under two or more national merger control laws should be notified with the Commission if they exceeded the proposed lower turnover thresholds – a half-way house between a threshold reduction and a solution to multiple filings. By 1996, most of the Member States had adopted pre-merger filing laws – at that time 11 Member States had such laws[12] – and the business community had started to experience the costs and burdens of multijurisdictional filings 'below the ECMR thresholds'. The issue of multijurisdictional filings was identified in the 1996 Green Paper as a problem in and of itself.[13] The fall-back proposal was meant to deal with this problem. Contrary to today, there was widespread opposition from business circles and lawyers because it was generally felt that the uncertainties of national merger control thresholds (in particular market share thresholds) should not be incorporated in the ECMR. Probably even more important in explaining the lack of support was that the fall-back proposal was just that – a fall-back – and industry and lawyers hoped that a clear-cut threshold reduction could be achieved. Instead the 'Italian' proposal prevailed and was incorporated into Article 1(3) of the ECMR: a new set of lower turnover thresholds intended to capture concentrations below the original Community dimension thresholds that nevertheless were likely to have a cross-border impact.[14] The most

9 See Council Notes on Regulation (EEC) 4064/89, reprinted in Supplement 2/90 of the Bulletin of the EC and also available at http://europa.eu.int/comm/competition/mergers/legislation/regulation/notes.html. In the proposal for a Merger Regulation, that the Commission submitted on 30 November 1988, the thresholds were still ECU1 billion (worldwide turnover) and ECU100 million (Community-wide turnover) and the exception for a concentration of turnover in one and the same Member State was still at 3/4 instead of at 2/3: see Amended proposal for a Council Regulation (EEC) on the control of concentrations between undertakings, OJ 1989 C 22/14. In the original 1973 Commission proposal, the threshold was simply a combined worldwide turnover of ECU1 billion and an exemption if the target undertaking had a turnover of less than ECU30 million: see Proposal for a Regulation (EEC) of the Council on the control of concentrations between undertakings, OJ 1973 C 92/1.

10 Report from the Commission to the Council on the Implementation of the Merger Regulation, COM (93) 385/final, 28 July 1993 and 7 September 1993: see *EC Merger Control Reporter* (Kluwer), Section D.

11 The Community Merger Control Green Paper on the Review of the Merger Regulation (the '1996 Green Paper'); see *EC Merger Control Reporter* (Kluwer), Section D.

12 The exceptions were Denmark, Finland, Luxembourg, and the Netherlands.

13 See, eg 1996 Green Paper, *supra* n 11, paras 51-57.

14 Council Regulation (EC) No 1310/97 amending Regulation (EEC) No 4064/89 on the control of concentrations between undertakings, 30 June 1997, 1997 OJ L 180/1.

characteristic feature of these secondary thresholds is that the parties to the concentration must have significant sales in three or more EU Member States.[15]

4. 2001 Green Paper

4.1 The 3+ proposal

In December 2001, the Commission published a second Green Paper on the Review of the Merger Regulation[16] but this time it no longer proposed a threshold reduction. Nevertheless, based on extensive surveys and consultations,[17] the Commission retabled a variant of its 1996 fall-back proposal: concentrations should be notified to the Commission if they would otherwise fall within the jurisdiction of three or more NCAs ('3+ proposal' or '3+ rule'). The proposal was backed up by statistics that showed two realities:

1. Article 1(3) ECMR has not remedied the problem it was meant to solve. For example, in 2000, only 20 cases were filed with the Commission based on the secondary thresholds in Article 1(3), while 75 cases were filed with three or more NCAs.[18] Those that had believed that with the new Article 1.3 it would be rare that concentrations had to be notified in three or more Member States were proven wrong.
2. A considerable number of cases still gave rise to a pre-merger filing in two or more Member States. In 2000, approximately 3,000 filings were made with NCAs in the EU. In 217 cases, filings were made in two or more countries (compared to 345 filings to the EU). In 75 cases, filings were made in three or more countries.[19]

4.2 Referral by the Commission to Member States

In return for this transfer of jurisdiction incorporated in the 3+ rule, the Commission proposed changes in the complex Article 9 referral criteria. Today, referrals remain relatively uncommon because they are subject to strict criteria.[20] The Commission proposed to facilitate referrals to Member States in order to allow them to vet concentrations that do not have significant cross-border effects:

15 Each of at least two undertakings to the concentration must have a €25 million turnover and all undertakings combined must have a €100 million turnover in at least three Member States.

16 See n 1 above.

17 The Green Paper followed the Commission's Report of 28 June 2000 to the Council on the application of the Merger Regulation, COM (2000) 399 final, issued on 28 June 2000, pursuant to Article 1(4) of the Merger Regulation which required the Commission to report to the Council on the Merger Regulation thresholds before 1 July 2000. The text of this Report is available at http://europa.eu.int/comm/competition/mergers/review/.

18 See Green Paper, *supra* n 1, para 24. See also Annex 1 to the Green Paper at para 52. The 2000 Commission Report on the Merger Regulation thresholds mentioned that in the period March 1998-December 1999 (ie 22 months), the number had been 45 or approximately nine per cent of all filings, while in 2000, the percentage had dropped to approximately five per cent. On the contrary, the numbers of filings in three or more Member States was, proportionally, on the rise: see Annex 1 to the Green Paper, paras 6 and 52.

19 *Id.*

20 Nevertheless, looking at year-by-year statistics, it is clear that in recent years significantly more cases were referred to Member States.

- A referral would no longer be subject to the Member State proving that the concentration threatens to create or strengthen a dominant position in a national or sub-national market. It would be sufficient to prove that the concentration would have a substantiated effect on competition in the Member State concerned and that the markets affected by the concentration are, at most, national.[21]
- The Commission could refer a concentration at its own initiative. A request from a Member State would no longer be necessary, although the Commission would envisage prior consultation with the Member State(s) concerned.[22]

Thus, potentially, every case that does not have significant cross-border effects, or the separable parts of a case that do not have cross-border effects, would be a candidate for referral, either at the request of a Member State or the Commission's own initiative.

4.3 Referral by Member States to the Commission

Finally, I should mention Article 22(3) of the ECMR. Article 22(3) provides for a mechanism allowing one or more Member States to refer a concentration without a Community dimension to the Commission. Member States can make a referral if they believe that the Commission is better placed to review a particular case, for example because the markets involved are larger than national. With regard to Article 22(3), the Commission did not propose any changes.[23] It must have assumed that, if the 3+ proposal were adopted, there would likely be very little scope for any application of Article 22(3), ie the referral to the Commission of a concentration without a Community dimension, at the request of one or more NCAs. Interestingly enough, since the publication of the Green Paper, Member States have twice submitted a joint request that a concentration filed at the national level be referred to the Commission.[24] In *Promatech/Sulzer Textil*, seven authorities made a joint request for a case where the markets were apparently European-wide.[25] In *GEES/Unison*, six authorities filed a referral request. The case concerned worldwide markets.[26]

21 Green Paper, *supra* n 1, para 81.

22 Green Paper, *supra* n 1, para 80.

23 Green Paper, *supra* n 1, paras 84-99. In its formal proposal of December 2002, the Commission envisages an increased use of Article 22 to allow the Commission to deal with those concentrations, without a Community dimension, that nevertheless have significant cross-border effects.

24 The ability to make such coordinated requests was facilitated by the creation of the European Competition Authorities (ECA) network among NCAs.

25 *Promatech/Sulzer Textil*, Case No COMP/M.2698, Commission decision of 24 July 2002. See also IP/02/1140.

26 See *GEES/Unison*, Case No COMP/M.2738, Commission decision of 17 April 2002. The press release (IP/02/578) mentions that there were seven NCAs who referred the case. Two authorities did not participate in the joint referral.

4.4 Replies to the Green Paper

The Commission received approximately 120 replies to its invitation to comment on the Green Paper proposals. A great many of these replies took a position with regard to the above-mentioned topics. According to the Commission[27]:

- There was 'broad support' for a division of jurisdiction along the following lines: the Commission should deal with concentrations where the markets are, or are becoming, wider than national and the NCAs should deal with 'purely national cases'.[28] This statement is, unfortunately, ambiguous, not least because it does not expressly address the question as to who should deal with a case where the markets are national but the concentration affects markets in several Member States.
- There was 'very strong support' for continuing to base ECMR notification thresholds on objective and transparent criteria, such as turnover thresholds, and for avoiding more subjective criteria such as market shares or the discretion of national authorities (Article 22).[29]
- There was 'considerable support', in particular among industry representatives, for the 3+ proposal. According to the Commission, 'a significant portion of each group of respondents' would be prepared to accept the proposal, but many believe that a mandatory 3+ rule could significantly reduce legal certainty.[30] Accordingly, the 3+ proposal should be made optional.[31]
- There was 'support' for at least some harmonisation of merger control rules at the national level, particularly relating to methods for establishing jurisdictional nexus, procedural rules on triggering events for notification, and on review periods.
- There was a mixed response to the proposals regarding Article 9. Most respondents agree that the test for a referral should be simplified. Member States generally favoured an expanded use of referrals but comments by industry, the legal profession and others were not supportive of a significant increase in referrals to NCAs. There was little (or at best qualified) support for the idea that the Commission would refer cases at its own initiative and there appeared to be a widespread aversion to partial referrals among industry representatives and lawyers.[32]

4.5 What should be the principles underlying case allocation?

The Green Paper calls for one general comment. The Commission proposes as the ultimate allocation criterion that a concentration be reviewed by the authority that is best placed to do so, in line with the principle of subsidiarity. In its view, the Commission is best placed to review concentrations that have cross-border effects and

27 See Green Paper on the Review of Council Regulation (EEC) No 3064/89 ('Merger Review') – Summary of the Replies Received, available at http://europa.eu.int/comm/competition/mergers/review/. The text of all replies is available on the same web page.
28 Summary of Replies, *supra* n 27, para 8.
29 Summary of Replies, *supra* n 27, para 8.
30 *Ibid.*
31 *Ibid,* para 22.
32 *Ibid,* paras 33-46.

NCAs are best placed to review those that do not have such effects.[33] This 'cross-border effects' criterion is relatively vague and ambiguous and indeed has been construed differently:

- The Commission seems to have in mind that a concentration has a 'cross-border effect' if the concentration (1) has an effect on competition in a market that is, or is becoming, wider than national, (2) has an effect on competition in a market that is national but such effects occur to a significant extent in more than one Member State, or (3) has an effect on competition in a national market but risks limiting entry from competitors in other Member States.[34]
- Others take a narrower view: the Bundeskartellamt ('BKartA') is very representative in this respect. The BKartA believes that the Commission should review deals where the markets are wider than national, and NCAs those where the markets are national or narrower. In fact, the BKartA mentions that many cases that are currently reviewed under the ECMR deal with national markets and should be reviewed by NCAs.[35]

In short, the controversy is about which level – the Commission or NCAs – should deal with concentrations in markets that are national. Despite market integration, in many cases markets are still national, so this controversy is not just theoretical. As a result of a move towards much more flexibility in the Article 9 referral mechanism, the outcome may prove important for case allocation purposes. In my view, it is erroneous to introduce case allocation principles borrowed from the modernisation reform, dealing with Articles 81 and 82 of the EC Treaty, and apply them to merger control. Merger control is different. The need for efficiency and a 'super' timely review is more overriding than in general antitrust law, not in the least because mergers cannot be implemented without prior clearance.

Instead of an undue focus on whether a concentration has 'cross-border effects', allocation should be guided by two simple principles: merger control should be effective and efficient[36]:

- *Merger control should be effective.* The authority that carries out the review must have the necessary experience and resources. There is consensus that the Commission is better placed to carry out reviews if the markets are worldwide, pan-European or wider than national because NCAs will always have a national perspective and may lack the tools to carry out an effective review beyond their

33 Green Paper, *supra* n 1, paras 16-20.

34 See also Recital 9 of the Merger Regulation. For more details, please see the Green Paper, *supra* n 1, paras 15-20. Interestingly, the 1996 Green Paper was less ambiguous about what must be understood by a 'cross-border' impact and made it very clear that concentrations that affect competition in several countries, even though the markets are national, should be considered to have a cross-border impact. Paragraphs 17-20 of the 2001 Green Paper are somewhat more ambiguous in this respect and coupled with the Commission's proposals concerning Article 9 give rise to concern about a 'swing back' in the Commission's thinking about case allocation. The Summary of Replies gives rise to a similar concern, *supra* n 27.

35 See Submission by the Bundeskartellamt in reply to the Green Paper. The text of this submission, as well as of all other comments on the Green Paper, is available at http://europa.eu.int/comm/competition/mergers/review/.

36 In its speech 'Review of the EC Merger Regulation – Roadmap for the reform project' delivered on 4 June 2002, Commissioner Monti suggested that its proposals on jurisdictional reform will be guided by these principles. The text of the speech is available at http://europa.eu.int/comm/competition/mergers/review/.

borders. We may assume that, in general, the Commission and NCAs are equally placed to review cases where the relevant markets are national. For sub-national markets, in certain specific cases, an argument can be made that based on resources, prior expertise, language, etc, NCAs may be better placed to review these cases. This recognition underlies the Article 9 referral procedure and, in years past, the Commission has referred many regional or local market cases to the NCAs if they asked for it.[37]

– *Merger control should be efficient.* Without jeopardising effectiveness, merger control in Europe should be organised in the most efficient, least burdensome way. The business community has underscored this need time and time again. Multijurisdictional filings are an inefficient way of organising merger control. In many instances, a filing with the European Commission will be more efficient, from the vantage point of the notifying parties, and possibly also from the regulators' perspective. The insistence of the business community on having more mergers reviewed by Brussels[38] demonstrates the strong conviction that a centralised filing for the whole of the European Union is, generally speaking, more efficient.

The need for having efficient and effective merger control in the European Union calls for support of the Commission's 3+ proposal.[39] It is simply not efficient for a firm to have to notify a deal in several – sometimes many – countries in the European Union, even if the relevant markets may be national.[40] In such instance, it should be possible for the notifying parties to elect to notify to the Commission and to avail themselves of the 'one-stop shop' facility offered by the ECMR. Therefore, it would be wiser to justify the 3+ proposal directly on the need to deal with the problem of multijurisdictional filings, not as a proxy of cross-border effects. Because of the extremely low nexus requirements in some national merger control laws, it is difficult to deny that the fact that a merger may have to be notified in three jurisdictions does not mean that it will produce significant cross-border effects. Nevertheless, even for those multijurisdictional filings that do not give rise to such cross-border effects, the costs and burdens of having to file in several jurisdictions are real and in many cases difficult to justify, given the fact that there is a merger control regime at Community level that may avoid or reduce these costs.

There may be need for a corrective measure – under the form of a referral to NCAs – but such referral mechanism should remain the exception and limited to instances where the Commission is not as well placed as NCAs to carry out an effective review. Moreover, if more cases are transferred to the Commission, the Commission must ensure that it has the resources to deal with these cases.

37 See, for a few recent examples, *Nehlsen/Rethmann/SWB/Bremerhavener Entsorgungsgesellschaft*, Commission decision of 30 May 2002 (see also IP/02/785); *Connex/DNVBV/JV*, Commission decision of 24 April 2002 (see also IP/02/627); *Govia/Connex South Central*, Commission decision of 20 July 2001 (see also IP/01/1048).

38 Summary of Replies, *supra* n 27, para 8.

39 The mechanism should be optional. If a merger can be reviewed at the central level, it should be. An optional transfer mechanism enhances efficiency without jeopardising effectiveness. I will revert to the need for an optional transfer mechanism below.

40 The 1996 Green Paper still contains a good overview of the reasons why multijurisdictional filings are not efficient: see 1996 Green Paper, *supra* n 11, paras 51-57.

5. The 3+ proposal should be optional

The Commission's proposal in the Green Paper envisages an automatic transfer: if three or more national merger control laws are applicable, irrespective of whether these laws provide for a mandatory or voluntary filing, the concentration would fall under the ECMR and the Commission would have to vet it. Many of the replies to the Green Paper endorse the 3+ proposal provided it is made optional.[41]

A strong case can be made for an optional mechanism. There are at least three major advantages of making the transfer optional:

1. Efficiency dictates that in the current state of play where some national filing regimes are voluntary and the costs and burdens involved in preparing each national filing still vary greatly, the notifying parties should have the choice. They should be allowed to pick the route which, depending on the circumstances, is the least costly and burdensome. For example, if filings are required in Austria, Germany, and the United Kingdom, the simplest route, especially in a case with no or minor competition issues, will be to file nationally rather than to the European Union. Filings to the Austrian and German competition authorities do not require the detail imposed by, for example, a Form CO and can consist of a short overview and analysis. Since filing is voluntary in the United Kingdom, the parties may legitimately decide that a filing will not be made.
2. It is not always easy to assess whether a filing is required, particularly in those Member States with a market share test. If the 3+ transfer rule remains optional, parties cannot be harmed as a result of their being wrong about the application of one or more national merger control laws. If they believe that they had to file in countries A and B while they should also have filed in country C, the filings with the NCAs in A and B remain perfectly valid. They will not have filed with the NCA in country C, while they should have, but their failure would not have different consequences from today. If the 3+ rule were mandatory, this would mean that the parties did not file to the Commission when they should have done so. Their failure may expose them, in principle, to fines pursuant to Article 14 of the ECMR. More relevant, such an error would mean that, as a matter of Community law, the transaction may not be valid pursuant to Article 7(5) of the ECMR.[42] With an 'optional' system, the question of validity would be limited to the country where no filing took place and, if the law of that country was not governing the transaction or no share transfer had to take place in that country, it would be of little significance in practice.
3. The notifying parties will be able to anticipate referrals 'down' (under Article 9 ECMR) or 'up' (under Article 22 ECMR) based on guidelines or consultation. This will avoid 'ping pong', and thereby have important consequences for timing and costs.

41 Summary of Replies, *supra* n 27, para 22.

42 Article 7(5) ECMR provides that the validity of any concentration put into effect without prior approval shall be dependent on the ultimate Commission decision taken in respect of this decision.

An optional transfer mechanism will not formalise 'forum shopping', as some critics suggest. Cooperation and coordination between European competition authorities, through such bodies as the European Competition Authorities (ECA), is already a reality that will only gain in importance. Moreover, substantive convergence is much further along than procedural convergence. Finally, there are the referral mechanisms under Articles 9 and 22 of the ECMR. Those who gamble on forum shopping do just that: 'gamble'.

6. Certifying the application of three national merger control thresholds

Some who have not endorsed the 3+ proposal have raised concerns regarding the implementation of such a proposal. These concerns can be summarised as follows:[43]

- The 3+ rule is not sufficient to indicate whether the merger has significant cross-border effects. Some national merger control thresholds do not require a sufficient nexus to ensure that a concentration has significant impact in a particular country and therefore the 3+ rule may capture concentrations where the effects are concentrated in one Member State.
- National merger laws are still too divergent for a 3+ proposal to make sense. In particular, (1) thresholds are very different, (2) different types of transactions are caught, (3) filing deadlines and suspension obligations are different.
- The 3+ rule would incorporate the uncertainties arising from national threshold determinations into the ECMR threshold determination. In several current and future EU Member States, jurisdictions depend on market share thresholds that are not objectively verifiable and on which information may not be readily available.
- It will be complex to have a mechanism to certify whether a particular transaction is notifiable in three or more Member States. Such certification will lead to delays and possible disputes and defeat an efficient merger control review.

6.1 Should cross-border effects form the justification for the 3+ proposal?

As explained above, the presence of significant cross-border effects should not be the foundation of the 3+ proposal. The 3+ proposal should be justified on *efficiency* grounds, as a measure to avoid the unnecessary costs and burdens of multi-jurisdictional filings. 'Significant cross-border effects' is too vague and imprecise to serve as the basis for case allocation and the problems associated with using this standard are only aggravated by the fact that there exists controversy over what should be meant by it.

6.2 Should there be harmonisation first?

While harmonisation of national merger control laws, in terms of jurisdiction, procedure and substantive test, would certainly be welcome, those who insist that national merger control laws should first be harmonised before a 3+ rule can be

43 See also Summary of Replies, *supra* n 27, paras 9-20.

introduced, advocate a *status quo*. Harmonisation is not a near-term project and Commission officials have indicated that such harmonisation will not be proposed at this time. I do not agree that harmonisation is required first for the 3+ proposal to work. Let us take the scope of the merger control laws as an example. It is true that the types of transaction covered by the respective national laws may vary from country to country. For example, German merger control law covers transactions that would not qualify as a concentration under the ECMR. However, the adoption of the 3+ proposal does not mean that these variations need to be incorporated in the ECMR jurisdictional criteria. Article 3 of the ECMR should remain unchanged. In other words, only if the transaction gives rise to a concentration as defined by the ECMR could a notification to Brussels be made. If a transaction is not a concentration in the sense of the ECMR, but in the unlikely event that it would nevertheless have to be notified with three or more NCAs under their respective merger control laws, the 'one-stop' facility would not be available, not even on an optional basis. For these transactions, the *status quo* would not change.

Likewise, the differences in filing deadlines should not be an impediment. If there are strict filing deadlines – for example, an obligation to file within one week after the conclusion of the agreement – it is for the notifying parties to work within these timing constraints. It will mean they may have to prepare a filing plan in advance in order to ensure that they know in time whether they should file at a national or Community level. My experience is that in most instances a verification, of which merger control laws may be applicable, is achievable with reasonable efforts and in a reasonable period of time.

In a similar vein, the differences in suspension obligations may be frustrating but the parties will have to work within those constraints. If they file with the Commission based on the 3+ facility, they will have to abide by Article 7 and wait until clearance is obtained to implement the concentration, unless a derogation is obtained.

6.3 Difficulties created by market share thresholds should not be exaggerated

The adoption of the 3+ proposal will mean that – for as long as certain EU Member States have market share thresholds – ECMR jurisdiction may depend on satisfying market share criteria. A few comments are in order. I will focus on the uncertainties arising from market share thresholds but the comments apply to all uncertainties associated with applying national thresholds, whatever their nature.

There is increasing consensus that market share thresholds are not an appropriate way of determining whether a concentration is notifiable. I will return to this consensus below when discussing the ICN-recommended practices. One may hope that market share thresholds will gradually disappear and indeed a few European countries have recently abolished them while others are likely to do so in the near future.[44] However, it would be wrong to wait until this convergence is brought about because the problem of multijurisdictional filings is pressing.

In many cases, market share thresholds will not be an issue. Since Community jurisdiction would depend on just three national merger control laws being applicable,

44 See n 6 above.

the test might well be satisfied by a number of jurisdictions that do not have market share thresholds. For example, a concentration may fall under the merger control laws of three EU Member States, based on the transaction exceeding turnover thresholds, and it may fall under the laws of two or three more Member States depending on the satisfaction of market share thresholds. In such a case, it is irrelevant, for jurisdictional purposes, what the relevant market is and what the market shares of the parties are, because the 3+ test has already been met by the first three countries. Moreover, if the parties decide to file with the European Union, they would avoid having to deal with the market share threshold issues.

Nevertheless, there would always remain a number of cases where it is necessary to ascertain that a certain market share threshold is met in order to determine whether the 3+ facility is available to the notifying parties. For some of these cases, there may be little scope for discussion because the relevant market and the parties' market shares may be readily ascertainable or the threshold would be met under every possible alternative.

Finally, there would be those cases where jurisdiction based on the 3+ rule will not be readily ascertainable because of the uncertainty associated with a market share threshold. Here, the optional variant of the 3+ proposal offers relief. With an optional 3+ rule, the parties can decide themselves whether they file with the Commission. If they do, they may need to have a discussion with certain NCAs about the relevant market and the application of their laws. The notifying parties may run the risk that Community jurisdiction would not be established, with the ensuing delays and lost efforts, or they may be well advised to file at the national level as they would have to do if a 3+ facility did not exist. In this respect, there should be put in place a sensible certification system that would not allow that the initial certification by a Member State would be reversed by a finding at the substantive stage that the market is wider than postulated for jurisdictional purposes. I will return to this issue below.

So, in conclusion, market share thresholds are an attack on the 'purity' of the ECMR's turnover-based thresholds, and their implicit incorporation through the 3+ facility into ECMR law should not be lauded. However, the real-life problems should not be exaggerated because, in most instances, the uncertainties that might arise as a result of their application will not be critical to the Community jurisdiction assessment. In any event, an optional 3+ rule would avoid much of the negative consequences that may arise from such uncertainties. All in all, the result may not be perfect but the desire for perfection should not be a pretext for inaction.

6.4 How should the application of national merger control laws be certified?

The Commission suggests that certification as to whether national merger control laws apply has to be done by the NCAs because it will be based on an interpretation of national law.[45] I believe very few people, if any, disagree with this proposed rule.

Even though other authorities than the Commission may thus become involved in deciding whether the ECMR applies, it must be done in an efficient, timely and non-bureaucratic way. Allow me to can make a few suggestions:

45 Green Paper, *supra* n 1, para 60.

- *No need to pass via the Commission.* The notifying parties should have the option to obtain a certification directly from the NCAs concerned, if they elect to do so. They could do so in order to settle any issues that may arise and obtain closure on jurisdiction prior to notification to the Commission. In doing so, they may eliminate the Commission as an unnecessary intermediary and save time. Alternatively, the parties could use the Commission as a 'clearing house', either during the pre-notification stage or at the time of notification, although in both instances the Commission should serve largely as a 'mailbox'. I believe these issues should be dealt with in practice guidelines and do not need to be incorporated in the ECMR or the Implementing Regulation.
- *Prior to notification.* NCAs should be prepared to issue a certification at any time prior to notification, and subject to strict confidentiality restrictions, without there being a need to have a binding agreement.[46] Such certification should be limited to the application of the thresholds and not concern jurisdiction as such. For example, the NCA should not pronounce itself on whether the transaction is a concentration. That question is up to the Commission to answer.
- *Short delay.* The NCA should issue its certification within a short period of time after it has received all information allowing it to do so. A week seems to be a sensible maximum period. If no decision is received within one week, it must be presumed irrevocably that the decision is positive ('opposition procedure').
- *Three certifications are sufficient.* The Commission should accept jurisdiction once it has received three certification letters issued by NCAs or equivalent proof that an NCA did not oppose a certification request. It would not be necessary to certify the application of all national merger control laws in the European Union. The Commission would not have the power to challenge this certification, although it remains obviously free to discuss the case with the NCA prior to the latter taking a certification decision. If the parties do not yet have three certifications at the time they notify with the Commission, the Phase I deadline should not start to run until that has happened.
- *Certification must be irreversible.* If during or after the Commission's review of a concentration it would appear that certification was based on a wrong determination, excluding the application of one or more national merger control laws, the Commission's jurisdiction should remain vested in the absence of intentionally misleading information provided by the parties.

In conclusion, I believe that straightforward administrative arrangements can be put in place that will lead to an efficient and timely confirmation as to which level should assume jurisdiction. In most cases, certification that the Commission has jurisdiction should not cause undue delay or even any delay at all. In this respect, it should not be forgotten that in quite a few cases uncertainty about a particular authority having jurisdiction may cause delays under today's framework. With a 3+ facility, these controversies can be avoided when it will be possible to ascertain readily that at least three NCAs have jurisdiction, obviating the need to determine whether others will too.

46 A certification procedure has as an advantage that the NCA needs to take a position. At present, some NCAs are prepared to give guidance or a ruling prior to notification, but others are not.

7. Referrals to Member States

A desire widely expressed by business associations and lawyers in the comments on the Green Paper is that referrals to Member States should remain an exception.[47] It is no longer contested that, in some specific and narrowly described circumstances, such referrals are proper but the Commission's proposals give rise to concern because they open the door to a greater number of referrals based on a theoretical assumption that NCAs are better placed to deal with cases where markets are at most national.

At present, the Merger Regulation provides several hurdles that ensure referrals are only requested and granted in a few cases:

- a referral must be explicitly requested by a Member State;
- in most cases, the requesting authority will have to prove that the concentration threatens to create or strengthen a dominant position in a national or sub-national market; even so, the Commission has discretion to refer the case[48];
- in other cases (ie where the market concerned is not deemed to be a substantial part of the Common Market), the requesting authority will have to show that the concentration affects competition; in this case, the Commission does not have any choice but to refer.[49]

The Commission proposals in the Green Paper suggest removing these three hurdles. There appears support for a change in the Merger Regulation that would no longer require Member States to prove that the concentration threatens to create or strengthen a dominant position.[50] Such substantive analysis has no place in what is largely a jurisdictional allocation mechanism.

It would be a significant step back if, based on misguided principles of decentralisation advocated in the area of general antitrust, the Commission would, in the future, refer significantly more cases to Member States than it does now. Referrals to Member States create time delays, upset the merger planning and in other ways they may add significant costs. Therefore, such referral should only be contemplated if there are compelling reasons that in the case in question an NCA is better placed to review.

It is worthwhile noting that several NCAs are opposed to referrals at the initiative of the Commission and insist that they have at least a say in whether such a referral may be made.[51] Since cases should only be referred if it is clear that the NCA is better placed to review it, it is imperative that the NCA has requested the referral. It would be odd that a review by an NCA is deemed more effective, if the NCA did not request to handle the case. The ECMR should keep the system of 'double approval': both the NCA involved and the Commission should be convinced that the NCA is better placed.

47 Until today, approximately 50 requests for referral were made. Approximately ten were rejected. Approximately 25 led to a partial referral and 15 to a full referral.

48 Article 9(2)(a) of the ECMR.

49 Article 9(2)(b) of the ECMR. It is very unlikely this test will be satisfied. For example, in *C3D/Rhone/Go-Ahead*, Commission decision of 20 October 2000, the Commission based the referral for a bus concentration in the South and South-West of London on Article 9(2)(a). See also IP/00/1195.

50 See Summary of Replies, *supra* n 27, para 32. Proving such a threat is required under Article 9(2)(a) but not Article 9(2)(b) ECMR.

51 See, eg comments from the following NCAs: Austria, Belgium, France, Germany, Spain, UK. See also Summary of Replies, *supra* n 27, para 38.

If Article 9 is changed, the Commission should issue guidelines that lay out in which cases it would consider a request favourably. If the referral test in the ECMR is lowered, along the lines proposed by the Commission, it should not imply that the Commission *should* refer cases in all instances that this test is met. The Guidelines should narrow the category of cases where the Commission is likely to refer. In my view, such guidelines should include:

- Guidance that the Commission will only refer cases where the competition effects are concentrated in one Member State. In other words, a concentration that has significant effects in two or more national markets would, generally speaking, not be referred.[52] There may be exceptions based on reasons mentioned below but in that instance the justification should be particularly compelling. In other words, notifying parties should not have to fear that cases are referred simply because the markets are national or sub-national. Such practice would undo the benefits of the one-stop shop facility incorporated in the ECMR.[53]
- Guidance that the Commission will not refer a case to more than one authority. If two authorities request a referral, it is a *prima facie* indication that the case produces significant effects in two or more countries.[54]
- Guidance that the Commission will not refer where the concentration has effects concentrated in one Member State but it is likely to make entry less likely from outside that Member State or in any other way adversely affect competition in other markets that are not confined to that Member State.
- For cases where the effects are concentrated in one country, it would have to be determined on a case-by-case assessment whether NCAs are better placed to carry out the review in the particular circumstances of the case. Factors could be:

  Prior expertise. The NCA has recently investigated the sector and therefore has pre-existing expertise about it.[55]

  Parallel investigation. The NCA is investigating another merger that affects the same market that the Commission has not.[56]

52 For a case where this guideline was not followed: see *SEB/Moulinex*, Case No COMP/M.2621, Commission decision of 8 January 2002. The Commission referred the acquisition of Moulinex by SEB to France as far as the French market was concerned and imposed remedies for a number of markets outside France. The French NCA did not impose any remedies. Interestingly, two third parties (Philips and BaByliss) filed an appeal against this decision, including against the referral decision: OJ 2002 C 144/56 and C169/35.

53 See, eg *Carnival Corporation/PO Princess*, Case No COMP/M.2706, Commission decision of 24 July 2002. See also IP/02/552. The referral was rejected even though the UK NCA was reviewing a parallel bid by Royal Caribbean. However, for a contrary approach: see *SEB/Moulinex, supra* n 52.

54 In the past the Commission has occasionally made such split referrals: see, eg *Lafarge/Redland*, Case No COMP/M.1030, decision of 16 December 1997, where the Commission referred part of the investigation to the UK and part to France.

55 See, for recent cases, eg *Metsaliitto/Vapo*, Case No COMP/M.2234, Commission decision of 8 February 2001. See also IP/01/183; *BP/E.ON*, Case No COMP/M.2533, Commission decision of 20 December 2001. See also IP/01/1247; *Haniel/ Fels*, Case No COMP/M.2495, Commission decision of 21 February 2002. See also IP/01/1438.

56 See, for recent cases, eg *C3D/Rhone/Go-Ahead, supra* n 49; *Preussag/Hapag-Lloyd*, Case No COMP/1001, Commission decision of 10 November 1997; *Gehe/Lloyds Chemists*, Case No COMP/M.716, Commission decision of 8 February 1996.

Local markets. The notification requires the investigation of local markets or supply arrangements.[57] In this respect, caution should be used not to assume that NCAs are always better placed to deal with regional or local markets. For example, there may be a need for developing a consistent approach at the Community level to issues raised in such sub-national market case(s).
Availability of resources. This reason is, as far as I know, not quoted in referral decisions but it may be a relevant one. A particular investigation may be so resource-specific or require knowledge of a local language (eg Greek) that the Commission would be less able to carry out an effective investigation.

- Guidance that the Commission and the NCA in question are prepared to discuss with the notifying parties prior to notification whether a referral is likely in order to allow the parties to prepare for it. Such early guidance should also avoid 'ping pong' whereby parties notify to the Commission under the 3+ rule, only to discover after notification that they are referred back to one or more Member States. In such instance, the parties may be well advised not to file to the Commission but to the NCAs that have jurisdiction.

8. ICN-RECOMMENDED PRACTICES ON JURISDICTION

The International Competition Network (ICN) is an organisation, established in October 2001, which comprises most antitrust agencies in the world. All current and future EU competition authorities, except Bulgaria, are members. The ICN has been designed as an inclusive organisation, and therefore private sector representatives, including lawyers, economists, academics and business associations, are members of the various working groups within it, and have a significant input. The ICN has a virtual structure, and does not operate as a 'bricks and mortar' organisation. By and large, the ICN operates by means of working groups which work remotely by e-mail and conference call. One of the ICN's working groups deals with mergers. It has three subgroups: (1) investigative techniques used in merger review; (2) the analytical framework for merger review; and (3) merger notifications and review procedures.[58]

The Subgroup Notifications and Procedures[59] has started to develop recommended practices for merger review. During its first working year, it focused on three recommended practices, which were endorsed in principle at the ICN's first Annual Conference in Naples last September.[60] The work that the ICN is carrying out on merger review best practices is focused directly on solving the problems of the costs and burdens of multijurisdictional filings.

The first set of recommendations deals with the following topics that are relevant for future case allocation in Europe:

- *Appropriate nexus for merger notifications.* The ICN recommends that merger notification thresholds incorporate appropriate standards of materiality as to the level of 'local nexus' required for merger notification. In particular, nexus should be based on activity within the jurisdiction concerned, as measured by

57 See, for recent cases, eg *Haniel/Fels*, *supra* n 56, *BP/E.ON*, *supra* n 55.
58 For more details, please see the ICN's website at www.internationalcompetitionnetwork.org.
59 The membership of this Subgroup includes the following EU authorities: the European Commission, Germany, France, Italy.
60 See http://www.internationalcompetitionnetwork.org/wg1_practices.html.

reference to the activities of at least two parties to the transaction in the local territory and/or by reference to the activities of the acquired business in the local territory.[61] Worldwide revenue or assets tests in the absence of a local nexus (eg revenues or assets in the jurisdiction concerned) should not be sufficient to trigger a notification requirement, nor should there be a requirement to notify on the basis of the acquiring company's local activities[62] only or the combined local activities of the parties.

- *Clear and understandable notification thresholds.* The ICN recommends that thresholds should be clear and easily understandable. The information needed to determine whether or not thresholds are fulfilled should be of the type that is available to the parties in the ordinary course of business. Sales and assets, but not market share, can be used, on the basis that these are objectively quantifiable and information to verify whether they are satisfied should be readily available.
- *Flexibility in timing of a merger notification.* The ICN recommends that parties should be able to notify transactions at any time provided they can submit appropriate indicia that they intend to proceed with the transaction. However, jurisdictions may make notification dependent on a definitive agreement being concluded but then parties should have the opportunity to discuss the transaction and the notification with the competition authority in order to facilitate a timely submission and review. There should be no deadline for filings in jurisdictions where there is mandatory suspension prior to clearance. Jurisdictions without suspension prior to closing should allow parties a reasonable time in which to file.

These recommendations do not have a binding force. Some of the recommendations involve practices that competition authorities may modify at their own initiative but recommendations with regard to jurisdictional thresholds will almost invariably require legislative changes in the countries concerned. EU Member States whose merger control thresholds do not comply with the recommended practices are not legally required to change their laws – an organisation whose membership consists only of competition authorities cannot adopt resolutions with such binding force – but it is hoped and expected that these recommended practices that have been endorsed by practically all competition authorities around the world will carry great authoritative weight. In any event, the successful adoption in Naples of these recommended practices means that all EU competition authorities have, in principle, endorsed the abolition of market share thresholds and 'low nexus' thresholds. One may expect that NCAs will recommend to their respective national ministries and parliaments that this change is implemented. Business circles, academics, lawyers and economists should join in the efforts. It is important to note that for the first time a wide consensus has emerged about basic principles with regard to allocating 'horizontally' jurisdiction in merger control cases.

61 Please note that the recommended practices have been written with an acquisition scenario and not a joint venture or merger scenario in mind.

62 There has been discussion about a scenario whereby the acquiring company has activities in the local jurisdiction but the acquired company does not yet do so. Some competition authorities feel that countries should not be discouraged from having thresholds that capture such a potential competition scenario.

To the extent merger control thresholds are revised to incorporate a more appropriate nexus, multijurisdictional filings will become less problematic. If the 3+ proposal is accepted, these changes will furthermore reverse a trend of case transfers to the Commission and bring about a rebalancing of the case allocation. In plain terms, if more countries incorporate appropriate nexus requirements in their merger control laws, it will occur less that concentrations fall within the scope of three or more merger control regimes, even though they may not give rise to significant effects in those countries. Therefore, over time the centripetal force of the 3+ facility will weaken. There will be fewer cases transferred to the Commission and less need for referrals. The implementation of the ICN-recommended practices is an integral part of an improved case allocation in Europe to the benefit of all stakeholders involved.

6

Dealing with Multijurisdictional Filings – Ensuring Legal Certainty

Lynda Martin Alegi

Baker & McKenzie, London

This brief paper focuses on the EC notification thresholds and argues that Article 1(3) of the Merger Regulation should be replaced by a definition providing that a concentration will have a Community dimension if it is certified by the notifying part(y)ies to qualify for notification in three or more Member States.

There are various attempts to define the ideal jurisdictional rule for merger control in Europe. Desirable characteristics are 'simplicity, predictability, consistency and rapidity'.[1] The rule should ensure that the authority best placed to carry out the investigation should deal with the case, consistent with the principles of subsidiarity, and the Commission's basic approach, that notifiability in three or more Member States indicates that there are more than national markets and interests concerned, is a good one.

Legal certainty requires that a jurisdictional rule establishing an obligation to notify the Commission should be so framed that a reasonably competent and well-advised party should be able to get it right first time and not be at risk of a notification being rejected or a notification requirement being missed.

The ICN Merger Notification and Procedures Sub-group recommends that merger notification requirements should be:

- clear and understandable;
- based on objective quantifiable criteria (not eg market shares or effects); and
- based on information readily accessible to the part(y)ies.

This ideal world is not yet a reality in the EEA. Any revised Merger Regulation threshold needs to take account of the current situation, as well as the increasing complexity which accession will bring in this regard, even if we may hope for harmonisation in the future. Current reality includes some countries which have market share tests (Greece, Portugal, Spain and the United Kingdom) and some where notification is voluntary (Norway and the United Kingdom).

In my view, the best way to ensure legal certainty without excessively costly and time-consuming pre-filing procedures is to define the Community dimension of a concentration by reference to meeting the Article 1(2) thresholds or to the case being certified by the notifying part(y)ies to the Commission as fulfilling the criteria of notifiability in 3+ Member States.

1 House of Lords Select Committee Report, 23 July 2002, para 33.

This approach would give the notifying part(y)ies the *option* to notify a merger to the Commission where they can certify that, to the best of their knowledge and belief,[2] the merger is one which meets the merger control thresholds, for mandatory or voluntary filing, in three or more Member States.

This is a practical, workable definition which ensures legal certainty. It avoids a couple of problems inherent in the Commission's original proposal:

1. A Merger Regulation filing will never need to be rejected because the part(y)ies honestly but wrongly thought that a threshold was met. Case example: the French and German thresholds are met and the part(y)ies, based on an assumption that the relevant geographical market is national, as established in prior cases, conclude that a Spanish filing is also required because the combined market share in Spain is over 25 per cent. The Commission, well into its investigation, concludes that the market has evolved and is now European in scope.[3] On this basis, only two Member State notifications would be required and the merger would not, after all, have a Community dimension. The part(y)ies, now out of time and liable to sanctions for late notification must start again, with new forms in local language in France and Germany.

   The opposition procedure proposed by the Commission would be an alternative for securing legal certainty in this type of case. But at a price. The Commission proposes that when parties indicate 3+ Member State notifiability, the Member States in question would have two weeks to object on an opposition basis. Considerable resources may be expended by Member State authorities in checking turnover and market share thresholds. The presumption created under this procedure would need to be absolute, applicable even in the extreme situation where, as in our example, the Commission decision on its face would show that the market share in Europe and hence in Spain was less than 25 per cent so that the merger would actually have been notifiable only in two Member States.

2. A Merger Regulation filing will never be discovered to be necessary when notifications have been made and proceedings are well under way in one or two Member States. Case example: after the part(y)ies have notified in France and Germany, a niche market is discovered where the parties have more than 25 per cent of the market in Spain.

   This situation of the late discovery of an additional filing requirement will not be unknown to anyone who has handled a volume of complex multijurisdictional cases. It is an irritating fact of life. The Commission's proposal would turn it into a nightmare. The French and German authorities, perhaps well along in their investigations, lose jurisdiction. All the time and effort of making and progressing those notifications is lost. The parties must start again in Brussels where they face sanctions for late filing.[4]

2 This is the level of certification already required for information on Form CO - section 12 Annex to Regulation 447/98.

3 See eg Pirelli/BICC.

4 Some of the responses to the Commission's Green Paper suggest that sanctions should not apply in this situation.

It is this situation which makes it essential that the Commission's jurisdiction in 3+ Member States notification cases be based on the bona fide certification of the part(y)ies.

If it is thus clear that the approach proposed in this paper avoids certain problems, does it create any?

- It does not require the Commission to interpret national laws.
- Forum shopping concerns are misplaced. One of the most common objections to an optional approach to Merger Regulation filing for multijurisdictional cases is that it would enable the part(y)ies to forum shop. However, the mere fact that parties have a choice of forum is not in itself a negative feature. Forum shopping is only problematic if the part(y)ies, by shopping around, can choose a particularly favourable jurisdiction where, whether based on their nationality or other factors, a full and rigorous review protecting competition in the Community will not take place. By definition, this will never be the case where a merger is reviewed by the Commission. Choosing to deal with the Commission will never enable the part(y)ies to escape proper scrutiny. It is equally far-fetched in practice to think that parties would opt for national filings with three or more Member States in an attempt to avoid rigorous review. The problems of forum shopping are generally linked to the fear that a party may find one jurisdiction which is unduly favourable to its position, for nationalistic or political reasons. This does not arise where three or more jurisdictions will review the case.
- It has been suggested that an optional filing would fundamentally change the structure of the Merger Regulation, which is based on mandatory filing. However, the proposal made would provide that once the parties have certified to the Commission that the merger is notifiable in three or more Member States they would be obliged to follow that with a full notification. So the proposal does provide for flexible, but still ultimately mandatory, filing.
- It does not create problems based on the different definitions of mergers covered by Member State law. Inconvenient though these differences in definitions are, they do not impact this proposal. Mandatory notification to Brussels would apply only to concentrations as defined by Merger Regulation. Only where there is a Merger Regulation concentration does the question arise whether it has a Community dimension because it falls within Article 1(2) or is certified to be notifiable in 3+ Member States.
- Finally, it has been observed that the 3+ test (as proposed by the Commission, but this concern would also apply to the test modified as suggested here) is anomalous since the Member States may unilaterally alter the Commission's jurisdiction.[5] However, it is surely not anomalous or objectionable that a rule designed to allocate jurisdiction, consistent with the principles of subsidiarity, to the authority best placed to carry out the investigation should take account of the need to avoid review by multiple authorities and hence necessarily must take account of the scope of jurisdiction of all of the authorities concerned.

5 M Broberg, 'Muddying the Clear Waters: on the Commission's Proposal for a New Delimitation of Jurisdiction in the Field of Merger Control' [2002] ECLR 429.

This paper will not consider the rules for reallocating cases under Articles 9 and 22 of the Merger Regulation save to say that once a case does have a Community dimension and has been notified to Brussels, legal certainty and practical considerations suggest that it should only exceptionally be transferred. The one-stop shop, largely achieved by the Merger Regulation, should be reinforced, not undermined. The Green Paper confirmed the results of the Commission's survey that even the possibility of an Article 9 referral had an impact on the time, financial and human resources needed to prepare Form CO and referrals entailed additional costs and resources in a substantial majority of cases. It would be particularly unsatisfactory to simplify the requirements for a referral request,[6] leading to cases undergoing a '*de facto* Phase II', four-month inquiry at national level when they did not even raise serious doubts or risk of creating or strengthening a dominant position.

6 Which Member States commenting on the Green Paper did not generally consider would even support a reduction in the three-week time limit.

Pre-Lunch Keynote Address: Mergers and Restructuring – the Consequences for Employment and Social Inclusion

Christa Randzio-Plath

Chair, Economic and Monetary Affairs Committee of the European Parliament

This is a very timely initiative and it offers us an opportunity to take stock of what has been achieved so far during more than a decade of remarkable European merger control policy, and to find answers to the new challenges facing us. Therefore I convey to you my best wishes for a successful Conference.

I would also like to transmit the support of the Economic and Monetary Affairs Committee regarding the quality of the work undertaken by the Merger Task Force since its creation and, in particular, during the difficult past few years of intensive merger activity.

The underlying aim of the Green Paper on the review of the Merger Control Regulation is to provide the necessary responses to the new challenges resulting from greater integration of European markets and economic globalisation, the immediate effect of which has been to increase the number and complexity of cases that the Commission is being called on to examine. The need to cooperate and work together with the authorities of the Member States and the additional challenge posed by the forthcoming enlargement of the Union add another dimension to the review.

Given these challenges, the European Parliament believes that certain points, in particular harmonisation of the fundamental provisions of national and Community legislation, should be tackled in parallel to the review itself. The Commission and the Council should determine the most appropriate bases and procedures with a view to embarking on such harmonisation because there is no specific legal basis for this in the Treaties under the heading of competition policy.

In general, the heart of the current reform can be said to be one focusing on jurisdictional matters and especially the alterations to the threshold system introduced under the 1997 reform in Article 1(3) of the Regulation. The Commission is rightly aware that no change should undermine 'effective, efficient, fair and transparent control of concentrations at the most appropriate level, in accordance with the principle of subsidiarity'. This attitude is very much welcomed by the European Parliament.

The recent merger control decisions by the Court of First Instance annulling Commission decisions have to be studied carefully. They invite reflection on better economic analysis. We feel that strengthening the role of economic analysis is necessary in order to cope with the challenges of globalisation on the one hand and increased integration in Europe on the other. But the European Parliament does not consider these judgments as disqualifying the work of the Commission. Court rulings are part of any system where the rule of law prevails. And regarding court judgments,

I would like to refer to a German saying that states that on the high sea and in a court you are in the hands of God. We consider that the current system of appeals to the Court of Justice does not work in an optimal way, and we ask the Commission to envisage the possibility of an independent body, such as a new judicial panel in accordance with Article 225a introduced by the Nice Treaty, in order to treat cases before the Court in a quick and effective way by judges with special knowledge of competition and state aid. One could also consider a new system whereby the final decision in a merger case, including the imposed conditions, should be subject to a preview by such an independent body in a fast-track procedure, giving a greater legal security for the companies involved and their competitors.

Competition policy as such is one of the methods laid down in the Treaty for attaining the Union's objectives, particularly those set out in Article 127 of the EC Treaty: 'The objective of high level of employment shall be taken into consideration in the formulation and implementation of Community policies and activities' and at the Lisbon European Council and should not only concern the competitiveness of European economies and companies but also the protection of consumer interests, as well as supporting the objectives of full employment.

The time has come to examine whether mergers and acquisitions (M&As) which took place during the past merger wave of the late 1990s have really produced the expected efficiency objectives that they were expected to achieve. And we all know that recent studies show that this has not been the case for the majority of them: on the contrary, in a great deal of merger cases in all sectors of the economy the results have been negative not only from the employment and economic perspective, which is the first to be affected, but also for all stakeholders' interests in the medium and long run. Most mergers and takeovers have been proven to be disappointments, compared to the expectations of them.

These results are clearly opposite to the strategic goals for the European Union as laid down in the Lisbon Summit in 2000, underlining the necessity for Europe 'to become the most competitive region in the world in order to ensure growth, full employment and social inclusion'. Indeed, competitiveness is important but at the same time, we have to ask ourselves whether there is not currently an obsession with competition being seen as an instrument rather than an objective, which is dangerous for the economy and for employment.

The Lisbon strategy, together with the Göteborg strategy on sustainable development and the Barcelona and Seville Summits, created the obligation to implement a policy mix of economic, employment, environmental and social coordination aimed at:

- sustaining the healthy economic outlook and favourable growth prospects by applying an appropriate macro-economic policy mix;
- stepping up the process of structural reform for competitiveness and innovation and by completing the internal market;
- preparing the transition to a knowledge-based economy and society by better policies for the information society and R&D;
- modernising the European social model, investing in people and combating social exclusion.

To ensure that decisions regarding corporate restructuring are based on long-term perspectives and take into account the strategy for full employment, we need to put in place a broad range of Community instruments – through both legislative measures and through contracts between social partners. Here, competition policy comes into play because it also has to serve the goals of growth, full employment and social inclusion.

It has to be clear from the outset that the parameters from which we start are no longer those we had after World War II, where the social contract philosophy was the prevailing rule. Without falling into protectionist temptations, it must be admitted that policies of economic liberalisation and globalisation have altered the relationship between the state, labour and industrial partners and that economic outcomes are now influenced – as stated by the ILO conference 1999 – more by market forces than by mediation through social actors, legal regulations or state intervention. One important question is how to deal with the social elements and consequences of industrial restructurings or mergers.

First, it has to be borne in mind that the restructuring processes must be realised with full respect for the economic value of the companies and the people involved in these activities. Second, and from a European perspective, this social rationalisation of industrial changes is widely enhanced and encouraged within the framework of the Strategic Goals set in Lisbon. Therefore the different EU policies must be further coordinated to achieve common and specific final objectives, and within this context competition policy has to make an effort to modify its philosophy accordingly.

At this point, there is a need to understand whether, in the case of the restructuring processes, the present regulatory and contractual framework on a European level is such as to ensure an efficient process of information, consultation and negotiation with workers' organisations.

Generally, it is national legislation that deals with issues of workers' rights to information and consultation. In Denmark, Germany, France, Austria and Portugal national legislation creates an obligation to inform elected worker representatives, generally work councils. In Belgium, Great Britain, Ireland, Italy and Sweden there is an obligation to inform trade unions and if there are no recognised unions in the company, workers representatives of the relevant company. In Finland, Greece, Luxembourg, the Netherlands, Norway and Spain both the elected worker representatives and trade unions are informed.

But the issue of workers' information and consultation has also been dealt with at European level in a number of directives, including the Merger Regulation. In short, there are five directives and one regulation. From the basis of the different instruments available we can focus briefly on the following basic needs:

1. The codification of the information and consultation provisions, in order to create a uniform European regulatory framework relating to the definitions of information and consultation.
2. The achievement of an effective implementation of the European Workers Councils Directive.
3. The identification of a new direction in the process of information, consulting and negotiation of M&A transactions at a European level, able to ensure the validity of the restructuring plan on an economic, financial, and social context.
4. The need to ensure a proper definition of both processes of information and consultations arises from the fact that those identified in Directive 2002/14/EC, instituting a general framework relating to worker information and consultation, are very poor.

5. There is also a need to implement the rules contained in the Directive setting up the European Workers Councils (Directive 94/45/EC).
6. Finally it is necessary to draw up a plan for the processes of information, consultation and negotiation of M&A on a European level, valid to ensure the efficiency of the transactions both from economic and social perspectives.

Indeed, the Merger Regulation itself has foreseen the possibility for employees or for Workers' Councils to express their views to the Commission during the course of an in-depth investigation. However, some constraints exist, coming mainly from the rigid deadlines for examination and from the object of the investigation itself as the consultation has to be limited to the likely economic impact of the operation. Therefore, we are aware that it is not legally possible for the Commission to assess the impact of M&A transactions on employment in a particular undertaking.

The European Parliament rightly requested the Commission not to allow mergers if the relevant company did not apply European social legislation, in particular the right to timely information and consultation of employees. At Community level the Commission's Green Paper on 'Promoting a European framework for corporate social responsibility' rightly underlines that anticipation of change is important and that workers have to be involved, and that their full and efficient participation in economic life should be guaranteed. During the present reform process of Regulation 4064/89, consideration has been given to the impact on the environment and on consumers, while the consequences on employment have unfortunately been completely ignored. A voluntary consultation procedure with workers' representatives is foreseen, but it continues to be limited purely to economic issues, excluding employment aspects. In this context, I would like to mention the positive example of the South African Competition Commission. The South African Competition Act is unique as it provides explicitly for trade union participation in merger proceedings before the competition authorities. The necessity accordingly to change the legal framework of the European Union, integrating the social and the economic aspects of M&A transactions, has nowadays become a prerequisite to obtain the complete picture of the whole implications of these transactions on the economy. The question should be then if this should be desirable in the future. It is at this point where competition and social policies should go together in line with the Lisbon strategic goals for the European Union.

1. Conclusions

I would not like to finish my intervention without recalling that:

- The last merger wave has produced heavy consequences for the world economy and that strategies must be created from the public and private levels to avoid repetition of this in the future.
- There is a responsibility for national governments and for European institutions to look to the well-being of the economy, and that trusting 'goodwill long-term' companies' strategies has proved to be a wrong attitude and that the unemployment bill has not shown so far to be counterbalanced by other market benefits.

- A key issue is to enhance the development of a new management culture and that corporate responsibility is an obligation which has to be shared by all actors involved in the company's decision-making processes, namely shareholders, management, and workers. This assumption is crucial for the success of any restructuring process.
- The social rationalisation of companies' restructuring plans, in particular when a merger originates them, is a step forward for the benefit of the companies and therefore for all stakeholders involved, employees and public authorities included.
- At the level of competition policy, mechanisms have to be implemented to seriously check the social rationalisation process when restructuring operations plans are put forward, and that the items pointed out today in this respect merit at least serious and consistent thought. I therefore make an appeal to the Commission and to the Council to take on board the social dimension of concentration operations in the next proposal for of the Merger Regulation.
- The reform of the Merger Regulation pays tribute to the new challenges by adapting the legal framework, the jurisdictional system and the economic analyses, and improving legal certainty and the level playing field for all cross-border mergers. That in this context, the enhanced cooperation between the competition authorities and the national and Community level courts on counts. That also the automatic Community competence and at the same time a more restrictive interpretation of the two-thirds rule and the possibility of the Commission to refer cases and the clear procedural time schedule are very much welcomed, but that the question of a modification of the substantive test should be handled very carefully due to the risk of legal uncertainty. Finally also that there is no separation between the investigating and decision-making authorities and that further improvements and speeding-up procedures should therefore be made to the current system with appeal to the Court of First Instance.

I firmly believe that changes are the motor of economic life. A good reform of merger control will certainly contribute to it. The European Parliament is waiting for your advice.

Recent CFI Rulings on Merger Cases, Interim Measures and Accelerated Procedures and Some Reflections on Reform Measures Regarding Judicial Control

Bo Vesterdorf

President, Court of First Instance of the EC, Luxembourg

Please note that this is a written version of oral observations formulated in the light of Commissioner Monti's opening address and in reply to certain questions raised during various panel discussions or from the floor.[1]

For the judges of the Court of First Instance of the European Communities (CFI), living a quiet but busy life in Luxembourg out of the limelight of the media, the last couple of weeks have been quite an experience. Never before has the media taken such an enormous interest in our judgments. This might of course to some seem quite flattering. I have to say, however, that unfortunately the media in certain instances gave a somewhat distorted picture of the reality. Let me in these circumstances use this opportunity to stress what ought to be obvious. The CFI does not send 'messages', the CFI does not 'fight' with the Commission, instead the CFI merely does what it is supposed to do. It renders judgments in cases submitted to it, no more, no less, and in doing so it does what the Treaty asks it to do, namely to verify the legality of the decision, be it a competition decision or otherwise, submitted for judicial review.[2] The CFI examines whether the defendant acted within its competence, if procedural rules were infringed or not, whether the Treaty or secondary law was violated and whether there was an abuse of power. This is the role of the CFI and just as the role of the Commission is unfettered by the recent rulings, so too is that of the CFI unchanged. The Commission is and remains under the Treaty and the relevant regulations the Community authority responsible for ensuring the application of the EC rules on competition in the marketplace and for ensuring that the necessary legislative framework is in place.

As regards the recent merger rulings by the CFI you will appreciate that I must refrain from commenting in any detail on those judgments. I sat in these cases and the Commission is, as we have understood from the speech of Commissioner Monti earlier, still considering whether or not to introduce an appeal in one or both of them. Suffice to say that the CFI in two of its most recent judgments and in the earlier

1 A number of footnotes have been added hereinafter containing information to which no reference was made in my oral comments at the Conference but which, it is hoped, will constitute useful references for the present written text. I would like to thank Noel Travers, Legal Secretary (Référendaire) in my chambers, for his assistance.

2 In this connection, it is perhaps useful to recall that the CFI is no longer a court that deals almost exclusively with competition cases as it was on its establishment in 1989.

Airtours judgment of 6 June 2002 in fact largely confirmed the legal principles on which the impugned decisions of the Commission were based but that, when it came to the evidence and the concrete economic analyses in all three cases, the CFI found certain deficiencies that necessitated the annulment of the decisions.[3] It is now for the Commission to draw the consequences – if any – of the judgments regarding the existing merger control legislative framework or administrative procedures. Obviously, the Commission may also just decide to bring the cases before the Court of Justice to see if that Court confirms the judgments of the CFI.

Let me now turn to what was the very interesting and important substance of the reform package which Commissioner Monti outlined this morning, as a result of reform considerations already begun with the publication – long before the three high-profile judgments – of the Commission's Green Paper on merger reform.

Although I shall concentrate on the latter part of the reform considerations which concerns the question of judicial review, I cannot refrain from observing that I am impressed by the extent to which the Commission DG Competition is drawing positive consequences from the responses it has received during the consultative process from industry, from academia, from governmental bodies, from conferences on the topic and, perhaps, even from the recent rulings. I also do not doubt that the various immediate measures which Commissioner Monti outlined this morning will, if implemented, lead to a strengthening and improvement of the administrative procedures to the benefit of the parties notifying a proposed merger and ultimately the common good.

Regarding the judicial review of merger decisions Commissioner Monti specifically mentioned five different elements. First, the question of the number of cases which can be dealt with by the CFI applying the fast-track procedure. Secondly, the question whether decisions by the CFI applying the fast-track procedure can be taken even more quickly. Thirdly, the possibility of creating a specialised chamber within the CFI to deal with these cases or, fourthly, the creation of a new Community competition court in the form of a judicial panel and, finally, the question whether it would be possible to strengthen the role of the judge hearing applications for interim measures.

Let me then first deal with the application of the expedited, better known as fast-track, procedure in the present circumstances of the CFI's jurisdiction and workload. As you know, the CFI introduced this new procedure in February last year precisely to allow for certain cases of a particularly urgent character to be dealt with in an expedited procedure. We had in mind in particular merger cases but not only such cases; in principle, any case of a particularly urgent nature may merit expedited treatment on the condition that the case, as presented to the CFI, lends itself to such a treatment and to the extent that the CFI, in view of its other workload, is in a position actually to deal with the case under that procedure.

3 See Case T-342/99, *Airtours v Commission* [2002] ECR II-2585, Case T-310/01, *Schneider Electric v Commission* [2002] ECR II-4071, Judgment of 22 October 2002, and Case T-5/02, *Tetra Laval v Commission* [2002] ECR II-4381, Judgment of 25 October 2002. As regards the challenges to the divestiture decisions adopted by the Commission in consequence of its prohibition of the merger operations at issue in *Schneider Electric* and *Tetra Laval* cases (see Case T-77/02, *Schneider Electric v Commission* [2002] ECR II-4201, Judgment of 22 October 2002 and T-80/02, *Tetra Laval v Commission* [2002] ECR II-4589, Judgment of 25 October 2002), the Commission's analysis in those divestiture decisions was not considered by the CFI as they were annulled as a logical consequence of the annulment of the prohibition decisions in question.

The CFI has, since the introduction of this new procedure, received (by the end of October 2002) 34 applications with a request for the use of the fast-track procedure. It has accepted 14 out of these, all of them except three in merger cases. With the four recent cases dealt with under that procedure now decided, we have seven such merger cases pending, some of them, however, will be dealt with jointly because of their connectedness. Experience has shown us that this is probably even more than we ought perhaps to have accepted in view of the extra problems this creates all around for the CFI's different services and the judges' chambers. On top of this, it should not be forgotten that each case to be dealt with under the new procedure means that at least one other case will be dealt with less quickly than otherwise. It needs therefore to be stressed that the CFI cannot with present resources and the total number of cases – probably close to some 400 new ones this year – in any way give a guarantee that it can decide every or even most merger case(s) under that procedure and that it is so even if the case as such, in principle, lends itself to being decided under that procedure. It is quite simply a question of resources.[4]

As concerns the wish for even more rapid decisions by the CFI in cases dealt with under the fast-track procedure, I have to stress that there is a limit to how quickly cases can be decided. This is so for several reasons of a different nature. We need to give the defendant, as a minimum, one month to prepare the defence; after all we are talking about very complex cases presented by highly specialised lawyers. If the case is presented to the CFI in a language other than French, our internal working language, ie even if in English, we need to have translations prepared into our working language and this takes time. The application in both of the recently decided cases, one of which was presented to us in French, was more than 80 pages long. We also need some time to study the two written pleadings with a view to seeing if we can go directly to the second phase, the oral hearing, or whether we might find it useful to invite the parties to an informal meeting with the judge-rapporteur or the chamber to identify the key issues for the oral hearing which is even more important in this kind of proceedings than would normally be the case. There is the possibility or 'risk' of interventions which will delay procedures and which often raise problems of confidentiality that have to be resolved prior to the hearing. The judge-rapporteur needs some time to prepare his report for the hearing which must be sent to the parties in due time before the hearing for their possible comments. We will have the hearing, deliberations thereafter in the relevant chamber, the drawing up of a draft judgment, new deliberations of the chamber and the final linguistic review of the judgment, and then, finally, translation into the language of the procedure, if it is not French, followed by a review of that translation by the judges. I can assure you that we needed every single day, hour and moment of the nine months it took from the introduction of the *Tetra Laval* cases to the day of the judgments and that was also very much the case in the

4 Of the 44 merger cases that have been lodged at the CFI since its inception in 1989, almost one year before the entry into force, on 21 September 1990, of Council Regulation (EEC) of 21 December 1989 on the control of concentrations between undertakings (OJ 1989 L 395/1, corrected version in OJ 1990 L 257/13), 23 cases, ie over 50 per cent of the total, have been lodged since the beginning of 2000, while the CFI has so far received some 13 cases this year alone, a figure that does not include Case T-310/01, *Schneider Electric v Commission* which was lodged just before last Christmas on 13 December 2001. If this level of increase in the merger case-load were to continue, then, with the present level of the CFI's resources, the application of the fast-track procedure would simply have to become exceptional.

Schneider Electric cases even though French was there the language of procedure. You will see that, unless a contested merger decision is very different from and less complex than those at issue in the above-mentioned cases, the CFI will not, realistically, be able further to expedite its decision-making procedures. One needs also to make sure that haste does not lead to an inadequate level of judicial control. That would certainly not be in the general interest of litigants.

Turning to specialised chambers within the CFI, this is a question which has often been put to the CFI not only concerning competition cases. Up until a few years ago the CFI rejected the idea altogether. However, a couple of years ago we proceeded to introduce a certain kind of specialisation insofar as Community trademark cases are concerned: they are now only dealt with by two chambers of the CFI and not by all five. This was decided provisionally by the CFI in order to ensure a high degree of consistency of the case law to be developed by the CFI in this novel area of Community law. I think I can say that this has proved to be a very useful decision. There is, nevertheless, a certain degree of hesitation among some of my colleagues, for reasons of principle, regarding the idea of a general specialisation of the CFI's chambers. It is felt that the judges of the CFI should deal with all kinds of cases thus avoiding a risk of fragmentation of the functioning of the CFI with the resultant risks for the interpretation of the principles of law of general application being applied. The judges who deal with Community trademark cases also deal with all other types of cases but with a smaller number of such other cases than their colleagues. I say this not to exclude the possibility of creating a specialised chamber for merger cases but simply to indicate that such a move would require the adoption of a new approach by the CFI. However, it must also be stressed that in the present circumstances there are other real obstacles of a practical nature which would make it difficult, if not impossible, for the CFI to establish such a chamber. We quite simply do not have enough chambers as it is to deal with the large number of new cases lodged every year. If a specialised chamber for merger cases were to have any meaning it should not have to deal with other cases since it would have to be able to deal with any merger case brought before the CFI at any time and in accordance with the fast-track procedure. It could therefore not also, in between so to speak, decide other cases because the treatment of such other cases would constantly run the risk of having to be postponed owing to the arrival of new, and by definition urgent, merger cases. It should, in that context, be recalled that merger cases do not come at regular intervals and in predictable numbers to the CFI.[5] Having regard to the amount of other cases to be decided for parties who also have a right to have their cases decided in turn and as quickly as possible, and certainly without unreasonable delay, we cannot simply reserve one chamber out of five for incoming merger cases whose time and rate of arrival are both unpredictable. Even after the enlargement which will allow us to create another three chambers it would be a serious problem since new Member States also inevitably mean new cases.

What other possibilities, realistically speaking, do we then have? The Treaty of Nice provides us with new means in this regard. It allows for the creation of so-called 'judicial panels' to be attached to the CFI and to deal with specific areas of Community

5 By the way, it should also be observed that the simultaneous or proximate arrival of a number of merger cases would even stretch the limits of a specialised CFI merger chamber to deal with each case by the fast-track procedure within a 'commercially' acceptable time limit.

law at first instance. The Commission is, at present, in the process of preparing a proposal for the establishment of such a new court for staff cases. When that staff court is established, it will relieve the CFI, on current statistics, of some 80 to 100 cases per year but we shall probably have to decide some 25 to 35 cases on appeal against decisions taken by that court. Furthermore, it should not be forgotten that the Court of Justice and the CFI have presented to the Council a document containing a, so far informal, proposal for a transfer of further jurisdiction to the CFI regarding direct cases brought before the Community courts by Member States. Once the Treaty of Nice enters into force the Council will decide, on a formal proposal in this respect from the Court of Justice, on whether to proceed with such a transfer. It would mean extra work for the CFI in cases which normally have a certain complexity and importance, particularly in the area of state aids.

What is important in the context of the forthcoming merger control reforms is, however, that there is now a possibility, simply by establishing a new competition court in the form of a judicial panel, to solve the problem of how to ensure sufficiently rapid treatment of merger cases by judges specialised in this area of law. This possibility merits, *in my personal opinion*, serious consideration since it would allow for the appointment of a sufficient number of judges with specific experience in this area of law. It would allow for new tailor-made procedures for treating such cases. Such a court could be given jurisdiction to deal with all kinds of competition cases, thus not only with merger cases, while the CFI would become the appellate court perhaps with the possibility, in such circumstances, of assigning one or two of its chambers specifically to hear such appeals.[6] It would thus also relieve the Court of Justice of the task of dealing with often very voluminous competition appeals, particularly in the big cartel cases.[7] This is not necessarily the type of case that the highest Community court should have regularly to spend its resources on, especially if, post-Treaty of Nice, it is to move, in the longer term, towards becoming something more akin at EU level to a national supreme or constitutional court.

I need to stress that the CFI has no position – at least so far – on whether or not the establishment of such a competition court would be desirable. However, if and when the Commission should decide to propose the setting up of such a new court, we must be heard but only heard. One issue to be addressed would be whether the eventual creation of such a new court should be accompanied by a transfer of preliminary reference competence in respect of Articles 81 and 82 EC and merger control cases to the CFI.

Let me then, penultimately, address the question of whether the possibility of obtaining interim measures offers some kind of solution to the problem of urgency raised by legal challenges brought in respect of merger decisions taken by the

6 It seems unlikely that the Council would be willing to countenance the creation of a new judicial panel charged with hearing merger cases alone. It is, thus, probably more realistic to consider the desirability of establishing a competition law court of first instance. Such a court should not, however, in my opinion at least, have jurisdiction in cases concerning state aids where the issues raised are very different from those involved in cases concerning Articles 81 and 82 EC or mergers having a Community dimension.

7 The ECJ would, of course, always retain the possibility to re-examine decisions of the CFI given on appeal pursuant to the novel procedure created by the Treaty of Nice (see the new Article 225(2), second indent, EC) where, exceptionally, it is considered that a particular judgment poses 'a serious risk' of affecting 'the unity or consistency of Community law'.

Commission, be they positive or negative, for the notifying parties. As indicated by the CFI when we proposed the introduction of the fast-track procedure into our rules of procedure, this new procedure finds in part its justification in the fact that interim measures in merger cases, probably more often than not, are of little avail. This is due to the fact that the suspension by the judge hearing an application for interim measure of a negative decision by the Commission cannot turn that decision into a positive, thus approving, decision. That would mean that the judge hearing the application for interim measures would effectively substitute his assessment for that of the Commission. On the other hand, the interim judge should not suspend a positive Commission decision because that would turn it, as regards its commercial effects, into something comparable to a negative decision, thereby jeopardising the economic importance of the approved merger operation. In any event, it would be hazardous for the parties to rely on such suspensions even if they were adopted given the economic importance of all mergers having a Community dimension and the financial risks thus at stake.

There are, however, possibly some measures which may be ordered by way of interim relief by the CFI. Take, for example, a case in which a positive decision has been attacked by a competitor who is able to show that he is directly and individually concerned by such a decision. In such a case the judge might perhaps order – under specific conditions designed to protect the interests of the parties to the notification – that the activities of the acquired company or companies (or parts thereof) be kept separate if and until the main case is decided according to the fast-track procedure. Take, on the other hand, the further example of a positive decision which is, however, formally conditioned on the divestiture by the parties of certain of their activities. In such a case the notifying parties might attack the decision asking for the annulment of the dispositive part of the decision in which the Commission imposes this obligation. In such a case the judge hearing an application for interim measures might – of course, on condition that he finds that there is *fumus boni juris* and urgency and that the balance of interest is in favour of the applicant – suspend that part of the decision under certain conditions to be set by him. There are, thus, at least some possibilities for the granting of interim measures. It would probably, however, require amendments to the existing merger legislation expressly to give the judge hearing interim-measure applications more power, in the event that this should be deemed necessary.

Let me say, finally, that the CFI remains open for discussion with the Commission as to the kind of amendments to the existing system that the Commission may find it useful or appropriate to discuss with us. I have, in the press, recently been cited for advocating a radical change in the direction of the US system whereby prohibition decisions have to be first approved by the courts. Let me use this opportunity to stress that we have plenty of work as it is and we do not seek such additional powers. In conclusion, let me express my appreciation of Commissioner Monti's indication this morning of the willingness of the Commission to support the case for extra resources to be allocated to the CFI should the choice in the end be made by the relevant political authorities not to establish a new court in the form of a judicial panel to deal with competition cases in first instance but, rather, to keep those cases before the CFI.

Hearing Officer: First Year under the New Mandate

Serge Durande

Hearing Officer, European Commission, Brussels

The organisers of today's event have allocated this time to the Hearing Officers to present their views on the first year after the new mandate. In a few minutes, my colleague will address you specifically on one of the most interesting and important issues in our function, the oral hearings.

As far as I am concerned, I have chosen to speak about the questions which the lawyers ask me most frequently when I meet them, bearing in mind that the questions are based on the current system as introduced on 21 May 2001.

There are two questions. The first one is: are you independent? The way the question is phrased, you can see that there is some scepticism involved. The second question is: what are you doing to help us, when we are faced with such a powerful DG? Let me say a few words about the independence question first.

Obviously, this is a very important and critical issue, which goes to the heart of the matter and makes the link with the other question, namely, one cannot be of much help if one is not independent.

One of the lawyers present today said two years ago at a conference that the answer to the Hearing Officer's independence question is a plain 'No', for two reasons. First, the Hearing Officer was part of the hierarchy of DG Competition, and secondly he was like the legal service, part of the Commission staff.

Let us concentrate for a minute on these two aspects. You will have noticed that under the new mandate, the Hearing Officer is no longer in the DG for Competition. He is attached directly to the member of the Commission in charge of competition matters, following the wording of the Commission's decision.

This brings with it a number of consequences. I am sure that you appreciate the difference. When you meet the people of the DG for Competition, you are not a straightforward colleague anymore, you are a distant one, certainly you are not seen as belonging to the DG.

You receive no instructions from the DG, you are perfectly free to express your views, and you do. This in my view deals with the first point.

In relation to the second point: we are Commission people, we are under the Statute of the European Civil Servants. I personally do not see that this would make me less independent, if only because the Hearing Officers' 'new wave' are *de facto* placed in a slightly different situation from most other civil servants.

I quote the mandate of the Hearing Officers, Article 2: 'The appointment of the Hearing Officers shall be published in the Official Journal of the European Communities'. Now comes the interesting bit 'any interruption, termination of appointment or transfer by whatever procedure, shall be the subject of a reasoned decision of the Commission. That decision shall be published in the Official Journal'.

As a matter of fact, I feel that this is a significant protective measure. Moreover, are we in the same position as the Legal Service, which is acting as an in-house counsel under the control of the President of the Commission? Of course not. The Legal Service advises the Commission and subsequently defends the legality of the decisions and the legislation before the courts.

The Hearing Officer simply does not have the same function. The Hearing Officer has a much more limited role, he looks at the competition cases when they are ripe, at the stage of the Statement of Objections, he organises the hearings, writes interim and final reports. He is not very visible or glorious, but he has a role, and I am pleased to say that neither my colleague nor me have received an instruction or anything that would look like it from Mr Monti in the past year. Let me develop this a little to make it very clear: being attached to Mr Monti, the Hearing Officers have periodical meetings with him in order to improve due process, but he does not give any instruction on specific cases.

In my view this deals with the second point, but I would not leave this theme without saying what I – independently – think.

Something more helps him tremendously in this quest for independence, and I am aware that when I say so, I may not be fashionable. This is the mere fact that being an established European civil servant he has a reasonably good salary, and he is not in a short-term contractual relationship with the institution. He has no fear at all for his own future.

I now leave it to you to decide for yourself whether this set of parameters makes him independent or not. My own answer is: yes, absolutely, he is as independent as one can be in the present institutional system.

Turning to the second question, less theoretical but maybe as or even more important for the legal community which I express again: what are you doing to help my client out in front of this very powerful DG indeed?

I believe I have done a number of things, bearing in mind though that the Hearing Officers, like each of you, are willing to see competition rules implemented. So it is not only a question of looking at the immediate interest of the companies concerned. It is about implementing the competition rules in a fair and transparent way because, yes, the system has to be fair, and the companies are entitled to have confidence in it. But, yes also, you are part of the enforcement system when you are Hearing Officer.

1. Recent actions

I will mention some of the actions taken in the past year which are of a horizontal nature, and say a few words about cases, or at least about the way in which the Hearing Officers are handling cases.

I will tackle actions of a horizontal nature first. In this respect, the Hearing Officers put in place at the end of last year a new system to increase the general level of awareness of the Directorate General in relation to the rights of defence, in order to make sure that the right to be heard is completely implemented. How? By asking the case teams to provide comprehensive tables to the Hearing Officer, before the hearing when there is one, and also before the final decision in any case, which clearly spell out all the arguments of the parties in response to the Commission's objections and, at the last stage, the answers which are given to them. I insist: all the arguments, not only the main ones. As you know, this goes beyond the requirements of the Court of First Instance (CFI).

More recently, I remember having defended the view that an access to file should be given in merger cases after having initiated proceedings and launched an in-depth inquiry, ie at the stage of the 6(1)(c) decisions.

You have just heard the Commissioner this morning saying that he would instruct the DG to put this into place. This is obviously a very interesting development, in terms of increasing the transparency of the decision-making process, and in helping the undertakings to better comprehend (at an early stage of the case) the Commission's competition concerns.

My last point will be to mention action by the Hearing Officers in specific cases. This may give them the privilege of being caught exactly in between the Directorate General, which is not pleased when you object to their argumentation and their behaviour in the wider sense, and the parties and/or third parties to a case, who are not pleased either when the Hearing Officer does not recognise their argumentation or claims for. This is a fact of life, and after all the job is not about pleasing everybody.

At this point in time I feel like saying that the denomination 'Hearing Officer' does not describe in full the reality of the function, while the French term 'Conseiller Auditeur' actually provides a much better understanding of what we do, because they contain the word 'conseil', ie 'advise'.

In this capacity, the Hearing Officer may advise the Commissioner in the first place, and also by way of consequence the Directorate General, when he considers that something wrong is in fact happening in a case. This follows Article 3 of the terms of reference of the Hearing Officer, according to which he may present observations on any matter arising out of any Commission competition proceedings, to the competent member of the Commission.

I must say that I regularly draw on this provision. This may be in terms of due process in the stricter sense, because there may be procedural issues, such as prescription or the quality of evidence in fines cases. The Hearing Officer can express his views on the consequences which may be drawn from what you perceive as being procedural flaws.

This may also be, although less frequently, on issues of substance. I am not sure I should mention the specific cases in which this happened, but I would like to quote Mr Monti in a recent press conference, where he said that – quote – 'as to the Hearing Officers, I am happy that we introduced a reinforced mandate because in several cases already this has helped us to see problems that we couldn't have otherwise and to correct them in due course' – end of quote.

In three of these cases, although of a very different relative importance, this has ended in the cases being dropped altogether, for one or for all the parties to the case. I mention in passing that there had been an oral hearing in each of these cases. I am also, of course, very pleased that the decision has been taken to give resources to the Hearing Officers. This can only lead to an improvement of 'due process' in the wider sense.

One last point which I would also like to mention in passing: although the experts of the Member States for competition matters recognised the interest of the Hearing Officers' functions under the new mandate, they also confirmed to us during an experts meeting that there is no equivalent in any of the Member States, of a person who would specifically be in charge of ensuring fairness in their procedures.

It's all food for thought. It may be that the Commission is in fact setting an example in this respect.

To conclude, I would say that of course Hearing Officers should not be looked at as a panacea; universal remedies curing all the diseases or the faults simply do not exist. But the Hearing Officers have a very serious role to play under the new rules and the parties can call on them if and when there is a real issue of fairness in the handling of their case.

Hearing Officer: First Year under the New Mandate – Oral Hearings

Karen Williams

Hearing Officer, European Commission, Brussels

There are a number of issues which the Hearing Officer may deal with in the course of a competition procedure. Decisions on whether third parties are to be heard, requests to extend the deadline to reply to a statement of objections and the resolution of disputes on access to file are part of the 'bread and butter' of the Hearing Officer's work. In addition, as Serge Durande has just indicated, we can be called on when any legitimate due process issue is at stake. Nevertheless, we remain most commonly associated with the function for which the role was originally created: the oral hearing. The Hearing Officer has exclusive competence for the organisation and conduct of the hearing. The Hearing Officer chairs the meeting, and reports to the Commissioner thereafter. This report deals with the right to be heard. In addition, the Hearing Officer is entitled to express a view to the Commissioner on the future progress of the case.

The essential purpose of the oral hearing is to enable the parties to exercise their rights of defence. It follows the Commission's Statement of Objections, setting out the competition concerns and the facts on which those concerns are based. The parties must have the opportunity to respond to these concerns – in writing and also orally. Given the general time constraints imposed by the legal deadlines in merger cases it would be reasonable to assume that the oral hearing would be especially important to parties in merger cases and would play a prominent role in the administrative procedure overall.

However, in a meeting held with competition lawyers earlier this year we were confronted with disillusion as to the value of oral hearings, in particular in merger cases. This disillusion was based essentially on the unlikelihood of the Commission changing its preliminary view as set out in the Statement of Objections. Lawyers complained, in particular, that parties face essentially the same case team at the oral hearing as all previous meetings on the case, with little indication that others would or could take an active role in the decision-making process. They also expressed a reluctance to expose clients to hearings, organised at their request and in the interests of their own defence, which could in the event provide too much of a platform for third parties hostile to their merger plans.

The complaints were not necessarily new, nor confined to the oral hearing as such. We do not necessarily accept the merits of all claims made. Nevertheless, the meeting was a thought-provoking experience for the new Hearing Officers. We ourselves have also noted a reluctance of parties in some cases to request an oral hearing (though merger cases have in general been rather thin on the ground this year). Moreover responses to the merger review and, of course, the recent judgment of the Court of

First Instance, require us to re-evaluate hearings, like all other parts of the competition procedure.

Accordingly, we are examining all aspects of the oral hearing in particular with a view to making hearings more focused, interactive and more useful generally for all concerned. Some measures have already been introduced in recent months, and are applicable to antitrust as much as mergers.

- To begin with, the layout has already changed. Whenever possible hearings are now held in meeting rooms with circular seating, as compared with the former podium-style layout. The DG Competition case-team has been clearly separated from the Hearing Officer and normally sits facing the parties.
- In addition, the Director responsible for the case is expected to be present. In future, the Deputy Director General may also participate. In appropriate cases the Merger Panel and Chief Economist should also attend. Directorate A is normally represented in any event. The extent to which these participants operate as checks and balances or are more closely allied to the investigation depends on their actual involvement in that process. In any event, this should in future dispel any notion that the case team is running the show alone. Of course the Legal Service, other associated services and the Member States, will continue to be also represented and are encouraged by the Hearing Officer to take an active role. The Hearing Officer is also listening closely.
- We have also started to introduce more structure and focus into hearings, at least by encouraging parties to concentrate on the main issues which need to be drawn out (especially factual issues). Presentations should not be overly lengthy and must be punctuated by frequent opportunities for questioning. Obviously more can be done in this respect. Indeed the mandate itself includes a number of provisions, not really exploited to date. In particular, pre-hearing meetings between the Hearing Officer and the parties should become standard in our view and the Hearing Officer should have a more pro-active role in the content of the hearing itself. The resources just announced by the Commissioner for the Hearing Officers will of course help to ensure that the hearing can be better prepared in future.
- In addition, there must be sufficient time made available to enable such preparation to take place.
- Traditionally, the Commission listens to the parties' arguments, and then presents questions. Member States are encouraged to ask questions too. Parties, and third parties, may comment on each other's statements. This does not preclude a dialogue and even, on occasion, some questions to the Commission. However, the process is not adversarial in nature. In future, parties should be able to make use of pre-hearing meetings to alert the Hearing Officer to specific issues that in their view need clarification. The Hearing Officer can invite the case-team to address these issues fully in presenting their case during the hearing. In addition, the parties (and third parties) may also be invited by the Hearing Officer to comment specifically and fully on particular issues.
- A distinct feature of the Commission's hearings is that interested third parties admitted by the Hearing Officer are also able to participate in the oral hearing and to present their views on the case – whether for or against the merger. This is a positive feature – it is efficient, and enhances transparency as between

companies actively contributing. Nevertheless, the Hearing Officer must be careful to retain the appropriate balance between the interests of the parties to the concentration as compared to third parties in the case.

The Hearing Officer's mandate states that the hearing should contribute to the objectivity of any decision taken thereafter. The Hearing Officer is required in particular to ensure that in any subsequent draft decision due account is taken of all the relevant facts. The measures I have spoken of today are intended specifically to promote this objective.

Of course the whole process can only come into play if the parties themselves decide to make use of their right to be heard orally. On this, I have to say that I believe the parties should be very hesitant to deprive themselves of this important step, especially in merger cases, if they want to defend themselves to the full. In doing so, they deprive themselves, and the Commission of the opportunity for an effective check and balance in the Commission's administrative system.

We look forward to discussing this subject further with you to our mutual benefit in the coming months.

Session 2

Due Process and Judicial Review – Contrasting Merger Control Systems

7

Strengthening External Checks and Balances in the EU Merger Control System

Paul Glazener

Allen & Overy, Amsterdam

1. Introduction

The Commission's Green Paper on the review of the Merger Regulation[1] was relatively brief on the issue of due process and 'checks and balances'. In contrast to its position on other subjects, where the Commission put forward proposals for modifications, the Commission in the section dealing with due process and 'checks and balances' confined itself to a description of the current system. This suggested that the Commission did not think that any modifications were necessary. The Commission's position changed since the judgments of the Court of First Instance in *Airtours,*[2] *Schneider*[3] and *Tetra Laval.*[4] At a press conference on 25 October 2002 following the *Tetra Laval* judgment, Commissioner Monti announced significant reforms, including detailed 'best administrative practices', the formalisation of a 'peer review panel' in Phase II cases, the nomination of a senior economist and a team of specialist economists and reinforced powers for the Hearing Officer.

There have been appeals from several sides, including the European Parliament,[5] for a more radical overhaul of the system, and to require the Commission to initiate proceedings before the Court of First Instance if it wants to block a merger, as in the United States. This is not possible without an amendment of the Treaty, and would imply a wholly new division of competences between the Commission and the Court. There is no good reason why such a change should be limited to merger decisions and not include decisions on the basis of Articles 81 and 82 EC. Clearly, this would require a more comprehensive exploration of the issues involved than was instigated by the Green Paper.[6]

If the Commission is to retain its dual role as investigator and decision-making body, effective judicial review is necessary to ensure that the system complies with Article 6 of the European Convention on Human Rights. The Commission will say that the judgments in *Airtours, Schneider* and *Tetra Laval* demonstrate that it is subject to effective judicial review. This does not apply to *Airtours,* where the judgment came

1 Green Paper on the review of Council Regulation (EEC) No 4064/89, COM (2001) 745/6 final.

2 Case T-342/99, *Airtours v Commission,* judgment of 6 June 2002, not yet published.

3 Case T-310/01, *Schneider Electric SA v Commission,* judgment of 22 October 2002, not yet reported.

4 Cases T-5/02 and T-80/02, *Tetra Laval v Commission,* judgments of 25 October 2002, not yet reported.

5 See the motion for a resolution of the European Parliament adopted by the Committee on Economic and Monetary Affairs on 8 October 2002.

6 See the report on the review of the EC Merger Regulation of the House of Lords' Select Committee on the European Union, p 45.

two-and-a-half years after the Commission prohibited the merger. The expedited procedure applied by the Court of First Instance in *Schneider* and *Tetra Laval* is a marked improvement. The judgments in these cases have been delivered in less than one year. However, this will in many cases still be too long to save the deal. Furthermore, the Court's judgment is in principle followed by a reopening of the Commission procedure pursuant to Article 10(5) of the Merger Regulation.

There are ways to make the judicial review more effective, but the time required to obtain a judgment will always remain a problem in the judicial review of merger decisions. It is important to note that this problem would not be solved by changing to a US-style system. In the United States, the agencies first have to obtain a preliminary injunction if they want to block a merger. Such preliminary injunctions can be issued relatively quickly. But they may be followed by a trial on the merits which takes at least as much time as (expedited) proceedings before the Court of First Instance. If the agencies fail to obtain a preliminary injunction, the merging parties may therefore still face the uncertainty of the outcome of the main action. If they implement their merger, they take the risk of a divestiture should the agencies succeed in the main action.[7] Arguably, their position is not fundamentally different from parties who have obtained a suspension of a prohibition decision by way of interim relief in the EU system.

To address this fundamental imbalance, it is also necessary to build more 'checks and balances' into the administrative process. Many useful suggestions have been made in the replies to the Green Paper, and it is to be welcomed that the Commission is now considering introducing certain reforms. However, if such additional checks and balances have to make up for the fact that effective judicial review is not always available, they will have to include *external* checks and balances from outside the Directorate-General for Competition. This calls in particular for a strengthening of the role of the Hearing Officer. The other reforms which the Commission appears to be considering will help to improve the quality of the Commission's decisions, but are not instrumental in counterbalancing the exercise of the Commission's powers under the Merger Regulation.

In my paper I will discuss in some more detail these two issues: the role of the courts and that of the Hearing Officer.

2. Judicial review: challengeable acts

There are numerous instances in the Commission's procedure under the Merger Regulation where the parties concerned can challenge a decision of the Commission. This right is not limited to formal decisions but exists with respect to any act of the Commission which is capable of bringing about legal effects.[8] In the following paragraphs I will discuss the possibilities to challenge some of the more important decisions which the Commission may take in the investigation of a merger, making

7 In the United States, many cases do not survive beyond the preliminary injunction stage, but that has practical reasons such as the costs, delay and uncertainty of a full-blown trial on the merits (see ABA Section of Antitrust Law, *Mergers and Acquisitions: Understanding the Antitrust Issues*, ABA 2000, p 358). The main action is an integral part of the system in the United States.

8 See Case 60/81, *IBM v Commission* [1981] ECR 2639.

a distinction between decisions on the substance of the case and procedural decisions.

2.1 Substantive decisions

2.1.1 Prohibition decisions

There have been several appeals of prohibition decisions, some of which are still pending. The Court of First Instance delivered judgments in six cases: *Gencor,*[9] *Kesko,*[10] *Endemol,*[11] *Airtours,*[12] *Schneider*[13] and *Tetra Laval.*[14] Appeals are still pending in two cases: *WorldCom/Sprint*[15] and *GE/Honeywell.*[16] In *Gencor* it took 33 months to obtain a judgment, in *Kesko* it took 35 months, in *Endemol* it took 41 months and in *Airtours* it took 33 months. With the exception of *Airtours,* the appeals were unsuccessful, but it is clear that the judgments would have come too late to resurrect the merger if the outcome had been different. This also applies to *Airtours* and two of the appeals which are still pending. (The appeal in *WorldCom/Sprint* was filed on 28 September 2000, the appeal in *GE/Honeywell* on 12 September 2001.) In *Schneider* and in *Tetra Laval* the Court of First Instance has applied the expedited procedure. *Schneider* and *Tetra Laval* are exceptional cases, where the merger was effected by means of a public bid which under French law cannot be made conditional on the Commission's clearance. (Implementation of a public bid is permitted under Article 7(3) of the Merger Regulation, provided the voting rights attached to the shares are not exercised.) Following its decision prohibiting the mergers, the Commission ordered Schneider and Tetra Laval to divest their shareholdings in Legrand and Sidel within a certain time frame. In such exceptional situations, where the shares have already been acquired, there may still be an opportunity to complete the merger in the event of a successful appeal. In most cases, however, the opportunity to implement the transaction will have disappeared by the time the Court of First Instance gives its judgment.

A further delay is caused by Article 10(5) of the Merger Regulation, which provides that, where the Court makes a judgment annulling a Commission decision, the time periods laid down in the Regulation start again from the date of the judgment. This provision was applied for the first time in *Kali und Salz.*[17] The Commission in that case took the view that under this provision a new notification had to be submitted and that the competitive assessment of the concentration had to be carried out *ex nunc,* ie a completely new competitive assessment based on facts pertaining to the current market circumstances.[18] The status of Article 10(5) of the Merger Regulation has become unclear with the judgment of the Court of First Instance in *Schneider.*

9 Case T-102/96, *Gencor Ltd v Commission* [1999] ECR II-753.
10 Case T-22/97, *Kesko v Commission* [1999] ECR II-3775.
11 Case T-221/95, *Endemol v Commission* [1999] ECR II-1299.
12 Case T-342/99, *Airtours v Commission.*
13 Cases T-310/01 and T-77/02, *Schneider Electric SA v Commission,* not yet published.
14 Cases T-5/02 and T-80/02, *Tetra Laval BV v Commission,* not yet reported.
15 Case T-310/00, *WorldCom v Commission* (pending case).
16 Case T-210/01, *General Electric v Commission* (pending case).
17 Case IV/M.308, *Kali und Salz,* on appeal Joined Cases C-68/94 and C-30/95, *France and Others v Commission* [1997] ECR I-1375.
18 See XXVIIIth Report on Competition Policy 1998, points 175 *et seq.*

In *Schneider* the Court rejected the Commission's analysis with respect to all the relevant national markets outside France.[19] With respect to the consequences of its judgment the Court held the following[20] (the judgment is as yet only available in French):

> 'En vertu de l'article 233 CE, il appartient, en effet, à la Commission de prendre les mesures que comporte l'exécution du présent arrêt d'annulation.
>
> Ces mesures d'exécution doivent respecter les motifs qui constituent le soutien nécessaire du dispositif de l'arrêt (voir arrêt de la Cour du 26 avril 1988, Asteris e.a./ Commission, 97/86, 99/86 et 215/86, Rec. p. 2181, point 27). Les motifs pertinents du présent arrêt impliquent notamment, dans l'hypothèse où serait repris l'examen de la compatibilité de l'opération notifiée, que Schneider soit mise à même, pour les marchés sectoriels nationaux affectés à propos desquels l'analyse économique contenue dans la Décision n'a pas été écartée par le présent arrêt, à savoir les marchés sectoriels français, de faire utilement valoir sa défense et, le cas échéant, de proposer des mesures correctives répondant aux griefs retenus et préalablement précisés par la Commission.'

The Court seems to say that with respect to the relevant national markets outside France, the case is closed and the Commission cannot take any further action. As both the prohibition decision and the divestiture decision adopted under Article 8(4) of the Merger Regulation have been annulled by the Court, this would imply that in those countries the transaction can be completed. Under Article 230 EC, the Court only has the power to annul a decision of the Commission. It cannot replace the Commission's decision by its own decision or order the Commission to take a particular new decision. However, Article 233 EC states that the institution whose act has been declared void shall be required to take the necessary measures to comply with the Court's judgment. In *Schneider*, the Court of First Instance refers to the judgment of the Court of Justice in *Asteris*,[21] in which the Court stated that to comply with the judgment and to implement it fully, the institution is required to have regard not only to the operative part of the judgment but also to the grounds. According to the grounds in *Schneider*, the Commission has not shown that the merger of *Schneider* and *Legrand* creates a dominant position in the relevant national markets outside France. In particular, the Court disagrees with the approach followed by the Commission, which had based its assessment of the impact of the concentration in relation to these national markets on general, transnational considerations, without demonstrating their relevance at a national level. Apparently, the Court of First Instance takes the view that because it has rejected the Commission's analysis in relation to these markets, the Commission is prevented from taking a new decision as far as these markets are concerned (which effectively means that the merger is cleared in these countries, because the time to take a prohibition decision has expired). This is also apparent from the press release of the Court of First Instance, which states the following:

> 'This judgement therefore annuls the prohibition decision. The Court of First Instance adds that, if the [concentration] were to be re-examined (if Schneider

19 See ground 419 of the judgment in Case T-310/01.

20 Grounds 464 and 465 of the judgment.

21 Joined Cases 97, 193, 99 and 215/86, *Asteris and Others v Commission* [1988] ECR 2181.

maintains its wish to acquire Legrand), the procedure must recommence with the drawing up of a precise statement of objections and relate only to French markets, which are the only markets to have been identified as being affected by the implementation of the merger.'

The Court of First Instance in its judgment does not mention Article 10(5) of the Merger Regulation. Its apparent finding that the Commission is prevented from taking any further action with respect to the markets outside France is not easily reconciled with Article 10(5), which provides that the time periods laid down in the Regulation start again from the date of the judgment. According to the Commission's interpretation in *Kali und Salz*, this would mean that if *Schneider* still wanted to acquire Legrand, it would have to file a new notification which would be examined by the Commission on an *ex nunc* basis. Possibly the Court of First Instance considers that Article 10(5) of the Merger Regulation can be set aside by Article 233 EC. This would also explain the Court's statement (which is more explicit in the press release than in the judgment itself) that in relation to the French markets, the procedure ought to recommence with a new statement of objections. If the time periods laid down in the Regulation start again, the first step is not a statement of objections, which is only issued towards the end of the investigation period.

The judgments of the Court of First Instance in *Airtours* and *Tetra Laval* shed no light on this issue. In these cases the Court simply annuls the Commission's decision without saying anything about the consequences.[22]

2.1.2 Decisions declaring a concentration compatible with the Common Market

An unconditional authorisation can be challenged by third parties if they are directly and individually concerned within the meaning of Article 230 EC. This includes competitors of the parties to the concentration under certain conditions.[23] The parties to the concentration will normally not have the right to challenge an unconditional authorisation.[24] Until now all appeals by third parties against unconditional authorisations have been rejected. However, if such an appeal is successful and the Court annuls the Commission's decision, the Commission will have to reopen the case pursuant to Article 10(5) of the Merger Regulation. This could mean, at least in theory, that the Commission will prohibit the concentration after all and require its divestiture. In relation to third parties, the time between the Commission's decision and the judgment of the Court of First Instance does not necessarily deprive the Court's judgment of its practical significance.

22 In its press release issued after the Court's judgment, Tetra Laval assumes that there will be a new Commission procedure. It is interesting to note that in *Tetra Laval* the Court concludes that the Commission overestimated the anti-competitive effects of the merger, insofar as the Commission justifies its prohibition by the likely immediate horizontal and vertical effects resulting from the merger. In this respect the Court takes into consideration that the commitments offered by Tetra Laval would have eliminated a horizontal overlap between the parties. If the Commission were prevented from further investigating the merger, the parties would be allowed to implement it without these commitments.

23 See, *inter alia*, Case T-3/93, *Air France v Commission* [1994] ECR II-121.

24 See Joined Cases T-125/97 and T-127/97, *The Coca-Cola Company and Coca-Cola Enterprises Ltd v Commission* [2000] ECR II-1733.

2.1.3 Conditional authorisations

Conditional authorisations can be challenged by the parties to the concentration and by third parties, provided they can show direct and individual concern. There have been two judgments relating to conditional authorisations, one of the Court of Justice in *Kali und Salz*[25] and one of the Court of First Instance in *Kaysersberg.*[26] In *Kali und Salz* the Commission raised a plea of inadmissibility against the application for partial annulment brought by SCPA. SCPA distributed Kali und Salz's products in France and participated with Kali und Salz in an organisation which coordinated exports to third countries outside the European Union. To prevent the Commission from prohibiting the concentration on the ground that it would give rise to a collective dominant position of Kali und Salz and Mitteldeutsche Kali AG, on the one hand, and SCPA, on the other hand, Kali und Salz had offered to withdraw from the export organisation and to terminate the distribution arrangement with SCPA. SCPA sought annulment of those commitments. The Commission argued that annulment of the conditions attached to the declaration of compatibility would 'alter the substance of the contested decision', as the conditions for authorising the concentration would no longer be satisfied, and would compel the Commission to revoke the decision in its entirety. *Kaysersberg* involved an appeal of a competitor, who argued that the Commission should have prohibited the concentration instead of authorising it conditionally, and did not raise similar issues of admissibility.

In *Kali und Salz* the Court examined the plea of inadmissibility together with the substance of the case. As to the substance of the case, the Court held that the Commission had not established to the necessary legal standard that the concentration would give rise to a collective dominant position. Then the Court turned to the question of partial annulment. It referred to earlier judgments (not concerning the application of the Merger Regulation) in which it had held that partial annulment of a decision, limited to the conditions it imposes, is possible if these conditions can be severed from the remainder of the decision. The Court also referred to Article 10(5) of the Merger Regulation, which expressly mentions partial annulment of decisions. The Court continued as follows:

> 'However, it does not appear that annulment limited to the section of the operative part of the contested decision which relates to the conditions and obligations set out in point 63 thereof is possible without the substance of the decision being altered.
>
> It follows from the decision and the documents in the case taken as a whole that those conditions and the declaration of compatibility in the operative part form an indivisible whole. The conditions are the result of a negative assessment by the Commission of the concentration as notified, and are regarded by that institution as essential if the concentration is to be declared compatible with the common market.
>
> Consequently, the whole of the operative part of the contested decision must be annulled.'

The Court did not follow the Advocate-General, who had argued in favour of partial annulment. It is not immediately clear why the Court did not just annul the commitments, after it had found that 'the Commission has not any view established to

25 Joined Cases C-68/94 and C-30/95, *French Republic and Others v Commission* [1998] ECR I-1375.
26 Case T-290/94, *Kaysersberg v Commission* [1997] ECR II-2137.

the necessary legal standard that the concentration would give rise to a collective dominant position on the part of K+S/MdK and SCPA liable to impede significantly effective competition in the market' (ground 249 of the judgment). It is possible that the Court's findings have been influenced by Article 10(5) of the Merger Regulation. As already noted, Article 10(5) provides for a reopening of the Commission procedure and a new examination of the concentration in the light of the current market conditions. If the Court annuls only the commitments, the concentration has effectively been authorised and there is nothing more to investigate. As we have seen, the Court of First Instance appears to give less weight to Article 10(5) in *Schneider*, insofar as it appears to rule out a reopening of the Commission procedure in relation to the relevant national markets outside France.

Kali und Salz involved an appeal by a third party. A decision authorising a concentration subject to commitments can also be appealed by the parties to the concentration themselves. Although they have offered the commitments, it would be wrong to deny them the right to appeal the Commission's decision on that ground. Clearly the parties to the concentration have not offered the commitments out of their own free will, but only to avoid an outright prohibition of their merger. The conditions attached to the authorisation have binding legal effects affecting the interests of the parties to the concentration, so they should have the right to appeal the decision under Article 230 EC. However, the Court's judgment in *Kali und Salz* appears to close the door to partial annulment not only in the specific circumstances of that case, but with respect to conditional authorisations in general. If that is correct, the parties to the concentration will not be able to obtain a partial annulment which would allow them to implement the concentration without the commitments, even if they can convince the Court that the Commission was wrong in finding that the concentration would give rise to a dominant position. Instead they will have to await the outcome of a new Commission investigation in light of the current market circumstances.

2.1.4 Conditional authorisations in Phase I

Under Article 6(2) of the Merger Regulation, the Commission may declare a concentration compatible with the Common Market in Phase I if the parties offer commitments that remove the Commission's serious doubts. By offering such commitments the parties can avoid a burdensome Phase II investigation which carries the risk of becoming a self-fulfilling prophecy.

So far there have been no appeals of conditional authorisations in Phase I. It is clear that such decisions can be appealed by third parties which are directly and individually concerned. For the reasons outlined above, I see no reason why such decisions cannot be appealed as well by the parties to the concentration themselves. Instead of showing that the Commission has not properly established the existence of a dominant position, they would have to show that the Commission has not properly established the serious doubts that prompted them to offer the commitments. Clearly the Commission is entitled to a considerable discretion in this respect, which will make it very difficult to show that the Commission had no reason to entertain serious doubts. Even if the parties can pass this hurdle, however, it follows from the foregoing that they may not be able to obtain a partial annulment of the conditions attached to the authorisation and will be faced with a reopening of the Commission procedure under Article 10(5) of the Merger Regulation.

2.2 Procedural decisions

There are many procedural decisions in a merger investigation that are capable of adversely affecting the interest of the parties to the concentration or that of third parties. Some examples are decisions to obtain information under Articles 11 and 13 of the Merger Regulation, to declare a notification incomplete, to initiate Phase II proceedings, etc. Such decisions are challengeable acts, but the parties will rarely avail themselves of the possibility to appeal such decisions to the Court of First Instance. They will not be able to obtain a decision before the Commission has completed its investigation, and as long as there still is a possibility that the Commission will issue a positive decision, they will be inclined to focus their efforts on the Commission's investigation. However, if they let the two-month period of Article 230 EC go by without filing an appeal, the decision may become final and they may lose the right to challenge it if the Commission eventually takes a negative decision on the substance of the case. Depending on the type of decision this may mean that they lose an opportunity to get the Commission's final decision annulled.

This was an issue in *Schneider*. The Commission had sent the parties a request for information containing 322 (!) questions to which they had to reply within five working days. When the replies were not received before the deadline, the Commission adopted a decision requesting the information pursuant to Article 11(5) of the Merger Regulation, which suspended the four-month period in Phase II. The final decision was taken six months after the opening of Phase II. *Schneider* challenged the Commission's decision on this basis and argued that the exceeding of the time period could not be justified by the Commission's decision pursuant to Article 11(5), which in Schneider's view was invalid. The Commission raised an exception of inadmissibility, arguing that the decision had become final because *Schneider* had not appealed it within the two-month deadline of Article 230 EC. The Court of First Instance did not have to rule on the exception of inadmissibility because it considered that the Commission had been entitled to request the information, and to take the decision suspending the time period when it was not received by the deadline. It therefore remains uncertain whether procedural decisions have to be appealed within two months, and to reserve their right to challenge such decisions the parties may have to file appeals during the Commission's procedure in anticipation of the final decision.

3. Scope of judicial review

In *Kali und Salz*, the Court acknowledged that the Commission enjoys a certain discretion in its competitive assessment of a merger:

> 'In this respect, however, the basic provisions of the Regulation, in particular Article 2 thereof, confer on the Commission a certain discretion, especially with respect to assessments of an economic nature. Consequently, review by the Community judicature of the exercise of that discretion, which is essential for defining the rules in concentrations, must take account of the discretionary margin implicit in the provisions of an economic nature which form part of the rules on concentrations.'

Under Article 2(2) of the Merger Regulation the Commission has to declare a concentration compatible with the Common Market if it does not create or strengthen a dominant position. Under Article 2(3) the Commission has to declare a concentration incompatible with the Common Market if it creates or strengthens a dominant position. So far the Commission does not appear to have any discretion. The discretion conferred on the Commission would have to be found in the assessment of the economic circumstances (including the circumstances referred to in Article 2(1) under (a) and (b) of the Merger Regulation) underpinning a finding of dominance (or the absence thereof).

In practice, however, the Court of Justice and particularly the Court of First Instance have not hesitated to conduct a detailed examination of the Commission's findings in light of the available evidence. The judgments of the Court of First Instance in *Airtours, Schneider* and *Tetra Laval* are a good illustration of this approach. The Court in these cases does not carry out a marginal review but a full assessment of the Commission's findings. Such an assessment fits within a system where it is up to the Commission to show that the concentration creates or strengthens a dominant position. Clearly the Court has to remain within the limits of the pleas advanced by the applicants and cannot conduct its own competitive assessment of the concentration. But within those limits the Court has to examine whether the Commission has shown to the requisite legal standard that the concentration creates or strengthens a dominant position. In principle, the economic nature of the Commission's findings is not a reason why the Court should exercise any reservation in this respect.

4. Judicial review: procedure

4.1 Expedited procedure

We have already seen that a normal procedure before the Court of First Instance and the Court of Justice takes far too long to make a difference for the implementation of a merger. In order to do something about this problem the Court of First Instance has introduced an expedited procedure. This procedure is designed to deal with cases of particular urgency. In this connection the Court specifically mentions decisions regarding merger control.[27] In these cases more emphasis is placed on the oral procedure. The written procedure is in principle limited to the application and the defence. Expedited procedures are given priority over other cases.

Parties who want to make use of the expedited procedure must file an application with the Court of First Instance. The Court decides on the application having regard to the particular urgency of the matter, the circumstances of the case and the question whether, in view of its complexity and the volume of the pleadings lodged, the case lends itself to essentially oral argument. The Court of First Instance has shown itself very restrictive in granting applications for an expedited procedure, going as far as placing limits on the number of pleas and the number of pages of applications. So far applications for the expedited procedure have been granted in two merger cases, *Schneider* and *Tetra Laval.* In *Schneider* the Court first refused the application for the expedited procedure in relation to the action for annulment of the prohibitive decision. But when it granted the application for the expedited procedure in relation to the Article 8(4) decision requiring the divestiture of Schneider's shareholding in Legrand, it also granted the application in relation to the prohibition decision after

27 See OJ 2000 C 34/39.

Schneider had reduced the number of pleas, in order to be able to decide both cases simultaneously.

In *Schneider* it took the Court ten-and-a-half months to give judgment, calculated from the date of the first appeal against the prohibition decision. In *Tetra Laval* the parties obtained a judgment in nine-and-a-half months, calculated from the date of appeal against the prohibition decision. Although this is an enormous improvement in comparison with the average duration of the normal procedure of two-and-a-half years, it is still quite long. A recent example from the United Kingdom shows it is possible to do it in less time: when Interbrew's acquisition of Bass was prohibited by the Competition Commission, Interbrew was able to obtain a judgment from the High Court ordering the Secretary of State to reconsider the question of remedies in less than five months.

4.2 Appeal

A judgment of the Court of First Instance can be appealed to the Court of Justice, but on points of law only. The possibility of an appeal to the Court of Justice may add to the uncertainty for merging parties. If they implement their merger after an annulment of the Commission's decision by the Court of First Instance, they take the risk that the judgment of the Court of First Instance is overturned by the Court of Justice in the event the Commission appeals the judgment. However, this risk will be remote if the Court of First Instance has annulled the Commission's decision for factual reasons. This has been the case in *Airtours*, *Schneider* and *Tetra Laval*, where the Court of First Instance did not disagree with the doctrines applied by the Commission and annulled the Commission's decisions because it had failed to substantiate these doctrines with facts.

4.3 Interim relief

An applicant who has brought an action for annulment can apply to the Court of First Instance for interim relief under Articles 242 and 243 EC. The application for interim relief is ancillary to the main action. The applicant has to establish a *prima facie* case and show that the requested measures are necessary to avoid grave and irreparable damage. Furthermore, the interests of the applicant must outweigh the interests of the other parties concerned by the contested act as well as the interest of the Community in the immediate implementation of the act. If these conditions are fulfilled, the President of the Court of First Instance (or in appeal, the President of the Court of Justice) can suspend the contested act or prescribe any necessary interim measures.

There have been several cases where third parties have sought interim relief in merger cases.[28] In all but one case these applications were unsuccessful. In *Kali und Salz* the President of the Court of Justice ordered the suspension of the condition

28 Case T-96/92R, *CCE Grandes Sources v Commission* [1992] ECR 2579; Case T-12/93 R, *CCE Vittel v Commission* [1993] ECR 449 and 785; Case T-83/92R, *Zunis v Commission* [1993] ECR 1169; Case T-88/94 R, *SCPA v Commission* [1994] ECR 263 and 401; Case T-322/94 R, *Union Carbide v Commission* [1991] ECR 1159; Case T-52/96 R, *Sogecable v Commission* [1996] ECR 797. In *Schneider/Legrand* and *Tetra Laval/Sidel*, Schneider and Tetra Laval filed applications to suspend the divestiture decision taken by the Commission pursuant to Article 8(4) of the Merger Regulation. The applications were withdrawn after Schneider and Tetra Laval reached an agreement with the Commission concerning the postponement of the time limit fixed for the divestiture.

requiring Kali und Salz to withdraw from an export organisation at the request of SCPA who participated together with Kali und Salz in this organisation. So far there have been no applications for interim measures by parties to the concentration.[29] They have the possibility to request the suspension of the decision prohibiting the concentration.[30] It will be difficult but not impossible to establish a *prima facie* case, as the President may already accept that this requirement is satisfied when it cannot be excluded that the applicant will succeed in the main action.[31] It is also conceivable that a decision blocking a merger causes grave and irreparable damage, although after the introduction of the expedited procedure it will be more difficult to argue that interim measures are necessary to avoid irreparable damage.[32] However, the real problem is the risk that the Court will reject the main action and that even if the main action will be successful, this may only have the effect that the Commission's proceedings are reopened. In the face of such uncertainties the parties to the concentration will be reluctant to rely on a suspension of the Commission's decision to implement their merger.[33]

Interim relief may be more meaningful in cases involving conditional authorisations. In such cases the parties to the concentration could apply for suspension of the conditions pending the main action. For example, a condition requiring the parties to divest a certain business could temporarily be suspended. As already noted, this form of interim relief was granted in *Kali und Salz*. The Court found that implementation of the condition to withdraw from the export organisation could entail the dissolution of that organisation, and that suspension of this condition would not seriously affect the interests of the other parties and the interest of the Community in the immediate implementation of the decision. *Kali und Salz* involved an application by a third party, but a similar application could be filed by the parties to the concentration themselves.

5. Conclusion on judicial review

It follows from the foregoing that the possibilities for judicial review are limited. To some extent this is unavoidable. Not many mergers will be able to survive a prolonged Commission investigation, a negative decision *and* a judicial review of that decision, however short and effective that judicial review may be. However, in some respects the current system can be approved.

29 With the exception of Case T-52/96 R, *Sogecable SA v Commission* [1996] ECR II-797, but in that case the parties to the concentration requested a suspension of a decision of the Commission to investigate a concentration under the Merger Regulation. There have not been any requests from parties to the concentration to suspend prohibition decisions or the conditions attached to authorisations.

30 See Francisco Enrique González-Díaz, 'Tenth Anniversary of the Merger Regulation: the Way Forward', in *EC Merger Control: Ten Years On*, Papers from the EC Merger Control 10th Anniversary Conference (London: IBA, 2000), p 415.

31 See, for example, Case T-65/98 R, *Van den Bergh Foods Ltd v Commission* [1998] ECR II-2641, ground 61: ('In view of all the foregoing, the pleas in law put forward by the applicant cannot be held prima facie to lack any foundation'). However, the case law in this respect is not consistent. For a discussion of the case law, see Lenaerts and Aarts, *Europees procesrecht* (2nd edn, Antwerpen, 1999), p 385 *et seq.*

32 See Rachel Brandenburger and Thomas Janssens, European Merger Control: Do the checks and balances need to be re-set (Fordham Corp L Inst, 2001) 135, at 180 (B Hawk ed 2002).

33 This is different in a situation like Schneider/Legrand and Tetra Laval/Sidel, where the merger has already been implemented. In such a situation a suspension of the Commission decision is useful to postpone the divestiture.

A significant improvement would in my view be to amend Article 10(5) of the Merger Regulation. As already noted, the judgement in *Schneider* has raised some uncertainty about the status of this provision. The Court's findings in *Schneider* can be interpreted to mean that after the Court has rejected the Commission's competitive assessment, the Commission is not entitled to reopen the procedure and the merger must be deemed to have been cleared. I already pointed out that it is difficult to reconcile this with Article 10(5) of the Merger Regulation.

There are cases where a reopening of the Commission procedure would not serve any useful purpose. *Airtours* is such an example. Everyone who has read this judgment will wonder what the purpose of a reopening of the Commission procedure could be in the (not very likely) event that the parties still wanted to implement the merger. After the Court of First Instance so strongly rejected the Commission's findings that the merger would give rise to a collective dominant position, it is difficult to imagine how the Commission could prohibit the merger again on this basis. In cases like this the Commission has no option but to clear the merger, unless the market structure has changed significantly since the Commission's original decision (which the Commission can take into account as part of its *ex nunc* assessment of the merger). That is, however, another anomaly of Article 10(5). Although I accept that in a new investigation it does not make sense to assess the merger on an *ex tunc* basis, I find it more difficult to accept that this may have the result that a merger, which should have been cleared when it was first assessed, can be blocked in view of developments which have occurred after the original investigation and are beyond the parties' control.

However, there are also cases where reopening the Commission procedure can be useful, for example if the Commission decision is annulled for insufficient reasoning but the Court's judgment does not exclude that the concentration gives rise to a dominant position, or if, as in *Schneider*, there is a discrepancy between the statement of objections and the final decision. *Tetra Laval* also falls into this category, insofar as the Court took into account in its annulment of the Commission's decision that the commitments offered by Tetra Laval would have eliminated every horizontal overlap between the parties. In such a case a reopening of the Commission procedure would allow the Commission to take a new decision incorporating the commitments.

A solution could be to amend Article 10(5) in such a way that a reopening of the Commission procedure would no longer be an automatism but would depend on the judgment of the Court. Ideally the Court would have the option to refer the case back to the Commission. It could let the decision whether or not to refer depend on whether it believes there is a need for a new investigation by the Commission. However, this would require an amendment of Article 230 of the Treaty. Under Article 230 the Court currently only has the power to annul, and not to refer a case back to the institution for further examination. In an indirect way a similar result could be achieved by providing in Article 10(5) that after an annulment of a Commission decision the Commission has the right to reopen the procedure depending on the Court's judgment. The Court would have to indicate clearly in its judgment the issues that require further examination and the issues in respect of which its judgment is meant to be final.

Such an amendment of Article 10(5) could also clear the way for a partial annulment of conditional authorisations. As previously noted, the finding of the Court of Justice in *Kali und Salz* that partial annulment of the conditions attached to an authorisation is not possible seems to have been influenced by Article 10(5). If a new investigation would no longer be an automatism, the Court could in appropriate cases only annul the conditions, thus allowing the parties to implement the concentration without having to comply with the conditions. In order to obtain such a partial annulment the parties would have to show that the Commission had not established to the necessary legal standard that the concentration would create or strengthen a dominant position, or in the case of a conditional authorisation in Phase I, that the Commission did not have sufficient reasons to entertain serious doubts.

The rights of interested parties to challenge Commission decisions could be further improved if the Court of First Instance adopted a less restrictive attitude towards expedited procedures. By placing severe constraints on the number and type of arguments that can be developed in an expedited procedure the Court is making it unattractive for interested parties to resort to this procedure. It is true that merger cases tend to be complex and involve a substantial amount of evidence. However, that does not exclude that such cases can be decided within a period of, say, six months. It should not be forgotten that the proceedings before the Court are preceded by an extensive Commission investigation, which has culminated in a long decision setting out all the issues in detail. The ground is therefore well prepared. If it is a question of resources there are ways to resolve this, for example by creating a special judicial panel to hear actions in merger cases on the basis of the new Article 225a that will be inserted in the EC Treaty when the Nice Treaty comes into effect.

Another, smaller, improvement would be the inclusion of a provision in the Merger Regulation stipulating that decisions taken by the Commission throughout the investigation of a merger can be appealed together with the Commission's final decision in the case. Such an amendment would obviate the need for parties to file appeals against, in particular, procedural decisions of the Commission to reserve the right to challenge these decisions if the final outcome of the Commission's investigation is negative.

6. Role of the Hearing Officer

The role of the Hearing Officer in competition proceedings has been strengthened with the new decision on his mandate that was adopted on 23 May 2001.[34] According to the new rules, the Hearing Officer no longer belongs to the Directorate General for Competition, but is directly attached to the office of the Competition Commissioner. The post of Hearing Officer can now also be filled by candidates from outside the Commission. In addition to organising and conducting the hearing, the Hearing Officer prepares a report on the respect of the right to be heard. Under the new rules the report of the Hearing Officer is communicated to the Member States, attached to the final draft decision and published with the final decision in the *Official Journal*. In this report the Hearing Officer also considers whether the draft decision deals only with objections in respect of which the parties have been afforded the opportunity of making their views known, and whether the 'market testing' of commitments proposed by the parties has been conducted in an objective manner.

The reports of the Hearing Officer which have been published since the extension of his mandate are quite succinct. They vary from a mere statement that the procedural rights of the parties have been respected to a brief discussion in general

34 OJ 2001 L 162/21.

terms of procedural issues that have arisen during the proceedings and how they have been dealt with. A number of respondents to the Green Paper have proposed to enable the Hearing Officer to express views on both procedural and substantive issues. This would certainly give more meaning to the reports of the Hearing Officer. His reports can be a useful check for all those who are not directly involved in the investigation but play a role in the final decision (the Member States, the Legal Service, other Commission services), whether the investigation by the Merger Task Force has been thorough and fair to all the parties concerned. A mere statement that procedural rights have been respected is not much to go by in this connection. The Hearing Officer's report would also have more impact if it were made available simultaneously to the Commission, the Member States *and* the parties as quickly as possible after the hearing and well in advance of the final decision, and if the Commission were required to set out in the final decision its views on the issues where it disagrees with the Hearing Officer.

Some respondents to the Green Paper have warned that widening the mandate of the Hearing Officer to include scrutiny of substantive issues might lead to a separate inquiry in parallel to that of the Merger Task Force.[35] I do not share that concern. The Hearing Officer could formulate his views on the basis of the statement of objections and the defence of the notifying parties. He would not have to conduct his own inquiry to give his opinion. On the other hand, the fact that the parties can turn to someone with an objective view that *counts* would in my opinion greatly enhance the confidence in the system.[36]

7. Concluding remarks

Accountability is fundamental to the integrity of the merger control system and to the way in which this system is perceived by the business community.[37] The opportunity of this review of the Merger Regulation should be grasped to make some real improvements in this area. The replies to the Green Paper contain many interesting suggestions for procedural reforms. However, the most important improvements would in my view consist of improving the external checks and balances. First of all this could be done by strengthening the role of the Court. I have made some suggestions for this in my paper. But as there will remain many situations where resort to the Court is not an option, the checks and balances in the administrative process should also be reinforced, particularly by expanding the role of the Hearing Officer. Such reforms are relatively easy to implement. Experience will show whether it is sufficient to enhance the procedural safeguards in the current system or whether more fundamental changes are necessary.

35 See, *inter alia*, the report of the House of Lords' Select Committee on the European Union on the review of the EC Merger Regulation, p 48.

36 Whether the Hearing Officer is attached to the office of the Competition Commission or has a completely independent status, as suggested by some, is in my view mostly a question of perception and not a major issue.

37 See the reply of Morgan Stanley to the Green Paper and Morris Tabaksblat, 'The EU Merger Regulation: Ten Years On' in *EC Merger Control: Ten Years On*, Papers from the EC Merger Control 10th Anniversary Conference (London: IBA, 2000).

8

Proposed Reform of the EU Merger Regulation: a US Perspective

JANET L MCDAVID

Partner, Hogan & Hartson LLP, Washington, DC; Past Chair of the Section of Antitrust Law of the American Bar Association

American antitrust lawyers who advise clients on mergers welcome many of the reforms proposed in the European Commission's recent Green Paper on reform of the European Union Merger Regulation.[1] The divergent merger review processes across some 60 countries have led to a number of reform initiatives, including the International Competition Network (ICN) and the US-European Commission bilateral merger working group. The Commission's proposed reforms meet objectives of multilateral convergence and are also consistent with the principles and best practices being considered by the ICN and other merger reform efforts. However, additional room for improvement remains, and based on recent announcements in Brussels, some of which may become official in December, it appears that the European Commission is moving in the right direction.

1. PROPOSED TIMING CHANGES

Today, formal notification under the EU Merger Regulation is not possible until the parties have executed a final binding agreement. In contrast, in the United States, Canada, and other jurisdictions parties can file on the basis of either a letter of intent or a memorandum of understanding. This allows the merger review process to begin even in advance of execution of a definitive agreement. The Green Paper proposes that earlier notification should be permitted based on a letter of intent or a memorandum of understanding. In the interest of timely merger review, and to facilitate companies' ability to coordinate their global merger filings, the European Commission should allow companies to notify transactions before signing a definitive agreement, provided the terms are sufficiently clear to allow the Commission to conduct its assessment. On 7 November, the European Commission announced that it was likely to do so. A related change that would be welcomed by US practitioners would be for the European Commission to abolish the deadline that requires a Form CO filing within one week after execution of a definitive agreement, which is almost never applied in practice and is unnecessary in a system that precludes closing pending clearance. Again, the European Commission has announced its willingness to consider this change. Final decisions are likely by the year end.

One of the best features of the Merger Regulation is the clear, strict deadlines for a decision on a proposed merger. Yet these deadlines have often posed problems for companies when it was clear that remedies were needed to address the Commission's

1 Green Paper on Review of Council Regulation (EEC) No 4064/89 (11 December 2001).

competition concerns. This was a problem in several transactions in recent years, including GE/Honeywell, EMI/Time Warner, and Volvo/Scania.[2] This 'time squeeze' may leave the parties with only a few days to come up with appropriate remedies, and the European Commission and Member States may be left with a very short time to assess the adequacy of proposed remedies.

In its Green Paper, the European Commission suggests allowing the parties to 'stop the clock' to allow more time to propose and consider remedies. US practitioners would welcome additional flexibility in the Commission's remedies deadlines – provided that the practice is not abused by routinely asking the parties to extend deadlines, which too often happens in the United States. The European Commission has recognised the value of the current merger review timetable, and therefore proposes only a limited time extension of 20 to 30 working days, which would be split proportionately between the Commission and the parties. The remedies procedure could be greatly enhanced if the Commission played a more active role in suggesting and discussing appropriate remedies.[3] The Commission has also proposed allowing additional time extensions at the request of the Commission and with the consent of the parties.

2. Due process reforms would be welcome

The Green Paper invited views on the effectiveness of the due process procedures provided under the Merger Regulation – particularly with respect to the parties' rights of defence. One of the most widely criticised aspects of EU merger review is that the European Commission's Competition Directorate and its Competition Commissioner are effectively investigator, prosecutor, and judge in merger investigations, and that due process checks and balances are inadequate.

There are some procedural protections in the review process, such as the Hearing Officer, whose task is to ensure that the proceedings safeguard the right of persons to be heard fairly and within a reasonable time; consultation with an Advisory Committee composed of representatives from the Member States' competition authorities before adopting a decision; consultation with the Commission's Legal Service on any proposed decision; and the requirement that the final decision in a second-phase investigation be adopted by the College of Commissioners.

In practice, however, the role of the Hearing Officer is not sufficient to provide effective independent review of the proceedings, in part because the Hearing Officer's powers are inadequate and the Hearing Officer is attached to the Competition Commissioners' Cabinet. Moreover, most parties do not find the hearing useful and often waive their right to a hearing, which limits the role of the Hearing Officer. The Advisory Committee's role is also an inadequate check on the powers of the Commission since its opinion does not bind the Commission, and it generally rubber-stamps the Commissioner's decisions. The same is true of the College of Commissioners. However, in one recent matter, Commissioner Monti convened a

2 See, eg, Janet L McDavid and Catriona Hatton, 'Antitrust: Globalization and the EU', Nat'l LJ (6 November 2000) at B7.

3 The European Commission has recently invited comments on proposed revisions in its remedies processes. *Commission Launches Discussion on Best Practice Guidelines for Divestiture Commitments in Merger Cases*, IP/02/1091 (18 July 2002).

separate review team to evaluate the preliminary conclusions of the merger team as outlined in the Statement of Objections.[4] This led to a decision reversing the preliminary conclusions outlined in the SO. Practitioners would welcome more regular use of such processes, and Commissioner Monti has recently said he would do so, in the wake of *Airtours, Schneider*, and *Tetra Laval*.[5] Director General Lowe has said that such panels will be formed in controversial cases, and provide input throughout the administrative review process.

The flaws in the Commission's processes were made particularly evident in the recent *Airtours* decision, in which the European Court of First Instance concluded that the Commission had failed to meet its burden of proof and that it had erred in its application of the facts to the law.[6] In particular, the Court was critical of the extent to which the Commission had adopted the position advocated by competitors without sufficient scepticism and analysis. Similarly, in *Schneider Electric*, the Court found 'several obvious errors, omissions and contradictions in the Commission's economic reasoning' and also concluded that the Commission's processes were flawed, which resulted in a denial of critical rights of defence.[7] Finally, in *Tetra Laval*, the Court concluded that the European Commission overestimated anti-competitive effects and failed adequately to evaluate whether there would be incentives to engage in leveraging.[8] Practitioners will carefully monitor the ways in which the Commission responds to these criticisms.[9]

An appeal from the Commission decisions to the European Court of First Instance is possible, and several appeals are currently pending. The *Airtours, Schneider*, and *Tetra Laval* decisions established that the Court is willing to reverse Commission decisions, and Commission officials have argued that *Airtours* establishes that the checks and balances in the EC system are sufficient.[10] However, despite recent reforms to expedite judicial review, the time required for an appeal means that most mergers will have been abandoned long before any decision can be secured. The *Airtours* appeal was decided almost three years following the Commission decision. Even under the expedited processes, the parties typically have abandoned the transaction long before a judicial decision can be reached. For example, under its expedited processes,

4 *Commission Clears Carnival's Takeover Bid for P&O Princess*, DN: IP/02/1141 (24 July 2002), reprinted at http://europa.eu.int/rapid/start/cgi/guesten.ksh?p_action.gettxt=gt&doc=IP/02/1141|0|RAPID&lg=EN; *Royal Caribbean Left Cruising for a Bruising*, Financial Times (25 July 2002) (the author is counsel to Carnival). As one commentator noted, 'when the Commission officials responsible had to present their argument to an internal panel, doubts were reportedly raised about their arguments'. *Court Rulings Should Prompt Antitrust Changes*, Wall Street Journal Online (22 October 2002), http://online.wsj.com/article/0,,BT_CO_20021022_005959,00html?mod= COMPANY.

5 Wall Street Journal Online (25 October 2002), http://online.wsj.com/article_print/0,,BT_CO_20021025_002067,00.html.

6 Case T-342/99, decision of 6 June 2002.

7 *Schneider Electric SA v Commission*, Cases T-310/01 & T-77/02, decisions of 22 October 2002.

8 *Tetra Laval BV v Commission*, Cases T-5/02 & T-80/02, decisions of 25 October 2002.

9 One commentator has suggested that the Commission's response to *Airtours* and *Schneider* will be critical to its future credability, 'If the Commission concedes slightly now and vows to fix the plumbing – and not just plaster over the leaks – there's an opportunity for Monti to be truly super, and for Europe to put in place a world-class antitrust regime'. WSJ Online, n 5 *supra*.

10 *Speech by Mario Monti to the British Chamber of Commerce* (4 June 2002), reprinted at http://europa.eu.int/rapid/start/cgi/guesten.ksh?p_action.gettxt=gt&doc=SPEECH/02/252|0|RAPID&lg=EN&display=.

the Court reversed the Commission's decision in *Schneider* a year after the parties abandoned the merger. While the Commission has expressed support for faster reviews, it is not clear that improvements are possible.

There have also been criticisms that the European Commission lacks sufficient economic analytical capability, and that its decisions are not subject to sufficiently rigorous economic review. This was one of the factors that the Court emphasised in its *Schneider* decision. The EC has recently proposed to enhance its economics staff,[11] and following *Schneider* and *Tetra Laval,* Commissioner Monti has said that he will appoint a chief economist.[12] Director General Lowe has announced that the chief economist will report to the Director General to review proposed merger decisions, and that economists will be added to case teams – moves that would be welcomed by US practitioners. A key unresolved issue, however, is the extent to which the economists will be able to recommend different outcomes than the case team and provide a genuinely independent voice – as they do in the United States.

There are many elements in the EU system that could serve as a model for other merger review systems, such as the fact that the parties receive a written Statement of Objections, have access to the Commission file, may request an oral hearing, and will receive a reasoned decision from the Commission. Most US lawyers find access to the file particularly useful because it allows the parties to understand the claims being advanced by third parties so the parties can respond more effectively. The Statement of Objections provides a detailed articulation of both the facts and theories that concern the staff. Both practices should be emulated by the US agencies.

However, there is a widespread view that the checks and balances in the Commission system are generally insufficient to ensure due process. For example, although the Statement of Objections and access to the file are useful, both events take place too late in the process to allow a meaningful response.[13] Similarly, the hearing typically occurs too late in the process to be useful. Access to the file would be far more useful if it was provided at the time the investigation moves into Phase II, and then on a rolling basis. Following *Schneider* and *Tetra Laval,* Commissioner Monti has promised reforms including systemic peer review, improved access to the file at earlier points in the process, greater transparency for the parties concerning complaints and concerns, and enhanced economic analysis. The Commission's willingness to remedy

11 Monti speech, n 11 *supra.* The Commission has recently sought proposals from private economists to consult with the Commission. See Call for Expressions of Interest from Competition Policy Experts: Merger Control, Specifically in Economic Analysis and Financial Analysis and Accounting, 2002/S 135-104760 (19 July 2002), reprinted at http://europa.eu.int/comm/dgs/competition/call_for_experts/2002_s_135_en.pdf. A recent report by the Select Committee on the European Union of the UK House of Lords also endorsed this concept: 'The Commission should certainly strengthen its overall capacity for economic analysis in merger cases. Given that how the Commission defines markets in merger cases is crucial in determining the fate of many mergers, we see merit in the Commission developing a dedicated economics branch within the MTF. In particular, DG Competition should appoint a Chief Economist, which could lend more weight to their decisions. We look forward to seeing what Commissioner Monti's proposal are in this area'. Session Report 2001-2001, 32nd Report (23 July 2002).

12 See n 6 *supra.*

13 Moreover, in *Schneider,* the Court concluded that the Commission's processes were flawed and denied the parties' rights of defence because the Commission changed its analysis following the Statement of Objections, which precluded the parties from offering effective remedies.

the flaws in the current system may be one indication of the success of the proposed reforms. Commissioner Monti's proposals are a good start.

3. Proposed substantive changes in the merger review standard

The Green Paper launched a debate on the merits of the current 'dominance test' in the EU Merger Regulation versus the 'substantial lessening of competition test' used in the United States under section 7 of the Clayton Act. There has been concern that the Commission's dominance test causes it to give greater weight to competitor complaints – a criticism heard frequently after *GE/Honeywell.* While the multilateral convergence process might be served by such a change, the real question is whether it would lead to more consistent decisions between the major antitrust authorities. There is no guarantee that the Commission's interpretation of the substantial lessening of competition test would be guided by US precedent; the United States and European Union might come to different results faced with the same set of facts and the same legal standard. Moreover, there would certainly be transitional difficulties given the lack of Commission precedents. Recognising these issues, Commissioner Monti has indicated that he recommends retaining the current standard, but also recommends adding recitals to ensure that it can apply to conduct that might otherwise fall into a gap.

The European Commission has been regarded as hostile to efficiencies – perhaps unfairly – and a competition test may enhance the Commission's ability to consider them. While a statement from the Commission on how it will assess efficiencies would be welcome, the Commission can follow a US-type approach to efficiencies without changing the dominance test. Commissioner Monti has confirmed the Commission's ability and willingness to consider efficiencies under the current test.[14] He has also committed to developing guidelines for consideration of efficiencies as part of guidelines on market power. US practitioners would welcome such guidelines.

Some have suggested that the dominance test has been stretched to encompass anti-competitive effects that may not involve dominance, and the Commission has made greater use of theories of collective dominance in recent years. But while some of the Commission's theories may not fit comfortably into the dominance sphere, there is some concern that a substantial lessening of competition test would facilitate over-regulation of mergers. It is also important to weigh convergence and the other objectives in moving to this test against the obvious downside – a period of legal uncertainty resulting from the application of the new test without established EU precedents.

The European Commission could achieve some of the objectives of moving to a substantial lessening of competition test by focusing on the second part of the current dominance test, ie whether 'effective competition will be significantly impeded in the common market'. This element of the test might allow consideration of efficiencies arguments and provide greater scope for economics-based analysis. In any event, if the Commission proposes to move to a substantial lessening of competition test, it is important that any such move is accompanied by guidelines on how the test is to be applied and whether US precedents are relevant to Commission analysis. This will become clearer in December, when the Commission makes formal proposals.

14 Monti speech, n 11 *supra*.

4. Filing fees

The Green Paper invited comments on whether the European Commission should follow the lead of several other jurisdictions and impose filing fees. US lawyers would oppose filing fees in the Commission. Most US lawyers object to the substantial filing fees imposed in the United States and believe that important antitrust law enforcement functions should be funded from government revenues.[15] Moreover, funding antitrust agencies from filing fees raises the risk of inadequate funding if the number of merger filings declines. The US Government set a bad example when it imposed merger filing fees, and the Commission should not follow that example.

5. Proposed changes in filing requirements may be complicated

When the EU Merger Regulation was adopted in 1989, one of the principal objectives was to provide a single review procedure in Brussels for large transactions with a cross-border European dimension (a 'one-stop shop'). Transactions that met the Merger Regulation thresholds were subject to review only in Brussels and did not have to be notified to various EU national authorities. Because the revenue thresholds that triggered an EU filing were set very high, however, many transactions fell outside the European Commission's jurisdiction, and companies were often faced with multiple merger filings with EU national authorities. The lower thresholds introduced in 1997 in an effort to address these concerns proved complicated to apply and did not capture a large number of transactions with a cross-border dimension.

In its recent Green Paper, the European Commission has proposed replacing this lower threshold with a three-country filing test, whereby transactions that do not meet the high threshold but that would require merger filings in at least three EU Member States would be subject instead to the EU Merger Regulation and therefore benefit from a one-stop shop.

While the objective of increasing the application of the European Union's one-stop shop is welcome, this proposed solution is problematic because it leaves companies with the burden of conducting an EU-wide assessment of whether a transaction triggers local merger filings. There will be some transactions for which the three-country filing test clearly will be met, but in the Member States the assessment can often be complex and burdensome because of the divergent and subjective triggers for merger filings. For example, some Member States use market share tests, while others assert jurisdiction based on worldwide revenues – even in the absence of any jurisdictional nexus to the Member State. In some Member States it is often not possible to determine whether a filing is required without consulting the national authority. The European Commission recently indicated that it recognises these concerns, and instead may propose a system of advance consultations and more regular cross-referrals. Practitioners will have to evaluate these options when more specific information becomes available.

Against this background, efforts to simplify merger review procedures and eliminate burdensome multiple filings would be better served by lowering and simplifying the EU thresholds. Furthermore, with the upcoming expansion of the

15 See, eg Report of the Section of Antitrust Law on Proposed Hart-Scott-Rodino Antitrust Improvement Act Amendments (11 April 2000), reprinted at http://www.abanet.org/antitrust/hsr_antitrust.html.

European Union, the European Commission could also seek further harmonisation of merger filing thresholds of EU Member States and accession countries. The EC should work towards the elimination of market-share tests as a basis for determining a country's jurisdiction over a merger and introduce clear revenue-based thresholds that require a minimum level of local revenue in the country concerned, which would be consistent with the approach being pursued by the ICN.

6. Conclusion

Many reform proposals under the Commission's Green Paper would be welcomed by US lawyers. The recent reversals in *Airtours, Schneider,* and *Tetra Laval* may enhance the European Commission's incentives to reform its processes and analysis. The Green Paper provides an important opportunity to improve merger regulation in the European Union and to take a significant step towards multilateral convergence. Following the recent court decisions, the EC seems committed to reforming its processes and enacting even more substantial reforms that would further enhance due process rights, fairness, timeliness, and efficiency under the Merger Regulation. American antitrust lawyers will watch these developments with interest.

9

Due Process and Judicial Review: a Member State System – Germany

Jochen B Burrichter and Markus M Wirtz*

Hengeler Mueller, Düsseldorf and Brussels

1. Introduction

In his treatise on *Law and Competition in Twentieth Century Europe*, David Gerber notes:

> 'While most European countries reacted to post-war conditions by creating competition law systems that were, at least initially, little more than minor components of economic policy, Germany moved in a new direction that would fundamentally alter the path of competition law in Europe. In 1957 the Federal Republic created a competition law system that was to play a new role and operate on a different set of principles. Its role was "constitutional" – to promote basic values and protect fundamental rights, and it was to operate at least as much on juridical as on administrative principles.'[1]

As *Gerber* rightly observes, the German system is an administrative/juridical mix. It is administrative in the sense that the statute relies primarily on the Federal Cartel Office (FCO) for application of its substantive norms. This is consistent with prior German practice and with the administrative model followed elsewhere in Europe. The FCO's rules and modes of operation are, however, highly juridical.[2] This ordo-liberal stance is reflected in many provisions of the German law, including merger control. In this paper we will provide an overview on the statutory safeguards which aim at securing due process and judicial review in German merger control.

We will first summarise the characterising features of the German merger control procedure. We will then describe the most important procedural rights of the notifying parties and the framework for conditions and obligations in German merger control. This will be followed by a discussion of the role of third party interveners. As concerns the judicial review of merger control decisions, we will first deal with appeals against the merger decisions of the FCO and finally with interim measures by the appeal court.

* Markus M Wirtz is a former associate of Hengeler Mueller and is now a partner at Taylor Wessing, Düsseldorf and Brussels.

1 Gerber, *Law and Competition in Twentieth Century Europe* (1998), p 266.

2 *Cf* Gerber, *op cit*, p 278, Bornkamm, *Judicial Control and Review of Antitrust Administrative Authorities*, 29th Fordham Corp Law Inst, New York, 31 October/1 November 2002.

2. Due process

2.1 Overview on the German merger control procedure

2.1.1 The FCO as decision-making body

In the discussions preceding the introduction of merger control rules in German law, one proposal provided for a separation between the investigative functions, which should be carried out by the FCO, and the decision-making functions, which should be performed by the courts. Others favoured a similar approach by envisaging the FCO to refer cases that raised concerns to a monopolies commission for investigation, leaving the final decision to the Minister of Economics.[3] Such proposals were rejected. Instead, both the investigative and the decision-making functions were conferred on the FCO. In addition to the organisational independence of the FCO, its internal set-up and its procedural rules provide for intra-institutional constraints on the exercise of the FCO's powers. Further, full judicial review of the FCO's merger decisions by the courts provides for effective external 'checks and balances'.

The FCO is an independent Federal High Authority. Merger decisions of the FCO are rendered by, currently ten, decision divisions that decide in bodies composed of a chairman and two associate members. Each decision division is competent for one or several industries. The divisions therefore have significant industry know-how. Although the FCO is part of the organisation of the Federal Ministry of Economics, neither the Minister nor the President of the FCO has reportedly tried to give instructions to the decision divisions in individual merger cases, and it appears doubtful whether they would be allowed to do so.[4] The decision divisions function like tribunals; they operate according to procedural rules that are similar to the rules for court proceedings.[5]

Approximately half of the members of the decision divisions are economists and half of them are lawyers. A case will normally be assigned to one member of the decision division as a case reporter. The case reporter will report his findings to the other members of the decision division and propose what actions to take. Problematic cases are further discussed in the chairmen's conference with the chairmen of the other divisions, and with the FCO's legal service. The process is coordinated by the General Policy Division of the FCO. This provides for an intra-institutional control mechanism, which aims at securing a consistent and sound application of the law, and which provides for a test as to whether the FCO has a strong case.

Whereas, therefore, investigative and adjudicative functions are not separated within the FCO, the independence of the decision divisions and the juridical procedural rules distinguish the FCO markedly from 'normal' administrative authorities and, arguably, from the Commission.

3 *Rittner* [1970] Der Betrieb, p 720 *et seq*; *cf* K Schmidt, *Kartellverfahrensrecht, Kartellverwaltungsrecht, Bürgerliches Recht* (1977), p 76.

4 *Cf* Schultz in Langen and Bunte (eds), *Kommentar zum deutschen und europäischen Kartellrecht*, Vol. 1, Sec 51 para 5 (9th edn, 2001). The Minister may give general instructions to the FCO, and the President issues rules of procedure, *cf* section 51 para 2, 52 ARC.

5 Section 51, section 54 *et seq*. Act against Restraints of Competition, *cf* Bornkamm, *Judicial Control and Review of Antitrust Administrative Authorities*, 29th Fordham Corp Law Inst, New York, 31 October/1 November 2002.

2.1.2 Notification and waiting periods

The parties to an envisaged concentration which satisfies the turnover thresholds of, on aggregate, €500 million worldwide, and €25 million of at least one party within Germany, have to seek prior authorisation from the FCO (provided the transaction will have effects on the German market, section 130 paragraph 2 of the Act against Restraints of Competition (ARC)). The parties are not allowed to put the concentration into effect or to participate therein prior to (1) its clearance by the FCO or (2) expiry of time limits for investigation by the FCO, section 41 paragraph 1 ARC.

Following receipt of a complete notification, the FCO must investigate within an initial period of one month (first phase) whether the concentration is likely to create or whether it strengthens a dominant position. The FCO may notify the parties at any time during the first phase that it has instituted second phase proceedings: section 40 paragraph 1 ARC. It should be noted that the FCO may institute second phase proceedings 'if a further examination of the concentration is necessary'. The reason for this may simply be that it did not have sufficient time to evaluate the concentration within the first phase.

If the FCO during the first phase should neither issue a clearance letter nor notify the parties in time that it has instituted second phase proceedings, the concentration is deemed to be cleared.

In the first phase the clearance decision consists of a simple letter stating that the conditions for a prohibition are not met and that the concentration may be put into effect. In case second phase proceedings are opened, the FCO has to either clear or prohibit a notified transaction by way of a formal reasoned decision within four months following receipt of the notification.

The FCO may clear a concentration during second phase proceedings subject to conditions and obligations: section 40 paragraph 1 ARC. The conditions and obligations must be structural and may not subject the undertakings concerned to the continuous supervision and control of the FCO.

As in EC law the FCO can prohibit a concentration without court intervention in an administrative procedure.

The operative part of decisions issued in the second phase proceedings will be published: section 43 no 2 ARC.[6]

In practice, the FCO normally seeks to conclude as speedily as possible merger control proceedings that do not lead to a prohibition, all the more since in case of a clearance decision in the first phase no reasons need to be given. If it is clear from the information submitted to the FCO, or already available to it, that a dominant position is not likely to be created or strengthened as a result of the notified transaction, the FCO will clear the merger within a short period of time after receipt of the complete notification. The FCO is not required by law to wait until the end of the one-month or four-month period, respectively. In unproblematic cases, clearance from the FCO can therefore be achieved within one to two weeks, sometimes even faster, depending on the workload of the competent officer.

6 Section 43 No 2 ARC only requires the FCO to make public the fact that it has issued a decision on a specific concentration and to provide some basic information. In practice, the FCO regularly publishes a non-confidential version of the full decision on its website (www.bundeskartellamt.de/fusion2003.html).

In 2001, the FCO received 1,519 merger notifications. Only in 79 cases did the FCO institute second phase proceedings. Out of these 79 concentrations, 35 were cleared unconditionally and 14 were cleared subject to conditions and obligations. Only two concentrations were prohibited.[7] Since 1990, the FCO has prohibited on average three concentrations per year. It has to be taken into account, however, that in critical cases the parties sometimes decide to withdraw the notification and give up the concentration project.

2.1.3 Publication of notifications

Until summer 2001, the notification of a concentration was not published. Since then, the FCO has published on its website (www.bundeskartell-amt.de/english_html, link 'list of merger projects') a list of notified concentrations indicating the parties and a short description of the markets concerned.

2.1.4 Notification prior to signing

Unlike the current Merger Regulation, German merger control law allows for the notification of a concentration prior to the signing of the agreement bringing about the concentration. It suffices to provide the FCO with the essential information which enables it to perform its controlling function, ie information on the parties, the form of the concentration and the basic elements of the transaction structure, and the necessary market data for the assessment of the effects of the transaction on competition. In its Green Paper on the Review of the Merger Regulation,[8] the Commission discussed whether the Regulation should be amended accordingly to allow for a more flexible approach to the timing of a notification. Many comments on the Commission's Green Paper, including those from the FCO,[9] have supported this proposal. The recently published draft Proposal for a new Council Regulation on the Control of Concentrations suggests to allow for the filing of a notification if the parties can demonstrate that they have a good faith intention to conclude an agreement bringing about a concentration.[10]

German merger control law therefore allows for some flexibility with regard to submitting the notification, so that in practice transactions have often already been cleared by the FCO before the agreements are signed. As the fact that a notification was submitted now will normally be published by the FCO (see above), confidentiality issues including obligations under German corporate law regarding ad hoc disclosure requirements will have to be taken into account for the timing of a notification. In exceptional cases, the FCO may agree not to publish the fact that a notification was submitted at all or only at a later point in time.

Merger projects can still be discussed in an informal and confidential guidance procedure, eg by submitting a notification in draft form.

The consummation of a cleared concentration has to be reported to the FCO and will be published.

7 The remainder of 28 concentrations was pending at the end of the year 2001.

8 Green Paper on the Review of Council Regulation (EEC) No 4064/89, COM (2001) 745/6 final, available on the internet: www.europa.eu.int/comm/competition/mergers/review/.

9 Available on the internet: www.bundeskartellamt.de/diskussionsbeitrage.html.

10 OJ 2003 C 20/4, available on the the internet: www.europa.eu.int/comm/competition/mergers/review/.

2.2 Important procedural rights of the notifying parties

The ARC provides for important procedural rights of the notifying parties.

2.2.1 Access to the file

The notifying parties are in principle and in practice entitled to inspect the files of the FCO at any time at least during the second phase proceedings: section 29 of the Administrative Procedures Act. Access to the file is often granted in the form of a continuous process and on an ad hoc basis. In practice, the FCO in problematic cases also grants access to certain parts of the file already during the first phase, namely to important submissions of third parties, however, subject to the respect of business secrets. This is a great advantage of the German merger control procedure over the current procedure under the Merger Regulation,[11] because the notifying parties will be able to identify and address potential concerns relating to competition at an early stage in the proceedings.

Business secrets of third parties and internal papers have to be kept confidential and are not subject to access to the file. However, such business secrets cannot be used against the parties. In case of an appeal the courts have to disregard the facts which are subject to business secrets, if they cannot be disclosed to the parties.

2.2.2 Right to be heard

The FCO must afford the notifying parties the possibility to make their views known before it adopts a decision prohibiting the notified concentration: section 56 paragraph 1 ARC. To this end, the FCO must inform the notifying parties about its concerns. In practice, the FCO issues a so-called warning letter, in which it gives detailed reasons for its preliminary view that the notified transaction is likely to create or strengthen a dominant position. The warning letter is similar to a final order both with regard to its form and contents, and can be compared to a Statement of Objections under the Merger Regulation. Normally, the warning letter has to be communicated approximately one month before the final decision. Shorter periods of time are permissible if the parties have been continuously informed about the concerns coming up during the procedure.

The notifying parties may comment in detail on the warning letter. If the comments lead the FCO to investigate further, it will have to grant the parties access to the files again and the possibility to comment on any new aspect that might justify a prohibition by issuing an additional warning letter.

The parties have the right to ask for a formal oral hearing: section 56 paragraph 1 ARC. For these hearings no special Hearing Officers are appointed. In most cases such formal hearings are not necessary because the parties are normally invited to meet the competent officers informally in order to keep them updated on the ongoing investigation.

11 In the recently published draft Best Practices on the Conduct of EC Merger Control Proceedings, the Commission, however, proposes to offer the notifying parties the opportunity to review, at the beginning of Phase II, all submissions received during Phase I, and prior to that, the possibility to review on an ad hoc basis at appropriate intervals in Phase I certain key documents submitted by third parties, in particular substantiated submissions and market studies; *cf* para 39 *et seq.* Draft Best Practices, available on the internet: www.europa.eu.int./comm/competition/mergers/others/.

2.3 Conditions and obligations

The FCO was originally not authorised to clear concentrations subject to conditions and obligations in the ARC itself. However, for more than two decades the FCO had abstained from prohibiting concentrations if the undertakings concerned had made commitments on the basis of a contract governed by public law with the FCO remedying the concerns relating to competition. Since the entering into force of the 6th Amendment of the ARC on 1 January 1999, the FCO has been explicitly granted the power to clear a notified concentration subject to conditions and obligations: section 40 paragraph 3 ARC. These shall not aim at subjecting the conduct of the undertakings to continued control. The difference between conditions and obligations is that in the event a clearance is granted by the FCO, on the fulfilment of a certain condition, the concentration may only be put into effect once the condition has been fulfilled, eg divestiture of certain production facilities. By contrast, obligations may be fulfilled after consummation. The FCO can force the notifying parties to fulfil obligations (as opposed to conditions) and regularly fixes a deadline for the fulfilment of the obligations. The FCO normally prefers to impose conditions rather than obligations.

In its recent decisions of 26 March 2002, in the cases *Haniel/Fels* and *Haniel/Ytong*, the FCO cleared the concentrations under the *condition* of substantial divestitures.[12] It stated that the conditions were necessary to prevent even a short-term dominant position, an aim which could not be achieved by means of an obligation.

In other cases, the FCO combined conditions or obligations for divestiture with conditions or obligations to enter into supply agreements (eg in *Federal Mogul/Alcan*[13]), to allow third parties access to its network and infrastructure facilities on reasonable and non-discriminatory business terms (eg in *RWE/VEW*,[14] *E.ON/Heingas*[15] and *Contigas/Stadtwerke Heide*[16]), to terminate agreements or to allow the customer to terminate (eg in the case *CP-ships/TMM (WITASS)*,[17] *Westfälische Ferngas*[18] and *Lekkerland/Tobaccoland*[19]).

In 2001, the FCO in 14 cases cleared the notified concentration subject to conditions or obligations.

In practice, the FCO will indicate its concerns relating to competition during the ongoing investigation and it is then up to the parties to put forward remedies and propose commitments. As conditions and obligations can only be attached to the formal second phase decisions, the FCO may not clear a notified transaction subject to conditions or obligations in the first phase.[20]

There are no statutory deadlines within which the notifying undertakings have to submit proposals for commitments within the second phase. If the proposal for

12 Available on the FCO's website: www.bundeskartellamt.de/archiv.html.
13 Available on the FCO's website: www.bundeskartellamt.de/archiv.html.
14 WuW/E DE-V 301.
15 WuW/E DE-V 360.
16 WuW/E DE-V 366.
17 WuW/E DE-V 122.
18 WuW/E DE-V 195.
19 WuW/E DE-V 116.
20 The notifying parties may, however – if necessary after having withdrawn their initial notification – restructure the notified transaction so as to remove the competitive concerns and thus secure clearance already in the first phase.

commitments or amended commitments is received by the FCO only at a very late stage in the proceedings, the FCO will normally ask the notifying undertakings to agree to an extension of the procedural deadlines. This is possible according to section 40 paragraph 2 no 1 ARC, pursuant to which the statutory deadline of four months shall not apply if the notifying undertakings have consented to an extension of the time limit. Unlike the Commission (at least for the time being), the FCO may therefore agree with the notifying undertakings on a *de facto* procedural 'standstill'.[21] This may be in the interest of the parties in order to secure merger clearance. In general it can be said that this procedural option has not been misused by the FCO as a means to circumvent the statutory deadlines.

If the FCO regards the commitments as sufficient to rectify its concerns relating to competition, it will state in its decision clearing the notified concentration that in view of the conditions or obligations the creation of a dominant position is unlikely to be expected, and it will explicitly set out in the decision which conditions or obligations the parties will have to fulfil. The FCO may revoke merger clearance if the parties do not comply with the conditions or obligations attached to the clearance, or if the clearance was based on incorrect information or was obtained by means of deceit.

Conditions or obligations can also aim at securing pro-competitive effects of the notified concentration which outweigh the disadvantages of dominance: section 36 paragraph 1 ARC.

It has not yet been decided whether the undertakings can challenge conditions and obligations by appealing to the court. This has been done in a recent case which is currently pending. As already mentioned, the notifying parties have to propose the condition or obligation. The court may thus have to answer the question of whether a party can challenge a commitment which was proposed by itself.

2.4 Role of third parties

The role of third parties in German merger proceedings has been significantly strengthened by the 6th Amendment of the ARC, which entered into force on 1 January 1999. Since then, parties which have been admitted to the FCO's proceedings as intervening parties may challenge the merger decision of the FCO in front of the court. The procedural rights of third parties in the FCO's proceedings are an important means to influence the outcome of the merger control process.

2.4.1 Admission as intervening party

On application, a third party has to be admitted by the FCO to the proceedings if its interests are materially affected by the notified transaction: section 54 paragraph 2 No 3 ARC. This requirement will regularly be fulfilled in the case of competitors which will be affected by the transaction but also by customers and suppliers of the notifying undertakings.

The admission to the proceedings as an intervening party is important because it is unclear whether third parties that have not been admitted to the FCO's proceedings have standing in front of the court to challenge the final decision or can be admitted as interveners during the court procedure. In addition, German merger law does not

21 The Commission's draft Proposal for an amended Merger Regulation now provides for the extension of the procedural deadlines for a maximum of 20 days: *cf* Art 10(3).

know any form of private suits. This means that third parties may neither sue the notifying undertaking for injunctive relief or damages nor request that the FCO investigates and prohibits a concentration.

The application to intervene may be made at any stage of the proceedings before the FCO.[22]

The FCO has been rather liberal in allowing third parties to intervene. The decision of the FCO rejecting or granting the admission to intervene, respectively, may be challenged in court.[22a]

Also, without formally being admitted as intervener, third parties in practice are invited to make submissions and have informal meetings with the FCO officers in charge of the case.

2.4.2 Access to the file

The competitors, customers or suppliers of the notifying undertakings which have been admitted to the proceedings as third party interveners have access to the files of the FCO. As for the notifying undertakings, there is no right to inspect the internal files of the FCO and files containing business secrets.

2.4.3 Right to be heard

Interveners have the opportunity to comment on the notified transaction. They may submit briefs and have the right to ask for and participate in an oral hearing: section 56 paragraph 1 ARC.

In the recent application by E.ON to the Federal Minister of Economics to grant ministerial authorisation for its acquisition of Ruhrgas, which was prohibited by the FCO, the Federal Minister of Economics granted the authorisation without giving the interveners the opportunity to comment on commitments offered to the Minister at a late stage in the proceedings after the – in this case mandatory – oral hearing. The appeal court granted interim relief against the authorisation. It held that in view of the mandatory oral hearing in this procedure, the intervening parties should have been heard on the important issues discussed between the notifying undertakings and the Minister that took place after the oral hearing. Although an oral hearing is not mandatory in merger control proceedings before the FCO, the decision of the court could be interpreted as to require the FCO to provide third party interveners the opportunity to comment on all commitments proposed by the notifying undertakings at any time before a final decision of the FCO.

2.5 Judicial review

In order to emphasise the juridical nature of the FCO's operations, as well as its special status outside the regular administrative hierarchy, the ARC makes its decisions reviewable by the regular courts (rather than the administrative court system that normally reviews administrative acts).[23]

22 And even after the FCO has issued a final decision, as long as the decision may still be challenged in court.

22a For further details *cf* Becker [2003] ZWeR p 199 *et seq.*

23 *Cf* Gerber, *Law and Competition in Twentieth Century Europe* (1998), p 278.

2.6 Appeals in merger cases

The decision of the FCO to clear a concentration during proceedings in the first phase is not issued by means of a formal order and cannot be appealed by third parties: section 63 paragraph 1 ARC.[24] By contrast, decisions of the FCO to clear or prohibit a concentration taken during second phase proceedings are issued by means of a formal reasoned order and may be appealed by the notifying or third party interveners, respectively, to the court of appeals, the Higher Düsseldorf Regional Court: section 40 paragraph 2, section 63 paragraph 1 ARC. Decisions in merger proceedings will be taken by the specialised Competition Senate of the Düsseldorf court.

Since merger decisions of the FCO have become appealable by third parties with the entering into force of the 6th Amendment of the ARC on 1 January 1999, several decisions clearing a concentration have been challenged by competitors, eg in the cases *Callahan/NetCologne*,[25] *Lekkerland/Tobaccoland*,[26] *Trienekens*[27] and *Blitz-Tip*.[28]

In the last ten years, 75 per cent of all merger decisions of the FCO have been appealed (clearance decisions have only been appealable since 1999). Until now, no third party action against a clearance decision has been successful.[29] On appeal from the notifying parties, the Düsseldorf court has found against the FCO in more than 60 per cent of the cases.[30]

The legal prerequisite for an appeal is that the appeal has to be filed in writing within one month with the FCO or the Higher Düsseldorf Regional Court. The appeal need not already be reasoned, however, the reasons have to be submitted within a further one-month period, which can be extended. The appeal can be based on new facts and new means of evidence: section 63 paragraph 1 ARC. Third parties may appeal the decision only if they have been admitted by the FCO as interveners to its merger proceedings. According to the decision of the Higher Düsseldorf Regional Court of 19 September 2001 in *Callahan/*NetCologne,14 third parties have standing only if they can also show that the decision affects their competitive position in a negative way thereby limiting their freedom of action.

2.7 Full judicial review

If the appeal is admissible (see above 2.6), the Competition Senate of the Higher Düsseldorf Regional Court will investigate the facts *ex officio*: section 70 paragraph 1 ARC. The standard of review is whether the FCO has appropriately interpreted and applied the ARC. The grounds for appeal are therefore not limited, and the court will undertake a full factual and judicial review of the decision without being limited to

24 *Cf* Kammergericht WuW/E DE-R 386 *Tobaccoland*.
25 WuW/E DE-R 665.
26 WuW/E DE-R 688.
27 WuW/E DE-R 681.
28 WuW/E DE-R 900.
29 In the *Lekkerland/Tobaccoland* case the decision of the appeal court to reverse the FCO's clearance decision is pending before the Federal Supreme Court on further appeal.
30 If the decisions of the Berlin Kammergericht, which had jurisdiction until the FCO moved to Bonn in 1999, are included in the statistics, the overall success rate for appeals will be less than 50 per cent. The Kammergericht had held in favour of the FCO in approximately 75 per cent of the cases; *cf* Bornkamm, *Judicial Control and Review of Antitrust Administrative Authorities*, 29th Fordham Corp Law Inst, New York, 31 October/1 November 2002.

reviewing 'manifest errors'. Thus, the court will evaluate whether the FCO's decision violates procedural or substantive law, in particular whether the FCO's conclusion concerning dominance is based on a sound assessment of all relevant facts: section 71 ARC. The court may also take into account additional considerations which may speak against or, conversely, in favour of the FCO's conclusion. It is not limited to the facts and evidence presented in the FCO's merger proceedings.[31] Rather, the court is obliged to investigate all relevant facts *ex officio*: section 70 ARC. If the court holds the decision of the FCO to be inadmissible or unfounded, it will reverse the decision.

2.8 Legal consequences of a successful action

If a decision of the FCO *clearing* a transaction is reversed by the court, the second phase will start anew and the FCO will have four months to complete its merger review taking into account the findings of the court: section 40 paragraph 6 ARC. In case of a *prohibition* order that was successfully challenged by the notifying undertakings in front of the court, the FCO (unlike the European Commission) has no possibility of prohibiting the transaction again and the notified transaction may be consummated, because the FCO has not rendered a valid prohibition decision within the statutory time limits.[32] This is a serious consequence because the FCO has no 'second shot'. In effect, it means that the shaping of German merger control is very much in the hands of the judges, who have traditionally shown reluctance towards certain fashions in economic thinking. This requires the FCO to base its decisions on actual facts and to demonstrate that the application of economic models and theories is justified in each individual case.

Decisions of the Higher Düsseldorf Regional Court may be appealed to the Federal Supreme Court (Bundesgerichtshof) on points of law only: section 74 ARC.

2.9 Interim relief

An appeal against decisions of the FCO to clear a merger has no suspensive effect. It goes without saying that appeals against prohibition decisions, on the other hand, do not terminate the prohibition to consummate the merger.

An appeal against a decision *prohibiting* a concentration will be time-consuming and may eventually frustrate the proposed transaction. For this reason, the appeal court may grant interim relief to the notifying undertakings by allowing them to consummate the transaction if the notifying undertakings put forward important reasons, in particular to prevent serious and irreparable damage to the notifying undertakings, *and* if there are serious doubts as to the legality of the appealed prohibition decision.[33]

In the event of an appeal by an intervening third party against a decision *clearing* the notified transaction there is a risk that the market structures will be irreversibly changed if the transaction is allowed to proceed pending the appeal. On appeal from a third party intervener the Higher Düsseldorf Regional Court therefore granted interim

31 *Cf* Werner in Wiedemann (ed), *Handbuch des Kartellrechts* (1999), Section 54 para 94 *et seq.*
32 *Cf* Kammergericht WuW/E DE-R 688, 690 *Habet/Lekkerland*; Art 10(5) of the Merger Regulation.
33 Sections 60 and 64 para 3 ARC; the list contained in section 60 ARC is not exclusive; *cf* Kammergericht WuW/E OLG 2419 *et seq, Synthetischer Kautschuk II*; WuW/E OLG 2571 *et seq, Gaslöschanlagen.*

relief and ordered the notifying parties not to consummate the transaction pending the appeal, based on the finding that there were serious doubts as to the legality of the appealed clearance decision.[34] Interim relief was also granted in the most recent appeal against the ministerial authorisation by the Minister for Economics in the matter of *E.ON/Ruhrgas*.[35]

2.10 Summary and conclusions

German merger control law contains important safeguards for the rights of the notifying parties and third parties which are affected by a notified transaction.

German merger control is administered by the FCO, which is an independent administrative body that operates according to quasi-juridical rules of procedure.

The notifying parties in principle have access to the file at any time at least during the FCO's second phase proceedings and usually in a continuous process. They will receive a warning letter and may comment on the concerns of the FCO in detail. It is up to the notifying parties to propose conditions or obligations in order to allay concerns relating to competition. There is no formal deadline for such proposals, and the notifying parties can agree with the FCO on an extension of the statutory time limits for the merger control procedure.

Third parties can be admitted as interveners to the proceedings of the FCO. They will have access to the file and may comment in writing and orally on the transaction.

Both clearance orders in the second phase and prohibition orders of the FCO can be appealed to the Higher Düsseldorf Regional Court, which will undertake a full judicial review of the order without being limited to reviewing 'manifest errors', also taking into account new facts and evidence. The court may grant interim relief. Decisions of the Düsseldorf court may be appealed further to the Federal Supreme Court on points of law.

The introduction of a fast-track procedure for the judicial review of the Commission's merger decisions was a first step to enhancing the effectiveness of judicial review in EC merger control. In addition, however, there seem to be possibilities to improve the Commission's investigation and decision-making process in merger cases. It would appear worthwhile for the Commission to consider some of the features of German merger control described above in the discussion of due process and increased transparency under the Merger Regulation, in particular better internal checks, more flexible timing of the notification, enhanced access to the file, extension of the deadlines if the parties agree, full judicial review, and no 'second shot' if a decision prohibiting a merger is reversed by the Court.

34 Section 65 para 3 ARC; *cf* WuW/E DE-R 665 *NetCologne*; WuW/E DE-R 681 *Trienekens*. This has been criticised by legal literature; *cf* Bechtold, GWB, Section 40 para 23 *et seq* (3rd edn, 2002).

35 WuW/E DE-R 926.

10

Due Process and Judicial Review: a View from Inside the Commission

Richard Wainwright*

Principal Legal Adviser, and Head of Competition Team, Legal Service, European Commission

> 'The history of liberty has largely been the history of observance of procedural safeguards'[1]

1. What is due process?

Due process is a term of US law which refers to fundamental procedural legal safeguards of which every citizen has an absolute right when a state or court purports to take a decision that could affect any right of that citizen. The most basic right protected under the due process doctrine is the right to be given notice, and an opportunity to be heard. The term is now also in use in other countries, again to refer to basic fundamental legal rights such as the right to be heard.[2]

2. Magna Carta[3]

This idea of due process can be traced in English law at least back to the Magna Carta. Article 39 of the Magna Carta provides: 'No freemen shall be taken or imprisoned or disseised or exiled or in any way destroyed, nor will we go upon him nor send upon him, except by the lawful judgment of his peers or by the law of the land.'

In the Magna Carta, due process is referred to as 'law of the land' and 'legal judgment of his peers.' Some US state constitutions continue to use these phrases.

Generally, due process guarantees the following: the right to a fair and public trial conducted in a competent manner; the right to be present at the trial; the right to an impartial jury; the right to be heard in one's own defence, that laws must be written so that a reasonable person can understand what is criminal behaviour, that taxes may only be taken for public purposes, that property may be taken by the government only for public purposes, and that owners of taken property must be fairly compensated.

* Thanks are due to Aliette Carré for help in the preparation of this paper. Any opinions expressed are personal to the author.

1 Justice Felix Frankfurter in *McNabb v US*, 318 US 332, 347 (1943).

2 Duhaime's legal dictionary.

3 Magna Carta 1215 http://www.bl.uk.

3. European Convention on Human Rights[4]

Due process is guaranteed by the European Convention on Human Rights (ECHR) in Article 6 on the right to a fair trial. In particular, Article 6 paragraph 1 provides: 'In the determination of his civil rights and obligations or of any criminal charge against him, everyone is entitled to a fair and public hearing within a reasonable time by an independent and impartial tribunal established by law. Judgment shall be pronounced publicly but the press and public may be excluded from all or part of the trial in the interest of morals, public order or national security in a democratic society, where the interests of juveniles or the protection of the private life of the parties so require, or to the extent strictly necessary in the opinion of the court in special circumstances where publicity would prejudice the interests of justice.'

It should be noted that the term 'determination of civil rights and obligations' has been held by the Court of Human Rights to include administrative decisions.[5]

4. Charter of Fundamental Rights of the European Union[6]

The right to an effective remedy and to a fair trial is provided for in Article 47 of the Charter (Chapter VI, Justice) in the following terms:

> 'Everyone whose rights and freedoms guaranteed by the law of the Union are violated has the right to an effective remedy before a tribunal in compliance with the conditions laid down in this Article.
>
> Everyone is entitled to a fair and public hearing within a reasonable time by an independent and impartial tribunal previously established by law. Everyone shall have the possibility of being advised, defended and represented.'

Due process within the administration is required under Article 41, paragraphs 1 and 2, on the right to good administration (Chapter V, Citizens' Rights):

> '(1) Every person has the right to have his or her affairs handled impartially, fairly and within a reasonable time by the institutions and bodies of the Union.
>
> (2) This right includes:
>
> - the right of every person to be heard, before any individual measure which would affect him or her adversely is taken;
> - the right of every person to have access to his or her file, while respecting the legitimate interests of confidentiality and of professional and business secrecy;
> - the obligation of the administration to give reasons for its decisions.'

Although there is controversy about the legal status of the Charter it has frequently been referred to in Opinions of the Advocate General at the European Court of Justice and in judgments of the Court of First Instance.[7]

4 Convention for the Protection of Human Rights and Fundamental Freedoms, Council of Europe, signed in Rome on 4 November 1950, entered into force on 3 September 1953.

5 *Ringeisen v Austria*, judgment of 16 July 1971, Series A, No 13; (1979-80) 1 EHRR 504.

6 Proclaimed by the European Parliament, the Council of the European Union and the European Commission at Nice on 7 December 2000 (OJ 2000 C 364/1).

7 Note, in particular, judgment of the CFI of 30 January 2002 in Case T-54/99, *Max Mobil Telekommunication v Commission* at § 48 where the Court described the Charter as 'confirmation' of the constitutional traditions common to the Member States.

5. How is due process ensured under the Merger Regulation at present?

5.1 Judicial review

Judicial review of decisions by the Commission under the Merger Regulation is guaranteed by Article 230 of the EC Treaty (ex-Article 173) which provides that the Court of Justice (including now the Court of First Instance) shall review the legality of acts of the Commission 'on grounds of lack of competence, infringement of an essential procedural requirement, infringement of the Treaty or of any rule of law relating to its application, or misuse of powers'. It should also be noted that under Article 16 of Regulation 4064/89 ('the Merger Regulation') the Court has 'unlimited jurisdiction' to review decisions whereby the Commission has fixed a fine or penalty payment, which it may cancel, reduce, or increase.[8]

Article 242 of the EC Treaty (ex-Article 185) provides that actions brought before the Court do not have suspensive effect but that the Court may, if the circumstances so require, suspend the operation of a contested decision. Under Article 243 (ex-186) the Court additionally has the power to prescribe 'any necessary interim measures'. To date there has only been one successful request for suspension under Article 242 – in the *Kali und Salz* case where the President of the Court of First Instance (CFI) ordered the suspension of a condition (in a decision authorising a joint venture) that the parties should withdraw from a common export organisation in which the applicant firm had an interest and on which it depended for its exports.[9]

Mention should also be made of the 'expedited procedure' introduced by the Court of Justice and by the CFI with effect from 1 February 2001.[10] This procedure has to be requested by one of the parties and is decided by the President in exceptional circumstances when required by the urgency of the case. In such a situation written pleadings are shortened and the Court may take particular organisational measures. The CFI has recently given two judgments under the expedited procedure in merger cases – on 22 October 2002 in Cases T-310/01 and T-77/02, *Schneider Electric v Commission* and on 25 October 2002 in Case T-5/02, *Tetra Laval v Commission.*

5.2 Administrative procedure

Due process during the administrative procedure of the Commission is guaranteed essentially by Article 18 of the Merger Regulation on hearing of the parties and of third parties, as follows:

1. Before taking any decision provided for in Article 7(4), Article 8(2), second subparagraph, and (3) to (5), and Articles 14 and 15, the Commission shall give the persons, undertakings and associations of undertakings concerned the opportunity, at every stage of the procedure up to the consultation of the Advisory Committee, of making known their views on the objections against them.
2. By way of derogation from paragraph 1, a decision to grant a derogation from suspension as referred to in Article 7(4) may be taken provisionally, without the

8 Based on Article 229 (ex-Article 172) of the EC Treaty.

9 Order of 15 June 1994, Case T-88/94R, *SCPA v Commission.*

10 Amendment of the Rules of Procedure, in particular Article 76a of the Rules of the CFI (OJ 2000 L 322).

persons, undertakings or associations of undertakings concerned being given the opportunity to make known their views beforehand, provided that the Commission gives them that opportunity as soon as possible after having taken its decision.

3. The Commission shall base its decision only on objections on which the parties have been able to submit their observations. The rights of the defence shall be fully respected in the proceedings. Access to the file shall be open at least to the parties directly involved, subject to the legitimate interest of undertakings in the protection of their business secrets.
4. Insofar as the Commission or the competent authorities of the Member States deem it necessary, they may also hear other natural or legal persons. Natural or legal persons showing a sufficient interest and especially members of the administrative or management bodies of the undertakings concerned or the recognised representatives of their employees shall be entitled, upon application, to be heard.

Also significant for due process during the administrative procedure before the Commission is Article 10 of the Merger Regulation on time limits for initiating proceedings and decisions. The effect of this Article is that the Commission must complete its examination of the proceedings/initiation of proceedings ('first phase') within one month (extendable under certain circumstances to six weeks).

If it initiates proceedings under Article 6(1)(c) on the basis of 'serious doubts' as to the compatibility of the concentration with the 'Common Market' it normally has a maximum further period of four months. If it misses these deadlines the concentration is 'deemed to have been declared compatible with the common market'.

5.3 Tenth anniversary of the Merger Regulation September 2000 'The way forward'

Two papers read at this Conference are of interest for due process: González Díaz on the administrative procedure and Marenco on judicial review.

5.3.1 Administrative procedure

González Díaz recalls that the Merger Regulation gives the Commission the serious responsibility to decide within very tight deadlines and in compliance with due process guarantees on the acceptability of proposals to effect, by merger or joint venture, durable changes to the structure of the market.

On the procedural front, two types of objectives have to be addressed: the preservation of the rights of the notifying parties to a proper assessment of the case within a reasonable period of time, including the possibility to modify their initial concentration plan, and the need to adopt a decision, with full knowledge of all the relevant facts, including submissions made by interested third parties.

The paper is very supportive of the current (as of 2000) regime especially regarding the number of checks and balances in the merger assessment, always taking into account the stringent deadlines. The list includes: the obligation to guarantee the notifying parties' rights of defence under the supervision of the Hearing Officer (embodied in the obligation to issue a Statement of Objections, to grant access to the Commission's file and to offer the possibility to reply to its objections both in writing and orally), the obligation to consult the Merger Task Force's associated services, including the Legal Service, and most importantly the competition authorities of the 15 Member States, the obligation to motivate its decisions and, finally, the possibility to appeal the final decision before the European courts.

Already, the idea of a 'stop-the-clock' provision is launched. González Díaz envisages it for complex cases whenever it is necessary to collect information from third parties who are not willing to reply in full to the Article 11 requests for information or whenever the discovery of new facts, not known to the notifying parties, warrants further investigation.[11]

5.3.2 Judicial review

Marenco analyses the case law of the Court and emphasises the fact that the Court often points to the Merger Regulation as being characterised by *strict* (*Grandes Sources*[12] interim measures, paragraph 30) or *short* (Zunis, CFI,[13] paragraph 38) time-limits, *the need for speed* (*Kaysersberg,*[14] para 113, *Endemol,*[15] paras 68 and 84) and *urgency* (*Dan Air,*[16] para 67).

On the rights of defence in the first phase *Generali,*[17] paragraphs 87-88 are cited: 'Despite the absence of provisions on the rights of undertakings during the first phase, the Court derives the necessity to respect such rights from fundamental principle of Community law.'

On access to file for notifying parties Marenco cites *Endemol* where the Court summarises the case law developed under Regulation 17 and goes on to say that the same principles are applicable under the Merger Regulation, 'even though their application may reasonably be adapted to the need for speed, which characterises the general scheme of that regulation'.

On the procedural rights of third parties, in particular competitors, Marenco recalls that the Court has ruled that, although their position cannot be equated with that of the interested parties, they do have a right to be heard by the Commission, if they so request, in order to make known their views on the harmful effects on them of the notified concentration plan, but such a right must nevertheless be reconciled with the observance of the rights of the defence and with the primary aim of the legislation which is to ensure effectiveness of control as well as legal certainty for undertakings to which it applies. Marenco concludes[18]:

> 'The case law is attentive to the protection of procedural rights. The rights of the defence are affirmed even where the Regulation is silent, and analogies with Regulation 17 exist. The court is not blind, however, to the fact that the strict

11 González Díaz, 'Tenth Anniversary of the Merger Regulation: the way forward' in *EC Merger Control: Ten Years On* (London: IBA, 2000), p 422.

12 T-96/92, *Comité Central d'Entreprise de la Société Générale des Grandes Sources v Commission,* judgment of the CFI, 27 April 1995, [1995] ECR II-1213.

13 T-83/92, *Zunis Holding v Commission,* judgment of the CFI, 28 October 1993, [1993] ECR II-1169.

14 T-290/94, *Kaysersberg SA v Commission,* judgment of the CFI, 27 November 1997, [1997] ECR II-2137.

15 T-221/95, *Endemol,* judgment of the CFI, 28 April 1999, [1999] ECR II-1299.

16 T-3/93, *Air France v Commission (Air France/Dan Air),* judgment of the CFI, 24 March 1994, [1994] ECR II-121.

17 T-87/96, *Assicurazioni Generali v Commission,* judgment of the CFI, 4 March 1999, [1999] ECR II-203.

18 G Marenco, 'Judicial Review in the First Ten Years of the Merger Regulation' in *EC Merger Control: Ten Years On,* n 11 above p 303.

deadlines contained in the Regulation necessarily colour the rights and obligations of all the players in the procedure, the Commission as well as the undertakings concerned, third parties as well as the Advisory Committee.'

5.4 The Hearing Officer

Under the current mandate,[19] the Hearing Officer is empowered, and frequently requested by the notifying and the third parties, to take decisions on a number of procedural matters including: rights of third parties to be heard (Article 6), the rights of parties to a formal oral hearing (Article 7), disclosure of documents in the Commission's possession (Article 8), confidentiality/business secrets (Article 9), extension of deadlines for reply (Article 10), admission of evidence and experts at the oral hearing (Article 12(3)), written evidence after the oral hearing (Article 12(4)), and objectivity of market test enquiries (Article 14). Article 5 of the mandate is particularly wide and allows the Hearing Officer to 'ensure in particular, that, in the preparation of draft Commission decisions, due account is taken of all the relevant facts whether favourable or unfavourable to the parties concerned ...'. The Hearing Officer also has the power to prepare and submit reports to the Competition Commissioner. His/her final report is attached to the draft decision considered by the College of Commissioners, is circulated to the Member States and is published along with the final decision in the Official Journal (mandate Articles 13, 15, and 16). The main novelties introduced by the new mandate are organisational separation (the post is removed from DG Competition) and made directly responsible to the Commissioner for Competition and the publication of his/her final report. There are also now two Hearing Officers.

5.5 Advisory Committee

The Advisory Committee consists of representatives of the Member States and is chaired by the Commission. It must be consulted before any second phase decision is taken by the Commission. The Commission must send the members of the Committee a summary of the case together with an indication of the most important documents and a preliminary draft of the decision and invite them to a meeting.

The Committee shall deliver an opinion on the draft decision and may recommend that its opinion be published. The Commission shall take the utmost account of the opinion and shall inform the Committee of the manner in which its opinion has been taken into account.[20]

6. Reforms envisaged in the Green Paper[21]

Some decisions of the Commission under the Merger Regulation have spurred companies and practitioners to criticise the merger control process. A high point was

19 Commission Decision of 23 May 2001 on the terms of reference of Hearing Officers in certain competition proceedings, OJ 2001 L 162/21.

20 Article 19(3) of the Merger Regulation.

21 Green Paper on the Review of Council Regulation (EEC) No 4064/89 COM (2001) 745 of 11 December 2001.

reached with the prohibition of the proposed GE/Honeywell merger in the summer of 2001.[22] The Green Paper acknowledges the criticisms and sets out a number of ideas and options with regard both to substance and to procedure and invited comments before 31 March 2002.

The most significant procedural suggestions concern an amendment of the timetable for the submission and discussion of commitments, both in first and second phase. There would be an option, at the initiative of the merging companies, to 'stop the clock' by an additional 20-30 days to allow them to propose commitments and to permit the Commission to market test their proposals.

With regard to due process the Green Paper recalls that the procedure established by the Merger Regulation is administrative rather than judicial, but emphasises that the apparent dual function of the Commission as investigation and decision-making body has been found not to contravene Article 6 of the ECHR on the right to a fair trial. In particular the Commission has been held to be subject to 'effective' judicial review by an independent and impartial judge.[23]

The Green Paper sets out the various mechanisms of relevance to due process, underlining in particular the role of the Hearing Officer whose role in safeguarding the right to be heard has been strengthened by the new mandate of May 2001. The Green Paper also sets out the various 'checks and balances' in the decision-making procedure, in particular the role of the Member States in the Advisory Committee.

With regard to judicial review the Green Paper recalls the expedited procedure adopted by the CFI on 6 December 2000 and concludes that it 'does not believe that the current system of judicial review fails to provide adequate judicial protection'. Nevertheless, it would consider suggestions aimed at enhancing judicial review as well as 'substantive reflection' on the relative merits of the overall procedural system provided for in the Merger Regulation as compared to merger control procedural systems employed in other jurisdictions.

7. Reactions to the Green Paper

DG Competition has made a summary of the reactions to the Green Paper and put them on its website.[24]

As summarised, the main reactions regarding procedure and due process are:

- the majority are in favour of a 'stop-the-clock' possibility in cases involving remedy issues;
- criticism focuses on the fact that decisions are taken by the same body that carries out the fact-finding investigation, including weak rights of defence, inadequate checks and balances, and the absence of a 'fresh pair of eyes' to examine critically the merits of the investigating conclusions at key stages;
- further criticism is levelled at the availability and effectiveness of judicial review, both because of the lengthy delays before judgments are rendered and because of an inadequate standard of review;
- a minority of correspondents favours a radical overhaul of the current system with the introduction of a US-style prosecutorial regime, whereby the

22 Case COMP/M.2220 decision adopted on 3 July 2001.

23 Case T-348/94, *Enso Espanola*, judgment of the CFI, 14 May 1998, [1998] ECR II-1875.

24 http://europa.eu.int/comm/competition/mergers/review/comments.htm.

Commission would have to challenge a proposed merger before the CFI or a specialised competition Court. The Court would then rule on the legality of the proposed transaction.

Mention should also be made of the Report of the Select Committee of the House of Lords of the UK Parliament published on 23 July 2002.[25] On due process and checks and balances its recommendations can be summarised as follows :

- the priority for ensuring an effective system of due process within the Merger Regulation should not be limited to trying to obtain speedier judicial review or a greater role for the courts. Efforts should focus instead on improving the internal checks and balances in the Merger Regulation regime. The concerns about due process are best addressed by enhancing the procedural safeguards in the current system (para 248);
- the Commission should divide responsibility for the consideration of cases in Phase I and Phase II (para 255);
- Hearing Officers should be required to produce fully reasoned reports that contain a full explanation of their conclusions (para 264);
- the Commission should strengthen its overall capacity for economic analysis in merger cases. In particular, DG Competition should appoint a Chief Economist (para 273).

8. Current ideas within the Commission

The current ideas within the Commission can be gleaned from a speech by Commissioner Monti to the British Chamber of Commerce in Brussels on 4 June 2002,[26] by a speech by Philip Lowe, Director General DG Competition, to the International Bar Association at Fiesole on 20 September 2002,[27] as well as by a press conference given by Commissioner Monti on 25 October 2002.[28] The Advisory Committee is also being consulted in particular on the basis of a document on due process drawn up by DG Competition. It is envisaged that the 'college' of the Commission should be presented before the end of the year with a package containing internal reforms of DG Competition, proposed amendments to the Merger Regulation, and new draft Guidelines. It appears likely at present that the main elements of this package would be:

(1) Internal organisation

- appointment of a chief competition economist
- best practice guidelines
- improvement of access to file after Article 6(1)(c) decisions
- triangular meetings between parties, third parties and the Commission
- more systematic peer review panels
- more time flexibility ('stop the clock').

25 European Union – 32nd Report, http://www.parliament.the-stationery-office.co.uk/pa/ld200102/ldselect/leeucom/165/16501.htm.

26 Review of the EC Merger Regulation – Roadmap for the reform project.

27 Future Directions for EU Competition Policy.

28 See *Financial Times*, 28 October 2002, p 13.

(2) Judicial review

- no change to US-style prosecutorial system
- support for additional resources and structural changes at the CFI
- examination of advantages/disadvantages of separate chamber of the CFI for competition/merger cases or specialised court for competition/merger cases under Article 225 A of the Nice Treaty
- support for generalised application of the 'expedited procedure' by the CFI to all merger prohibition cases where parties can show urgency irrespective of the complexity and volume of the pleadings
- support for further shortening of expedited procedure (at most six months) by specialised chambers or a change in linguistic regime of the CFI
- examination of deadlines for Court judgments (example Sweden)
- clarification of role of interim measures proceedings within the expedited procedure
- more attention to preparation and performance at oral procedure of the Court.

9. Analysis and conclusions

In the context of an overall reform of merger control due process and judicial review cannot be entirely separated from other aspects of the reform. It is clear from the reaction to the Green Paper that there are other points of criticism of the working of the Merger Regulation. There are issues of jurisdiction as between the Commission and the national competition authorities, there is the question of the 'substantive test' (whether there should be a move to a 'significant lessening of competition' test and whether an 'efficiencies' defence should be allowed), there are the 'stop-the-clock' suggestions which are not strictly issues of due process but which have an effect on due process. The success of the reform, if and when it is implemented, will be judged on the basis of the whole package and not just on one of its elements.

Nevertheless, due process and judicial review are obviously of prime importance and certainly justify separate treatment at this Conference.

9.1 Administrative due process

The current ideas of Mr Monti and DG Competition which I have already outlined in the preceding section of this paper, if adopted by the Commission and translated, so far as necessary, into new legislation by the Council of Ministers would certainly make a useful contribution to the fairness and transparency of the administrative procedure. In particular the 'stop-the-clock' ideas appear to have been generally welcomed although, by adding to the length of the procedure, they go against another important requirement of the whole process: the speediest possible conclusion in order to enable the parties to 'keep their transaction alive'.

It is worth, however, examining in greater detail two suggestions which at present appear not likely to be retained in the reform package – the further strengthening of the role of the Hearing Officer and the separation of the teams within DG Competition that examine mergers in the first and second phase.

9.1.1 Hearing Officer

Most respondents to the Green Paper called for changes to the role of the Hearing Officer – for his[29] independence to be enhanced, for his resources to be increased, and for his function to be enlarged. One particular suggestion was that the Hearing Officer should chair the negotiations on remedies, acting as a mediator between the parties and the Commission.[30] While having some doubts as to whether the Hearing Officer would be willing or able to carry out this particular function, I think it is undeniable that a strengthening of his/her independence and resources together with an enlargement of his/her functions could improve administrative due process within the Commission.

9.1.2 Separation of the teams in first and second phase

Numerous suggestions were made as to changes that might reconcile what was seen as an inherent conflict between the Commission's role as both investigator and decision-maker. In particular, many stressed the importance of a 'fresh pair of eyes' being brought critically to bear on the merits of the investigators conclusions. The most common suggestion was that the investigation should be handled by different case teams in first and second phase. Indeed this suggestion was specifically supported in the concluding Summary of Recommendations of the Select Committee of the House of Lords.[31]

The current thinking within the Commission appears to be that this would involve too important a dilution of resources with a consequent reduction in efficiency. It is therefore envisaged that the requirement for a 'fresh pair of eyes' should be met by a systematic use of informal peer review 'merger panels' following an Article 6(1)(c) decision. These merger panels would consist of Commission officials with expertise in competition policy, drawn mainly but not exclusively from DG Competition

Personally I do not feel in a position to question this appreciation, which should combine the benefits of a 'fresh pair of eyes' with continuity in the investigation.

9.2 Judicial review

The heat has probably gone out of the debate on the *adequacy* of judicial review by the CFI in merger control cases as a result of three recent landmark judgments – *Airtours,*[32] *Schneider Electric*[33] and *Tetra Laval.*[34]

In its *Airtours* judgment the CFI concluded that the Commission's prohibition decision was 'vitiated by a series of errors of assessment as to factors fundamental to any assessment as to whether a collective dominant position right be created' (para 294).

In *Schneider Electric* the CFI found that there were errors of analysis and appreciation which undermined the Commission's economic appreciation of the impact of the merger (para 411) and that, on the French market, the Commission had

29 Also read 'her'.
30 See, in particular, Report of the Select Committee of the House of Lords, para 211.
31 Paragraphs 250 and following and 302 of the Report.
32 T-342/99, *Airtours plc v Commission*, judgment of the CFI, 6 June 2002.
33 Already cited.
34 Already cited.

not properly respected Schneider's rights of defence in its drafting of the Statement of Objections (paras 454 to 459).

In the *Tetra Laval* judgment the CFI found that the Commission committed a manifest error of assessment in concluding that the proposed merger would create a dominant position on the distinct PET equipment market ('conglomerate effect') (para 308) and that the Commission had not shown that the merged entity's position would be strengthened *vis-à-vis* competitors on the carton market (para 333).

With regard to *speed* it has to be recalled that the *Airtours* judgment was given more than three years after notification of the proposed merger to the Commission (29 April 1999). There was thus no hope of 'saving the transaction'. The *Schneider* and *Tetra Laval* cases were different in that in both cases the control of the target company had already been acquired under the 'public bid' exception of Article 7(3) of the Merger Regulation and in both cases the Court used the new 'expedited procedure' to give judgment within ten months of being seized of the case. In the case of a merger which is suspended pending and after a Commission prohibition decision or which is subject to commitments which are considered overly burdensome it seems unlikely that the CFI would be able to give judgment even under the expedited procedure in the four or five months which many correspondents appear to consider the maximum period for keeping a transaction alive.

Apart from the question of the adequacy and speed of judicial review there remains a fundamental unease with regard to an administrative procedure under which the Commission is apparently both prosecutor and decision taker. The question of a move to a US-style prosecutorial system will not therefore go away. Indeed the Committee on Economic and Monetary Affairs of the European Parliament has recently produced a report[35] in which:

- it considers that the current system of appeal to the Court of Justice in merger control cases does not work in an optimal way; and
- asks the Commission to consider a new system whereby a final decision in a merger case, including the imposed conditions, should be subject to a 'preview' by an independent judicial body.

In this case the Parliamentary Committee appears to envisage a hybrid system under which the Commission would act as a prosecutor in relation to transactions it proposes should be prohibited while retaining its decision-making powers in all other cases.

Personally I am not convinced that a radical change to a full or even a hybrid prosecutorial system for merger control would be desirable at this stage. To paraphrase one of the respondents to the Select Committee I do not believe that the present system is so 'broken' that it cannot be 'fixed' and I have some doubts as to whether a court is better suited than an administrative body to analysing and taking decisions on the economic issues which arise in merger control cases.[36] In any event such a radical change would appear to require an amendment to the EC Treaty itself since there must be a doubt as to whether Article 83 (ex-Article 87) of the EC Treaty would be a sufficient legal basis.

35 Report of 10 October 2002 on the Commission's XXX1st Report on Competition Policy, paras 5 and 6 (A5 – 0352+2002) – rapporteur Alain Lipietz.

36 See Report of Select Committee, paras 234 to 240.

Indeed if there were to be a transfer of powers to the Court in the field of competition there are more compelling arguments that this should be carried out for the imposition of fines for illegal agreements under Article 81 of the EC Treaty or abuses of dominant position under Article 82. This would particularly be the case if ever it were envisaged to introduce prison sanctions on individuals.[37]

37 See Wouter Wils, 'Does the effective enforcement of Articles 81 and 82 require imprisonment?' in *The Optimal Enforcement of EC Antitrust Law* (Kluwer, 2002), para 8.7.4.5.

Session 3

Substantive Tests – Are the Differences between the Dominance and SLC Tests Real or Semantic?

11

Dominance versus SLC: A Subtle Distinction?

Nicholas Levy*

Cleary Gottlieb Steen & Hamilton, Brussels

In its Green Paper on the Review of Council Regulation 4064/89 (the 'Green Paper'),[1] the European Commission (the 'Commission') initiated a debate on the merits of changing the substantive test in the EC Merger Regulation (ECMR) from 'dominance'[2] to a 'substantial lessening of competition' (SLC), the test employed in several jurisdictions, including the United States[3] and Canada.[4]

The first section of this paper describes the background to the European Union's decision to adopt a dominance test and explains that its adoption was due largely to the familiarity of the concept and the Commission's strong reluctance to consider non-competition criteria, rather than to any disinclination to employ an SLC test. The second section describes the practical approach taken by the Commission in applying the dominance test under the ECMR and explains that the broad and flexible interpretation given to the dominance standard has narrowed any differences between dominance and SLC to a point where they may be expected to arise only exceptionally. The third section considers three questions:

1. Does the SLC test better articulate the proper focus of merger control?
2. Is there an enforcement 'gap' between the concepts of dominance and SLC?
3. Would an SLC test have any material implications for EC competition law enforcement?

In answer to the first question, this paper concludes that the wording of the SLC test is more closely wedded to the key economic issue in merger control (ie whether a concentration creates market power that is likely to be used to lessen

* I am extremely grateful to a number of my colleagues at Cleary Gottlieb Steen & Hamilton, including, in particular, Mark Leddy, David Gelfand, Robbert Snelders, Stéphanie Hallouët, Christopher Cook, Robert O'Donoghue, and Simon Pritchard. I bear sole responsibility for the judgments, opinions, and any errors.

1 Review of Council Regulation 4064/89, COM (2001) 745/6 final.

2 Article 2(3) ECMR provides that 'a concentration which creates or strengthens a dominant position as a result of which effective competition would significantly be impeded in the common market or a substantial part of it shall be declared incompatible with the common market'.

3 Section 7 of the Clayton Act, 15 USC § 18 (2000) provides that 'No person ... shall acquire ... the whole or any parts of the assets of another person ... where in any line of commerce or in any activity affecting commerce in any section of the country, the effect of such acquisition may be substantially to lessen competition, or to tend to create a monopoly'.

4 Other countries with merger control regimes that incorporate an SLC test include Australia, Ireland, New Zealand, South Africa, and Spain (the Spanish test refers to the 'maintenance of effective competition'). The United Kingdom is in the process of replacing the existing public interest test with one based on SLC.

competition and lead to higher prices, reduced output, or less innovation). However, the practical implications of applying a standard that is more firmly grounded in economics are probably not that significant since the dominance and SLC tests pursue largely similar ends (ie the prevention of market power) and reach similar outcomes in most cases.[5] If both tests permit essentially the same types of transactions to be challenged, the practical consequences of adopting a standard that conforms more closely to economic theory may be slight.

In answer to the second question (ie is there an enforcement 'gap' between the concepts of dominance and SLC?), this paper explains that the SLC test comprehends the dominance test in virtually all situations. There may, however, be a small category of transactions that substantially lessen competition but which do not fit neatly into either single-firm or collective dominance. This is because the notion of single-firm dominance, as applied by the Community courts, envisages a situation where only the leading firm may be dominant in any market, while the definition of collective dominance, as defined in *Airtours*,[6] cannot be applied in all market contexts (eg oligopolistic markets with no risk of tacit collusion). As a result, it is uncertain whether the dominance test could be applied in a cogent fashion to transactions that have unilateral effects falling short of single-firm dominance in markets where joint dominance may be excluded. The dominance test might nevertheless be employed in various ways to challenge such transactions, although the Community courts' view of such analytical frameworks is uncertain. Adoption of an SLC test would remove that uncertainty.

As to the third question (ie would an SLC test have any material implications for EC competition law enforcement?), this paper considers the following questions:

1. Would an SLC test more readily permit the Commission to take positive account of efficiencies under the ECMR?
2. Would an SLC test avoid the possible prejudice of a dominance finding under the ECMR for purposes of Article 82?
3. Would adoption of an SLC test affect international convergence in merger control?

As to the treatment of efficiencies under the ECMR, this paper suggests that the dominance test should not prevent the Commission from taking positive account of efficiencies in assessing a transaction's compatibility with the Common Market, but recognises that the Commission may be constrained from applying an 'efficiencies defence' once it has determined that a dominant position will be created or strengthened by the lack of explicit wording in the ECMR and statements made by the Commission that there is 'no real legal possibility of justifying an efficiency defence under the [ECMR]'.[7] In regard to Article 82, this paper concludes that the practical consequences of detaching a finding of dominance under the ECMR from

5 See, eg Dr William Bishop cited in *The Review of the EC Merger Regulation*, 32nd Report of the House of Lords Select Committee on the European Union, HL Paper 165, Session 2001-02, para 102 ('[there is] very little difference in practice between the two tests').

6 *Airtours plc v Commission* ('*Airtours*'), Case T-342/99, judgment of 6 June 2002 (not yet reported), para 62.

7 *Competition Policy and Efficiency Claims in Horizontal Agreements*, European Commission Delegation to the OECD, November 1995 (http://www.oecd.org/pdf/M00007000/M00007744.pdf), p 53.

Article 82 would probably not be significant. As to international convergence, this paper concludes that the European Union's adoption of an SLC test would be unlikely to have either the beneficial or the adverse effects claimed by proponents and critics, respectively.

While this paper identifies subtle differences between the dominance and SLC tests, it concludes that the practical implications of replacing the current test would not be significant. Moreover, following the courts' judgments in *Airtours*, *Schneider*,[8] and *Tetra Laval*,[9] the Commission's principal enforcement priorities should be:

1. to develop a sound analytical framework that is firmly grounded in economic science[10];
2. to ensure that its decisions are based on firm evidence, solid investigative techniques, and are tested against 'the cold metal of economic theory'[11]; and
3. to issue clear and comprehensive guidelines that explain the enforcement standards on which the Commission intends relying.

On 11 December 2002, shortly after the Conference for which this paper was originally prepared, the Commission proposed a 'far-reaching'[12] reform of the ECMR that, among other things, sought to 'clarify' the dominance standard.[13] Although the Commission decided against replacing the dominance test with the SLC test, in an effort to 'improve legal certainty', it proposed a new Article 2(2) to the ECMR that is intended to 'clarify the concept of dominance' by expressly capturing transactions that occur in oligopolistic markets where there is no risk of tacit collusion and where the merging companies will not necessarily have a leadership position post-transaction, but where the merged undertaking will be in a position to raise prices and thus exercise market power (ie 'unilateral effects' in oligopolistic markets where a position of single firm dominance will not be created or strengthened). The Commission also proposed revising the ECMR to take positive account of efficiencies. The final section of this paper describes these proposals.

1. Adoption of the dominance test under the ECMR

The concept of a 'dominant position' was first recognised in Community law in the 1951 Treaty of Paris that established the European Coal and Steel Community (the 'ECSC Treaty'), Article 66(7) of which permitted the High Authority to issue recommendations to 'public or private undertakings which, in law or fact, hold or

8 *Schneider Electric SA v Commission* ('*Schneider*'), Case T-310/01, [2002] ECR II-4071.

9 *Tetra Laval BV v Commission* ('*Tetra Laval*'), Case T-5/02, [2002] ECR II-4381.

10 See, eg William J Kolasky, Former Deputy Assistant Attorney General, Antitrust Division, US Department of Justice, 'Sound Economics and Hard Evidence: The Touchstones of Sound Merger Review', American Bar Association, 14 June 2002.

11 J A Schumpeter, *Capitalism, Socialism, and Democracy* (1942).

12 Proposal for a Council Regulation on the control of concentrations between undertakings, COM (2002) 711 (the 'Draft ECMR').

13 See Mario Monti, Member of the Commission responsible for Competition Policy, 'Commission Adopts Comprehensive Reform of EU Merger Control' (Commission Press Release IP/02/1856 of 11 December 2002).

acquire in the market ... a dominant position shielding them against effective competition in a substantial part of the Common Market'. Elements of this test, notably 'dominant position' and 'effective competition in a substantial part of the Common Market', found their way into successive drafts of the Commission's merger control instrument. ECSC merger control, for its part, spoke of the analogous concept of an 'artificially privileged position'.[14]

Unlike the ECSC Treaty, the Treaty establishing the European Community (the 'EC Treaty') contains no specific provisions applying competition rules to concentrations. Prior to the adoption of the ECMR, the Commission's doctrine, as set out in its 1966 Memorandum on Concentrations, was that Articles 81 and 82 were not 'sufficient to control all operations which may prove to be incompatible with the system of undistorted competition envisaged in the Treaty'.[15] Taking note of a trend towards the formation of larger companies, the Commission considered that mergers 'may prevent competition from functioning or excessively limit the freedom of choice and activity of consumers, suppliers, and buyers ... [and] affect the conditions of existence of many small and medium-size companies'.

In 1973, the Court of Justice confirmed in *Continental Can* that Article 82 could be applied to concentrations that strengthened a pre-existing dominant position.[16] The Court concluded that 'an abuse may therefore occur if an undertaking in a dominant position strengthens such [a] position in a way that the degree of dominance reached substantially fetters competition, ie that only undertakings remain in the market whose behaviour depends on the dominant one'. The Court further held that 'the strengthening of the position of an undertaking may be an abuse and prohibited under Article [82] of the Treaty, regardless of the means and procedure by which it is achieved, if it has the effect mentioned above'.

Seizing the momentum provided by *Continental Can* in February 1973, the Commission proposed a first draft merger control regulation in July of the same year.[17] The draft contained no express reference to dominance, but instead provided that concentrations that permitted the undertakings concerned to 'acquire or enhance the power to hinder effective competition in the common market' would be prohibited.[18] The 1973 proposal also envisaged the possibility of exempting concentrations that were deemed 'indispensable to the attainment of an objective which is given priority treatment in the common interest of the Community'. The notion of a 'common interest' was defined in Recital 12, which

14 A proposed transaction was to be authorised under the ECSC Treaty if it: 'will not give to the persons or undertakings concerned the power ... to determine prices, to control or restrict production or distribution or to hinder effective competition in a substantial part of the market for those products; or to evade the rules of competition instituted under this Treaty, in particular by establishing an artificially privileged position involving a substantial advantage in access to supplies or markets'. (Article 66(2).)

15 'EEC Competition Services Study No. 3, Brussels' [1966] 26 CMLR 1-30.

16 *Europemballage and Continental Can v Commission*, Case 6/72, [1973] ECR 215, paras 26-27.

17 Commission Proposal for a Regulation of the Council on the Control of Concentrations between Undertakings (OJ 1973 C 92/1).

18 The 'power to hinder effective competition' was to be assessed 'by reference ... to the extent to which suppliers and consumers have a possibility of choice, to the economic and financial power of the undertakings concerned, to the structure of the markets affected, and to supply and demand trends for the relevant goods or services' (Article 1).

stated that 'it may be found necessary, for the purpose of reconciling objectives to be attained in the common interest of the Community, especially within the frame of common policies, to exempt certain concentrations from incompatibility, under conditions and obligations to be determined case by case'.

Discussions on a merger regulation continued through 1974 and 1975. Conflicting Member State views as to various issues, including the jurisdictional scope of a Community-wide instrument for merger control and the extent to which non-competition criteria should be taken into account, scuttled the debate,[19] and no text was adopted. The Commission did not venture a revised proposal until 1981,[20] although it did apply *Continental Can* to assess a small number of transactions under Articles 81 and 82.[21] The 1981, 1984, and 1986 proposals were based on the same substantive test suggested in 1973, including the notion of 'common interest', and there continued to be support for requiring the Commission to take account of non-competition criteria in its assessment of reportable concentrations.[22] The 'dominance' criterion emerged in a revised draft submitted by the Commission in March 1988, which proposed that '[c]oncentrations shall not be compatible with the Common Market where they give rise to or strengthen a dominant position in the Common Market or in a substantial part thereof'.[23] In a further revised version issued a few months later, dominance was no longer the central criterion, but one of the ways a concentration could impede competition: 'Concentrations ... which are found, notably as a result of the creation or strengthening of a dominant

19 See Comments of the French Delegation to the Working Party on Economic Questions of 25 July 1974: 'Le nud du problème consiste en fait à savoir dans quelle mesure les besoins de la politique de concurrence sont compatibles avec les besoins d'autres aspects de la politique économique'. Memorandum of the Working Party on Economic Questions, 5 June 1975: 'les délégations françaises et du Royaume-Uni ... ont estimé que toute décision en matière de contŗle des concentrations ... ne devrait pas priviliégier les aspects de concurrence, mais tenir compte également ... d'autres considérations relevant des politiques de restructuration industrielle, d'équilibre régional et de sauvegarde de l'emploi'. See too the Commission's Working Party on Economic Questions, 25 July 1974: 'le représentant de la Commission a de plus admis qu'il ne serait pas possible de tenir compte des seules considérations relatives à la concurrence'. A number of Members of the European Parliament were unenthusiastic about a pure competition-based test. See Reports of a Debate on Commission Documents 263/73 and 264/73 on 15 January 1974 (Lord O'Hagan's contribution is representative of a powerful sentiment at the time: 'There is a suspicion amongst some of us who are enthusiasts for the Community that there is too much emphasis on competition policy as a science or an art and not as a tool for the creation of a Community').

20 Amended Proposal for a Council Regulation on the Control of Concentrations between Undertakings (OJ 1982 C 36/3). See the Council's Response to a Written Question (225/79, 18 June 1979) enquiring why no merger control regulation had been adopted. Among the reasons cited, the Council noted that 'the conditions for securing consistency between industrial, social and regional politics and whatever decisions might be taken at Community level for the control of concentrations still need to be defined'.

21 See, eg *Pilkington/BSN-Gervais-Danone*, Xth Report on Competition Policy (1980), paras 152-155; and *Amicon Corp/Fortia AB/Wright Scientific Ltd*, XIth Report on Competition Policy (1981), para 112.

22 See, eg the Opinion of the Economic and Social Committee on Community Competition Policy in the light of the Current Economic and Social Situation (OJ 1981 C 322/3), which opined that '[b]usiness mergers should be vetted, though many cyclical and structural factors, including at the present time employment difficulties, militate in favour of policies free of legal and other rigidities'.

23 Amended Proposal for a Council Regulation on the Control of Concentrations between Undertakings (OJ 1988 C 130/4).

position, to impede or render more difficult the maintenance or development of effective competition, shall be declared incompatible with the common market'.[24]

By the November draft of the same year, the prevailing view was that 'the decisive criterion' for merger clearance ought to be whether a concentration 'impedes effective competition'[25] and the word dominance was not included.[26] The basic objective of the Commission remained unchanged, as the then-Commissioner for Competition Policy, Peter Sutherland, noted with respect to the November draft:

> 'Article 2(2) speaks of creating or strengthening "a position as a result of which the maintenance or development of effective competition would be impeded..." This is not quite the same thing as the wording which is contained in Article [82], but the underlying concern about ability to disregard competitive pressures is essentially the same and is the essence of the regulations and the concerns which it expresses.'[27]

In the final negotiations during late 1988 and 1989 leading to the adoption of the ECMR, the substantive test was one of the last major points agreed on. The principal debate at the time was between those favouring a competition-based test and those urging that explicit account be taken of social, industrial, and employment considerations, certain of whom envisaged the possibility of an Article 81(3)-type exemption. The debate is recalled by the then-Commissioner for Competition Policy, Sir Leon Brittan QC, now Lord Brittan:

> 'As I looked around the Member States and spoke to Ministers, I found very different approaches to merger policy; some tended to see it as a tool of industrial, regional and social policies, a way of shaping industrial structure and location, an opportunity to create European champions to compete overseas with American and Japanese giants. Others saw it as a pure expression of competition principles: monopolization and market domination should be stopped, everything else should be allowed to proceed.' [28]

24 Proposal of June 1988 attached to the Minutes of the Meeting of the Council Working Party on Economic Issues, 30 August 1988.

25 Report of the Council Permanent Representatives Committee, 10 November 1988.

26 Amended Proposal for a Council Regulation on the Control of Concentrations between Undertakings (OJ 1989 C 22/16) (the relevant wording was: 'create or strengthen a position as a result of which the maintenance or development of effective competition would be impeded in the common market'). There remained a strong body of opinion that favoured taking explicit account of non-competition criteria. See, eg the Opinion of the Economic and Social Committee on the Amended Proposal for a Council Regulation on the Control of Concentrations between Undertakings (OJ 1988 C 208/11), which disclosed support for the application of non-economic criteria, stating that 'the problem of controlling concentrations must ... be approached on a "case-by-case" basis within the framework of general principles and having regard to the economic and social provisions of the Treaty'. The authors proposed that the Commission be required to consider 'the importance of competition in promoting healthy economic growth (and the) satisfaction of the economic, social and regional needs of the population of the Community'.

27 Peter Sutherland, Member of the Commission then responsible for Competition Policy, *Merger Review*, 6th Report of the House of Lords Select Committee on the European Communities, HL Paper 31, Session 1988-89, para 109.

28 Sir Leon Brittan QC, now Lord Brittan, Member of the Commission then responsible for Competition Policy, *The Development of Merger Control in E.E.C. Competition Law*, speech of 9 February 1990.

After intense last-minute debate, the ECMR was adopted in December 1989 and came into force on 21 September 1990. The ECMR's substantive test is whether reportable concentrations 'create or strengthen a dominant position as a result of which competition would be substantially impeded'. As the historic narrative set out above amply demonstrates, the principal policy debate over the 16 years of 'arduous negotiations'[29] did not concern nuances in different competition-based tests, but focused instead on the extent to which the Commission should be required to take account of non-competition criteria.[30] To assuage those who had supported a test based on social, industrial, employment, and other non-competition criteria,[31] Recital 13 of the ECMR requires the Commission to 'place its appraisal within the general framework of the achievement of the fundamental objectives referred to in Article 2 of the Treaty, including that of strengthening the Community's economic and social cohesion',[32] while Article 2(1)(b) of the ECMR refers to the 'development of technical and economic progress'.[33]

The most plausible explanation of why a dominance test was chosen as opposed to any other competition-based test was its essential familiarity. The notion of dominance had been established under Article 82 and defined by the Court of Justice, and the familiar terminology was considered at the time as providing a useful precedent and being conducive of legal certainty.[34] The concept of dominance was also consistent with German competition law's emphasis on

29 XXIIIrd Report on Competition Policy (1993), p 35.

30 See, eg *Merger Review*, n 27 above, para 71: 'The Committee also had regard to the existing position in the United Kingdom, where, although the principal criterion is in practice that of competition, a wide range of other public interest issues can be taken into account in appropriate cases both by the Secretary of State and, if a reference is made, by the MMC. After careful discussion, however, the Committee concluded that it would not be appropriate to include such wider criteria in a competition Regulation based on the competition provisions of the Treaty. There are other provisions of the Treaty with social objectives and other measures of Community social and regional policy.'

31 See, eg the Opinion of the Economic and Social Committee on the Amended Proposal for a Council Regulation on the Control of Concentrations between Undertakings (OJ 1988 C 208/11), which stated that the Council was prepared to accept the form of merger control regulation proposed by the Commission on various conditions, 'foremost among these [being] the requirement that the needs of industry and society be taken into account in establishing a system of concentration control'.

32 See too XIXth Report on Competition (1989), Annex 265-268 ('The Commission states that among the factors to be taken into consideration for the purpose of establishing the compatibility or incompatibility of a concentration – factors as referred to in Article 2(1) and explained in Recital 13 – account should be taken in particular of the competitiveness of undertakings located in regions which are greatly in need of restructuring owing *inter alia* to slow development').

33 See Barry E Hawk, 'The EEC Merger Regulation: The First Step Toward One-Stop Merger Control' (1990) 59 Antitrust LJ 195 ('[Recital 13 and Article 2(1)(b)] reflect the Council of Ministers' inability to resolve completely the differences between Member States favouring industrial, regional and social policy considerations (eg Spain, Portugal and France) and Member States favoring a competition-based analysis more akin to the U.S. model of antitrust review (eg Germany and the United Kingdom)'). See too James A Venit, 'The 'Merger' Control Regulation: Europe Comes of Age...or Caliban's Dinner' [1990] 5 CMLR 7 ('[Recital 13] suggests that factors other than competition law may, to some extent, be taken into consideration in assessing concentrations').

34 See, eg *Merger Review*, n 27 above, para 67: 'As regards competition criteria, the Committee agrees with those witnesses who preferred the July 1988 Commission draft of Article 2 [referring to the creation or strengthening of a dominant position]. ... This language was based on Article [82] EEC and had the advantage to legal practitioners that it was clear that the jurisprudence of the European Court of Justice interpreting these words would apply to the new Regulation. Since Commissioner

market structures and the creation of 'market-dominating positions' (*Marktbeherrschende Stellungen*).[35] (Indeed, the German Government's view at the time was that its delegation had 'succeeded in anchoring the regulatory approach of German cartel law in European merger control'.[36]) At least some commentators, however, recognised the limitations inherent in the notion of 'dominance', although opinion was divided as to whether such limitations were desirable[37] or unsatisfactory.[38] Sir Leon Brittan QC, now Lord Brittan, Member of the Commission then responsible for Competition Policy, suggested in May 1990 that the Commission's approach under the ECMR would be likely to differ from the concept of dominance developed under Article 82:

> 'The question is bound to be asked whether it is sufficient to know what Article [82] means to understand the dominant position test or whether the qualification "as a result of which effective competition would be significantly impeded" gives rise to a new test altogether. In my view, we are at the beginning of a new legal development and the Council did not wish to create a pure dominant position test.'[39]

Sutherland said that the underlying concern of the Commission was the same even though the wording was not identical to that of Article [82], the Committee believes that the familiar terminology should be retained. The different formulation in the Commission's December 1988 draft [not referring to dominance] would create a risk of legal uncertainty.'

35 The Bundeskartellamt remains wedded to the notion that competition law should focus on market structure. See ICN Subgroup Analytical Framework for Merger Review, Contribution by the Bundeskartellamt, 29 April 2002 (www.internationalcompetitionnetwork.org/AFSGgermany.pdf): 'The [antitrust] aim ... is to maintain competitive market structures and ensure that the scope of action of companies is sufficiently controlled and does not impinge on the substantive freedom of action of other firms and consumers ... competition free of power positions leads to an optimum in welfare in the long term' (p 4).

36 See Janicki, 'Die EG-Fusionskontrolle auf dem Weg zur praktischen Umsetzung' (1990) 3 Wirtschaft und Wettbewerb 195; cf Hölzler, EG Fusionskontrolle: Konzepte und Konsequenzen, Wertpapier Mitteilungen, 1990, pp 489 and 491.

37 See, eg a representative of the English Bar testifying before the House of Lords Select Committee in December 1988 suggested that it would be preferable to 'tie the text to dominance' to avoid a situation where, in a market with a firm holding a 60 per cent share, the merger between the two remaining competitors having a 20 per cent share each would risk being considered as 'affecting the maintenance or development of effective competition'. Testimony of David Vaughan QC, representing the English Bar, op cit, para 232.

38 See, eg William Baxter, Assistant Attorney General for the Antitrust Division of the US Department of Justice at the time the 1982 US Merger Guidelines were adopted: 'Most puzzling is the central role accorded to dominance by the Regulation ... Apparently, the dominance must be of a type that leaves the firm "independent of its rivals". Very few firms enjoy such a market position ... [It] is not until you get up to firms with market shares in the vicinity of 80% that it is realistic to suppose that dominance of that type is present ... So, it is a savagely restrictive notion of dominance that involves independence from competitors. Why should the EEC be limited to such rare cases?' Substantive Review under Merger Regulation [1990] Fordham Corp L Inst 561, p 563 (Barry E Hawk, ed, 1991).

39 Sir Leon Brittan QC, now Lord Brittan, Member of the Commission then responsible for Competition Policy, 'The Law and Policy of Merger Control in the EEC' (1990) 15 EL Rev 351, at 354.

2. The evolution of the dominance test under the ECMR

The substantive test under the ECMR is whether a concentration 'creates or strengthens a dominant position as a result of which effective competition would be significantly impeded in the Common Market or a substantial part of it'.[40] Dominance is not defined in the ECMR, although the Commission and the Community courts have extensively developed the concept.

A dominant position has been defined by the Court of Justice for purposes of Article 82 to mean situations where a company has 'the power to behave to an appreciable extent independently of its competitors, customers and ultimately of its consumers'[41] (in other words, will be largely free from competitive constraints). This definition has also been employed under the ECMR, although there are two important differences in the Commission's approach to dominance under Article 82 and the ECMR. First, the analysis under the ECMR is necessarily prospective, whereas Article 82 focuses on past conduct and therefore requires an assessment of the situation at the time of the alleged abuse. The second difference is that the ECMR contains an explicit additional element in the substantive assessment, namely that a dominant position should 'significantly impede competition'. In common with the Commission's approach under Article 82, the ECMR concept of dominance does not require the absence of all competition, but rather the ability to exercise market power, in particular over prices.

The Commission has emphasised that 'the dominance test is not some immovable and absolute measurement against which the future effects of a merger can be assessed', but is rather 'a highly sophisticated tool that requires us to understand the dynamics of competition and to identify the key competitive factors in the markets concerned'.[42] As a practical matter, the Commission's approach has evolved over the last decade and, in recent years, less reliance has been placed on market share data and greater emphasis has been given to evaluating the competitive characteristics of the market, the dynamics of competition between the merging parties, and the competitive effects of reportable transactions. The Green Paper explained this evolution in the following terms:

> 'Since the adoption of the Merger Regulation in 1989, the application of the notion of dominance has evolved, allowing it to be adapted both to developments in economic theory and to refinements of the now available econometric tools to measure market power. This implies that merger assessment today can be less reliant on the rather blunt and imprecise market share test than it was 10 years ago. The fact that the dominance test has undergone such an evolution is natural, and Article 2 has so far proved

40 Article 2(3) ECMR. Under Art 2(2) ECMR, 'a concentration which does not create or strengthen a dominant position as a result of which effective competition would be significantly impeded in the Common Market or in a substantial part of it shall be declared compatible with the Common Market'.

41 *United Brands v Commission*, Case 27/76, [1978] ECR 207, para 65. See too *Hoffmann-La Roche v Commission*, Case 85/76, [1979] ECR 461, para 38; and *Michelin v Commission*, Case 322/81, [1983] ECR 3461, para 30.

42 Professor Mario Monti, Member of the Commission responsible for Competition Policy, The Main Challenges for a New Decade of EC Merger Control, 10th Anniversary Conference, 15 September 2000 (Commission Press Release SPEECH/00/301).

sufficiently flexible to accommodate an effects analysis made on the basis of more sophisticated micro-economic tools, instruments and models developed by econometric and industrial organisation research.'[43]

The Commission's market-oriented approach to the application of the test of dominance has manifested itself in a number of ways. First, the Commission has consistently declined to take account of social, industrial, political, and other non-competition criteria in its assessment of reportable transactions. Secondly, the Commission has eschewed structural presumptions and has instead endeavoured to base its assessments on an understanding of the market characteristics and dynamics. Thirdly, the Commission has in recent years employed microeconomic analysis and 'unilateral effects' considerations in an effort to quantify merged entities' ability to raise price and limit output. As a result, the Commission has interpreted dominance in such a way as to capture readily the large majority of transactions that might be challenged under an SLC test.

2.1 A pure competition test

From the outset, the Commission focused purely on competition concerns in assessing reportable transactions. In statements published shortly after the ECMR's adoption, the Commission maintained a diplomatic tone towards those Member States that had sought to inject industrial and regional policy considerations into the ECMR.[44] In practice, however, the Commission resisted suggestions that it should take account of such considerations to exempt or permit concentrations that would create or strengthen a dominant position.[45] (In contrast, at the national level, certain Member States have maintained systems that permit political intervention to over-turn determinations made by competition agencies.[46]) The Commission has consistently emphasised that its decision-making would be based on competition criteria alone. Commissioner Brittan made this point most emphatically: 'Let there

43 Green Paper, para 163.

44 See Notes on Council Regulation 4064/89, where the Commission stated that, 'among the factors to be taken into consideration for the purpose of establishing the compatibility or incompatibility of a concentration – factors as referred to in Article 2(1) and explained in Recital 13 – account should be taken in particular of the competitiveness of undertakings located in regions which are greatly in need of restructuring owing inter alia to slow development'.

45 See, eg Sir Leon Brittan QC, now Lord Brittan, Member of the Commission then responsible for Competition Policy, Principles and Practice of the Merger Regulation, extracts of a speech at the Centre for European Policy Studies, 24 September 1990 (Commission Press Release IP/90/751): 'no words plucked from the Regulation can give rise to a defense against the finding that there is a dominant position as a result of which competition is significantly impeded. ... I do not see how a dominant position which impedes competition could give rise to technical or economic progress of the sort which competition policy could endorse.'

46 Under the German Act against Restraints on Competition (Gesetz gegen Wettbewerbs-beschränkungen), the Bundeskartellamt is limited to assessing the competitive aspects of a concentration and does not take account of public interest considerations, eg the creation or protection of jobs. Public interest considerations may, however, be considered if the Bundeskartellamt has prohibited a concentration and the undertakings concerned apply for Ministerial approval. The Ministerial approval procedure allows the Minister of Economic Affairs and Technology to set aside prohibition decisions rendered by the Bundeskartellamt if: (1) the concentration offers advantages to

be no doubt: the fundamental analysis to be carried out by the Commission is whether the merger impedes competition.'[47]

The ECMR requires the Commission to appraise mergers on the basis of, among other things, 'the development of technical and economical progress provided that it is to consumers' advantage and does not form an obstacle to competition'.[48] In the years following the ECMR's adoption, this provision gave rise to extensive discussion among commentators, the principal debate being whether economic efficiencies could in any circumstance constitute a defence to a merger that might otherwise restrict competition. The prevailing view of Commission officials at the time and subsequently was that this provision did not permit an 'efficiencies defence' and that 'any kind of derogation [is] totally excluded'.[49] Among other things, the Commission cited the Council's omission from the ECMR of language considered in earlier drafts that would have permitted the Commission to authorise mergers that would 'contribute to the attainment of the basic objectives of the Treaty in such a way that, on balance, their economic benefits prevail over the danger they cause to competition'.[50]

This focus on pure competition criteria found its first unambiguous expression in *Aérospatiale-Alenia/De Havilland*, the Commission's first prohibition decision, which was adopted notwithstanding political pressure from the French and Italian Governments.[51] Following this decision, fears that the Commission would not confine itself to applying competition considerations appeared unfounded.[52] In recent years, the growing confidence of the Commission, the increasing complexity

the economy as a whole which offset any harm to competition; or (2) there is an overriding public interest. The Ministerial approval procedure has been sought in only 16 cases and has been successfully invoked on only six occasions. It was recently applied in *E.ON/Ruhrgas*, a transaction concerning the German gas and electricity markets. Following the prohibition of the transaction by the Bundeskartellamt at the beginning of 2002 (FCO decision of 17 January 2002, B 8 – 109/01 – *E.ON/Ruhrgas I* and FCO decision of 26 February 2002, B 8 – 149/01 – *E.ON/Ruhrgas II*), the Minister approved the transaction subject to certain remedies in essence based on two public interest arguments (Ministerial decision of 5 July 2002, I B 1 – 22 08 40/129 – *E.ON/Ruhrgas*). The Minister found that the concentration would: (1) guarantee Ruhrgas' competitiveness in international gas markets; and (2) safeguard German gas supplies in times of shortage or crisis. The Minister rejected other public interest aspects, including the creation and protection of jobs and the protection of the environment. An appeal against the Ministerial approval is currently pending before the Düsseldorf Court of Appeal.

47 Sir Leon Brittan QC, now Lord Brittan, Member of the Commission then responsible for Competition Policy, 'The Law and Policy of Merger Control in the EEC', n 39 above, at 352.

48 Article 2(1) ECMR. See Pierre-Emmanuel Noel, 'Efficiency Considerations in the Assessment of Horizontal Mergers under European and U.S. Antitrust Law' [1997] 8 ECLR 498.

49 H Colin Overbury, then-Director of the Merger Task Force, EEC Merger Regulation, Panel Discussion, [1992] Fordham Corp L Inst 605 (Barry E Hawk, ed, 1993). See also Christopher Jones and Francisco Enrique González-Díaz, *The EEC Merger Regulation* (Sweet & Maxwell, 1992), pp 153-156.

50 Amended Proposal for a Council Regulation on the Control of Concentrations between Undertakings (OJ 1989 C 22/14), Recital 16.

51 Case IV/M.053, Commission decision of 2 October 1991 (OJ 1991 L 334/42).

52 Even today, the pressure for merger control to take account of employment, social, and industrial considerations remains strong. For example, although clearly focused on competition criteria, the proposed new UK merger control provisions include the possibility to create exceptional public interest gateways 'which can allow consideration of wider effects'. See Dr John Vickers, Director-General of Fair Trading, The Enterprise Act: Aspects of The New Regime, speech to the Regulatory Policy Institute Summer Conference, 27 June 2002.

of many cases, and the Commission's determination to insulate itself from political pressures have reduced the incidence of lobbying activities of this kind, even in high-profile cases. Commissioner Monti has resisted political pressure in a number of important cases, including *General Electric/Honeywell*,[53] *Volvo/Scania*,[54] and *Schneider/Legrand*,[55] and has explained his reasons for so doing in the following terms:

> 'I would be very hesitant in calling the EU merger control system a political or even politicized one: the Regulation is based solely on a competition-based test, unlike some other systems that apply various "public interest tests". Moreover, there is no possibility for a political authority to intervene in first or second phase and, in any case, decisions are subject to a system of judicial review by independent courts.'[56]

2.2 A dynamic approach to the concept of dominance

The Commission has consciously adopted a dynamic approach to identifying dominance under the ECMR and has 'developed and exploited progressively'[57] its interpretation of the dominance standard. This has been the case since the earliest decisions,[58] and at the end of the first full year following the ECMR's implementation, the Commission acknowledged that the significance of high market shares depended on:

1. the presence and strength of competitors;
2. the existence or absence of purchasing power;
3. the probability of market entry; and
4. market dynamism (eg demand growth, technological evolution).[59]

53 Case COMP/M.2220, Commission decision of 3 July 2001 (not yet reported). See Commission Press Release IP/01/855, where Commissioner Monti stated: 'I deplore attempts to misinform the public and to trigger political intervention. This is entirely out of place in an antitrust case and has no impact on the Commission whatsoever. This is a matter of law and economics, not politics. ... The nationality of the companies and political considerations have played and will play no role in the examination of mergers, in this case as in all others.'

54 Case IV/M.1672, Commission decision of 14 March 2000 (OJ 2001 L 143/74) (a reported attempt by the Swedish Government to intervene in favour of the merging parties apparently reinforced the Commission's resolve to prohibit the transaction).

55 Case COMP/M.2283, Commission decision of 10 October 2001 (not yet reported) (a reported intervention by the French Government on behalf of the parties failed to change the Commission's decision to prohibit the transaction).

56 Quoted in interview with Commissioner Monti, [2001] 15 Antitrust 6.

57 See evidence of Götz Drauz, Director of the Merger Task Force, cited in *The Review of the EC Merger Regulation*, n 5 above, para 139.

58 See, eg *Alcatel/Telettra*, Case IV/M.042, Commission decision of 12 April 1991 (OJ 1991 L 122/48) (approval of a transaction leading to an 83 per cent combined share, primarily on grounds of countervailing monopsonistic buyer power), where the Commission rejected any notion of an implicit 50 per cent dominance 'threshold' or 'presumption' that might be derived from the Court's Article 82 jurisprudence.

59 XXIst Report on Competition Policy (1991), p 363.

While this approach was not novel – the Court of Justice had recognised in *Hoffmann-La Roche*[60] that the significance of market share in determining dominance varies depending on the market structure – the Commission made clear from an early stage that it did not intend applying a rigid approach to the dominance analysis.

Less obvious but also significant was the Commission's departure from what might have been viewed as persuasive 'precedent' under German merger control. Such precedent was potentially powerful because of the two systems' shared heritage and the common catalogue of analytical criteria found in the ECMR and German merger control law.[61] Nevertheless, in its early decisions the Commission declined to adopt the market-share based presumptions present in German merger control. In 1991, the Commission approved the *Alcatel/AEG Kabel* transaction notwithstanding a request from the Bundeskartellamt that it be permitted to review the transaction on the basis of a 'dominant oligopoly' theory, noting that the ECMR, unlike German law, did not operate on the basis of formal presumptions of dominance:

> 'Where three companies have a combined market share exceeding 50% there is a legal presumption under German law that no substantial competition exists between these companies and that consequently they form a dominant oligopoly. Under the Regulation such a presumption which amounts to a reversal of the burden of proof does not exist. On the contrary, the Commission would have to demonstrate in all cases that effective competition could not be expected on structural grounds between the leading companies in a highly concentrated market.'[62]

Thus, from the outset, the Commission articulated a distinctive approach to dominance that differed from the more formalistic or schematic dimensions of German merger control.[63]

60 *Hoffmann-La Roche v Commission, supra,* para 41, where the Court noted that 'although the importance of market shares may vary from one market to another the view may legitimately be taken that very large market shares are in themselves, and save in exceptional circumstances, evidence of the existence of a dominant position'. A similar approach was taken in Michelin, supra, as well as other Article 82 cases subsequent to the entry into force of the ECMR.

61 The Bundeskartellamt used the occasion of the adoption of the ECMR to issue detailed multilingual guidelines explaining its 16-year experience in applying a 'creation or strengthening of a dominant position' test to cases of single-firm and oligopolistic dominance, stating that it was 'us[ing] this occasion to take stock of its experience won during sixteen years of merger control, and to present its result to the public ... in the form of a checklist which can be used to examine whether a merger will create or strengthen a market-dominating position'. See Remarks of W Kartte, President of the Bundeskartellamt, Foreword to Checklist for Merger Control Procedures, reprinted in [1990] Fordham Corp L Inst 161 (Barry E Hawk, ed, 1991).

62 Case IV/M.165, Commission decision of 18 December 1991, para 22. The Commission made these statements without prejudice as to whether the ECMR applied to oligopolies, and also disagreed with the Bundeskartellamt's evaluation of various market conditions in support of the latter's finding of oligopolistic dominance (paras 22-27).

63 See, eg Dr Rainer Bechtold, Antitrust Law in the European Community and Germany – An Uncoordinated Co-existence? [1991] Fordham Corp L Inst 343, pp 353-355 (Barry E Hawk, ed, 1992): 'German [merger control] applies rigid standards to the interpretation of the terms "market

2.3 Dominance as a synonym for market power

There is substantial consensus among economists that the principal purpose of merger control law is to prohibit mergers that threaten to confer market power on the merging firms or, by increasing concentration, facilitate tacit collusion among oligopolists. Both the US agencies and the Commission have applied their respective tests in terms that emphasise market power, although, as a formal matter, the Commission has often expressed the concept of dominance under the ECMR using the terminology of 'appreciable freedom of action'.[64] This has remained the case even in recent decisions that have described dominance in the language of 'independence',[65] but have focused on market power (ie the potential for a merger to raise prices, restrict output, and retard innovation). The Commission's July 2002 Glossary of Competition Terms confirms this interpretation:

> 'A firm is in a dominant position if it has the ability to behave independently of its competitors, customers and suppliers and, ultimately, the final consumer. A dominant firm holding such market power would have the ability to set prices above the competitive level, to sell products of an inferior quality or to reduce its rate of innovation below the level that would exist in a competitive market.'[66]

This definition conforms to the Court's definition of dominance, while explicitly articulating the Commission's primary focus on market power.[67] In so doing, it mirrors the definition of market power under the 1992 US Horizontal Merger

domination" and "strengthening of market domination". ... [T]he term "superior market position" is interpreted in a static and very structured manner [and] may even apply to situations in which substantial competition [is not called] into question. ... [Moreover,] strengthening [of a dominant position] ... [need] not necessarily [be] "appreciable", ... an interpretation ... related to the Resource Theory, which provides that every infusion of financial or technical resources is made to establish a reinforcement of the dominant market position regardless of whether the reinforcement actually occurs. ... [U]nder Community law, [such strengthening] is assumed only if the lessening of competition is concretely demonstrated.'

64 See, eg the Commission's commentary on *Aérospatiale-Alenia/De Havilland* ('the test of dominance is to be understood as an appreciable freedom of action uncontrolled by actual or potential competition'). XXth Report on Competition Policy (1990), p 362.

65 See, eg *Carnival/P&O Princess*, Case COMP/M.2706, Commission decision of 24 July 2002 (not yet reported) and *Volvo/Renault V.I.*, Case COMP/1980, Commission decision of 1 September 2000, which do not use the term 'market power'.

66 Glossary of Terms Used in EU Competition Policy – Antitrust and Control of Concentrations (2002), p 14 (http://europa.eu.int/comm/competition/publications/glossary_en.pdf).

67 See too the UK Office of Fair Trading's Guidelines to the Competition Act. Paragraph 2.10 concerning the 'Assessment of Market Power' states that 'an undertaking is unlikely to be dominant if it does not have substantial market power', while para 1.2 states that 'Market power describes a situation where the constraints which would usually ensure that an undertaking behaves in a competitive manner are not working effectively. As a matter of convenience, however, this guideline usually refers to market power as the ability to raise prices consistently and profitably above competitive levels'.

Guidelines, thereby bringing the dominance test closely into line with the SLC test employed in the United States.[68]

The 2002 Glossary formulation does not represent a new position, but is rather a reflection of how the Commission has interpreted dominance in closely contested merger decisions over recent years. This has manifested itself in two ways. First, the Commission has moved away from the pre-existing conventional wisdom that combined shares below 40 per cent would generally not support a finding of single-firm dominance, and has subjected to careful scrutiny a number of transactions involving post-transaction shares below 40 per cent.[69] Secondly, the Commission has increasingly focused on the direct substitutability of the merging parties' products,[70] and has cast its assessment in terms of assessing the 'unilateral effects' of a merger.[71]

Two decisions involving Volvo's trucks business illustrate how unilateral effects considerations can 'tip the scale' towards or away from a finding of dominance

68 US Horizontal Merger Guidelines, § 0.1 (1992 and revised 1997) state that 'the Guidelines focus on the one potential source of gain that is of concern under the antitrust laws: market power. The unifying theme of the Guidelines is that mergers should not be permitted to create or enhance market power or to facilitate its exercise. Market power to a seller is the ability profitably to maintain prices above competitive levels for a significant period of time'.

69 See, eg *Carrefour/Promodes*, Case COMP/M.1684, Commission decision of 25 January 2000 (Commission concerned that two supermarket chains with 28 per cent of the French market for procuring consumer goods sold through retail outlets would have substantial bargaining power over suppliers). See too *Nestlé/Ralston Purina*, Case COMP/M.2337, Commission decision of 27 July 2001 (Commission regarded 35 per cent as a level above which dominance concerns might arise); *Unilever/Bestfoods*, Case COMP/M.1990, Commission decision of 28 September 2000 (Commission required divestitures to remedy horizontal overlaps leading to combined shares of 35-45 per cent); and *Bayer/Aventis Crop Science*, Case COMP/M.2547, Commission decision of 17 April 2002 (not yet reported) (Commission concerns arose in several markets where the parties' combined shares would have been below 40 per cent, including certain markets in which the increment in share was small (as low as two per cent)). *Bayer/Aventis Crop Science* considered directly whether the merged firm would have the 'power to raise prices', and casts it conclusions in the language of 'market power'. See, eg para 165 and the analysis at paras 175 et seq.

70 The Commission's preparedness to focus on projecting a merger's likely effect on prices through unilateral effects has precedent in some of the early decisions rendered under the ECMR. Perhaps the earliest prominent example is *DuPont/ICI*, Case IV/M.214, Commission decision of 30 September 1992 (OJ 1993 L 7/13) (Commission required remedies on the basis of a 43 per cent combined share and the distinctive features of the parties' products as compared to their competitors). Another early example is *Kimberly-Clark/Scott Paper*, Case IV/M.623, Commission decision of 16 January 1996 (OJ 1996 L 183/01) (Commission concerned about the nature of head-to-head competition between the merging parties, based on the competitive strengths of their respective brands).

71 The assumption here is that if the firms' products are particularly close substitutes, then the merged entity could more likely profitably raise the price of Product 1, because it would recoup lost sales of Product 1 as a large proportion of purchasers switch to Product 2. The converse is also true: even if the parties' combined market share is high, the merged entity may lack the power to raise price unilaterally if the parties' products are not close substitutes. Under this line of reasoning, the dominance analysis focuses on the transaction's effects on the merging parties' pricing incentives.

when moderately high market shares are involved.[72] In both *Volvo/Scania*,[73] where the notified transaction was prohibited, and *Volvo/Renault*,[74] where the transaction was approved, the Commission focused on the degree of substitutability between the parties' heavy trucks and considered direct evidence of substitutability (by surveying customers' perceptions of the trucks' characteristics), as well as economic evidence (including studies of market share fluctuations and econometric pricing models). In *Volvo/Scania*, evidence showed that the parties' trucks were each other's closest substitute, which became a significant factor in the Commission's prohibition decision. On the other hand, in *Volvo/Renault* the Commission concluded that the transaction raised no concern on the French heavy truck market despite a combined share of 49 per cent – a share that would have been sufficient to trigger opposition in *Volvo/Scania* – primarily on the basis of evidence showing that the parties' trucks were *not* particularly close substitutes.

In sum, recent developments show how, notwithstanding language in its decisions that suggest continued adherence to the concept of 'independence', the Commission's application of the dominance test has in practice evolved towards a 'market power' standard that focuses less on structure and more on the transaction's predicted effect on price, output, and innovation. In addition to bringing the Commission more closely into line with the methodological framework applied in the United States, this analytical approach has expanded the range of situations that may be caught by the dominance test.[75]

72 See too *Carnival/P&O Princess*, Case COMP/M.2706, Commission decision of 24 July 2002 (not yet reported). During the investigation, there was considerable debate as to whether the relevant market for UK oceanic cruises should include both 'premium' and 'economy' offerings or whether the different classes should comprise separate markets. The Commission ultimately adopted the broader definition (on which the parties' combined share was 35-45 per cent), but examined in detail the nature of head-to-head competition between the merging parties within that market in order to assess the merged entity's ability to raise prices. The Commission found evidence showing that customers did not regard the parties' offerings as being uniquely close substitutes for each other, with many customers citing other cruise operators as the closest substitute for the parties.

73 Case COMP/M.1672, Commission decision of 15 March 2000 (OJ 2001 L 143/74), para 82: '[W]hen examining the situation in Nordic countries, it is clear that over a long period of time (1989-1998) ... most variations in the market share of one of the two companies correspond to a variation (in the opposite direction) of the other one. These graphs ... are indicative of the fact that they are each other's closest substitutes.' Volvo and Scania products are characterised as close substitutes in several product and geographical markets; see paras 282, 297, 315, and 323.

74 Case COMP/M.1980, Commission decision of 1 September 2000, paras 33-34.

75 See, eg William J Kolasky, Former Deputy Assistant Attorney-General US Department of Justice, 'Conglomerate Mergers and Range Effects: It's a Long Way from Chicago to Brussels', speech before the George Mason University Symposium, Washington DC, 11 September 2001, p 5 ('We understand the EU's concept of dominance to be more or less synonymous with our concept of market power. Dominance is defined in EU case law as "a position of economic strength enjoyed by an undertaking which enables it to prevent effective competition being maintained on the relevant market by affording it the power to behave independently of its competitors, its customers and ultimately of the consumers". Similarly, U.S. law defines market power law as the ability to raise price and exclude competitors. Both definitions are somewhat inexact from the perspective of a professional economist – not even a monopolist can behave wholly independently of its rival and customers – but both seem designed to describe verbally the same basic economic position – ie monopoly').

3. AN ASSESSMENT OF THE ISSUES RAISED BY THE SLC TEST

This section considers five questions raised by the Green Paper's initiation of a debate on the merits of replacing the dominance test with an SLC test:

1. Does the SLC test better articulate the proper focus of merger control?
2. Is there an enforcement 'gap' between the concepts of dominance and SLC?
3. Would an SLC test more readily permit the Commission to take positive account of efficiencies under the ECMR?
4. Would an SLC test avoid the possible prejudice of a dominance finding under the ECMR for purposes of Article 82?
5. Would adoption of an SLC test affect international convergence in merger control?

3.1 Does the SLC test better articulate the proper focus of merger control?

The concept of dominance as defined by the Community courts is not grounded in economics. As a result, application of a dominance test must confront the economist's objection that 'independence' lacks utility for the task required of it, namely a means to distinguish a dominant firm from a non-dominant one.[76] All firms face constraints on their freedom of action – even a monopolist confronts the fact that as it raises price, customers will buy less (how much less depends, of course, on demand elasticity). Thus, while the extent of constraints and thus the level of a firm's profit-maximising price will vary, the 'dominance as independence' concept provides no clear guidance for determining where dependence (and thus non-dominance) becomes independence (and thus dominance). The UK Director-General of Fair Trading has commented as follows:

> 'Dominance is not an ideal test for considering the impact of a merger on competition. Narrowly interpreted it would be far too permissive. The Commission has therefore been creative in applying the dominance test, particularly when looking at oligopolistic markets. But the concept of joint or collective dominance is not without difficulties.'[77]

In contrast, the SLC test focuses more directly on the principal economic question raised by a merger, namely whether competition is likely to be reduced to a point where prices may be expected to rise or output to fall.[78] Put another way, the SLC test directly measures the 'delta', ie the degree of change in the dynamics

76 See, eg João Pearce Azevedo and Mike Walker, 'Dominance: Meaning and Measurement' [2002] ECLR 363, pp 364-65. See too *The Review of the EC Merger Regulation*, n 5 above, paras 130-135, which reports proponents of SLC having contended that it is an 'economic concept', which is 'rooted in economic theory' and has the 'attraction' of 'directness'. By contrast, dominance is said to be an 'artificial' and 'indirect' test.

77 Dr John Vickers, Director-General of Fair Trading, *International Mergers: The View From A National Authority*, [2001] Fordham Corp L Inst (Barry E Hawk, ed, 2002, forthcoming).

78 Economics suggests that mergers between competitors may be expected to lessen competition not only as between the merging parties (where such competition as existed previously will inevitably be lost), but also as between the merged entity and its competitors in concentrated markets. See, eg letter from various economists on the Green Paper (J Crémer, D Encaoua, M Ivaldi, M Motta, D Neven, P Rey, L-H Röller, P Seabright, E Van Damme, F Verboven and X Vives): 'A merger between

of competition posed by a merger, while the dominance test in essence measures how much competition is left over, as opposed to how much has been lost.[79] As a practical matter, however, there is no reason to suppose that the European Union's adoption of an SLC test would facilitate the Commission's placing any greater emphasis than it does today on inter-firm competitive dynamics, empirical evidence, or economic analysis. What it would do, though, would be to avoid the Commission's having to 'go through the mental contortions'[80] of fitting its assessment into the dominance prism.

3.2 Is there an enforcement 'gap' between the dominance and SLC tests?

Experience under the ECMR has shown that the dominance test is a flexible tool capable of capturing a wide range of potentially anti-competitive concentrations. In *Kali und Salz*[81] and *Gencor*,[82] the Community courts endorsed an extensive interpretation of the concept of dominance. Under the courts' interpretation, the intention of the ECMR's drafters may be overridden to ensure the full 'effectiveness' of the ECMR and thereby fill potential 'gaps'. [83]

> 'A concentration which creates or strengthens a dominant position on the part of the parties to the concentration with an entity not involved in the concentration is liable to prove incompatible with the system of undistorted competition laid down by the Treaty. Consequently, if it were accepted that only concentrations creating or strengthening a dominant position on the part of the parties to the concentration were covered by the Regulation, its purpose ... would be partially frustrated. The Regulation would thus be deprived of a not insignificant aspect of its effectiveness, without that being necessary from the perspective of the general structure of the Community system of control of concentrations.'[84]

rivals lowers the competitive constraint any firm faces. When the management of a company resulting from the merger of two firms considers a price increase, it will know that its current customers face less alternative choice than before (the number of competitors is reduced). Hence, fewer current customers will now turn to competitors after a price increase, making it more profitable, and hence likely to take place.'

79 See too Dr John Temple Lang, *Oligopolies And Joint Dominance in Community Antitrust Law*, [2001] Fordham Corp L Inst, 310 (Barry E Hawk, ed, 2002, forthcoming): 'The Regulation as it is now written would not easily apply to a merger merely by reference to the fact that it made the market substantially less competitive than it had previously been. The Regulation is based on the result (dominance or increased dominance) rather than the significance of the change resulting from the merger. Substantially reduced competition is not necessarily dominance: dominance is a result of how much competition is left, not how big the change has been.'

80 Dr William Bishop in *The Review of the EC Merger Regulation, Minutes of Evidence*, n 5 above, p 26.

81 *France and Others v Commission*, ('*Kali und Salz*'), Joined Cases C-68/94 and C-30/95, [1998] ECR I-1395.

82 *Gencor v Commission*, Case T-102/96, [1999] ECR II-753.

83 As the Chairman of the UK Competition Commission has said: 'if there is a substantial lessening of competition, that is something that should be investigated', Dr Derek Morris, Chairman of the UK Competition Commission, cited in The Review of the EC Merger Regulation, n 5 above, para 109.

84 *Gencor v Commission, supra*, para 151. See too *France and Others v Commission* ('*Kali und Salz*'), *supra*, para 167 ('[T]he travaux préparatoires ... cannot be regarded as expressing clearly the intention of the authors of the Regulation as to the scope of the term "dominant position"').

There may, however, be a small category of transactions that substantially lessen competition but which do not fit neatly into either single-firm or collective dominance. As explained more fully below, to the extent there is an enforcement 'gap' between the SLC and dominance tests, it arises in those rare cases where:

1. characteristics of joint dominance do not exist;
2. the merging firms would not be the leading supplier post-transaction;
3. the merging firms are close substitutes and would be able to impose a price increase post-transaction; and
4. other aspects of the market (entry, shifting preferences, repositioning by other competitors, etc) would not defeat this price increase.

The clarity given by the Court of First Instance in *Airtours* to the circumstances in which collective dominance may arise has limited the Commission's scope for challenging transactions in concentrated markets where there is no risk of tacit collusion.[85] Any enforcement 'gap' between the dominance and SLC tests may therefore arise in markets that are not readily conducive to tacit collusion (as defined in *Airtours*). In such cases, the focus will necessarily be on the 'unilateral effects' of the merger, ie the possibility that the merged entity will alone be able to raise or reduce prices. Although the dominance test is well suited to addressing situations where the merged entity will be the leading supplier post-transaction, it is less effective in cases where the merged entity will not be the leading supplier, but the elimination of rivalry between the merging parties could lead to higher prices, reduced output, or less innovation. Such transactions may substantially lessen competition, even if they do not involve single-firm dominance.

This fact pattern arose in the recent *Heinz/Beech-Nut* baby food transaction that the US Federal Trade Commission (FTC) challenged successfully.[86] In that case, there was a clear market leader (with 65 per cent of sales) and vigorous competition between merging #2 and #3 parties to be the second baby food producer on supermarket shelves. (For various reasons, there are seldom more than two baby food brands on supermarket shelves.) In this situation, the merger of the #2 and #3 suppliers (which had shares of 17 per cent and 15 per cent, respectively) was expected to lessen competition and was, accordingly, challenged by the FTC. This fact pattern would not neatly be caught by the dominance test. The Commission has questioned the likelihood of such a situation arising in

85 The judgment did not call into question the theoretical idea of collective dominance, but did expound strict criteria that the Commission will have to satisfy in order to defend a finding of collective dominance. The Court stated that three conditions must be met if there is to be a finding of collective dominance: (1) each member of the alleged dominant oligopoly must have the ability to know how the other members are behaving in order to monitor whether or not they are adopting a common policy. According to the Court, this required 'sufficient market transparency for all members of the dominant oligopoly to be aware, sufficiently precisely and quickly, of the ways in which the other members' market conduct is evolving'; (2) the situation of tacit collusion must be 'sustainable over time, that is to say there must be an incentive not to depart from the common policy on the market'; and (3) the 'Commission must also establish that the foreseeable reaction of current and future competitors, as well as of consumers, would not jeopardize the results expected from the common policy'. In short, tacit collusion must be feasible and it must be sustainable, both internally (within the dominant oligopoly) and externally (the competitive pressures from fringe firms and customers must be sufficiently weak). Airtours, supra, para 62.

86 *FTC v H J Heinz & Co*, DC Circuit Docket No 00-5362 (decided 27 April 2001).

practice,[87] and has stated that 'experience in applying the dominance test has not revealed major loopholes in the scope of the test'.[88] If confronted with such a situation, the Commission would presumably seek to employ the dominance test to challenge the transaction on the basis of one of the following three analytical frameworks.

First, it might endeavour to challenge the transaction on the basis of collective dominance. Indeed, in *Heinz/Beech-Nut*, the FTC endeavoured to do exactly that and the first limb of its complaint challenged the transaction on the ground that '[t]he effect of the proposed acquisition, if consummated, may be to substantially lessen competition in markets for the manufacture and sale of prepared baby food and segments thereof, specifically jarred baby food, in the United States and smaller geographic markets therein by, among other things ... substantially increasing concentration, and further heightening barriers to entry, thereby increasing the likelihood of successful anticompetitive coordinated interaction, and actual or tacit collusion among the two remaining firms'.[89] Market dynamics might, however, exclude a finding of collective dominance as defined in *Airtours*.

Secondly, the Commission might define a narrow market (eg a 'market' for secondary baby food brands in the *Heinz/Beech-Nut* case). Since the 'core purpose of market definition is to help assess questions about market power, or in the case of mergers, changes in market power',[90] the Commission could plausibly contend that if the merging parties could raise prices post-transaction by five to ten per cent, then the relevant market should be defined in such a way as to reflect that market power. The following line of reasoning might be advanced: (1) in *Kali und Salz* and *Gencor*, the Community courts endorsed an extensive interpretation of dominance intended to avoid anti-competitive mergers escaping challenge[91]; (2) the notion of dominance may be equated with market power (ie the power to raise price, reduce output, or chill innovation); and (3) if a merger confers power to raise prices, the merging companies can effectively act independently of competitive

87 Green Paper, para 166 ('while interesting as a hypothetical discussion, the Commission has so far not encountered a situation of this kind'). This confidence may be somewhat misplaced given the fact patterns in *Airtours/First Choice* (Case IV/M.1524, Commission decision of 22 September 1999 (OJ 2001 L 093/1), para 72 (three firms would together have accounted for around 80 per cent of UK sales of short-haul package holidays (Airtours/First Choice (34 per cent), Thomson (30 per cent), and Thomas Cook (20 per cent)) and Abbey National/Lloyds (UK Competition Commission Report, Cm 5208, 10 July 2001), where the merger would have increased the market share of Lloyds TSB from 22 per cent to 27 per cent and the share of the four largest banks from 72 per cent to 77 per cent. The UK Competition Commission prohibited the merger, but Dr Derek Morris, Chairman of the UK Competition Commission, told the House of Lords Select Committee on the European Union that it would have been 'extremely difficult' for it to have done so under the dominance test, even though there was clearly a substantial lessening of competition: The Review of the EC Merger Regulation, n 5 above, para 150.

88 Green Paper, para 167.

89 See *FTC v H J Heinz & Co and Milnot Holding Corp*, DC Circuit Civil Action No 00-1688 (JR) (complaint dated 14 July 2000) (http://www.ftc.gov/os/2000/07/heinz.htm), para 12(e).

90 Dr John Vickers, Director-General of Fair Trading, Competition Economics and Policy, speech at Oxford University, 3 October 2002.

91 See too Explanatory Memorandum to Draft ECMR, para 54 and fn 17 ('It should also be noted that the Court of Justice has not explicitly ruled on, and therefore not explicitly excluded, the possibility of addressing the effect of mergers in (non-collusive) oligopolies with no single firm being significantly larger than the others under the current dominance test. In the past, the Court has

constraint and should therefore be considered 'dominant' on a market defined in such a way as to reflect that market power. Such an analytical framework has not to date been tested before the Community courts.[92]

Thirdly, the Commission might contend that the merger increases the dominant position of the #1 player by reducing the competition it faces. Such a concept of third-party dominance was used by the Commission in *Exxon/Mobil*[93] and considered elsewhere.[94] Citing *Kali und Salz* and *Gencor* as authority for the proposition that the ECMR applies to the strengthening of the dominant position of a third party, the Commission acknowledged in *Exxon/Mobil* that these two judgments lend only indirect support as both cases dealt with oligopolistic dominant positions.[95] The Community courts have not to date confirmed the validity of the 'third party dominance' theory.

In conclusion, as explained above, to the extent there is an enforcement 'gap' between the SLC and dominance tests, it may arise only with respect to

shown a willingness to adopt a teleological interpretation of the notion of dominance in order not to deprive it of its effet utile. Such a teleological interpretation has been particularly applied in the context of the Merger Control Regulation where the Court has held that it applies "to all concentrations with a Community dimension insofar as they are likely, because of their effect on the structure of competition within the Community, to prove incompatible with the system of undistorted competition envisaged by the Treaty". *France v Commission* ('*Kali und Salz*'), Case C-68/94, [1998] ECR I-1375, para 170)').

92 A similar line of reasoning was raised on appeal in *Airtours, supra*. One of Airtours' grounds of appeal was that the Commission had attempted to apply a new legal theory in prohibiting the Airtours/First Choice merger because the decision was not based on collective dominance concerns but on a more general objection that there would be less competition between the leading market players post-merger, ie akin to unilateral effects within an oligopoly. There is some evidence for this in the Commission's decision. (See, eg para 138: 'Absent the merger, First Choice would very probably develop quickly into a more powerful, fully integrated competitor in addition to the existing three, who have already ... more or less completed their vertical integration strategies' and 'the proposed merger would eliminate First Choice as an independent competitor at this critical juncture, leaving only three vertically integrated players.') The Court did not deal with the point expressly as it conflated this ground of appeal with the ground concerning the Commission's application of collective dominance.

93 Case IV/M.1383, Commission decision of 29 September 1999 (not yet reported), paras 225-229. Exxon held a non-controlling 25 per cent equity interest in Gasunie, the dominant player in the Dutch natural gas business. As a result of the transaction, Exxon would obtain control over Mobil's Dutch gas marketing subsidiary, which had a three per cent share of natural gas sales in the Netherlands. The Commission considered that the merged entity would no longer compete with Gasunie and that the elimination of the competition from Mobil would strengthen Gasunie's dominant position.

94 See, eg *RWE/Hidroelectrica Del Cantàbrico*, Case COMP/M.2353, Commission decision of 19 March 2002, para 10.

95 The Commission's reasoning in *Exxon/Mobil, supra*, paras 225-227, is worth setting out in full: 'It can be noted that Article 2(3) of the Merger Regulation states that a concentration which creates or strengthens a dominant position is to be declared incompatible with the Common Market. Article 2(3) is thus, in terms, not limited to the prohibition of an operation which will give rise to the creation or reinforcement of a dominant position on the part of one or more of the parties to the concentration – see also Recitals 1, 5 and 7 in the Preamble to the Regulation. The reasoning by the Court of Justice in the *Kali und Salz* judgment and of the Court of First Instance in Gencor does lend indirect confirmation to the above conclusion. The Commission acknowledges that the support is indirect as both cases deal with oligopolistic dominant positions. However, the Court, in point 171 of the Kali und Salz judgment, confirms in general terms that the dominant position that is created or strengthened does not need to be one of the parties to the concentration.'

transactions that have 'unilateral effects', but which would not confer single-firm dominance and affect markets where tacit collusion may be excluded. Because such transactions can reasonably be expected to arise only rarely, this 'gap' is not likely to be very large on any basis. In any event, there may be scope for dealing with such transactions under the dominance test, although the Commission's ability to do so is not entirely free from doubt. Adopting an SLC test would resolve any uncertainty and give the Commission explicit power to challenge transactions of this kind. As described in greater detail in 'The Commission's December 2002 proposals' below, in December 2002 the Commission announced its intention to amend the ECMR by 'clarifying' the dominance standard so as to make clear that it expressly captures transactions that have unilateral effects falling short of single-firm dominance in markets where joint dominance may be excluded.

3.3 Would an SLC test more readily permit the Commission to take positive account of efficiencies under the ECMR?

There is widespread agreement that the promotion of efficiency is a central aim of competition law.[96] The importance of efficiencies as part of sound economics-based merger analysis has been recognised for over a quarter of a century,[97] and efficiencies have, at least implicitly, been taken into account under the US Guidelines for many years.[98] The US agencies seek to integrate efficiencies fully into their competitive effects analysis to determine the likely effect on competition given both the increased market power and the efficiency effects, and the US Horizontal Merger Guidelines recognise an 'efficiency defence' in certain circumstances:

> 'The [reviewing] Agency will not challenge a merger if cognizable efficiencies are of a character and magnitude such that the merger is not likely to be anti-competitive in any relevant market. To make the requisite determination, the Agency considers whether cognizable efficiencies likely would be sufficient to reverse the merger's potential to harm consumers in the relevant market, eg by preventing price increases in that market.'[99]

96 See, eg Richard A Posner, *Antitrust Law* 2 (2nd edn, 2001), p 2 ('Efficiency is an important social value ... the only goal of antitrust should be to promote efficiency in the economic sense'). See also Competition Policy and Efficiency Claims in Horizontal Agreements, European Commission Delegation to the OECD, November 1995 (http://www.oecd.org/pdf/M00007000/M00007744.pdf), p 1: 'The basic objective of competition policy is to protect competition as the most appropriate means of ensuring the efficient allocation of resources – and thus efficient market outcomes – in free market economies.'

97 See, eg Robert H Bork, *The Antitrust Paradox* 91 (1978) ('The whole task of antitrust can be summed up as the effort to improve allocative efficiency without impairing productive efficiency so greatly as to produce either no gain or a net loss in consumer welfare'). See too Phillip E Areeda, Herbert Hovenkamp and John L Solow, *Antitrust Law* (1998), pp 22-25.

98 See Joseph Farrell and Carl Shapiro, 'Scale Economies and Synergies in Horizontal Merger Analysis' (2001) 68 Antitrust LJ 659. The US Horizontal Merger Guidelines state at § 4 that '[t]he primary benefit of mergers to the economy is their potential to generate efficiencies ... [that can] enhance the merged firm's ability and incentive to compete, which may result in lower prices, improved quality, enhanced service, or new products'.

99 US Horizontal Merger Guidelines, § 4 (1992 and revised 1997). In determining whether efficiencies claimed by merging parties are 'cognizable' for the purpose of balancing their effects against the risk of anti-competitive harm, the agencies consider only those efficiencies that are likely to be

Efficiency gains may be taken into account at two separate points in the analytical framework: (1) where they increase rivalry in the market so that no dominant position would result from a merger;[100] or (2) where they do not avert the creation of a dominant position but, because they are expected to be passed on to consumers, are deemed to outweigh the adverse effects of the transaction.[101] As to (1), it is clear that the Commission is free to take account of efficiencies in assessing whether a dominant position would be created or strengthened.[102] The debate surrounds the possibility under the ECMR for applying an 'efficiencies defence' following a finding of dominance (ie situation (2) above).

In contrast to the view taken by the US agencies, the Commission has been ambivalent at best as to the scope for an 'efficiencies defence' under the ECMR. Although the Commission has in a number of cases considered the ECMR's Article 2(1)(b) 'development of technical and economic progress' provision, in no case has it found that such developments would counteract the creation or strengthening of a dominant position. On the contrary, the Commission has consistently rejected notifying parties' attempts to rely on efficiencies arguments to counterbalance anti-competitive effects of proposed mergers.[103] In some cases, the Commission has

accomplished with the proposed merger and unlikely to be accomplished in the absence of either the proposed merger or another means having comparable anti-competitive effects. These are termed 'merger-specific efficiencies'. The US Horizontal Merger Guidelines instruct the agencies not to recognize efficiencies that flow from an anti-competitive reduction in output. In other words, saving costs by closing plants may not be recognised as an efficiency. The Guidelines go on to say that, under the balancing test, efficiencies are most likely to make a difference in cases where adverse effects in the absence of the efficiencies are not great. Accordingly, as a practical matter, the 'efficiencies defence' rarely works in merger-to-monopoly or near-monopoly situations.

100 See, eg US Horizontal Merger Guidelines, § 4 (1992 and revised 1997) ('[t]he Agency will not challenge a merger if "cognizable efficiencies" are of a character and magnitude such that the merger is not likely to be anti-competitive in any relevant market').

101 See, eg UK Office of Fair Trading's Mergers: Substantive Assessment – A Consultation Paper, OFT Paper 506, October 2002, para 4.35. The US Horizontal Merger Guidelines, § 4 (1992 and revised 1997) refer to 'efficiencies likely would be sufficient to reverse the merger's potential to harm consumers in the relevant market, eg by preventing price increases in that market'.

102 Competition Policy and Efficiency Claims in Horizontal Agreements, European Commission Delegation to the OECD, November 1995 (http://www.oecd.org/pdf/M00007000/M00007744.pdf), p 53 ('Any efficiency issues are considered in the overall assessment to determine whether dominance has been created or strengthened and not to justify or mitigate that dominance in order to clear a concentration that would otherwise be prohibited').

103 See, eg *Aérospatiale-Alenia/de Havilland*, Case IV/M.053, Commission decision of 2 October 1991 (OJ 1991 L 334/42), paras 65-69, where the Commission addressed in the following terms the parties' submissions that the transaction would reduce procurement and other costs: '[T]he Commission does not consider that the proposed concentration would contribute to the development of technical and economic progress within the meaning of Article 2(1)(b) of the Merger Regulation. Even if there was such progress, this would not be to the consumers' advantage. The consumers will be faced with a dominant position, which combines the most popular aircraft families on the market. Choice will be significantly reduced.' See too Frédéric Jenny, *EEC Merger Control: Economies As An Antitrust Defense Or An Antitrust Attack?*, [1992] Fordham Corp L Inst 591 (Barry E Hawk, ed, 1993): '[The Commission's] reasoning [in the 1991 merger cases] supposes that if a merger is likely to allow the merging firms to offer a new product or service with a better price/quality ratio than the products or services that their competitors can offer (either because the new product has superior performance or because the new service is less costly to consumers), then the merger is incompatible with the common market.'

determined that efficiencies would be more likely to strengthen the merging parties' post-transaction position.[104]

More recently, the Commission has indicated that appropriately substantiated efficiency claims should be regarded as positive factors that support mergers.[105] In September 2001, the Director of the Merger Task Force 'categorically reject[ed] the criticism that the European Commission does not recognize an efficiency defence',[106] and Commissioner Monti has hinted that the Commission endorses and applies the notion of an 'efficiency defence':

> 'We distinguish clearly between – on the one hand – mergers leading to price reductions that are the result of strategic behavior on the part of a dominant firm, the purpose of which is to eliminate or marginalize competitors with a view to exploiting consumers in the medium term, and – on the other – mergers which will objectively lead to significant and durable efficiency gains that are likely to be passed on to the consumer.'[107]

These statements appear to endorse some form of US-style merger efficiencies analysis. Indeed, the Green Paper invites comment not on whether efficiencies should form part of the Commission's merger analysis, but on 'how, and the extent to which' they should be taken into account. From the Commission's perspective, the broad issue would appear to have been resolved. The question nevertheless remains whether the ECMR can be read in such a way as to provide for an 'efficiencies defence'. As recently as 1999, the Commission stated in *Danish Crown/ Vestjyske Slagterier* that '[t]he creation of a dominant position in the relevant markets ... means that the efficiencies argument put forward by the parties cannot be taken into account in the assessment of the present merger'.[108] This view echoed the categoric position taken by the Commission in 1995:

104 See, eg *British Telecom/MCI (II)*, Case IV/M.856, Commission decision of 14 May 1997 (OJ 1997 L 336/1), paras 58-59 (operational synergies and the ability to 'benefit from the more efficient use of transmission capacity' cited as factors contributing to merged entity's dominant position); and *AT&T/NCR*, Case IV/M.050, Commission decision of 18 January 1991, para 30 ('it is not excluded that potential advantages flowing from synergies may create or strengthen a dominant position').

105 Professor Mario Monti, Member of the Commission responsible for competition policy, Merger Control: Issues Highlighted in the Context of the GE/Honeywell Merger, speech at 'The Future for Competition Policy in the European Union', 9 July 2001 (Commission Press Release SPEECH/01/ 340): '[The Commission is] not against mergers that create more efficient firms. Such mergers tend to benefit consumers, even if competitors might suffer from increased competition.'

106 Götz Drauz, Director of the Merger Task Force, *Unbundling GE/Honeywell: The Assessment of Conglomerate Mergers under EC Competition Law*, [2001] Fordham Corp L Inst (Barry E Hawk, ed, 2002, forthcoming). Mr Drauz rejected the contention that General Electric/Honeywell had been prohibited because of the Commission's expectation that the transaction would create efficiencies. According to Mr Drauz, the parties had consistently argued that the transaction would not create efficiencies of the kind normally relied on by competition law authorities, ie long-run structural reductions in the marginal cost of production that would be passed on to consumers in the form of lower prices, but had instead identified only cost savings that could be anticipated to flow from any merger.

107 Professor Mario Monti, Member of the Commission responsible for Competition Policy, *Antitrust in the US and Europe: A History of Convergence*, American Bar Association, 14 November 2001 (Commission Press Release SPEECH/01/540).

108 Case IV/M.1313, Commission decision of 9 March 1999 (OJ 2000 L 20/1), para 198.

'There is no real legal possibility of justifying an efficiency defence under the Merger Regulation. Efficiencies are assumed for all mergers up to the limit of dominance – the "concentration privilege". Any efficiency issues are considered in the overall assessment to determine whether dominance has been created or strengthened and not to justify or mitigate that dominance in order to clear a concentration which would otherwise be prohibited.'[109]

It is common ground that the ECMR does not explicitly provide for an 'efficiencies defence'.[110] Various ways have, however, been envisaged to construe the current language of the ECMR to provide for such a defence, of which the most commonly proposed would involve the Commission's relying on Articles 2(1)(b) and 2(3) of the ECMR.[111] It has been suggested that, once it had made a finding of dominance, the Commission could apply Article 2(1)(b) and the second limb of Article 2(3) to examine whether the transaction would also significantly impede competition.[112] At this stage of the analysis, the transaction's anti-competitive effects could be balanced against the anticipated efficiencies. As with an SLC test, the Commission would have to determine that a dominant firm would

109 Competition Policy and Efficiency Claims in Horizontal Agreements, European Commission Delegation to the OECD, November 1995 (http://www.oecd.org/pdf/M00007000/M00007744.pdf), p 53. See too Dr Derek Morris, Chairman of the UK Competition Commission, cited in The Review of the EC Merger Regulation, n 5 above, para 176 ('A merger that clearly has substantial synergistic gains but creates a very substantial degree of market power such that there really would be no particular incentive or pressure to pass those benefits on, would have benefits that would be unlikely to count'); and Alex Jacquemin, 'Horizontal Concentration and European Merger Policy' (1990) 34 Eur Econ Rev 539 ('Given that the criterion of technical and economic progress can be used only if it is perfectly compatible with competition and consumers' interests, it is difficult to see how an operation which creates or reinforces a dominant position could be accepted because the negative anticompetitive effects outweigh the positive effects of such a progress').

110 In contrast, section 36(1) of the German Act against Restraints of Competition reads: 'A concentration which is expected to create or strengthen a dominant position shall be prohibited by the Federal Cartel Office unless the participating undertakings prove that the concentration will also lead to improvements of the conditions of competition, and that these improvements will outweigh the disadvantages of dominance.'

111 See Green Paper: Summary of the Replies Received, para 117: 'There is widespread support for the view that the ECMR provides a legal basis for taking into account efficiency benefits likely to result form a proposed merger, and that no amendment of the Regulation would be required in order to allow for such assessment. In this regard, reliance is normally placed on the 2nd limb of the dominance test in Articles 2(2) and 2(3) (significant impediment to competition) and/or on the wording of Article 2(1)(b)' (http://europa.eu.int/comm/competition/mergers/review/comments/summary_publication.pdf.). Article 2(1) states that, in assessing whether a concentration is compatible with the Common Market, the Commission shall take into account the development of technical and economic progress, while Article 2(3) provides that in order to be declared incompatible with the Common Market, a concentration must satisfy two cumulative conditions: (1) it must create or strengthen a dominant position; and (2) the creation or strengthening of that dominant position must significantly impede competition in the common market or in a substantial part of it.

112 The Community courts have made clear that Articles 2(2) and 2(3) require the Commission to undertake a two-stage analysis of a notified concentration. See *Air France v Commission ('TAT')*, Case T-2/93, [1994] ECR II-323, para 79, confirmed in *Kaysersberg v Commission*, Case T-290/94, [1997] ECR II-2137, para 158: 'It follows from [Articles 2(2) and 2(3) of the ECMR] that the Commission is required to declare a concentration compatible with the Common Market where ... the transaction in question does not create or strengthen a dominant position and ... competition will not be significantly impeded by the creation or strengthening of such a position.'

have an incentive to pass on to customers the efficiencies achieved by the transaction (eg because merger-specific efficiencies would lower a merged company's marginal costs in circumstances where that company would have the ability and incentive to increase output and lower prices).[113]

In conclusion, the dominance test does not prevent the Commission from taking positive account of efficiencies in assessing a transaction's compatibility with the Common Market where such efficiencies avert the creation or strengthening of a dominant position. The Commission's ability to apply an 'efficiencies defence' following a finding that a dominant position would be created or strengthened is, however, less clear in light of the absence of any explicit wording in the ECMR, uncertainty as to the Community courts' view, and statements made in the past by the Commission to the effect that the ECMR does not permit an 'efficiencies defence'. Adoption of an SLC test would resolve this uncertainty and clarify the situation.

3.4 Would an SLC test avoid the possible prejudice of a dominance finding under the ECMR for purposes of Article 82?

Both Article 82 and Article 2 of the ECMR refer to a 'dominant position'. (Indeed, as described above, one of the main reasons why the dominance test was adopted in the ECMR was because of its 'familiar terminology'.[114]) Although there are certain conceptual differences between Article 82 and ECMR cases, the identical wording means that, in principle, findings made under the ECMR may be relevant for Article 82, and vice versa. (Indeed, the Court in *Tetra Laval* recognised the relationship between a finding of dominance under the ECMR and Article 82.[115]) As a result, a dominance finding under the ECMR may have implications for the legality of a company's commercial practices.[116] In the case of collective dominance, firms that were not parties to the notified concentration (and may have no standing before the Community courts) may find themselves entrusted with the 'special responsibility' assigned to dominant undertakings.[117] The UK Government has articulated the following concerns:

113 This is because the profitability of each unit sold goes up, so the incentive is to sell more units. In other words, maintaining the monopoly price is no longer as attractive due to the lost profits on the lost unit sales. Put another way, the firm's marginal cost curve shifts to the right and intersects the marginal revenue curve at a (lower price)/(higher output) point.

114 See *The Review of the EC Merger Regulation*, n 5 above, para 152: 'When the ECMR was first established, one of the reasons the Committee was in favour of the dominance test was on account of its "familiar terminology" (1989 Report, p 21)... After over a decade and some 2000 decisions made under the ECMR, it is necessary to reconsider whether or not this link between the language of Article 86 (now 82) and the substantive test in the ECMR is still beneficial.'

115 *Tetra Laval, supra,* para 157.

116 See *Michelin v Commission, supra,* para 57 (a dominant undertaking 'has a special responsibility not to allow its conduct to impair genuine undistorted competition on the common market').

117 See Dr John Temple Lang, *Oligopolies and Joint Dominance in Community Antitrust Law,* [2001] Fordham Corp L Inst (Barry E Hawk, ed, 2002, forthcoming): 'If joint dominance is proved, each company is subject to substantially the same kind of duties under Article 82 as in the case of single dominance. One jointly dominant company can commit an abuse which is contrary to Article 82 even if the others do not.'

'Under Article 82, a party that holds a dominant position is under a special obligation as to its future commercial conduct. This obligation applies to parties found to be either singly or collectively dominant. The increasingly broad interpretation of the concept of collective dominance under the existing ECMR is, therefore, placing numbers of undertakings under a special responsibility under Article 82 even if they themselves hold a relatively small market share, since they have been found to be in a position of collective dominance. A move to SLC under the ECMR would prevent this situation being aggravated any further, since the direct read-across to Article 82 would be removed.'[118]

Thus, there is a legitimate concern that a dominance finding rendered under the ECMR may be employed by the Commission (or a national authority or court) in pending or future Article 82 cases. The possible prejudice of such a finding under the ECMR is exacerbated by the limits that have been placed by the Community courts on the possibilities open to companies found dominant under the ECMR for appealing such determinations other than in cases where an adverse decision had been rendered under the ECMR.[119] The question, however, is whether that prejudice would be materially reduced by an SLC test, and the answer is probably 'no, it would not be'. This is because the risk of 'cross-contamination' between the ECMR and Article 82 is likely to be little different with an SLC test. After all, a finding that a company (or group of companies) had market power under the ECMR in circumstances where the dominance test had been replaced by an SLC test would probably have broadly similar implications under Article 82 to a dominance finding under the ECMR.

On examination, the concerns surrounding the relationship between a dominance finding under the ECMR and Article 82 relate more to the scope of application of Article 82 than to the wording of the substantive test applied in the ECMR. This reflects two principal factors, detailed consideration of which is beyond the scope of this paper: (1) the uncertainty surrounding the Commission's

118 *The Review of the EC Merger Regulation*, n 5 above, para 153.

119 See *The Coca-Cola Company and Coca-Cola Enterprise Inc*, Joined Cases T-125/97 and T-127/97, [2000] ECR II-1733; and *Dutch Banks*, Case T-138/89, [1992] ECR II-2181. The Court of First Instance rejected as inadmissible an appeal brought by The Coca-Cola Company (TCCC) and Coca-Cola Enterprises (CCE) against findings of the Commission that TCCC's UK bottler, Coca-Cola & Schweppes Beverages Ltd (CCSB), held a dominant position. The Commission had made these findings in a decision unconditionally approving CCE's acquisition of CCSB. The Court dismissed the parties' contention that the challenged findings might prejudice their position in future cases before both the Commission and national authorities or courts. The Court further held at para 81 that any such findings did not constitute a legally binding precedent for the Commission or national authorities or courts, but instead represented 'the outcome of an analysis of the structure of the market and of competition prevailing at the time the Commission adopts each decision'. The Court determined that, in any future proceeding, 'the Commission must define the relevant market again and make a fresh analysis of the conditions of competition which will not necessarily be based on the same considerations as those underlying [a] previous finding' (para 82).

application of Article 82 to certain commercial practices[120]; and (2) the application of collective dominance under Article 82. As to the first issue, to the extent there is uncertainty, the Commission should develop clear and cogent guidelines on its interpretation of Article 82. As to the second issue, the policy and legal question is whether collective dominance should be applied under Article 82. This question has for the time being been resolved by the Community courts, which have determined that joint dominance can apply independently under Article 82.[121] Thus, even if the European Union were to change the substantive test under the ECMR from dominance to SLC, the potential application of Article 82 to situations of joint dominance would remain. In this circumstance, the practical consequences of detaching the substantive test under the ECMR from the dominance standard under Article 82 would probably not be significant.

3.5 Would adopting an SLC test help or harm international convergence?

A wide array of views have been expressed as to the possible effect of switching to an SLC test for international convergence and consistency in decision-making. Proponents of an SLC test have suggested that the European Union's adoption of the US test would create a 'transatlantic harmony in terms of language'[122] that would avoid or, at a minimum, lessen the risk of divergent decisions with respect

120 See, eg Dr John Temple Lang and Robert O'Donoghue, *Defining Legitimate Competition: How to Clarify Pricing Abuses Under Article 82 EC*, [2002] Fordham Int LJ (Inna Nazarova, ed, 2003, forthcoming): 'The case-law and practice has arisen pragmatically, and largely in response to complaints to the European Commission and appeals to the Community courts against Commission decisions adopted on the basis of such complaints. With the exception of specialized Notices and guidance in the telecommunications and postal sectors, the Commission has not attempted to develop any kind of general or comprehensive statement on abusive behavior. There have been several consequences of this unplanned growth. First, the Commission and the Community courts have dealt with individual cases that were said to raise questions of abuse by reference to the facts of the individual case, seemingly without having any clear general analytical or intellectual framework for doing so. Second, a number of basic questions have not been answered or even discussed, because due to the accidents of litigation or otherwise they did not arise in any of the cases that have been decided. Finally, the influence that economic thinking has had on the Community rules on distribution, horizontal agreements, and mergers has not been felt, to the same extent or at all, in the interpretation and application of Article 82.'

121 *Società Italiano Vetro and Others v Commission, ('Italian Flat Glass')*, Joined Cases T-68/89, T-77/89 and T-78/89, [1992] ECR II-1403. By contrast, in the United States, the lower courts have rejected a theory under which a group of firms that collectively possess monopoly power could be found liable for 'joint monopolization' under section 2 of the Sherman Act. See American Bar Association, *Antitrust Law Developments* (5th edn, Vol I, 2002), p 312; and Phillip E Areeda and Herbert Hovenkamp, *Antitrust Law, An Analysis Of Antitrust Principles And Their Application*, Vol IIIa (1997).

122 See submission of UK Office of Fair Trading cited in The Review of the EC Merger Regulation, n 5 above, para 127.

to the same transaction,[123] of which *General Electric/Honeywell* is the most prominent example. Conversely, proponents of the status quo have contended that the European Union's adoption of an SLC test would create a risk of inconsistent decision-making across the European Union since a number of Member States have adopted dominance tests.[124] On examination, the arguments advanced by both proponents and opponents of an SLC test appear overstated and the effect on convergence in decision-making would be likely to be minimal in either event.

The contention that the European Union's adoption of an SLC test would reduce the risk of the Commission's and US agencies' forming different views of the same transaction is, for the following reasons, exaggerated:

1. very significant convergence on substantive and procedural issues has been achieved over the last decade notwithstanding the existence of different standards[125];
2. other than with respect to the treatment of efficiencies[126] and conglomerate

123 See Green Paper, para 160: 'From a procedural viewpoint, the main reason proposed in favour of such a re-evaluation is that it could allow an alignment of the Merger Regulation's appraisal criteria with those applied in other major jurisdictions, such as the US, Canada and Australia, which rely on a concept of substantial lessening of competition ("the SLC-test"). Such an alignment towards a global standard for merger assessment holds certain attractions. It would, for example, facilitate merging parties' global assessment of possible competition issues arising from contemplated transactions, by obviating the current need to argue their case according to differently formulated tests. This would in turn provide competition agencies with a better basis on which to build effective cooperation in cases that are notified in several jurisdictions. Moreover, as a common test would tend to highlight the actual application of the test, rather than the test itself, it would provide for better bench-marking of the activities of competition authorities and courts, as well as facilitating the development of competition-oriented research and modelling.' See too The Review of the EC Merger Regulation, n 5 above, paras 122-129.

124 See Green Paper, para 161: 'Another possible complication relates to the fact that most Member States (as well as the Candidate Countries) have aligned their merger control provisions to the current dominance test. Thus, unless national rules were also amended, changing the Merger Regulation's competition test could have the awkward effect of creating greater alignment internationally, while leading to greater disparity within the Community.' See too *The Review of the EC Merger Regulation,* n 5 above, paras 118-121.

125 See, eg the publication on 31 October 2002, by the Commission and the US competition agencies of a set of best practices on cooperation in reviewing mergers that require approval on both sides of the Atlantic with a view to 'enhancing the good relationship developed over the last decade' (Commission Press Release IP/02/1591). See too the establishment in October 2001 of the International Competition Network (ICN). In the field of merger control, the ICN has formed a Merger Review Working Group to promote the adoption of best practices in the design and operation of merger review regimes so as: (1) to enhance the effectiveness of each jurisdiction's merger review mechanisms; (2) to facilitate procedural and substantive convergence; and (3) to reduce the public and private time and cost of multi-jurisdictional merger reviews.

126 As explained below, in December 2002, the Commission proposed revising the ECMR to take positive account of efficiencies, thereby aligning the European Union's approach with that of the US agencies.

mergers,[127] the substantive differences between the EU and US agencies are modest[128];

3. convergence is not necessary for its own sake and, if there are differences in the underlying economic approach between the European Union and other jurisdictions, these will not be resolved by their adopting substantive tests with similar wording; and
4. where differences have arisen, these have been primarily attributable to differences in the application of common underlying principles to a given transaction.[129]

The contention that abandonment of the dominance test would frustrate alignment among national agencies within the European Union is, for the following reasons, also not persuasive:

127 With respect to conglomerate effects, the differences between the Commission and the US agencies' positions can be overstated. There continue to be cases characterised as vertical mergers by the US agencies that share similar features to those viewed as being conglomerate mergers in the European Union. By way of example, the FTC conducted a lengthy investigation in 2002 into the acquisition by Synopsys Inc, which provides 'front-end' electronic design automation tools for integrated circuit chip design, of Avant! Corp, which creates 'back-end' physical design and transistor-level design tools for integrated circuit chips. The FTC investigated, over the course of six months, whether: (1) the transaction would give Synopsys an incentive to frustrate competing back-end tools from communicating with Synopsys' front-end tools; and (2) whether the transaction would have any other adverse effect. The FTC permitted the transaction to proceed on 4 June 2002, but continued its investigation for several further weeks to determine whether to bring an administrative complaint. The FTC ultimately voted to close its investigation (see FTC Press Release of 26 July 2002, http://www.ftc.gov/opa/2002/07/avant.htm), although three FTC Commissioners issued statements indicating that the FTC would continue to watch the industry.

128 The unilateral effects and coordinated interaction tests described under the US Guidelines are very similar to the single firm dominance and collective dominance tests applied under the ECMR. Indeed, the US Guidelines define a 'substantial lessening of competition' as 'creating or enhancing market power', which is very similar to 'creating or strengthening a dominant position'. See too Commissioner Thomas B Leary, A Comment on Merger Enforcement in the United States and in the European Union, speech at Transatlantic Business Dialogue Principals Meeting, 11 October 2001 ('there may be as much agreement between the United States and the European Union in competition matters as there is between the federal and state governments within the United States').

129 The divergence between the Commission and the US agencies in General Electric/Honeywell, for example, cannot be attributed to differences in the respective substantive tests, but rather to the application of different underlying philosophies. The fact that the European Union and the United States reached opposing conclusions was almost certainly not a function of the wording of their respective substantive tests for merger review, but more likely reflects different philosophies on the application of the underlying principles and their assessment of the future effects of the transaction on the market. (See William Kolasky, Former Deputy Assistant Attorney General, Antitrust Division, US Department of Justice, Conglomerate Mergers and Range Effects: It's a Long Way from Chicago to Brussels, George Mason University Symposium, 9 November 2001.) See too Charles A James, then-Assistant Attorney General, Antitrust Division, US Department of Justice, International Antitrust in the Bush Administration, speech to the Canadian Bar Association, Annual Fall Conference on Competition Law, 21 September 2001: 'The different results in General Electric/ Honeywell, therefore, were not attributable to failings on the part of the two agencies to coordinate on the facts and analysis. Rather, they flowed from a substantive difference between the two agencies on the proper scope of antitrust enforcement.'

1. differences exist between agencies that apply the same substantive test but have varying views on the employment of market share presumptions;
2. different conclusions may be reached by agencies applying the same substantive test to the same transaction where the factual situation varies[130];
3. a number of Member States have SLC tests (or variants thereof) so the alleged disadvantage of the Commission's adopting an SLC test would not be universally felt in any event; and
4. there is no reason to suppose that the coexistence of an SLC test at the EU level and dominance tests in certain EU countries would retard analytical convergence, which is the more important policy objective.[131]

4. The Commission's December 2002 proposals

In November 2002, the Commission announced that it did not intend proposing that the dominance standard be replaced with an SLC test,[132] but would instead seek to 'clarify' the existing language of the ECMR to make specific reference to 'unilateral effects' in situations where a position of single firm dominance would not be created or strengthened. (Certain commentators criticised the Commission's proposal and continued to urge adoption of an SLC test.[133])

On 11 December 2002, the Commission adopted the Draft ECMR and Draft Horizontal Mergers Guidelines.[134] The Draft ECMR proposes that the dominance test be clarified to make clear that it applies to all transactions that have 'unilateral effects', including those occurring in oligopolistic markets where there is no risk of tacit collusion and the merging companies will not hold a position of single firm dominance post-transaction, but where the merged undertaking would be in a

130 By way of example, in 1999, the proposed acquisition by The Coca-Cola Company of the non-US commercial beverage brands of Cadbury Schweppes was notified in a number of Member States and approved in some (eg the United Kingdom and Ireland), but not others (eg Belgium and Italy), largely because the factual background and competitive assessment differed as between Member States, rather than because of any differences in the applicable substantive tests.

131 Clearly, though, the requirement that any change to the ECMR should have the unanimous support of the Council might create political difficulties in modifying the dominance test in the event of opposition from Member States that currently apply that test.

132 Mario Monti, Member of the Commission responsible for EU Competition Policy, speech at the Fordham Annual Conference on International Antitrust & Policy, New York, 31 October 2001 (Commission Press Release SPEECH/02/533) ('I believe that the issue of choice among the two tests, dominance and substantial lessening of competition, has been excessively dramatized. I attach definitively more importance to the adoption of guidelines on the assessment of horizontal mergers, which will give clarity and predictability to the Commission policy').

133 See, eg John Vickers, UK Director-General of Fair Trading, 'How to reform the EC merger test?,' speech at the International Bar Association Conference, Brussels, 7-8 November 2002 ('In sum, it cannot safely be assumed that the existing ECMR dominance test covers all anti-competitive mergers of concern. The test needs to change....[The Commission] has said that it will propose a clarification of the meaning of "dominance" in the merger test. This clarification is said to have the advantage of not being linked to future Court interpretations of dominance under Article 82. Perhaps the word "dominance" will then be free to mean different things. But directly incorporating SLC in the EC merger test might do more for clarity and legal certainty').

134 Draft Commission Notice on the appraisal of horizontal mergers under the Council Regulation on the control of concentrations between undertakings, OJ 2002 C 331/03, http://europa.eu.int/eur-lex/en/dat/2002/c_331/c_33120021231en00180031.pdf.

position to raise prices and thereby exercise market power.[135] The Draft ECMR explains the Commission's thinking in the following terms:

> 'In view of the consequences that concentrations in oligopolistic market structures may have, it is all the more necessary to maintain effective competition in such markets. Many oligopolistic markets exhibit a healthy degree of competition. However, under certain circumstances, the elimination of important competitive constraints that the merging parties exerted on each other, as well as the reduction of competitive pressure on the remaining competitors, may, particularly in these markets, be detrimental to competition unless these effects would be constrained by the reaction of competitors, customers or consumers.
>
> For that purpose, the notion of dominance within the meaning of this Regulation should, therefore, encompass situations in which, because of the oligopolistic structure of the relevant market and the resulting interdependence of the various undertakings active on that market, one or more undertakings would hold the economic power to influence appreciably and sustainably the parameters of competition, in particular, prices, production, quality of output, distribution or innovation, even without coordination by the members of the oligopoly.
>
> In making this appraisal, account should be taken of the specific features of the markets under examination, such as the level of capacity constraints, the degree of product differentiation, or the functioning of the bidding process. Consideration should also be given to, *inter alia,* the likely reactions of actual and potential competitors, as well as of customers, and any efficiencies brought about by the merger.'[136]

Accordingly, the Draft ECMR proposes that the Regulation's substantive test expressly provide that 'one or more undertakings shall be deemed to be in a dominant position if, with or without coordinating, they hold the economic power to influence appreciably and sustainably the parameters of competition, in particular, prices, production, quality of output, distribution or innovation, or appreciably to foreclose competition'.[137] As a practical matter, this wording would 'plug' any 'enforcement gap' between the dominance and SLC tests. In addition, by 'closely follow[ing] the characterization of a dominant position given by the Court of Justice', the Commission's proposed wording seeks to 'maintain the sizeable body of case law and case practice which has been built up over the years'.[138] According to the Commission, '[t]his approach has the additional advantage of not linking the definition of dominance under the Merger Regulation to any future interpretations given by the [Community courts] to the concept of dominance under Article 82'.[139]

135 See Explanatory Memorandum to Draft ECMR, paras 53-58.
136 Draft ECMR, Recital 21.
137 Draft ECMR, Article 2(2).
138 See Explanatory Memorandum to Draft ECMR, para 56.
139 See Explanatory Memorandum to ECMR, para 57.

Adoption by the Council of the Draft ECMR in the form proposed by the Commission would clearly establish that the dominance standard may be applied to the following three categories of transactions:

1. transactions resulting in the creation or strengthening of a single firm with a 'paramount market position', including transactions having vertical or conglomerate effects;
2. transactions giving rise to situations of oligopolistic dominance where effective competition is absent from a market as a result of parallel conduct in the form of tacit collusion; and
3. transactions that occur in oligopolistic markets where there is no risk of tacit collusion and the merging companies will not have a leadership position post-transaction, but where they would be in a position to raise prices and thereby exercise market power.

Finally, with respect to efficiencies, the Explanatory Memorandum to the Draft ECMR discloses the Commission's opinion that 'it is legally possible to deal explicitly with the issue of efficiencies under the present substantive test and with the present and proposed wording of the Merger Regulation'.[140] The Commission's view is that Article 2(1)(b) of the Control Merger Regulation provides a legal basis in that respect by stating that the Commission shall, *inter alia*, take account of 'the development of technical and economic progress provided it is to consumers' advantage and does not form an obstacle to competition'. Accordingly, the Draft ECMR includes specific language signalling the Commission's willingness to take account of efficiencies.

> 'In order to determine the impact of a concentration on competition in the common market, it is appropriate to take account of any substantiated likely efficiencies put forward by the undertakings concerned. It is possible that the efficiencies brought about by the concentration counteract the effects on competition, and in particular the potential harm to consumers, that it might otherwise have and that, as a consequence, the concentration does not create or strengthen a dominant position as a result of which effective competition would be significantly impeded in the common market or in a substantial part of it. The Commission should publish guidance on the conditions under which it may take efficiencies into account in the assessment of a concentration.'[141]

In indicating a preparedness to approve transactions that might otherwise raise competition issues by reason of claimed efficiencies, the Commission has effectively aligned EU policy with that applied in the United States. The extent to which this policy will be applied in practice will of course only emerge over time.

140 See Explanatory Memorandum to ECMR, para 60.
141 Draft ECMR, Recital 24.

12

Substantive Tests – Are the Differences between the Dominance and SLC Tests Real or Semantic?

Caroline Montalcino

Deputy Director for Competition and Legal Affairs, General Directorate for Competition, Consumer Affairs and Fraud Control, Paris

This paper will put forward the views of the General Directorate for Competition, Consumer Affairs and Fraud Control in France on the substantive tests and, perhaps more importantly, on the main differences between them.

I would like to offer two preliminary observations. The first is that the question of the substance of the test is addressed to a system that does not have to answer it. It's not very easy for a French competition authority to address this topic, because we have written our law in order that we can explicitly use both tests. The wording of the test is that 'a merger that can lessen competition, especially by creating or strengthening a dominant position' is considered harmful. Some might think that we have avoided choosing between tests or that we thought, when drafting the law in 1986, that the dominance test might not catch all anti-competitive mergers.

To be completely truthful, we have used the dominance test to assess simple and collective dominance most of the time. Nevertheless, issues such as unilateral effects have been addressed explicitly in recent decisions, mixing 'substantial lessening of competition' (SLC) and dominance for the assessment of a merger. We found that an analysis from the perspective of unilateral effects is more appropriate in non-uniform competition settings (markets with differentiated products and services) and when the definition of relevant markets might be, for the same reason, an arduous task.

Secondly, when discussing the issue at hand, it seems important to bear in mind two points:

1. Both tests proved to be effective for reviewing mergers and the lack of major discrepancies between them is widely acknowledged.
2. Both tests aim at evaluating the probability of an increase in market power because of the merger under review. The dominance test will evaluate the changes of market structures and how they will affect the way the market works; the SLC test will evaluate directly the consequences of the merger on prices, on productivity and on welfare.

But there are differences that stem from a survey of the implementation of the two tests. I would like to point out three of them:

1. Are there some anti-competitive effects that are analysed differently according to the test which is used?
2. Are the two tests different in the time frame they take into account for the purpose of the competitive analysis?

3. Is the role given to the efficiencies question inherently different in the two tests?

1. Are there any anti-competitive effects that are analysed differently according to the test used for the assessment of a merger?

Anti-competitive effects of the immediate evolution of prices and of 'unilateral effects' might not be analysed as well within the scope of 'dominance tests' as within 'SLC tests'.

The SLC test has a broader scope of analysis because it refers in practice to quantified estimation. The 'dominance' criterion is more rarely backed by measurement of the direct effects of the merger on prices or welfare.

The 'dominance test' refers to a firm's ability to behave without taking into account its competitors, suppliers or customers and that starts with determining the *market share* of the new entity.

The first tool of an SLC test is usually also to look at the cumulated market share.

But this static computation is completed by another. The concept of SLC allows an evaluation of the reduction of competition by the change in prices through 'unilateral effects'.[1] It assesses whether merging firms could unilaterally impose a profitable post-merger price increase and whether rivalry might weaken without any kind of collusion. 'Unilateral effects' are systematically referred to in most recent decisions in the United States. It allows the taking into account of the impact of efficiency gains on the immediate change in prices.

Until now, the EC Merger Regulation (ECMR) has not appeared explicitly to allow such an approach. That could explain why unilateral effects have not been clearly discussed so far in Commission decisions even though some hints of a 'unilateral effects' reasoning may be found in a couple of decisions (*MAN/Auwarter* or *Barilla/Kamps* for instance). Yet the European Commissioner for Competition, Mario Monti, announced recently that it would be clearly specified in the revised ECMR that the test will cover analysis of 'unilateral effects'. It is then possible to think that the potential gap between the two tests might be closed, though exactly how is still under review.

2. Are the two tests different in the time frame they take into account for the purpose of the competitive analysis?

Another difference that could be a substantial difference in the way merger control is implemented on both sides of the Atlantic is the time frame of analysis. In practice, SLC tests focus more on short-run competition whereas dominance tests focus on long-term competition.

Addressing collective dominance, which is based on repeated interactions over time before a 'Nash equilibrium' is reached requires, for instance, a longer time frame than addressing immediate 'unilateral effects'. From that respect, the European test of 'dominance' seems to be more prospective than the American implementation of the 'SLC' test.

1 'Unilateral effects' include the whole loss of welfare caused by a merger after firms have moved their prices behaving independently from one another.

So there is clearly a difference in the time frame of the analysis, and a focus on the mid-long term effects of a merger in the dominance test.

3. Are efficiencies taken into account differently in the two tests?

A third difference of scope between the two tests is the room left to efficiency gains and their analysis when examining a merger. So far, European decisions do not offer examples of economic efficiency reasoning. European analysis rather focuses on the effects of mergers on the 'demand side'. From that point of view, I would like to express my satisfaction about the announcement made by Commissioner Monti of a better recognition of merger-specific efficiencies to the direct benefit to consumers in the ECMR.

However, computation of efficiency gains is extremely difficult especially as regards the long-term forecast. Empirical studies do not prove the effectiveness of efficiency gains after a concentration either. In other words, the potential divergence on that subject is rather minor: it seems that American competition authorities have very seldom based a clearance on the grounds of efficiency gains, in spite of the adverse effects on competition of a merger.

To conclude on that point, when assessing the impact of efficiency gains on general welfare, it should be kept in mind that in the short run, assuming 'pass-on to consumers' is taken into account, efficiency gains may have a positive impact, through a reduction in production costs and prices. However, in some market configurations, it may trigger a further concentration movement in search of economies of scale. If barriers to entry on the market are high, the resulting increased market concentration shall in turn lead to higher prices. While avoiding the 'efficiency offence' trap, the consequences of efficiency gains on market functioning have to be fully evaluated, in the short run as well as the long run.

***

So far, we find almost no examples in the past – except for the '*baby food*' case of 1992 – showing that dominance and SLC tests do not lead to the same conclusions in merger analysis. However, and to conclude, I would like to stress that the reasoning leading to the final decision is different in the two tests. From that respect, the conclusion could be drawn that differences between both tests are more substantial than semantic, although one of the core issues focuses more on the time frame in which the analysis is led. A comparison from that respect between cases reviewed on both sides of the Atlantic could usefully fuel the debate.

Yet, for the time being, the implementation of different tests on the two sides of the Atlantic or even within the European Union had no consequences on the ability of different authorities using different tests to cooperate, to converge and finally to reach consistent decisions.

At the end of the day, it seems that there are indeed differences between the two tests, that they are real enough in the process of analysis, and that there might be a gap between them. But, ultimately, they nearly always lead to consistent conclusions. And we must bear in mind that the issues of the review of the European Merger Regulation are broader than the sole comparison between the two tests of dominance and SLC.

13
How to Reform the EC Merger Test?

John Vickers

Chairman, Office of Fair Trading, London

> 'When *I* use a word', Humpty Dumpty said, in rather a scornful tone, 'it means just what I choose it to mean – neither more nor less.'
>
> 'The question is', said Alice, 'whether you *can* make words mean so many different things.'
>
> 'The question is', said Humpty Dumpty, 'which is to be master – that's all.'
>
> Lewis Carroll, *Through the Looking Glass*, 1872

1. Introduction

Are the differences between the dominance and substantial lessening of competition (SLC) tests real or semantic? This is a question about the meaning of words. Ultimately, it is for the courts to determine the meaning of words – they are the master.

I do not know for sure the meaning of words such as 'collective dominance'. It is increasingly widely accepted, however, that it cannot safely be assumed that the existing EC Merger Regulation (ECMR) dominance test covers all anti-competitive mergers of concern. My plan is to review the reasons for this conclusion and then to ask what can best be done to reform the ECMR – Article 2 in particular – to ensure that EC merger policy can securely achieve its goal. The SLC/dominance debate needs to move on to this question, since the case for change has, I believe, been made.

2. Mind the Gap?

Whether or not there is a gap between the dominance and SLC tests depends in good part on whether, in situations of oligopoly, 'dominance' goes beyond tacit coordination.

'Dominance' clearly captures the situation of several firms acting *as* one – by coordinating their behaviour – as well as the situation of single firm dominance. But does it capture all-important instances of 'unilateral effects', where firms continue to act independently, without coordination, but substantially less competitively? The jargon here is unfortunate inasmuch as 'unilateral' effects can well have *multilateral, market-wide* consequences, eg for the prices charged not just by the parties to the merger, but by other firms too.

Before the CFI judgment in *Airtours*, this was an open question. Some think it still remains an open question. Others take the view that the limits of 'dominance' in oligopolistic markets have now been set – at tacit coordination, where firms act collusively to exercise market power. In that case, anti-competitive mergers in oligopolistic markets not involving tacit coordination may be caught neither by collective dominance, nor by single-firm dominance because no market leader 'capable of acting independently of customers and competitors' has been created.

On this view, there is a considerable gap in policy, and a serious one if the aim of merger control is indeed to ensure that the competitiveness of markets is not significantly weakened by mergers. The prime exemplar of the gap – the US baby foods case – underplays its potential importance. For example, what about last year's *Lloyds TSB/Abbey* banks case in the United Kingdom? What about all the actual *and potential* cases where it can be shown with proper rigour that competition is likely to be substantially lessened, but where lessening-of-competition-via-increased-probability-of tacit-coordination is not demonstrable to that standard? Such a gap, if it be so, is certainly one to mind about. Even those who believe that the meaning of 'dominance' might still be so broad that there is no gap cannot be sure that this is so.

In sum, *it cannot safely be assumed that the existing ECMR dominance test covers all anti-competitive mergers of concern.* The test needs to change.

It is worth noting that, from a wider perspective, there is positive merit in there being a gap between the meanings of 'dominance' and 'SLC'. If they did generally mean the same, then there would be awkward consequences for EC competition law and policy as a whole. Article 82 policy would be too interventionist. Any firm or firms that had market power to a degree the prospect of which would invoke SLC-based merger policy would be dominant. Such firms would carry the special responsibilities that fall on all dominant firms, and if they engaged in conduct that counts as abusive, then they would face serious penalties and possibly private actions for damages.

Competition policy would then fail to discriminate between the accumulation of market power by successful product market competition and, on the other hand, the acquisition of market power by merger. It is one thing to win customers over time by serving them well in the product market, quite another to acquire them at a stroke in the stock market. Policy would also fail to distinguish between *ex ante* measures to maintain competitive incentives and *ex post* intervention to curb and penalise abuse of dominant market power.

From the point of view of the economic incentives of firms, and on general grounds, that would seem rather odd. The threshold of market power that triggers intervention to maintain competitive incentives by preventing anti-competitive structural changes in markets ought to be lower than that which triggers liability for the breach of competition law prohibitions on firms that have become dominant.

Put differently, merger regulation would seem logically to be a closer relative of Article 81 than Article 82. A merger is the ultimate agreement between firms. This does not mean that, say, horizontal mergers should be treated as strictly as horizontal price-fixing, since the latter, but not the former, is almost always anti-competitive. But even leaving aside hard-core anti-competitive agreements like horizontal price-fixing, it would be bizarre to recast Article 81 to apply only to agreements that created or strengthened a dominant position. Policy towards anti-competitive agreements would then be far too lax. This is not to say that merger control should be aligned with Article 81. It is, however, to query whether merger control should be based on the same key concept as Article 82.

How, then, should the EC merger test change? There is a straightforward way to change the test, and no doubt there are indirect solutions with more or less the same practical result.

3. How Article 2 could be revised

The simple and direct method to solve the ECMR problem is to use the language of SLC. Article 2(3) could read simply:

> 'A concentration shall be declared incompatible with the common market if, and only if, it would have the effect, or be likely to have the effect, of substantially lessening competition in the common market or in a substantial part of it.'

4. Legal uncertainty

A possible objection to such a change is that, in view of the accumulated case law, the dominance test has advantages over the SLC test in respect of legal certainty. I question this.

First, the meaning of 'dominance' – collective or otherwise – is not clear. This is demonstrated not least by the fact that various experts appear to have very different views as to its meaning at present – as conferences such as this illustrate. Secondly, this uncertainty has the danger of spilling over to Article 82. Thirdly, the key jurisprudence dates back only a few years, notably to the *Gencor* judgment in 1999, which in any event stands as relevant jurisprudence on coordinated effects. Further, the decades of EC case law on matters such as market definition would carry over straightforwardly to an SLC test for mergers. Fourthly, SLC is not a new creature internationally, or among EU Member States, and its application can be underpinned by guidelines – such as those long familiar in the United States or those recently issued for consultation in the United Kingdom.

Commissioner Monti said yesterday that he will propose a clarification of the meaning of 'dominance' in the merger test. This clarification is said to have the advantage of not being linked to future Court interpretations of dominance under Article 82. Perhaps the word 'dominance' will then be free to mean different things. But directly incorporating SLC in the EC merger test might do more for clarity and legal certainty.

5. Conclusion

I doubt that it is possible for merger policy to have all three of the following:

- the current 'dominance' wording of the ECMR;
- the effect of catching all (and only) SLC mergers; and
- rigorous case analysis.

The third of these is imperative, as the Court of First Instance has recently underlined. The second should be the aim of merger policy. So the first should change. The most straightforward change would be to adopt the language of SLC.

14
Merger Analysis: SLC versus Dominance

Kevin R Sullivan and Brian R Meiners

King & Spalding LLP, Washington, DC

1. Introduction

In the world of merger control, antitrust authorities in the United States and the European Commission ('EC') employ two distinct tests to review proposed mergers that are phrased in quite different language, but which seek to achieve the same goal: to identify the few combinations that present a high risk of harm to consumers from the many that do not. The EC has adopted a market dominance test ('dominance test') while US law asks whether a merger will substantially lessen competition ('SLC test').[1] The relevant strengths and weaknesses of these tests as vehicles for merger review became a point of discussion for antitrust authorities throughout the world, precisely because the regulators are increasingly unable to restrict their investigations to their own soil and markets.[2] Therefore, the problem is not which test is the better test, but the fact that there are two tests.

Over 60 countries around the world currently review mergers, and many deals are reviewed in multiple jurisdictions, thereby creating the risk of inconsistent outcomes and potentially unnecessary procedural burdens.[3] Multinational review of mergers and joint ventures has become commonplace, and arrangements for sharing information, cooperating at the investigative stages and, in some instances, deferring to the judgment of sister enforcement agencies, has also developed. Yet, agreement on a set of uniform international competition laws for mergers faces seemingly overwhelming obstacles rooted in political, cultural, and philosophical factors.

The desire to analyse critically the current environment and to move towards a common understanding of merger policy within the European Union has prompted the EC to issue a Green Paper inviting respondents to express their views on the perceived divergence in merger control regulations and to suggest alterations that increase transparency across regulatory authorities.[4] The EC's willingness to open its existing regulatory system to review is to be commended. It reflects a sincere effort to accommodate the business community's desire to reduce transaction costs and uncertainty when contemplating a merger, acquisition, or joint venture. There were a number of comments submitted urging the adoption of one test over another. Still

1 Clayton Act, ch 323 § 7, 38 Stat 730, 731-32 (1914) (current version at 15 USC § 18 (1994)).

2 Stefan Schmitz, 'How Dare They? European Merger Control and the European Commission's Blocking of the General Electric/Honeywell Merger' (2002) 23 U Pa J Int'l Econ L 325.

3 See *What is the International Competition Network?*, at http://www.internationalcompetitionnetwork.org/news_bk.html.

4 Green Paper on the review of Council Regulation (EEC) No 4064/89, 11 December 2001, COM (2001) 745 final.

others urged that because the two systems seek to promote the same objectives, they should continue to exist harmoniously. The perceived difference in merger regulations can perhaps best be reflected in the issue of collective dominance that is becoming an increasing concern of antitrust authorities everywhere.

These comments will compare the EC dominance test with the US SLC test and will examine arguments in favour of each, concluding that the two systems are sufficiently similar despite the difference in nomenclature, such that changes to an established legal system should be carefully considered and implemented only if the EC concludes that its current dominance test does not provide a basis to challenge a sufficiently comprehensive set of possible competitive outcomes that are viewed as undesirable.

2. Assessing mergers

Any person or agency charged with the task of reviewing a proposed merger is faced with a challenge involving a myriad of uncertainties. The uncertainties arise because markets can operate in ways that tend towards either competition or monopoly. Predicting in advance which way a merger will propel a market is far from an exact science. It is important for merger control to be able to distinguish as accurately as possible between pro-competitive and anti-competitive outcomes. This is inherently difficult because merger review is a predictive exercise, requiring a consideration of the likely change in behaviour of the firms in the market as a result of the change in the structure of the market brought about by the merger. For example, under the European Merger Control Regulation (ECMR),[5] the first stage assessment has to be made in four weeks. Even allowing for possible pre-filing discussions, this is relatively little time in which to decide whether there are doubts about the compatibility of a merger with the market that would prompt competition authorities seriously to consider blocking the closing of the transaction.

Assessing the nature of competition in the context of merger control in a given industry is a multifaceted inquiry. A number of market characteristics are relevant in evaluating whether a firm or a group of firms possess market power or may gain market power either unilaterally or by reason of tacit coordination as a result of a merger. After authorities determine that a merger requires thorough investigation, determination of the correct standard of review of the merger becomes relevant. As noted above, the two critical and rival tests used to assess changes in competition are the SLC test and the dominance test. Mergers involving large multinational corporations have gained the most consideration from the world's most prominent competition authorities (the American Department of Justice (DOJ) and Federal Trade Commission (FTC) and the Commission of the European Union (the 'Commission')).

There is considerable debate as to which test should be used and whether these two standards have the same practical effect. The two tests share a focus on increasing market power as the harm to be prevented. Market power, in the context of merger analysis, may be defined as the ability to increase prices without an effective challenge to profitability (via an output reduction (or reduced quality, innovation, choice, or other ways in which competition may be inhibited)) over pre-merger levels for a significant

5 Council Regulation 4064/89 EEC of 21 December 1989 on the Control of the Concentration between Undertakings, OJ 1990 L 257/13, as amended by Council Regulation 1310/97 EC of 30 June 1997, OJ 1998 L 180/1 (hereinafter ECMR).

period of time. This may arise through the individual decisions of the merged firms and their competitors or through increased opportunity for coordinated behaviour.

2.1 Merger control in the EC – dominance test

Under the ECMR, mergers with a 'Community dimension'[6] must be notified to the Commission, and may not be implemented before a clearance decision is granted declaring the proposed concentration compatible with the Common Market. The Merger Task Force of the Commission is obligated to perform a substantive review of all of these mergers. The ECMR prohibits any combination that 'creates or strengthens a dominant position as a result of which effective competition would be significantly impeded in the Common Market or in a substantial part of it'.[7] It is in this test where there exists the divergence between European merger control and its equivalent in the United States. US law asks, of course, whether a merger will substantially lessen competition.[8]

The ECMR provides for a two-stage process to review the effects of the merger in the markets concerned, the characteristics of the merging firms,[9] and the post-merger position of the new entity. First, the Commission must identify product and geographical markets in which the parties operate. Secondly, having defined the relevant markets, the Commission will consider whether either or both of the parties already enjoy a dominant position which will be strengthened by the merger, or whether the merger will create a dominant position in any of the markets previously identified.

Market share in the European arena remains the determinant factor in assessing the dominant position of a merger participant. In order to determine whether a merger creates or strengthens dominance, the Commission must inevitably consider how the merger will affect market share. Without any specific guidelines in the ECMR as to levels of market share that create market dominance, the Commission has, over the years, identified an unofficial *prima facie* level of 40 per cent market share as the threshold for dominance.[10] Market share is still the focal point of merger analysis under the ECMR, although the Commission looks at various other factors for establishing market dominance. The essential prerequisite, however, is always dominance.

It is only after a finding of dominance is made in the European system, that the Commission has to look beyond the presence of dominance. The merger authority has to address the effect of dominance on competition. The European Court of Justice (ECJ) seems to agree with this view. In *French Republic v Commission*, the Court acknowledged the need to address aspects of a merger beyond the mere presence of dominance by stating that the introduction of the additional criteria in merger review

6 Council Regulation 1310/97 of 30 June 1997, OJ 1997 L 180/1 (amending Merger Regulation to reach mergers in which the undertakings have a combined worldwide turnover of at least $2.5 billion ECU; in which each undertaking has an EC-wide turnover of at least 100 million ECU; and other requirements respecting turnover in at least three Member States).

7 *Id.*

8 See Clayton Act, *supra* n 1.

9 See ECMR, *supra* n 5.

10 See European Commission, *XXIXth Report on Competition Policy* 4-5 (1999); Barry E Hawk *et al*, 'Recent Developments in EU Merger Control' (2001) 15 *Antitrust* 24.

is 'intended to ensure that the existence of a causal link between the concentration and the deterioration of the competitive structure of the market can be excluded only if the competitive structure resulting from the concentration would deteriorate in similar fashion even if the concentration did not proceed'.[11]

Thus, aside from the question of dominance, the Commission actually has to review other aspects of a merger.[12] First, it has to establish that competition will be negatively affected by a merger which creates or strengthens a dominant position. Secondly, a causal link must exist between those negative effects and the dominant position. Finally, and this is the bottom line, the impediment to competition must be significant.[13] It is this third requirement which brings European law closer to the SLC test applied in US law by emphasising the actual impact on competition by a merger rather than by first having to determine whether there exists market dominance.[14] However, when evaluating the post-merger consequences, the Commission, like the US authorities, does have a certain latitude as to those features of the merger on which it will base its final decision. In the final analysis, therefore, European merger control is actually not very different from its counterpart in the United States. The main difference between the two is that the Europeans have to establish market dominance first, without which a merger could not be stopped.[15]

2.2 Merger control in the United States – SLC

The substantive test in merger control in the United States is whether or not competition would be substantially lessened by any merger proposal. Mergers are prohibited if their effect may be to 'substantially lessen competition or tend to create a monopoly in any line of commerce . . . in any section of the country'.[16]

The market shares of the merging firms and concentration levels in the relevant market are the starting points in assessing the competitive impact of mergers in the United States. The courts and the enforcement agencies, however, have disavowed exclusive reliance on market share in favour of 'a more reasoned analysis of the likely competitive effects of individual transactions based on real-life experiences'.[17] As the 1992 *Merger Guidelines* make clear, the competitive impact of a merger cannot be determined solely by reference to levels of market concentration.[18]

The 1992 *Merger Guidelines* describe a five-step analytical process by which the federal enforcement agencies determine whether to challenge a particular transaction. These steps are:

11 *French Republic v Commission (Kali and Salz)* [1998] ECR I-1375, para 106, [1998] 4 CMLR 829 (1990).
12 Schmitz, *supra* n 2, at 347.
13 *Id* at 347-48.
14 *Id.*
15 Schmitz, *supra* n 2, at 348.
16 Clayton Act § 7, 15 USC § 18. (Mergers may also be challenged under the Sherman Act, 15 USC § 1 or the Federal Trade Commission Act, 15 USC § 45; the analytical framework would be the same.)
17 Timothy J Muris, Chairman, Federal Trade Comm'n, *Antitrust Enforcement at the Federal Trade Commission: In a Word, Continuity*, Prepared Remarks Before American Bar Ass'n Antitrust Section Annual Meeting (7 August 2001), available at www.ftc.gov/speeches/muris/murisba.htm.
18 US Dep't of Justice & Federal Trade Comm'n, *Horizontal Merger Guidelines* § 0.1 (1992) (hereinafter '1992 *Merger Guidelines*').

1. defining a relevant market and determining the extent to which the proposed transaction would increase concentration in that market;
2. assessing, in light of both the impact of the proposed transaction on market concentration and other factors, whether the transaction would raise competitive concerns;
3. assessing whether entry by additional firms into the market would counteract these competitive concerns;
4. considering whether the proposed transaction would likely result in otherwise unachievable efficiencies; and
5. determining whether, but for the merger, either firm would be likely to fail, causing its assets to exit the market.[19] Courts generally have followed the same basic approach.[20]

The concept of SLC captures a situation where a merger may increase the market power of the merged firm and (some of) its remaining competitors, allowing each of them to increase prices unilaterally in the face of reduced competition. Under a concept labelled unilateral effects, the conduct of the firms is not coordinated; they are simply competing less vigorously with one another. In sum, a merger in a concentrated market can substantially lessen competition other than through tacit coordination by dulling competition among the remaining competitors in the market (and ending such rivalry as existed between the merged party themselves).

3. SLC VERSUS DOMINANCE

3.1 Arguments in support of SLC

3.1.1 Collective dominance

One of the most echoed critiques of the dominance test is that it does not adequately address tacitly coordinated conduct which may result from excessive concentration. The SLC test, on the other hand, addresses both single firm market effects (including dominance) as well as coordinated market effects. The ECMR does not specify whether the concept of dominance applies to the merging parties solely or also jointly together with one or more competitors (often referred to as collective dominance). The relevant concern with respect to collective dominance refers to the impact of the merger on the possibilities for competing suppliers to engage in coordinated behaviour with the intention of exercising collective market power. This concept has been described as follows:

> 'Market power may be exercised either unilaterally by a single firm, or coordinated among firms. The unilateral exercise of market power does not depend on the cooperation of other market participants. A firm with unilateral market power can assume that its rivals will behave competitively in response to market prices, but nevertheless, their capacity to defeat a rise in price is limited. In contrast, the

19 1992 *Merger Guidelines, supra* n 21, § 0.2.

20 See, eg *FTC v Cardinal Health, Inc*, 12 F Supp 2d 34 (DDC 1998); *New York v Kraft Gen Foods, Inc*, 926 F Supp 321 (SDNY 1995).

coordinated exercise of market power depends on the cooperative or accommodating actions of other market participants.'[21]

The lack of reference to collective dominance by the ECMR has not foreclosed this issue from being addressed in the EC, however. The assessment of mergers in oligopolistic markets has become a mounting concern of the Commission since confirmation by the Court of First Instance (CFI) in 1998 that the ECMR can be applied to mergers which create or strengthen a position of collective dominance.[22] Moreover, the debate continues about the interpretation of collective dominance that has been stirred by the decision in the *Airtours/First Choice* case in which the CFI found that:

'A collective dominant position significantly impeding effective competition in the common market or a substantial part of it may thus arise as the result of a concentration where, in view of the actual characteristics of the relevant market and of the alteration in its structure that the transaction would entail, the latter would make each member of the dominant oligopoly, as it becomes aware of common interests, consider it possible, economically rational, and hence preferable, to adopt on a lasting basis a common policy on the market with the aim of selling at above competitive prices, without having to enter into an agreement or resort to a concerted practice within the meaning of EC Article 81 . . . and without any actual or potential competitors, let alone customers or consumers, being able to react effectively.'[23]

While the Commission and the CFI seem to be addressing the issue of collective dominance, pro-SLC respondents to the Green Paper seem to take the view that the lack of measures in the ECMR to address collective dominance result in 'gaps', or at least potential ones, in the scope of the dominance test. In other words, they feel that there are serious competition problems which mergers may engender that are not capable of being reconciled under the dominance test. Most of these respondents are of the view that the SLC test is an inherently more appropriate test for dealing with the many different competition problem scenarios that may arise as a result of a merger. In particular, some Green Paper respondents have expressed the view that it may not be possible to extend the concept of collective dominance to the control of unilateral effects arising from such collective dominance; they see a risk that the concept might only encompass collusive coordinated effects.

Examples given by Green Paper respondents of scenarios that might not be caught by the dominance test include that of the merger of two firms producing differentiated or branded products that are close substitutes within a broader relevant market, but where the market does not exhibit characteristics normally associated with oligopolistic dominance.[24]

3.1.2 Economic considerations

The proponents of the SLC test argue that the underlying principle of competition policy requires that mergers that are likely to substantially lessen competition should be prohibited. It is argued that this lessening of competition can be best measured by

21 1992 *Merger Guidelines* (at para 5.11).

22 *Societa Italiana Vetro*, Joined Cases T-68/89, T-77/89 and T-78/89.

23 *Airtours plc v Commission of the European Communities*, Case T-342/99.

24 Green Paper on the review of Council Regulation (EEC) No 4064/89, Summary of the Replies Received.

analysing basic economic principles that drive the marketplace. Some believe that that the SLC test is a more appropriate standard for taking economic factors into account, avoiding what some view as the legal 'straight-jacket' of establishing dominance. In other words, the dominance test is too focused on corporate size and industry concentration, and doesn't allow for consideration of other economic factors. As indicated by the nomenclature of the test, European merger control attempts to prevent market participants from becoming dominant or increasing their dominance through a merger. The dominance test seems to be a focused test that does not leave room for other considerations such as efficiencies that may be attained as a result of a merger.[25] This is another difference from the United States where a well made 'efficiency defence' could carry the day for a merger that leads to improvements in its industry.[26]

These economic considerations have resulted in some Green Paper respondents advancing the position that the SLC test is the emerging global standard for merger assessment. These commentators regard the SLC test as one whose merits are gaining wider acceptance internationally than the dominance test. This has been evidenced in the adoption of the SLC test recently in leading jurisdictions such as the United Kingdom, Ireland, and New Zealand.

3.2 Arguments in support of dominance

A great number of Green Paper comments sum up their views of a proposed change to an SLC standard as being simply unnecessary. This argument can be summarised by the phrase, 'If it ain't broke, don't fix it'. These commentators take the view that the two tests, while differently worded, mean essentially the same thing. Both seek the same result and that is to ensure that mergers do not produce serious adverse effects on competition. Many of these commentators argue that the test itself is not really what matters. Rather, the theories of harm to competition that are used in application of a given test are of the utmost importance. In other words, if the dominance test can accommodate an analysis of competitive harm, then no change is needed. Thus, these commentators view the SLC versus dominance debate as a mere conflict of semantics.

Many observers also point out that a switch from the dominance test that is already in place is unnecessary because EC officials subscribe to a fundamental proposition of US antitrust law: that antitrust and competition laws are intended to protect competition, not competitors.[27] It is not, however, a great stretch to imagine broadly different interpretations in the hands of creative minds. What tends to counter the possibility of such widely differing outcomes is the similarity of the economic rationale exercised by enforcement agencies and courts in the two jurisdictions. Interestingly, those in favour of maintaining the dominance test in Europe also use the

25 *Cf* Thomas L Greaney, 'Not for Import: Why the EU Should Not Adopt the American Efficiency Defense for Analyzing Merger and Joint Ventures' (2000) 44 St Louis LJ 871, 889.

26 The DOJ/FTC Merger Guidelines recognise that efficiencies are valuable in considering mergers involving substantial increases in concentration.

27 16-FALL *Antitrust* 26, at 30.

matter of collective dominance as a vehicle to show that a switch to SLC is unwarranted.[28]

In the United States, the danger of collective dominance can be observed by looking at whether a merger is likely to diminish competition by enabling firms in a given market to engage, more successfully or more completely, in coordinated behaviour that harms consumers. Such coordinated interaction consists (in the words of the Merger Guidelines) in 'actions by a group of firms that are profitable for each of them only as a result of the accommodating reactions of the others. This behavior includes tacit or express collusion, and may or may not be lawful in itself'.[29]

As noted above, the ECMR does not make direct reference to the circumstances of collective dominance in the same manner as the US Merger Guidelines. It has been said, however, that the US Merger Guidelines summarise the EC approach to this scenario.[30] The Commission has always understood the dominance test as also applying to collective dominance.[31] As in the United States, the EC examines whether it is likely that the terms of a merger could be taken advantage of by oligopolists. Among other things, the Commission looks at market specific factors such as the extent of product homogeneity, the degree of market share symmetry between the oligopolists, the types of transactions usually concluded in the industry, the extent of structural links, market transparency in terms of pricing, and other marketing parameters, among others.[32] All of these elements are considered by US agencies in assessing the possibility of coordinated post-merger interaction.

Many in the European arena are opposed to the idea of change, fearing in particular the uncertainty that would result, at least for a transitional period. Some also fear that an SLC standard would give the Commission too broad a margin of discretion, and that it could result in what they fear might be an unacceptably interventionist merger control policy.[33]

The Green Paper also recognised that a change to the SLC test in the ECMR might involve some practical drawbacks. In particular, it was acknowledged that such a change might give rise to a degree of uncertainty or unpredictability about how the courts would exactly interpret the new standard. A considerable body of precedent in the EC (emanating from both the Commission and the courts) has been built up under the ECMR dominance test. Another possible complication relates to the fact that many Member States have aligned their merger control provisions to the dominance test.

4. Conclusion

When the SLC and dominance tests are placed side-by-side, one notices that there are fairly small differences between the two methods. As former FTC Chairman Robert Pitofsky stated: 'Many do not appreciate that antitrust authorities in Brussels and in Washington are enforcing two different statutes with modestly different emphases. In

28 Mario Monti, *Antitrust in the US and Europe: A History of Convergence*, Speech presented at the General Counsel Roundtable of the American Bar Association (14 November 2001), available at http://www.eurinion.org/news.

29 See *Horizontal Merger Guidelines 1992*, available at http://www.usdoj.gov (2 April 1992).

30 Monti, *supra* n 28.

31 *Id.*

32 *Id.*

33 Id.

Europe, the concern is with mergers that increase the leverage that can be exercised by a dominant firm and the possible impact of the merger on competitors.'[34] The case for and against a change in the EC from a dominance test to an SLC test would appear to be a closely balanced decision when one weighs all of the considerations. The EC dominance test is certainly not as rigid in terms of what is prohibited in a merger situation as some argue. In practice, however, the Commission seems to consider the issues in a way that is consistent with US merger policy.

If left in its current state, the European system's perceived flexibility could either prove to be helpful or to be lacking in guidance for authorities wrestling with complex merger concerns. For that reason, careful consideration must be given to the pros and cons of recommending a shift to the favour of one test over another in the EC. It should be clear that the discussion should not revolve around which system is better. Rather, the discussion should focus on ensuring that both systems are properly equipped to analyse mergers with the same competitive and economic goals in mind. Perhaps a better solution would be to modify the regulatory authority of the EC to ensure the dominance test is sufficiently robust to address any perceived gap in modern economic theory, without the potential cost associated with voiding a generation of jurisprudence.

34 Robert Pitofsky, Chairman, FTC, Staples and Boeing: What They Say About Merger Enforcement at the FTC (23 September 1997).

Session 4

Efficiency Considerations – What is Their Proper Role in Merger Control?

15

Efficiency Arguments in Merger Cases: Some Issues that Transacting Parties Should Consider

R Shyam Khemani*

Adviser, Competition Policy, Investment Climate Department, The World Bank Group, Washington, DC

The vast majority of the mergers and acquisitions (M&As) that take place in advanced industrial economies proceed confronting little or no regulatory obstacles. Even in cases where the transactions meet certain size thresholds and have to be notified to the competition authorities, a very small proportion of these mergers are actually prohibited or require the parties to restructure the deal, and/or make certain commitments.[1] In some jurisdictions, the competition laws contain provisions that allow for the negative competition effects to be tolerated and be balanced against the efficiencies that may result from the merger.[2] However, it may be noted that there have been only few such cases.[3]

In light of these facts, some businessmen may wonder if it is really that critical to incorporate efficiency arguments as part of the merger filings before the competition authorities. And whether focus may not be better placed on discussing primarily the market structure and competition aspects of the merger instead.

* Until recently, the author was Director, LECG (UK) and has also served as the Chief Economist and Director of Economics and International Affairs, Canadian Competition Bureau. The views expressed in this paper are those of the author and do not necessarily represent the views or position of any officials in his current or past institutional affiliations. The author can be contacted by e-mail at rskhemani@worldbank.org or rskhemani@aol.com.

1 For example of the 2,231 merger filings made to the EC's Competition Directorate over the past 12 years, only 18 merger transactions (ie less than one per cent) were prohibited, and 62 cases (less than three per cent) proceeded with commitments by the merging parties. Similar magnitudes of cases subject to merger investigations are reported by other jurisdictions such as Australia, Canada and the United States.

2 Most notably Canada and the United States. Other jurisdictions such as Australia and New Zealand also have provisions for considering efficiency arguments in merger cases. In Canada the 'total welfare' standard is applied whereby the efficiency gains (surplus) likely to accrue to producers and to consumers are taken into account. In the United States only the consumer welfare/surplus standard is applied. In Canada proposals to replace the total welfare approach with a consumer welfare approach are currently being discussed. For further discussion of these concepts see the papers by Katz and Venit in this volume. In the EC, Commissioner Mario Monti has indicated that efficiencies may provide a basis for approving a merger that may otherwise be viewed as being anti-competitive. See Mario Monti, 'Review of EC Merger Regulation-Roadmap for the Reform Project', Conference on Reform of Merger Control, British Chamber of Commerce, Brussels (4 June 2002). Also the paper by Rakovsky in this volume.

3 For Canada, see *Commissioner for Competition v Superior Propane Inc.* While efficiency arguments have been considered in several merger cases, this is the only fully litigated case which entailed balancing of the efficiency gains against the substantial lessening of competition. The Competition Tribunal ruled in favour of the merging parties and after an appeal to the Federal Court, the case was referred back to the Tribunal which upheld its initial decision, and the merger transaction proceeded to completion. In the

The short answer is that it is important to identify and discuss the efficiencies that are likely to arise from the merger as an *integral* part of the submissions to the competition authorities. This is beneficial for both the merging parties and the competition agency. By presenting credible and properly documented arguments on the competitive dynamics of the industry, *and* the merger specific efficiencies, costly and prolonged litigation can be avoided or at least cut short.

In advancing efficiency arguments, merging parties need to take into account a number of issues, some of which are highlighted in the ensuing discussion.

1. Advantages of incorporating efficiency arguments

My experience with a wide range of M&A cases in different jurisdictions suggests that there are several advantages in incorporating efficiency arguments as an integral part of the review process.

First, analysis of the efficiency and the competitive effects delineates and brings into sharp focus the business strategy and rationale for the merger, and the critical issues that the transacting parties and their advisers need to address in different markets and sub-markets. In doing so, it reduces the incidence of subjective arguments being put to the competition authorities. Moreover, when the data used in the analysis is primarily drawn from public or third party sources, the credibility of the objectives of the merger increases.

Secondly, it may be noted that competition regulators generally rely heavily on the information filed by the merging parties regarding the competitive implications of the proposed transaction. While maintaining business confidentiality, the staff of the competition office will vet this information in the marketplace by contacting customers, suppliers, competitors, and other interested parties. A properly prepared merger filing should anticipate this and, where necessary, be ready to identify measures to address the concerns that may be raised. However, more importantly, the brief being filed should be viewed as an opportunity to put forward the 'theory of the case'. This can establish the framework in which both the merging parties and the competition authorities will analyse the transaction.

Thirdly, the 'comfort level' of the competition authorities increases when they are confronted with some 'hard facts'. Indeed, there are two types of errors in merger cases that officials wish to avoid. One is permitting an anti-competitive merger to proceed, and the other is preventing a pro-competitive merger. It is human nature – regulators do not like their decisions to be the subject of negative publicity that is likely to follow in industry circles and the business press, or have the matter re-examined through the legal appeal process. This also leads to mentioning another type of error – that of a 'non-decision'. Namely, the competition authorities have to take such a long time in reviewing the case by gathering (versus vetting) information that one or both of the transacting parties throw up their hands and abandon the merger.

United States, efficiency arguments were extensively discussed in the case of *FTC v Heinz Co and Beechnut Co.* The decision by a lower court allowing the merger between the two companies was overturned in the court of appeals. For discussion of various other cases see Robert Pitofsky, 'Efficiencies in Defense of Mergers: 18 Months After', Remarks made at the Antitrust Symposium: The Changing Face of efficiency, George Mason Law Review, 16 October 1998; and William Kolasky and Andrew Dick, 'The Merger Guidelines and Integration of efficiencies into Antitrust Review of Horizontal Mergers', US Department of Justice, Celebration of the 20th Anniversary of the Guidelines, 10 June 2002.

Merging parties can avoid such an outcome by conducting and presenting as detailed an analysis as is possible. Indeed, in many jurisdictions, the internal and external briefs in merger cases tend to mirror each other in almost a standard format.

The fourth advantage of incorporating appropriate efficiency and other economic analysis relating to the merger filing is that it is likely to expedite the regulatory decision-making process. This can result in significant savings to both the business parties and taxpayers. Given the large sums of moneys involved in M&A transactions in terms of the acquisition price, the interest payments charged for lines of credit, the professional fees, and the like, even one day's cost savings can be a substantial amount.

2. Some types of efficiencies that matter

Although the wording of competition laws differs across countries, their general purpose is to maintain and encourage competition in order to foster economic efficiency and consumer welfare. In countries where phrases such as 'public interest' or 'public benefit' are used, economic efficiency and consumer welfare are an important sub-set of the basic objectives of the law. While Canada and the United States have different standards, the 'merger guidelines' allow for economic efficiencies to be balanced against the negative effects that may result from the substantial lessening of competition. However, in jurisdictions where such guidelines do not exist, or there are no explicit procedures for weighing the positive/negative aspects of M&A transactions, it is still useful to present such analysis for reasons mentioned before. A review of merger cases in the United Kingdom and European Union shows that merging parties do mention efficiency reasons for undertaking the transaction, and the regulators have noted or commented on the arguments put forward. However, the arguments that are advanced are often not convincing or cogent enough. And one error, whether by design or optimism or lack of application of relevant economic methods, is that the efficiencies claimed tend to be exaggerated in the majority of cases.

In presenting economic efficiency arguments, two major points need to be borne in mind. The first is that the efficiencies being identified must be 'real' and not 'pecuniary', that is the efficiencies should result in real savings of resources such as producing a given level of goods and services with less inputs. And they should not be pecuniary cost savings associated with extracting lower prices from suppliers, due to the superior bargaining power of the merging parties. The latter is a transfer of income from the suppliers to the merging firms, and does not necessarily result in less inputs being used in the production process. In some situations, however, the merging parties may be able to reduce the transaction costs of doing business with suppliers such as standardising and simplifying contracting procedures so less time is spent, employing less staff in the purchasing department, etc, in which case these are real cost savings. The second point is that the economic efficiencies should be merger specific, that is they cannot be achieved through alternative business arrangements. For example, firms often put forward arguments that the merged entity can avoid duplication in R&D or access new technology when the same objectives could be achieved through joint ventures and cooperative agreements. However, even in such cases credible arguments relating to the need for business secrecy, patent rights, licensing fees, and other factors can be put to the competition authorities for consideration.

There is a checklist of various sources of economic efficiencies. These are: *economies of scale* associated with producing goods and services at lower unit costs. These could be *plant specific*, which may entail more intensive use of existing machinery and equipment and/or *product specific*, resulting from longer production runs of a specific product. One problem frequently encountered in manufacturing is that firms produce multiple products using given machinery and equipment, and costs are incurred when production is switched from making one product to another. In a case relating to the manufacture of several types of bottles and jars for the brewing, wine, soft drink, and processed food industries, a merger between firms enabled different plants to specialise in specific types of bottles, reduce switching/re-tooling costs, and charge lower selling prices. Product-specific economies have also been identified in other merger cases relating to the manufacture of large and medium-sized power transmission equipment and steel products. Another source of efficiencies is *economies of scope*. These arise from the joint production or provision of complementary products. In a case involving an integrated financial services firm, it was found more economical to provide deposit taking, consumer loan, mortgage, and other services in one operation than if each of these services were being done by a less integrated firm. Economies of scope also arise in airline, trucking and other transport service industries – it is less costly to transport passengers on one flight from London to Montreal, and fly onwards to Chicago than having two separate flights to these destinations. However, if there is a significant volume of passengers through pooling arrangements and code sharing with other airlines, then *economies of density* can be attained to warrant separate flights. There can also arise economies of *capacity utilisation and/or capacity expansion*. In a recent beer merger case, it could be demonstrated that production in two under-utilised plants could be consolidated to yield significant efficiencies. In another matter relating to gypsum wallboard, the acquiring firm was operating at full capacity and had difficulties meeting customer demand while the target firm had non-utilised capacity. In this case, and another one relating to polyethylene manufacturing, there were also unexploited *transport cost savings* that were easily attained by post-merger rearranging of the product shipments made by plants in different locations. Then there are *synergies*, namely, when two firms have different competencies which when combined can lead to better market performance. The motivation for the acquisition of a software firm by a computer equipment manufacturer was that it facilitated joint marketing efforts. It also allowed for extending the firm's reputation and knowledge base. *Transaction costs and R&D* related efficiencies were mentioned before. The latter also relates to *dynamic efficiencies*, which pertain to product innovation, process technology, and quality improvements. Depending on the case, these sources of efficiencies can reduce costs, facilitate entry, expand existing markets or create markets for new products and services.

The majority of these efficiencies are quantifiable. Once the estimated cost savings have been arrived at, they can be used to quantify the extent (or lack thereof) of the competition effects that could arise from the merger. Arguments can be advanced on the *pass thru' rate* of cost savings and the extent to which these are likely to be passed on to customers – if not in terms of prices then in the form of improved services and quality. This information can also be used to allay concerns customers and competition regulators may raise, and put forward measures for entering into various undertakings should the transaction be allowed to proceed on a conditional basis.

3. Frequent business pitfalls

The point that merging parties often tend to exaggerate efficiencies was mentioned earlier. If doing this is based on the premise that the competition authorities are going to discount the claimed efficiencies anyway, then it is a bad business strategy. It runs the risk of losing credibility on even the efficiencies that may be legitimate.

The burden of presenting (or 'proving') efficiencies falls primarily on the acquiring firm. Even with *due diligence* on part of the transacting parties, there will be information gaps regarding the full nature of the operations of the target firm. This information asymmetry and the 'probable' nature of some of the efficiencies being claimed should be explicitly recognised. This cuts both ways – the claimed efficiencies can be understated or overstated, the former being better and more likely to be accepted by the competition authorities.

The claimed efficiencies and the lessening of competition or dominance are assessed in the relevant market in which the transaction is being reviewed. If competition concerns arise in the market for product 'A', the efficiencies being claimed must also relate to the production and sales of product 'A' in that market. Efficiencies relating to product 'B' are unrelated unless A and B are complements, there are economies of scope, production indivisibilities and other such factors, in which case certain efficiencies may need to be apportioned if there are no negative competition effects in the market for product 'B'. In instances of geographically segmented markets, efficiencies realised in geographical market 'X' are not likely to be acceptable and balanced against the negative competition effects in geographical market 'Y'. This results in depriving the benefits of competition to consumers in market Y where as those in market X may enjoy benefits from efficiency gains. It is better to avoid making such interpersonal or interregional comparisons and subjective value judgments.

Efficiency arguments are more likely to be accepted by regulators in declining or stable markets than in rapidly expanding markets – although the latter scenario is not necessarily ruled out. If markets are growing, competition authorities normally like to know why expansion cannot be attained by making new investments.

The timing of when the efficiencies will be realised matters. Regulators may accept some 'inter-temporal' lessening of competition if the claimed efficiencies are going to be realised in the not-too-distant future. Longer time frames may be accepted with certain behavioural commitments and if backed by industry-specific data indicating such factors as the gestation periods for plant and equipment to become efficiently operational.

The business and performance track record of one or both the merging firms matters. Claims of 'dynamic' efficiencies are not likely to be accepted if neither has been innovative, patented or has been a below average industry performer. Yet in merger filings businesses often advance dynamic efficiency claims.

4. Concluding remarks

The measurement and presentation of credible arguments that the efficiencies identified are indeed attainable should not be underestimated. Experience matters. It is advisable to engage appropriate economic experts to work alongside lawyers and corporate management early in the preparation of the merger brief. Generally speaking, empirical experience suggests that the acquiring firm management tends to be overly optimistic of the efficiencies to be realised, and competition regulators tend to be sceptical. A way to bridge this gap is to apply techniques that can be easily understood, quantify the efficiencies in terms of 'mini-max' estimates, and present 'worst case' or conservative post-merger scenarios. Also, draw on industry information sources, past experience, and where possible refer to similar transactions in other jurisdictions. A merger filing or brief presenting cogent efficiency arguments can, and should be used as an *affirmative defence or a statement on the objectives* of a proposed transaction. This is regardless of whether or not there exist official guidelines or provisions in competition law, which allow for efficiency arguments to be put forward. This is because it can better articulate the main reason for the merger (versus trying to acquire 'market power') and expedite the case review process There is a convergence in methods employed to assess mergers, even though laws and legal standards differ across countries. The use of quantitative and qualitative industrial organisation economic techniques can radically change the competition regulators' perspectives of the proposed merger transaction. It can become the key factor in their decision to allow the deal to go through.

16
Comments on the Role of Efficiencies in EC Merger Control

Claude Rakovsky and Vincent Verouden

Merger Task Force, European Commission, Brussels

In recent years, an important debate has taken place on the question of how to include efficiency considerations in EC merger control. It is a great pleasure for me to participate in this panel with such knowledgeable colleagues, some of whom have, in a very helpful way, contributed to this topic in response to the consultation launched by our Green Paper.

I would like to start out by making the observation that there appears to be widespread consensus among the panellists that there is a need to clarify the role of efficiency considerations in EU merger control. This reflects, with very few exceptions, the view of the respondents to the consultation on the Green Paper. I can only share this view: efficiency considerations are a natural part (although not the easiest) of a coherent economic appraisal of mergers. As such, it is appropriate that the Commission should look both at the creation of market power as a result of a proposed merger and at the possible efficiencies that mergers can bring about.

When I say that it is desirable to deal more explicitly, and more clearly, with efficiency claims in EU merger review, this evokes the question: why wasn't the Commission doing this before? One might think perhaps that legal constraints were in the way of doing so, but in my view this is not the case. The current wording of the European Merger Regulation (ECMR) does allow for an explicit treatment of efficiencies into EU merger control. Indeed, it appears to be legally possible to introduce an explicit treatment of efficiencies into EU merger control without changing the substantive test or even the present wording of the Merger Regulation. This view was also shared by many respondents to the Green Paper. Article 2(1)(b) of the ECMR provides a legal basis by stating that the Commission shall take account, among other things, of 'the development of technical and economic progress provided it is to consumers' advantage and does not form an obstacle to competition'. The Commission could therefore already consider efficiency claims by the parties under the notion of technical and economic progress and take them into account if they fulfil the two conditions set out in this provision.

I would say that the answer to the question why the European Commission will be taking efficiencies into account more explicitly in the future than it has done in the past is that it is a natural development of our practice. And this is so in two respects.

First, one should not forget that the European Commission only became active in the field of merger control about 12 years ago. In the beginning, it was extremely important to convey the message that EU merger control was about a competition test, not some kind of broad industrial policy or public interest test. In this light, it may not be surprising that the Commission has been somewhat cautious to pay too much attention to efficiency claims. It is a consequence of the evolution of the European Commission as a competition authority reviewing mergers, that we have now reached a stage in which we are more confident that all people concerned understand what EU merger control is about and what it is not about. Furthermore, I believe it is fair to say that the Commission now has sufficient experience and know-how to make its merger review process gradually more sophisticated and to fine-tune it to specific merger cases involving efficiencies.

Secondly, I would say the current development is fully in line with the Commission's endeavour to enhance its economics-based analysis of mergers. The stronger focus on the actual impact that mergers are likely to have, in conjunction with the analysis of the structural factors of the market, naturally makes the case for explicitly considering the efficiencies that a merger can bring about more appropriate.

Some people say that the 'dominance language' used in Article 2 of the ECMR may not allow for efficiencies being taking into account as a defence or counterbalance to anti-competitive effects. With Jim Venit, I am of the view that this issue should not be outcome determinative.

On the face of it, there appear to be essentially two possible approaches, not necessarily exclusive from each other, as to the exact treatment of efficiency considerations brought forward by the parties under the current test of Article 2(3) of the ECMR.

Under a first approach, efficiencies are taken into account in order to assess whether or not the concentration would lead to the creation or the strengthening of a dominant position. In that perspective, pro-competitive efficiencies would be balanced with other elements indicative of a dominant position. For instance, efficiencies may lead to the conclusion that, in spite of the loss of a competitor, it is unlikely that a collective dominant position (featuring anticompetitive co-ordination post-merger) would be created or strengthened. This kind of approach has, to a greater or lesser extent, already been explored by the Commission, eg in *Airtours/First Choice* (para 146), where the Commission envisaged the possibility that, as a result of the synergies expected by the parties, their incentives to compete with the two remaining players on the market would be increased. This possibility was dismissed, however, as the Commission found that the cost savings would be too limited (and mainly related to overhead and other fixed costs) and that, as a consequence, they would not materially change the overall cost structure of the merged entity.

Under the second option, the parties could also rely on the efficiencies the merger is likely to bring about, in order to 'rebut' a finding of dominance. In other words, parties could demonstrate that their merger would produce efficiencies of such a magnitude that they would counteract the otherwise negative effect of a dominant position, which is to impede competition significantly. Many respondents to the consultation on the Green Paper shared the view that this interpretation of Article 2(3) as a 'two-fold test' should be applied in order to take account of efficiencies as a mitigating factor to dominance.

This legal debate should, however, not be outcome determinative. Some efficiencies would arguably lead us to conclude that a dominant position would not be created or strengthened, others would allow us to conclude that they would counteract the otherwise negative effect of a dominant position, which is to impede competition significantly. The factors that will lead us to these conclusions will, in most cases, be overlapping.

Let me now turn to points of substance. It is clear that the choice as to what type of efficiency claims would be recognised, depends to a large extent on the precise objective of merger control, in other words, on the welfare test to be applied. As we have seen in the preceding papers, one commonly distinguishes between a 'total welfare' standard and a 'consumer welfare' standard, and variants lying in-between.

The choice of welfare standard affects how often an efficiency rebuttal can be expected to be used. Under a total welfare standard, cost savings can lead to an increase in producers' surplus that outweighs a reduction in consumers' surplus. Consequently, efficiencies could be invoked even to justify mergers that will result in negative consequences for consumer choice, service and price (see eg the famous Canadian *Propane* case). By contrast, the consumer welfare standard normally requires relatively large cost savings or other, more dynamic, efficiencies in order to counteract the increase in market power that is brought about by the creation or strengthening of a dominant position. If one looks at the US experience (at least as far as the litigated cases are concerned – the ones we know most about), the consumer welfare standard would limit the number of cases where such an efficiency rebuttal can be successfully recognised. It would imply that a 'consumer pass-on', like a price decrease or some sort of innovation, is one of the requirements for allowing efficiencies to be taken into account.

In my view, the consumer welfare standard would seem to be consistent with the legal wording of Article 2(1)(b) of the ECMR, which explicitly refers to 'the interests of intermediate and ultimate consumers' and to the condition that technological and economic progress must be to the 'consumers' advantage' in order to be taken into account. Furthermore, it would also be consistent with the assumption that EC competition law aims at promoting consumer welfare, as is also expressed in Article 81(3) which makes exemptions subject to the condition that consumers receive a 'fair share of the resulting benefit'. In this respect, it would appear that efficiencies have to benefit consumers, in principle in the relevant markets where a dominant position is likely to be created or strengthened. A question which is relevant in this respect is: should we go further and, in exceptional cases, also consider efficiencies in other relevant markets? This might seem inconsistent with our current practice. For example, the Commission never trades off pro-competitive effects in the United Kingdom with anti-competitive effects in the Netherlands. It would make sense, however, where for instance products are complementary and where efficiencies would, therefore, benefit the same group of consumers.

Apart from the requirement that efficiencies should be substantial enough, in the end, to benefit consumers, one also has to consider incorporating other elements for an efficiency defence to be operational. Here I come to the usual requirements that efficiencies should be merger-specific, timely and verifiable before they can be taken into account.

Merger specificity of efficiencies means that these efficiencies should come as a direct result of the merger and that they could not be effectively achieved through other means. Such a requirement would constitute a safeguard to avoid unnecessary anti-competitive effects and would be consistent with the general Community law principle of proportionality.

Secondly, it seems important to me that efficiencies materialise in a timely way. The longer efficiencies are projected into the future, the less weight the Commission can assign to the efficiencies being brought about.

Thirdly, and this is obviously an essential point (and probably the most difficult), efficiencies have to be verifiable so that the Commission can be reasonably certain that the efficiencies are indeed likely to materialise. In this respect, a choice has to be made on the required standard of proof as regards the efficiencies claimed by the parties. Most of the relevant information, which could allow the Commission to assess whether the merger will bring about the sort of efficiencies allowing a merger to be cleared, is uniquely in the possession of the merging parties. It would make sense, therefore, to make it incumbent on the notifying parties to provide the relevant information necessary to demonstrate that the efficiencies are merger specific, substantial, timely, and verifiable. Similarly, it would seem natural that it is for the notifying parties to provide evidence as to why the efficiencies will counteract the adverse effects on competition that might otherwise result from the merger. This is all the more important since the Commission, whether it accepts or rejects efficiency claims, will have to reason its decisions, decisions that can be appealed by the merging parties, as well as by third parties.

Before inviting my colleagues to react, if they so wish, on these particular aspects, I would finally like to put forward a last point about timing and procedure. For example, up to what point in the procedure would it make sense to be willing to accept the submission of efficiency claims? To me it is obvious that efficiency claims should preferably be made early in the process and certainly not at a stage where it is no longer possible for the Commission to have a reasonably careful look at them. Moreover, consideration of efficiencies might help competition enforcers to understand more effectively the rationale of the merger and to assess more accurately the impact on market power. The earlier competition enforcers start looking at efficiencies, the better.

Most of the views I have just developed are reflected, in a more systematic and elaborated way, in the draft notice on horizontal mergers that we are about to publish for consultation. I would, therefore, be most interested to hear from the other panellists, and from all of you, your first reactions on these very complex but stimulating matters.

17
The Role of Efficiency Considerations in Merger Control: What We Do in the United States

Michael L Katz*

Deputy Assistant Attorney General for Economic Analysis, US Department of Justice, Washington, DC

1. Introduction

This paper addresses two questions. The first, posed by the title of the conference session, asks: what is the proper role of efficiency considerations in merger control? The answer is that substantiated projections of merger-specific efficiencies should be factored into an integrated analysis of the likely welfare effects of a merger. The second question, posed by the session moderator, asks: what do you do in the United States? Ideally, one could answer this second question simply by replacing 'should be' with 'are' in the answer to the first question. The United States comes close, but there are some differences between reality and the ideal.

One can summarise the US treatment of merger efficiencies as follows:

- *There is an 'efficiencies defence'.* However, it is not based on economic efficiency, and it is not a defence. 'Efficiencies' is a misnomer because the antitrust calculus is based on certain categories of cost reduction rather than on changes in economic welfare. 'Defence' is a misnomer in the sense that efficiencies cannot be used to trump a conclusion that a proposed merger would lessen competition.[1] Instead, efficiencies are one factor that can be used to rebut the government's *prima facie* case that the increase in

* This paper does not draw on any confidential materials or information. The author would like to thank Andrew Dick, Edward Eliasberg, and Gloria Jenkins for helpful comments and assistance. The views expressed are those of the author and do not necessarily represent the views of those just thanked or the US Department of Justice. This paper is based on remarks delivered at the European Commission Directorate General for Competition's 'EC Merger Control Conference', 8 November 2002.

1 The Supreme Court stated: 'a merger the effect of which "may be to substantially lessen competition" is not saved because, on some ultimate reckoning of social or economic debits and credits, it may be deemed beneficial. A value choice of such magnitude is beyond the ordinary limits of judicial competence, and in any event has been made for us already, by Congress': *United States v Philadelphia Nat'l Bank*, 374 US 321, 371 (1963). And in *Federal Trade Comm'n v Procter & Gamble Co*, the Supreme Court stated: 'Possible economies cannot be used as a defense to illegality. Congress was aware that some mergers which [sic] lessen competition may also result in economies but it struck the balance in favor of protecting competition.' *Federal Trade Comm'n v Procter & Gamble Co*, 386 US 568, 580 (1967).

concentration resulting from the proposed merger would lessen competition.[2]

- *Efficiencies are assessed within an integrated framework.* The Antitrust Division of the US Department of Justice (the 'Division') assesses 'efficiencies' in a framework that integrates the analysis of changes in market power and cost levels to predict the net effects of a merger. This approach is consistent with both sound economics and the fact that efficiencies are not a defence against a finding that a proposed merger would lessen competition.
- *There is no 'efficiencies offence'.* Although economic theory can identify situations in which cost reductions are harmful to consumer welfare and economic efficiency, the Division and the Federal Trade Commission (FTC) proceed with extreme caution before using these theories as the basis of opposing a cost-reducing merger. A reduction in marginal costs triggered by a merger is almost always counted as a benefit, not harm, from a merger.
- *Most mergers get credit for creating efficiencies.* This is so even though merging parties often do little to substantiate their claims regarding projected cost savings from proposed mergers.

Below, I expand on these points.

2. We look at consumer surplus (sort of)

In the United States, mergers today are generally evaluated under a consumer-welfare standard. For example, the Division and FTC's *Horizontal Merger Guidelines* state:

> 'The Agency will not challenge a merger if cognizable efficiencies are of a character and magnitude such that the merger is not likely to be anticompetitive in any relevant market. To make the requisite determination, the Agency considers whether cognizable efficiencies likely would be sufficient to reverse the merger's potential to harm consumers in the relevant market, e.g., by preventing price increases in that market. [Internal footnote omitted.]'[3]

There are strong legal and political arguments for applying a consumer-welfare standard to merger evaluation. However, such a standard does not conform to an economic efficiency standard. As long as the income effects associated with a

2 That is, some federal district and appellate courts have recognised efficiencies as a 'defence' against the government's *prima facie* case: 'whether an acquisition would yield significant efficiencies in the relevant market is an important consideration in predicting whether the acquisition would substantially lessen competition. ... [T]herefore, ... an efficiency defense to the government's *prima facie* case in section 7 challenges is appropriate in certain circumstances.' *Federal Trade Comm'n v Staples, Inc*, 970 F Supp 1066, 1088 (DDC 1997) quoting *Federal Trade Comm'n v University Health, Inc*, 938 F 2d 1206, 1222 (11th Cir 1991). See also *United States v Rockford Mem Corp*, 717 F Supp 1251, 1288-92 (ND Ill 1989), *aff'd*, 898 F 2d 1278 (7th Cir 1990), *cert denied*, 498 US 920 (1990).

3 US Dep't of Justice & Federal Trade Comm'n, *Horizontal Merger Guidelines* (rev ed 1997) ('*Merger Guidelines*'), § 4, available at http://www.usdoj.gov/atr/public/guidelines/horiz_book/hmg1.html. This quotation also illustrates that efficiencies are incorporated into the analysis of whether a merger will have anti-competitive effects, as opposed to being a distinct factor that is weighed against anti-competitive effects.

merger are sufficiently small and antitrust policy is not intended as a means of income redistribution, an economic efficiency standard would focus on a proposed merger's projected effects on total surplus, the sum of consumer surplus and producer surplus.[4] Under a consumer-welfare standard, efficiencies count only to the extent that they affect the quality-adjusted prices paid by consumers. Under a total-surplus standard, even cost savings that were not passed on to consumers would count as benefits. And under such a standard, pure monetary transfers between the firm and consumers would be excluded from the decision calculus.[5] For these reasons, the evaluation of 'merger efficiencies' typically is not about economic efficiency. Instead, there is a focus on changes in marginal or incremental costs, as these are most likely to affect the pricing and output decisions of a profit-maximising firm.

The choice of welfare standard is above my pay grade, so I will confine my remarks to several observations concerning how the consumer-welfare standard is applied in the United States. First, the Division and the FTC do not focus solely on short-run price effects. For one thing, they also consider long-run price effects.[6] Consideration of long-run effects makes it necessary to think carefully about what constitutes a marginal or incremental cost. As the supplier's decision horizon lengthens, more decisions become variable and fewer remain fixed. For example, a merger might combine assets that allow the post-merger firm to lower the fixed costs of operating a production facility. In the short run, these cost reductions might have no effect on pricing. But in the long run, they would be relevant to the decision of how many plants to operate and thus could affect prices and production quantities. In addition to short- and long-run price effects, the agencies also recognise that merger-induced efficiencies can give rise to positive non-price effects, such as increased product quality or additional innovation.[7]

My second observation concerns monopsony power. Under US merger policy, monopsony considerations tend to come to the fore in agricultural markets (eg effects of food processor mergers on the prices paid to farmers) and medical

4 For the classic analysis, see Oliver E Williamson, 'Economies as an Antitrust Defense: The Welfare Tradeoffs' (1968) 58 Amer Econ Rev 18.

5 Suppose, for example, that a proposed merger would raise the price by $10 per unit and that post-merger sales would remain at 1 million units. The additional payment of $10 million resulting from the merger would be pure transfer from consumers to suppliers. Under a total-surplus standard, there would be no net effect: the loss to consumers would exactly offset the gain to suppliers.

6 Footnote 37 of the *Merger Guidelines* reads: 'The result of this analysis over the short term will determine the Agency's enforcement decision in most cases. The Agency also will consider the effects of cognizable efficiencies with no short-term, direct effect on prices in the relevant market. Delayed benefits from efficiencies (due to delay in the achievement of, or the realization of consumer benefits from, the efficiencies) will be given less weight because they are less proximate and more difficult to predict.'

7 I would argue that changes in equilibrium product quality and R&D levels are not themselves efficiencies. Rather they are the consequences of efficiencies that lead suppliers to change their competitive strategies. The importance of this distinction will become clear in the third section below.

industries (eg mergers' effects on fees paid to doctors by third-party payers).[8] Unfortunately, the treatment of monopsony power in the *Merger Guidelines* is neither clear nor sophisticated:

> 'Market power also encompasses the ability of a single buyer (a "monopsonist"), a coordinating group of buyers, or a single buyer, not a monopsonist, to depress the price paid for a product to a level that is below the competitive price and thereby depress output. The exercise of market power by buyers ("monopsony power") has adverse effects comparable to those associated with the exercise of market power by sellers.'[9]

Care must be taken in assessing the consumer-welfare effects of increased monopsony power. First, if the merging parties were considered to be the consumers, then any increase in monopsony power should be considered to be a benefit of the merger.[10] Suppose instead that one interprets the 'consumer' to be the final purchaser of goods and services provided by the merging parties. In some monopsony models, a buyer's recognition that it is not a price taker results in a marginal factor cost curve above the input price and thus results in an output reduction analogous to the standard monopoly output restriction. In these cases, the prices of final goods and services can be expected to increase as a result of the increased monopsony power. However, in other situations, a larger buyer may better be able to play suppliers off against one another, and thus an increase in monopsony power can raise the input quantities purchased at the same time that it lowers input prices. In these circumstances, output in the final market may rise and prices in that market fall. Thus, here too, increased monopsony power can be a benefit under a consumer-surplus standard. In short, the *Merger Guidelines* focus on price rather than on marginal factor cost and quantity is misplaced.

My next observation and the one following both arise from confusion between the consumer-surplus standard and a total-surplus or efficiency standard. The first of these observations concerns the mistreatment of pecuniary cost savings and is related to the confusion surrounding the treatment of monopsony power. Suppose a merger is projected to lower input prices. Even if monopsony power is not raised as an objection to the merger, some might argue that the cost savings should be ignored on the grounds that they are 'pecuniary' rather than 'real' cost savings. As long as input quantities were not affected, such an argument would be correct *if* the welfare measure were *total* surplus. However, under a consumer-surplus

8 See, eg Complaint at 9 and Competitive Impact Statement at 7, *United States v Cargill, Inc and Consolidated Grain Co*, 199CV01875 (GK) (DDC 23 July 1999) available at http://www.usdoj.gov/atr/cases/f2500/2552.pdf and http://www.usdoj.gov/atr/cases/f2500/2584.pdf ('significant changes in concentration among grain trading companies can have an anticompetitive impact upon prices received by farmers and other suppliers') and Competitive Impact Statement at 12, *United States v Aetna Inc et al*, Civil Action No 3-99CV1398-H (ND Tex 16 July 1999) available at http://www.usdoj.gov/atr/cases/f2500/2571.pdf ('The proposed acquisition thus would give Aetna the ability to unduly depress physician reimbursement rates in Houston and Dallas, likely leading to a reduction in quantity or degradation in the quality of physicians' services').

9 *Merger Guidelines*, § 0.1.

10 This is another example of a difference between the consumer-welfare standard and an economic-efficiency standard.

measure, pecuniary savings count to the extent that they are passed on to consumers. Consider, for example, the acquisition of a small supplier by a much larger firm. The parties might claim that the larger firm had a lower cost of capital. To the extent that this lower cost of capital reflected transactions cost savings, the efficiencies would be real. But much of the reduction in the cost of capital might not be a cost saving at all. Instead it could be redistribution of risk to the existing equity and debt holders of the acquiring firm. Nonetheless, under a consumer-welfare standard, the lower cost of capital would still count as a benefit to the extent that it led to lower prices in the relevant market *and* was merger specific.[11]

My final observation is that half-hearted attempts to apply a total-surplus standard sometimes lead to misguided weightings of various factors. Specifically, it is sometimes suggested that fixed cost savings should be counted as an offset to harm to consumers, at least in cases where the harm to consumers is small. Apparently, this approach picks up on the fact that, under a total-surplus standard, efficiencies count whether or not passed through to consumers. However, this approach forgets that pure transfers between consumers and suppliers do not affect total surplus and thus would not count under a total-surplus standard. If one really meant to examine changes in total surplus, one would compare the cost savings with losses in allocative inefficiency (the so-called deadweight loss triangle, which depends on the change in purchase quantities due to the merger) and would ignore the pure transfer that equals the price change times the post-merger purchase quantity.

3. We conduct an integrated balancing test

In analysing the effects of merger costs savings on consumers, the Division conducts an integrated analysis. That is, a proposed merger's effects on the parties' costs are taken into account in projecting the merger's net competitive effects. Unfortunately, the *Merger Guidelines* are somewhat unclear on this point and can be read to suggest a different approach, under which one calculates the adverse competitive effects of a merger and then weighs these effects against the efficiency benefits:

> 'In conducting this analysis, the Agency will not simply compare the magnitude of the cognizable efficiencies with the magnitude of the likely harm to competition absent the efficiencies. The greater the potential adverse competitive effect of a merger ... the greater must be cognizable efficiencies in order for the Agency to conclude that the merger will not have an anticompetitive effect in the relevant market. When the potential adverse competitive effect of a merger is likely to be particularly large, extraordinarily great cognizable efficiencies would be necessary to prevent the merger from being anticompetitive. [Internal footnote omitted.]'[12]

11 One might also address whether the cost of capital would be driven up for the acquiring firm's other products.

12 *Merger Guidelines*, § 4.

While the Guidelines state that the agencies do not conduct a simple, one-for-one balancing, the language is still suggestive of a weighing of two separately calculated quantities.

The misimpression that one can weigh so-called efficiencies (ie cost savings passed on to consumers) against harm from increased market power is further created by the nature of federal court proceedings. In litigation, the government first attempts to establish a presumption that the challenged merger would be likely to harm competition. This presumption is largely established by showing that the merger would significantly increase concentration in one or more defined relevant antitrust markets. The defendants then attempt to rebut the presumption by pointing to evidence of significant efficiencies, easy entry, or other factors. Although this process has the superficial appearance of calculating competitive harms and then seeing if efficiencies outweigh the projected harms, the rebuttal stage, done correctly, is an integrated analysis.

It is important to conduct an integrated analysis because the separate-balancing approach can lead to misleading conclusions about consumer-welfare effects. This is so for several reasons. First, it makes little sense to compare the cost reduction due to merger-specific efficiencies with the predicted price change due to merger-induced changes in market power. At a minimum, one would want to compare the price effects of the cost changes with the price effects of the market power changes. The change in the price due to a cost reduction divided by the cost reduction is known as the *pass-through rate*.

Depending on the market structure and the nature of firm interaction, the pass-through rate may be smaller or larger than one. Suppose, for example, that the merger lowers a maverick's marginal costs and triggers a price war. Then even a small change in marginal cost might lead to a large change in the equilibrium price. In other models of oligopolistic interaction, a cost change might lead to a very low pass-through rate because the supplier did not want to upset the existing tacit agreement among producers. The theoretical possibility of a wide range of pass-through rates does not rely on coordinated interaction. It is a trivial exercise in economic theory to show that even a monopolist may change its equilibrium price by an amount greater than the cost reduction in some cases and less in others.

Although the economics are straight out of an introductory text, there continues to be confusion among some antitrust practitioners about this last point. Some people appear to believe that a supplier with market power will not pass through cost reductions in the form of lower quality-adjusted prices.[13] However, economic theory does not predict that a firm with more market power is likely to pass through less of the cost saving. Indeed, a perfectly competitive firm facing a highly elastic demand curve will pass through essentially none of its cost savings, while a monopolist typically will find it profitable to lower its price in response to a decline in marginal cost.[14]

13 See, eg *Federal Trade Comm'n v Tenet Healthcare Corp*, 17 F Supp 2d 937, 948 (ED Mo 1998), *rev'd on other grounds*, 186 F 3d 1045 (8th Cir 1999) ('the merged hospital is unlikely to pass these savings on to its consumers absent competitive pressure to lower prices').

14 See, eg Paul L Yde and Michael G Vita, 'Merger Efficiencies: Reconsidering the "Passing-On" Requirement' (1996) 64 Antitrust LJ 735, or virtually any microeconomics textbook.

The predicted pass-through rate will depend on the model of industry behaviour used to generate the prediction. The need for coherence dictates that the same analytical framework used to predict the effects of a change in market power should also be used to predict the effects of a cost change. To do otherwise runs the risk of making predictions about the effects of cost changes and the effects of market power changes that are inconsistent with one another. The common analytical framework can be a broad conceptual scheme used to undertake a coordinated effects analysis, a formal merger simulation conducted as part of a unilateral effects analysis, or the identification of critical values of key parameters coupled with qualitative evidence about the values of those parameters.[15] In all cases, it is essential to tie the analysis to a careful look at the facts of the market.

A second problem with making separate determinations of efficiencies and competitive effects is that a small change in cost can lead to a large change in consumer welfare. This relationship arises when a small cost change tips the balance in favour of a supplier's undertaking a discrete investment that generates a large amount of consumer surplus. For instance, the parties to the proposed EchoStar/DirecTV merger argued that the merger would allow them to provide an array of services that they would not otherwise offer.[16] In principle, the consumer surplus generated by these new services could have exceeded the merger-specific reduction in the costs of offering these services.[17] In general, the same relationship could hold for efficiencies that made it profitable for a firm to engage in greater innovation post merger. Again, the analysis of efficiency effects should be conducted within the overall framework used to predict the net competitive effects of the merger.

4. We do not have an efficiencies offence

In the United States, the role of economics in antitrust enforcement generally, and merger control specifically, has steadily increased over the last four decades.[18] In the bad old days of the 1960s and 1970s, antitrust enforcement was often based

15 For an example of the last approach, see Gregory J Werden, 'A Robust Test for Consumer Welfare Enhancing Mergers Among Sellers of Differentiated Products' (1996) 46 J of Industrial Economics 409.

16 See, eg Consolidated Application for Authority to Transfer Control, EchoStar Communications Corp *et al*, Federal Communications Comm'n (December 2001), available at http://www.fcc.gov/transaction/echostar-directv/echostarappli.pdf.

17 This matter is offered only as an illustration of possible outcomes. I am offering no opinion as to the validity of any efficiency claims made by the parties. The Division announced its intention to challenge the proposed merger (Press Release, US Department of Justice, Justice Department Files Suit to Block EchoStar's Acquisition of Hughes Electronics (31 October 2002), available at http://www.usdoj.gov/atr/public/press_releases/2002/200412.pdf), and the parties abandoned it (Press Release, EchoStar Communications Corp, EchoStar and Hughes Terminate Proposed Merger Agreement; EchoStar pays Hughes $600 million; Hughes to Keep PanAmSat Interest (10 December 2002), available at http://www.corporate-ir.net/ireye/ir_site.zhtml?ticker=dish&script=410&layout=-6&item_id=362779).

18 For an insightful history of the Division's treatment of merger efficiencies see William J Kolasky and Andrew R Dick, *The Merger Guidelines and the Integration of Efficiencies into Antitrust Review of Horizontal Mergers* (10 June 2002), available at http://www.usdoj.gov/atr/hmerger/11254.pdf.

more on attorneys' intuitions than on economic analysis. Antitrust enforcers treated big as automatically bad, and anything that strengthened a dominant firm – including a merger that increased production efficiency – was highly suspect.[19] One could fairly state that the United States had an efficiencies offence. The rise of the use of economic analysis in the assessment of mergers led to a great improvement in enforcement policies. Cost reductions were recognised as generating beneficial effects, and both the antitrust enforcement agencies and the courts recognised that mergers and other practices could strengthen competition even if some competitors were harmed in the process.[20] However, in some ways the continuing development of economic theory has outstripped our ability to apply it.

Today it is relatively easy to construct a theoretical model in which cost reductions reduce welfare. A bedrock principle of American antitrust policy is that it is intended to protect competition not competitors.[21] Because it is so good at identifying market failures and strategic misbehaviour, modern economic theory runs the danger of being abused by a competitor who wants to portray a merger by other firms that harms its profitability as a threat to competition. Moreover, it can be extremely difficult reliably to predict this type of harm even after a detailed investigation of market conditions. For instance, for those theories of harm that entail driving the merging parties' rival suppliers from the market, it may be very difficult to predict the range of counter-strategies available to these rivals, such as mergers of their own or significant increases in R&D to re-establish their market positions. Further, enforcement authorities would have to balance the projected post-exit harms against the projected consumer gains that would arise during any period in which the merged firm enjoyed the efficiencies and its rivals were still viable competitors.

Given the importance of innovation and productivity improvements to the long-term level of economic welfare, policy makers should be extremely cautious about either blocking the realisation of efficiency benefits or of threatening to do so and thus undermining investment incentives. Even if firms are eventually allowed to merge, detailed investigations impose a tax on mergers, including potentially large costs of delay. Moreover, the mergers about which rivals are most likely to complain to antitrust enforcers are those mergers most likely to generate efficiency benefits for society.

19 In *Brown Shoe* the Supreme Court opined that Congress was willing to sacrifice efficiency to preserve small businesses and thus the fact that a merger would make a large, national firm a more effective competitor was a harm from the merger: *Brown Shoe Co v United States,* 370 US 294, 344 (1962). In *Procter & Gamble,* the Supreme Court also considered lower costs to pose a threat to competition: *Federal Trade Comm'n v Procter & Gamble Co,* 386 US 568, 578-79 (1967).

20 See, eg *Spectrum Sports, Inc v McQuillan,* 506 US 447, 458 (1993) for a statement in a non-merger case.

21 Of course, the definition of 'competition' is subject to interpretation. In *Brown Shoe,* the Supreme Court stated that 'It is competition, not competitors, which [*sic*] the [Clayton] Act protects': *Brown Shoe Co v United States,* 370 US 294, 344 (1962). Yet the Court objected to the merger in part on the grounds that the resulting efficiencies would make the merging parties a more effective national competitor. The majority rationalised their view by asserting that 'we cannot fail to recognize Congress' desire to promote competition through the protection of viable, small, locally owned business'. *Id.*

The US antitrust enforcement agencies have reacted to this situation by:

- Ignoring the fact that a cost-reducing merger of two small firms can: (a) lower productive efficiency and total surplus by increasing the merging parties' market share[22]; and (b) harm consumers by making it unprofitable for a dominant firm to undertake significant new investments in a new plant or better products and technologies.[23]
- Not considering the strengthening of a dominant firm's competitive advantage in itself to be objectionable.
- Recognising that a merger that lowers the costs of an already dominant firm can facilitate predatory strategies or even non-predatory exit-inducing behaviour,[24] but attacking that behaviour separately *if* it occurs and is illegal.[25]
- Recognising that lower costs can facilitate oligopolistic coordination, but trying to deal with such problems in ways that allow the realisation of efficiencies. In a recent merger investigation, the Division concluded that variation in cost structures among the major competitors was an obstacle to coordination and that the acquisition under scrutiny would more closely align those cost structures and thus increase the likelihood that coordination would successfully raise prices and restrict output.[26] This conclusion runs the danger of sounding like a reincarnation of an American efficiencies offence.[27] However, in stark contrast to the bad old days, the Division recognised the potential cost savings due to vertical integration as a benefit and structured a remedy to allow the realisation of these cost savings while addressing the competitive concerns.[28]

22 This effect can arise when the cost reduction shifts share to the merging parties but their costs remain higher than those of their rivals. See, eg Michael L Katz and Carl Shapiro, 'On the Licensing of Innovations' (1985) 16 Rand J of Economics 504.

23 Consider the following theoretically possible, but rather unlikely, scenario. There is a dominant firm with a large, old plant that is deteriorating. The firm is choosing whether to build a new plant. The merger of two smaller firms would increase their capacity and thus depress the profitability of the dominant firm's possible new plant. As a result of the merger, the currently dominant firm chooses not to construct the new plant and exits the business as its old plant reaches the end of its economic life, leaving the two small firms as monopolists.

24 The basic logic is that if one firm becomes more efficient, it may increase its market share to such a degree that rival suppliers no longer find it profitable to make the R&D or facility investments necessary to continue competing. Once these rivals have dropped out, or are limping along, the more efficient firm will be able to raise its prices.

25 This discussion cannot help but bring to mind the sharply diverging approaches that the Division and European Commission took with respect to General Electric Company's attempted merger with Honeywell International Inc. Fortunately, this experience has strengthened and improved the relationship between the two agencies, rather than weakened it as one might have feared.

26 *Competitive Impact Statement at 9, United States v Premdor, Inc et al,* Civil No 01-01696 (DDC 3 August 2001), available at http://www.usdoj.gov/atr/cases/f9000/9017.htm.

27 In *Procter & Gamble,* for example, the court relied in part on the theory that, by lowering the dominant supplier's costs, the proposed acquisition would facilitate increased coordination through price leadership: *Federal Trade Comm'n v Procter & Gamble Co,* 386 US 568, 578 (1967).

28 *Proposed Final Judgment, United States v Premdor, Inc et al,* No 01-01696 (DDC 3 August 2001), available at http://www.usdoj.gov/atr/cases/f8900/8908.pdf.

- Generally ignoring the possibility that a fall in costs could lower consumer welfare by making it profitable for a supplier to undertake actions that allow it to extract a larger percentage of gross consumption benefits for itself and thus lower consumer surplus, say by facilitating price discrimination.

In summary, the US approach to potential harms from efficiencies is as follows. First, it is not considered a harm that competitors' profits may fall because they compete with a more efficient firm once the merger is consummated. Secondly, we are very cautious about applying complex theories of harm to block a merger. Thirdly, if a problem is identified, then to the extent possible we impose remedies that offset any potential problem while allowing the merger to be consummated and the efficiencies realised. Finally, if there is a concern for potential problems, we look for policy approaches that treat them *ex post*. Even though merger policy tends to be proactive, this is an area where watch and wait is a more prudent approach.

5. We have merging parties that often have trouble substantiating their claims

Parties often encounter difficulties making credible claims of efficiencies both before the enforcement agencies and before the courts.[29] 'The majority of courts have considered efficiencies as a means to rebut the government's *prima facie* case that a merger will lead to restricted output or increased prices. These courts, however, generally have found inadequate proof of efficiencies to sustain a rebuttal of the government's case.'[30] Indeed, in appearances before antitrust enforcement agencies, many parties do not even try to claim efficiencies. In part this situation arises because credibly projecting efficiencies is an inherently difficult exercise: it involves potentially complex predictions, and our understanding of the theory of the firm and why mergers should affect costs is still limited.[31] And in part it arises because corporate executives may think more in terms of sweeping 'strategic

29 See, eg *Federal Trade Comm'n v University Health, Inc*, 938 F 2d 1206, 1223-24 (11th Cir 1991), *Federal Trade Comm'n v Staples, Inc*, 970 F Supp 1066, 1089-90 (DDC 1997), and *Federal Trade Comm'n v H J Heinz Co*, 246 F 3d 708, 721-24 (DC Cir 2001).

30 ABA Antitrust Section, *Mergers and Acquisitions: Understanding the Antitrust Issues* (2000), 152, as quoted by *Federal Trade Comm'n v H J Heinz Co*, n 29 above, at 720.

31 In the bad old days, the Division took the view that economies of scale from increased size were the only possible source of efficiency gains and that size generally could be achieved through internal expansion. US Department of Justice, 1968 *Merger Guidelines* at 8 (1968) available at http://www.usdoj.gov/atr/hmerger/11247.pdf. However, at least since 1937, a fundamental point of the transactions cost theory of the firm has been that bringing more functions within a single firm can enhance efficiency when it is less costly to organise the transactions involved within the firm than through open market exchanges. See Ronald Coase, 'The Nature of the Firm' (1937) 4 *Economica* 386, reprinted in Ronald H Coase, *The Firm, the Market, and the Law* (1988). ('A firm will tend to expand until the cost of organizing an extra transaction within the firm becomes equal to the cost of carrying out the same transaction by means of an exchange on the open market or the costs of organizing another firm.') Unfortunately, the extent to which and why the firm's boundaries matter still is very imperfectly understood. Moreover, developments in computing and communications technologies, as well management practice, are constantly changing the relationships between firms, their suppliers, and their customers.

visions' than in terms of cost savings or specific actions (eg the introduction of new products) that these cost savings can render profitable. Thus, there is often a lack of contemporaneous business documents indicating the parties planned to realise efficiencies from their proposed merger.

Although the problem will remain difficult, I can offer a few suggestions in the form of dos and don'ts:

- *Don't create ex post rationalisations.* That is, don't have executives or outside counsel and consultants claim efficiencies that were never considered by the executives when choosing to undertake the proposed merger. Although it is logically possible for a merger to have large efficiency effects that the executives failed to consider when making their business decisions, such claims are likely to elicit sceptical reactions from enforcement agencies and courts alike.[32]
- *Do provide copies of contemporaneous business documents projecting efficiencies.* Ideally, the documents would include implementation plans for achieving these efficiencies.
- *Do analyse the effects of the merger on transactions costs.* Efficiencies derive from transactions costs savings.[33] In addition to relying on contemporaneous business documents, outside economic consultants can be used to: (a) identify incentive and information problems that arise with certain market transactions, and (b) explain how the proposed merger would reduce costs by bringing those transactions within a single firm.
- *Do document why transactions costs would be higher for non-merger alternatives.* It is particularly helpful for establishing that efficiencies are merger specific if one can show that alternatives to merging were seriously evaluated and found to be more costly or less effective.
- *Do point to experience in realising efficiencies, where possible.* Firms that make repeated acquisitions may be able to establish reputations for being accurate forecasters of efficiencies and/or for being successful at realising efficiencies. It may also be possible to point to other firms that have realised efficiencies similar to those projected in the merger under consideration. Of course, detailed data concerning other firms are very likely to be hard to obtain.

32 The efficiencies claims put forth by the defendants in *Federal Trade Comm'n v Staples* provide an instructive example of what can go wrong. In his opinion granting a preliminary injunction against the proposed merger, Judge Hogan declared that he did not find the defendants' efficiencies claims credible. The following are just some of the reasons he gave: 'First, the Court notes that the cost savings estimate of $4.947 billion over five years which was submitted to the Court exceeds by almost 500% the figures presented to the two Boards of Directors in September 1996, when the Boards approved the transaction. The cost savings claims submitted to the Court are also substantially greater than those represented in the defendants' Joint Proxy Statement/Prospectus "reflecting the best currently available estimate of management," and filed with the Securities and Exchange Commission on January 23, 1997, or referenced in the "fairness opinions" rendered by the defendants' investment bankers which are contained in the Proxy Statement.' *Federal Trade Comm'n v Staples, Inc*, 970 F Supp 1066, 1089 (DDC 1997).

33 Transactions costs savings could include the realisation of economies of scale when customer bases are meaningful assets or there are other specialised assets that have to be combined to achieve scale.

6. We give most mergers implicit credit

US antitrust enforcers credit mergers with potential efficiencies more often than is generally appreciated. The vast majority of mergers are not challenged by the antitrust agencies.[34] Yet, in the absence of efficiencies, most horizontal mergers can be expected to have (possibly very small) adverse consequences for competition and consumers. The agencies let these mergers go unchallenged based on some combination of the beliefs that: (a) many mergers give rise to at least some efficiency benefits (including improved managerial incentives due to the workings of the market for corporate control),[35] and (b) in the absence of a strong prediction of harm to competition and consumers, the government should not interfere with private transactions, even if they are motivated by managerial utility maximisation (eg empire building) rather than potential efficiencies.[36]

It is interesting to note that some prominent commentators believe that explicit consideration of efficiencies in merger control is a mistake because evaluating efficiency claims is beyond the competence of the judiciary and/or it creates additional discretion for potentially misguided antitrust enforcers.[37] Instead, these commentators would prefer that the enforcement agencies and the courts impose high thresholds for the degree of projected competitive harms (ignoring any efficiency effects) that would have to be met in order to challenge and block a merger.

7. We are beset with paradoxes

I will close with the observation that, at least according to various attorneys and economists who come before the antitrust enforcement agencies representing parties to proposed mergers, the United States economy is beset with paradoxes. Because time is short, I will offer only a few:

- Market power is not a threat to consumers because even a monopolist passes through cost savings, yet the fact that a client has lowered its price proves it cannot have market power.

34 For example, in 2001, the Division received 2,376 Hart-Scott-Rodino Pre-merger Notifications and opened Preliminary Investigations in response to only 106 of them, or 4.5 per cent. Fewer than half of the Preliminary Investigations advanced to Second Requests, and there were only seven merger case filings. US Dep't of Justice, *Antitrust Division Workload Statistics FY 1992-2001*, available at http://www.usdoj.gov/atr/public/10108.pdf.

35 Another indication that antitrust policy broadly recognises the potential for mergers to create efficiencies is that mergers are subject to a rule-of-reason standard, while price-fixing is *per se* illegal.

36 In contrast, the well-known business strategist Michael Porter has suggested that antitrust enforcers take a sceptical approach to mergers on the grounds that they often serve managerial rather than shareholder interests and that efficiencies, particularly dynamic efficiencies, often fail to be realised. See, eg Michael E Porter, *Competition and Antitrust: A Productivity-Based Approach* (rev May 2002), § IV.1, unpublished draft, available at http://www.isc.hbs.edu/053002antitrust.pdf. An earlier version of this essay was published in *Antitrust Bulletin*, Winter 2001.

37 See, eg Robert Bork, *The Antitrust Paradox: A Policy at War with Itself* (1979) at 124-29. For a recent expression of this viewpoint in the context of the European Commission, see Kai-Uwe Kuhn, *Reforming European Merger Review: Targeting Problem Areas in Policy Outcomes* (2002) at 31-35 available at http://www.law.umich.edu/centersandprograms/olin/abstracts/discussionpapers/2002/KUKuhn%2002012.pdf.

- A client's fixed cost savings will be passed on to consumers through increased investment yet a merger that harms a rival's cash flow should not be considered to weaken competition.
- A client's proposed merger can be vital to maintaining the parties' competitive viability at the same time that the loss of an independent competitor poses no threat to competition because entry is easy – anyone can readily purchase or develop the needed assets on their own.
- A client's merger can create efficiencies because rivals will not transact with one another even when there are big gains from trade, yet vertical foreclosure is not a threat because even rivals will transact with one another when there are gains from trade.
- Partial ownership by a client will lead to significant efficiencies and competitive benefits, but there is no reason to be concerned about harm to competition because the partial ownership interest will have no effect on decision-making at either firm.

Notwithstanding these paradoxes, the United States has made tremendous strides in taking efficiencies into account in evaluating the competitive effects of mergers. However, much work remains to be done by the antitrust enforcement agencies, the courts, and the attorneys and economists who represent merging parties.

18

Some Thoughts on the Role of Efficiencies in Merger Control

Nadia Calviño

Deputy Director General, Spanish Competition Authority, Madrid

The main objective of this paper is to elaborate on the extremely short presentation made in the EC Merger Control Conference which took place in Brussels in November 2002.

Following the structure of the above-mentioned presentation, this paper puts forward some very basic questions on the role of efficiencies for merger control in order to conclude with two or three clear ideas which could be useful for policy making in this area. Finally, the paper includes a short appendix on the treatment of efficiencies under Spanish law.

WHY DO MERGERS TAKE PLACE ?

- **Economies of Scale**
- **Economies of Scope**
- **Transactional Efficiencies**
- **Dynamic Efficiencies**
- **Financial Efficiency** → **- Investment**, **- Synergies**, **- Diversification**

The main objective of mergers is their potential to generate efficiencies

1. Efficiencies as the objective of mergers

The choice by a firm of taking over or merging with another is clearly an investment decision. As such, it is usually based on an economic rationale. Although some other aspects of a personal or strategic nature which are difficult to formulate can also play a part, virtually all mergers are put forward to the Board and to competition authorities because they will increase the market value of the firm not only because of its bigger size but also because it will enable the generation of synergies or the increase of productive efficiency.

This economic rationale can be illustrated by the very attractive idea that one plus one is more than two. Synergies or increased efficiency are generated from various sources which can be classified in the following groups.

1.1 Economies of scale

These economies are related to the idea that average production cost decreases the bigger the number of units of a certain good or service produced. The reduction of the average production cost can be easily explained by the indivisibility of certain inputs, such as management or marketing or fixed assets.

From a purely theoretical point of view, there would be an optimum production size which would minimise long run average costs, thus liberating resources which could be invested in new methods or new products and so lead to economic and social progress.

These efficiencies usually underlie horizontal mergers and lead to an increase in the market share of the acquiring party and on the concentration ratio of the market.

1.2 Economies of scope

These economies are linked to the idea that average costs can diminish by the joint production of different goods or services, because of sharing inputs such as the distribution network, marketing, commodities, and so on. Therefore, they can explain mergers of firms operating in different product markets or offering different brands of the same sort of product.

1.3 Transactional economies

The main idea underlying these economies is that going to the market is expensive. Establishing the sort of relations needed for enjoying a stable environment for business can be very costly in terms of money, time or risk covering. Therefore, the integration in the same group of subsequent phases of production can lead to a lower cost.

These efficiencies are usually linked with vertical mergers.

1.4 Dynamic efficiency

A different source of efficiency is of a dynamic nature and calls to the idea that market processes that favour innovation can lead to a reduction of costs and the increase of the quality or quantity of output in the long run.

Although the question of which market structure favours innovation the most is not at all closed, in the field of mergers this dynamic efficiency is often linked to the productive efficiency of the merged company liberating financial resources that can be devoted to R&D.

1.5 Financial efficiency

The decision to acquire a firm can simply respond to the need to invest financial resources in a productive way, or to diversify the portfolio of activities of a firm. This last idea of diversification explains conglomerate mergers and the rise of 'multi-utilities firms' in the last years. Financial synergies can also be based on the presumption that the merged entity will be bigger and thus have a cheaper access to capital markets.

Efficiencies can also be of a financial nature when the economic resources of a big firm are invested in the production or marketing a product which has been developed by a small competitor which will on its own not be able to reach the global market.

1.6 Other efficiencies

Sometimes mergers are based on the idea that the management of the target firm is not effective and thus its performance will improve after the takeover. The rationale is therefore the removal of inefficiencies and has a clear link with the 'failing company' defence.

GRAPH 1: SHOULD EFFICIENCIES BE CONSIDERED?

☆ **Productive Efficiency**

☆ **Dynamic Efficiency**

☆ **Allocative Efficiency**

Williamson's trade off model

A merger will only have a negative allocative effect if the <u>net</u> reduction in consumer surplus derived from increased market power exceeds the real economies generated.

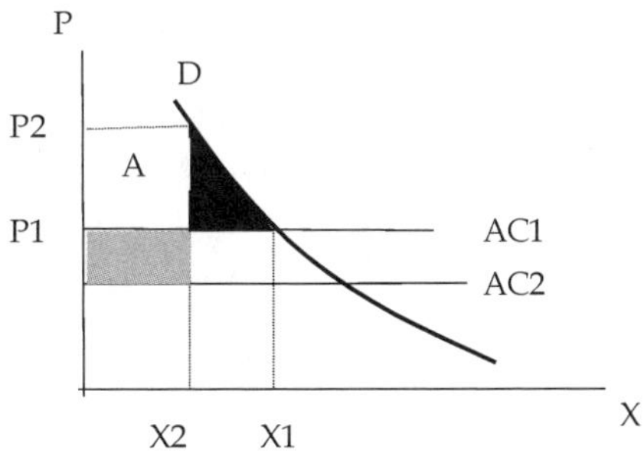

2. Efficiencies from the point of view of economic theory

Mergers can lead to two sorts of efficiencies which are considered in one way or the other under the neoclassic welfare theory.

2.1 Productive efficiency

The main underlying economic concepts could be intuitively explained by the idea that productive inputs can be assigned in an optimal way so that it is not possible simultaneously to increase the output of two alternative goods.

Therefore there is an optimal production size which leads to equilibrium: the minimal cost for a given output or alternatively the maximum output for a given cost. Naturally, the broader the market the bigger the optimal size.

Growth can be achieved either through internal development or by the acquisition of other firms. It is then easy to conclude that transnational mergers are the logical answer to an increasingly global market and that there might be some markets, which are called natural monopolies, where the optimal plant size will lead to a stable equilibrium of only one operator. This productive efficiency can have the different sources which have been mentioned before and is usually linked with scale, scope or transactional economies.

2.2 Allocative efficiency

Productive or dynamic efficiencies usually result in a cost reduction that increases profitability of the firm. Nevertheless, these internal benefits must be related to the final effect on social welfare.

The main objective of welfare economics is to look for the optimal allocation of resources within society; that is, which will maximise not only output but also utility or welfare as a whole.

Although many have been the theoretical and practical developments of this sort of analysis since Williamson produced his simple model in 1969, it is still a very useful tool for analysing this broad approach to allocative efficiencies.[1]

Graph 1 shows the effect of a merger which generates productive efficiency shown by average cost reduction (AC1 to AC2) and leads to a lessening of competition shown by the reinforcement of market power of the firm and the subsequent reduction in output (X1 to X2) and price increase (P1 to P2). Net cost reduction is shown by the grey rectangle. The consumer welfare loss derived from the lessening of competition is shown by total consumer surplus reduction, the area including the black triangle and square A. Nevertheless, square A also represents the profit increase for the firm and is therefore a transfer of wealth from consumers to the merged company which has a zero effect on total welfare. The net welfare loss would then be the black triangle and efficiency gains would offset the lessening of competition as long as the grey rectangle exceeds the black triangle, that is:

$$[(AC1 - AC2) * X2] - [1/2\ (P2 - P1)\ (X1 - X2)] > 0$$

The effect will depend on elasticity of demand so that the more inelastic the D curve (that is the less price sensitive the consumers), the bigger the efficiency gains needed to offset the welfare loss derived from the lessening of competition.

1 Oliver E Williamson, 'Economies as an antitrust defense: The welfare Tradeoffs' [1969] *American Economic Review* 18.

SHOULD ALL EFFICIENCY GAINS BE TAKEN INTO ACCOUNT ?

It is a very simple model based on the idea that efficiency gains can effectively be quantified and compared to the consumer welfare loss, that the welfare of consumers weighs the same as that of firms (after all, an entrepreneur is also a consumer in his/her leisure time), and also that the loss of consumer welfare in terms of output reduction or price increase can be foreseen when the merger takes place.

These three ideas can be and have been discussed but the model is nevertheless useful as a tool for reflecting on the issue from the point of view of policy makers and trying to set some objective criteria on which efficiency gains should be taken into account when assessing a merger.

POSSIBLE CRITERIA :

- **Reduction of unit-costs**
- **Merger-specific**
- **Verified / Verifiable**
- **Substantial / Significant**
- **Do not arise from anticompetitive conduct**
- ☆ **Are likely to be passed on to consumers**

3. Efficiencies from the point of view of policy making

The treatment of efficiencies under merger control varies from one country to another and has evolved significantly in the last decades. Nevertheless, there is a common feature in their legal assessment that is the search for objective standards which would enable the quantification of those efficiencies which should be compared to the consumer surplus loss in order to decide whether or not to block a merger.

These standards usually limit those efficiencies which will be considered to those which are merger specific, that is, that cannot be achieved through other means such as internal changes within the firm. Also, the dimension and nature of efficiencies is relevant so that only those which are substantial and verifiable will be taken into account. Of course, the assessment will not consider those efficiencies arising from anti-competitive conduct such as cost reductions resulting from abuse of a dominant position as a buyer of the merging firm.

Finally, some systems consider that efficiencies should be passed on to consumers, thus adopting a 'consumer welfare approach' as opposed to those which have a 'total welfare approach'. This requirement can be useful from a purely practical point of view as it has a relatively objective nature and can base conditions or commitments by the merging firms.

SOME THOUGHTS ON THE ASSESSMENT OF EFFICIENCIES UNDER MERGER CONTROL

- ☆ **Competition policy aims at promoting market competition as the best way to achieve an efficient allocation of resources**
- ☆ **The main objective underlying mergers is increasing productive efficiency**
- ☆ **Efficiencies should be taken into account under merger control:**
  - **When assessing whether the merger would reduce effective competition in the market**
  - **When assessing whether increased efficiency would offset the negative welfare effect derived from increased market power**
- ☆ **Only those efficiency gains that are likely to be passed on to consumers should be taken into account – The role of behavioural remedies**

4. Basic conclusions

Competition policy is based on the principle that effective competition is the best way to achieve an efficient allocation of scarce resources and thus maximise social welfare.

Promoting efficiency is therefore at the core of competition policy and it should not be ignored in merger control. Its final aim is not to predetermine or stop the decision-making of firms which can produce bigger operators or change of market structure but to ensure that they do not lead to a lessening of effective competition which will damage social welfare.

Therefore, whereas antitrust is based on the fact that some conduct is forbidden by law, merger control is of a preventive nature and has a positive approach towards mergers, which are considered to be part of a dynamic market economy. In fact, competition authorities only study those mergers which exceed certain thresholds and most of them are cleared within a short period of time with or without an explicit analysis of their efficiency enhancing nature.

Whereas the generation of synergies or increased efficiency is the ultimate goal of most mergers, competition authorities should ensure that they are not only productive for the firm but also lead to an efficient allocation of resources for society as a whole. When looking for criteria in this regard, some authorities have stated that efficiencies should be merger-specific, significant or 'cognisable'. Nevertheless, given that it is sometimes difficult to foresee and quantify in advance efficiency gains, it can be useful to work on the requirement that they should be passed on to consumers. This criterion could be relevant when considering whether a merger should be blocked or not but mostly when setting the conditions or compromises under which the merger should be cleared.

5. Appendix: The treatment of efficiencies under merger control in Spain

In line with most European countries, the proceedings for merger control are conducted in two phases in Spain.

In the first phase, the *Servicio de Defensa de la Competencia* analyses the operation in view of its foreseeable impact on effective competition in the affected market and submits a report to the Minister of Economy who will resolve within a month after the filing of the case whether to refer the operation to the *Tribunal de Defensa de la Competencia.*

The technical report which is the basis for this decision is made public on the website of the *Servicio* after deciding on the confidentiality concerns of the notifying parties.

If the case is refered to the *Tribunal,* the second phase starts with an in-depth study of the operation where all interested parties can participate and a non-binding report is issued by the *Tribunal de Defensa de la Competencia* in a two-month period. Once this report is produced, the Spanish Council of Ministers will in a month's time make the final decision. The report of the *Tribunal* is made public after the final decision is made.

Spanish competition law expressly provides for the analysis of efficiencies by the *Tribunal de Defensa de la Competencia,* which must assess whether the merger can improve production or distribution systems, can foster technical or economic progress, reinforce the international competitiveness of national industry or benefit consumers and users and these efficiencies can offset the restrictive effects on competition of the merger.

The *Tribunal de Defensa de la Competencia* analyses these efficiencies in the vast majority of cases in an independent chapter of its reports and considers them when making a final assessment on the case. The burden of proof is on the companies.

The assessment of efficiencies usually considers whether they are merger-specific, whether they would lead to a significant improvement of production systems or consumer welfare, and whether they are likely to be passed on to the consumer or user.

Efficiencies are also considered in a non-specific manner by the *Servicio de Defensa de la Competencia* when making the initial assessment of the merger in first phase cases.

Finally, the Council of Ministers will decide on the basis of the technical report of the *Tribunal de Defensa de la Competencia* and can decide whether to clear the operation, to forbid it or else to authorise it subject to compliance with certain conditions which contribute to economic and social progress so that the lessening of competition is offset. For more information, see www.mineco.es.

19
The Role of Efficiencies in Merger Control

JAMES S VENIT*

Skadden Arps Slate Meagher & Flom, Brussels

1. INTRODUCTION

The Green Paper on the Review of the European Merger Control Regulation[1] (ECMR) released by the Commission in December 2001 sought comments on the proper role and scope of efficiency considerations in EU merger control proceedings.[2]

Despite the fact that Article 2(1)(b) of the ECMR expressly provides for the Commission to take into account in its assessment of notified concentrations 'the development of technical and economic progress provided that it is to consumers' advantage and does not form an obstacle to competition', the issue of efficiencies has to date been raised in only a limited number of cases under the ECMR. Where raised, efficiencies have been included in the substantive analysis of dominance considerations, rather than as a defence for a transaction found to raise anti-competitive concerns.[3] The European Commission to date has never explicitly taken efficiencies into account to approve a merger it would otherwise have blocked.[4] Indeed, at times the Commission has come close to suggesting that the possibility that a merger may make a firm with a leading market position more efficient is itself a reason for challenging the transaction.[5]

* The author thanks his colleagues Nathalie Denaeijer for her outstanding assistance in the preparation of this paper and Patrick Rey, Henry L Huser and Frederic Depoortere for their constructive comments and suggestions.

1 Council Regulation (EEC) No 4064/89 of 21 December 1989 on the control of concentrations between undertakings, OJ 1989 L 395/1(as amended).

2 COM (2001) 745/6 final (11 December 2001), at ¶170-2.

3 See below pages 241-246 for a discussion of ECMR cases that involved efficiencies considerations.

4 In 1996, the Commission stated that it is not legally possible under the ECMR to justify an efficiency defence and that efficiencies cannot justify or mitigate dominance in order to clear a merger that would otherwise be prohibited. OECD, *Competition Policy and Efficiency Claims in Horizontal Agreements*, contribution from the European Commission, at p 53 (OECD/GD(96) 65).

5 This has been referred to as the 'efficiency offence'. See, eg F Jenny, *EEC Merger Control: Economies as an Antitrust Defense or an Antitrust Attack?*, in 1992 Fordham Corp L Inst 591 (B Hawk, ed); and W J Kolasky, *North Atlantic Competition Policy: Converging Toward What?*, address before the BIICL Second Annual International and Comparative Law Conference, London, England (17 May 2002), available at www.usdoj.gov/atr/public/speeches. The Director of the Merger Task Force and Commissioner Monti, however, have denied that the Commission applies an efficiency offence. See, eg G Drauz, *Recent Development in the Assessment of Dominance*, speech delivered at the EC Merger Control 10th Anniversary Conference, Brussels (14-15 September), at p 9, available at www.europa.eu.int/comm./competition/speeches; G Drauz, *Unbundling GE/Honeywell: the Assessment of Conglomerate Mergers under EC Competition Law*, 2001 Fordham Corp L Inst (B Hawk, ed); M Monti, *Review of the EC Merger Regulation – Roadmap for the Reform Project*, speech delivered to the Conference on Reform of European Merger Control, British Chamber of Commerce (4 June 2002), available at www.europa.eu.int/comm/competition/speeches.

The European Union's approach is often contrasted with the current practice of the antitrust agencies and courts in the United States and Canada. Although the US merger statute does not provide for an explicit efficiency defence,[6] under the Revised 1997 Horizontal Merger Guidelines[7] the agencies can decide not to challenge a merger that substantially lessens competition if it generates efficiencies that are cognisable and verifiable,[8] and reverse for consumers the harm resulting from the lessening of competition.[9] The US courts are also increasingly examining efficiencies claims put forward by parties defending their transaction against a challenge by the FTC or the DOJ (while in the past they mostly rejected them outright),[10] although to date no court has approved on the basis of efficiencies a transaction that would otherwise have been prohibited for substantially lessening competition. In Canada, the statute expressly permits (and even mandates) the consideration of efficiencies and the courts have applied the efficiency defence to authorise transactions that raised very substantial competitive issues.[11]

Recent statements by Competition Commissioner Monti and the Director of the Merger Task Force indicate that DG Competition now supports the introduction of an efficiency defence under the ECMR.[12] Indeed in June 2002, Commissioner Monti specifically announced that the Commission intended to release Market Power Guidelines that will address, *inter alia,* the role and scope of efficiencies under the ECMR before the end of the year.[13]

In this context, the Commission's willingness to open the efficiencies debate to practitioners, economists, business representatives and other antitrust agencies as part of the discussions on the Green Paper is certainly welcome. This debate will assist the Commission in identifying conceptual and practical issues that must be addressed in

6 Section 7 of the Clayton Act prohibits transactions that may substantially lessen competition or tend to create a monopoly, but does not mention a possible efficiency defence for transactions that would be found to have such effects.

7 The US practice before the adoption of the 1997 Revision of the Merger Guidelines was sceptical of efficiencies. See, eg ABA, Mergers and Acquisitions: Understanding Antitrust Issues (2000), pp 143-165; and W J Kolasky and A R Dick, The Merger Guidelines and the Integration of Efficiencies into Antitrust Review of Horizontal Mergers, available at www.usdoj.gov/atr/hmerger/11254.htm.

8 See below pages 237-241.

9 There are indeed cases where the agencies exercised their prosecutorial discretion and on the basis of efficiencies decided not to challenge a transaction, or even not to issue a second request. See R Pitofsky, Efficiencies in Defense of Mergers: 18 Months After, Remarks before the George Mason Law Review Antitrust Symposium: The Changing Face of Efficiency, Washington, DC, 16 October 1998, available at www.ftc.gov/speeches/pitofsky/pitofeff.htm, at p 2.

10 Prior to the 1997 Revision of the Merger Guidelines, lower courts often refused to consider an efficiencies defence on the basis of three 1960s judgments in which the US Supreme Court appeared to reject the defence. See *United States v Philadelphia National Bank,* 374 US 321 (1963); *FTC v Brown Shoe Co,* 384 US 316 (1966); and *FTC v Procter & Gamble Co,* 386 US 568 (1967).

11 Canada's most recent experience in analysing the proper role and scope of efficiencies is galvanised in the *Superior Propane* decisions. See below pages 248-249 and 259.

12 See G Drauz, Recent Developments in the Assessment of Dominance, speech to the EC Merger Control 10th Anniversary Conference, Brussels (14-15 September 2000), available at www.europa.eu.int/comm/competition/speeches; and G Drauz, *Unbundling GE/Honeywell: the Assessment of Conglomerate Mergers under EC Competition Law,* 2001 Fordham Corp L Inst (B Hawk, ed).

13 See M Monti, n 5 above; and M Monti, The Future for Competition Policy in the European Union, speech delivered at Merchant's Taylor's Hall, London (9 July 2001) – both available at www.europa.eu.int/comm/competition/speeches.

devising an effective approach to the issue of efficiencies while also ensuring that the enforcement powers of the Commission under the ECMR are based on sound policy and economics.

After examining the economic and policy considerations supporting the introduction of the analysis of efficiencies in EC merger control, this paper identifies the three main issues that the Commission will face in designing its policy towards efficiencies. In the second section below, we examine the various types of efficiencies that may result from a concentration. In this section, we also summarise the current approach towards efficiencies in the United States, Canada and the European Union. In the third section, we examine the various standards under which efficiencies can be evaluated. Last, in the fourth section, we address the various methodological and procedural issues that can arise in the analysis of efficiencies. In particular, this section examines how the evaluation of efficiencies relates to the substantive test applied in the evaluation of mergers and some of the issues arising in the measurement and assessment of competitive harm and efficiencies.

2. Efficiencies in merger control: economic theory and policy considerations

The debate on the role of efficiencies in merger control is as much a political as it is an economic debate. For antitrust enforcers and policy makers, as well as for economists, the issue is whether there should be a trade-off between what are perceived as positive and negative effects of the same transaction on competition, economic efficiency and ultimately welfare.

Economists generally recognise that mergers can yield efficiency gains in several ways thereby resulting in an overall increase of welfare.[14] For example, mergers can optimise and rationalise production and as a result generate economies of scale, lower costs and improved capacity utilisation rates; lower transport costs by optimising distribution networks; enhance technological progress by enabling firms to develop new products that would not otherwise exist by combining expertise that is not easily transferred among non-integrated firms; generate economies of scope from newly available joint production or marketing possibilities; increase the bargaining power of the merging firm; and/or improve the efficiency of management.[15] To most economists, these effects of a merger cannot simply be ignored if it is also found that a merger increases market power. Rather, it may be relevant to consider the trade-off between the increase of market power resulting from a merger and the related deadweight loss to society and the potential gains to society resulting from the

14 However, some economists also recognise that not all mergers will yield efficiencies. See L-H Röller, J Stennek and F Verboven, Efficiency Gains from Mergers, in 'The Efficiency Defense and the European System of Merger Control,' a study prepared for the Directorate General for Economics and Financial Affairs, No 5, 2001 (hereinafter 'the DG ECO-FIN Study'), at p 58 (after a review of empirical evidence of alleged efficiency gains in mergers, the authors state that 'there seems to be no support for a general presumption that mergers create efficiency gains.'). The DG ECO-FIN Study is available at www.europa.eu.int/comm/economy_finance/publications/european_economy/ 2001/eers0501_en.pdf.

15 See F Ilzkovitz and R Meiklejohn, European Merger Control: do we need an efficiency defence?, in the DG ECO-FIN Study, at pp 8-9; and L-H Röller et al, n 14 above, at pp 42-49.

merger's announcement of efficiencies.[16] This is particularly the case when the efficiency gains are of such a magnitude that consumers benefit in addition to the merging firms.

As they become increasingly aware of the economic and social value of efficiencies, policy makers confront the problem of designing a merger control system that effectively balances the efficiency gains arising from mergers against any anti-competitive effects. This question is directly related to the objective of the applicable antitrust law, into underlying welfare assumptions, and the substantive test and competitive harm theories applied in the assessment of mergers.

The willingness of the antitrust authorities to consider efficiencies in merger control has been intimately linked with the abilities of firms within their territorial jurisdiction to compete in the global market. For example, concerns have been raised about the current absence of an efficiency analysis in the EU merger control system and its negative impact on the competitiveness of the European industry, particularly in high-tech industries (such as the aerospace and the information technology industries).[17] Last, to the extent that industrial policy concerns may (if only implicitly) find their way into merger decisions, the introduction of a formal efficiency analysis could improve the transparency of the decision-making process.[18]

3. Identifying types or categories of legitimate efficiencies

In devising its policy towards efficiencies and their role in merger analysis, the Commission will need to identify and define the categories or types of efficiencies that it will be willing to consider and weigh against the anti-competitive effects of a merger. The Commission will also need to identify whether efficiencies must meet particular conditions to be considered (eg whether they must be merger-specific, and must be passed on immediately to consumers). Indeed definition of the scope of permissible efficiencies seems necessary to facilitate a predictable and reasonably expeditious review.

16 See P Camesasca, 'The Explicit Efficiency Defence in Merger Control: Does it Make the Difference?' [1999] ECLR 14, at p 16 (identifying O Williamson as the economist at the origin of the trade-off concept).

17 See F Ilzkovitz and R Meiklejohn, n 15 above, at pp 10-11 (citing, eg to European Commission, 'The European aerospace industry: meeting the global challenge', Commission Communication, COM (97) 466, 24 September 1997; and European Commission, 'The competitiveness of European enterprises in the face of globalization – how it can be encouraged', Commission Communication, COM (98) 718, 20 January 1999). See also the Opinion of the Economic and Social Committee on the 'Green Paper on the Review of Council Regulation (EEC) No 4064/89', COM (2001) 745 final, OJ 2002 C 241/130, at para 3.2. Similar concerns were raised in the United States before the adoption of the 1997 Revisions to the Horizontal Merger Guidelines. See, eg R Pitofsky, 'Proposals for Revised United States Merger Enforcement in a Global Economy' (1992) 81 Geo LJ 195, 198 (stating that 'the [early] failure of United States enforcement agencies and courts to take into account efficiency ... considerations in merger analyses was the principal cause of American firms' difficulties in international trade'). The Canadian Merger Guidelines also acknowledge the link between efficiencies and international competitiveness. Section 5 of the Guidelines on the Efficiency Exception refers directly to the purpose clause of the Canadian Competition Act, which in turn provides that the Act encourages 'competition in Canada in order to promote the efficiency and adaptability of the Canadian economy, in order to expand opportunities for Canadian participation in world markets ...'. Section 1.1 of the Competition Act, quoted in Section 5.1 of the Merger Enforcement Guidelines.

18 See P Camesasca, n 16 above.

Below we identify the principal categories of efficiencies that have been acknowledged in economic and antitrust literature. We also summarise the approach to efficiencies adopted under the US Merger Guidelines and the Canadian Statute and Merger Guidelines.

3.1 Categories of efficiencies

The antitrust and economic literature traditionally distinguish between productive, dynamic or innovative and transactional efficiencies. Other possible categories of efficiencies used in the US and Canadian Merger Guidelines and practice include distribution, promotional, procurement, management and capital cost efficiencies.

3.1.1 Productive efficiencies

Production is said to be efficient when goods are produced at the minimum possible cost. Mergers have the potential to increase productive efficiencies by enabling the merged firms to reduce costs through a more cost-effective combination of resources,[19] for example via production rationalisation, economies of scale, economies of scope and synergies. Productive efficiencies can benefit consumers by lowering the cost of goods and services or by increasing their value.[20] Production efficiencies are generally easier to measure than other types of efficiencies.

Efficiencies from *rationalisation* of production result from the reallocation of output between plants of the merged firms. The idea is to shift production from plants with high marginal costs to plants with lower marginal costs. Production is fully rationalised when the marginal costs are equalised at all the plants of the merged firm.[21] Rationalisation can also lead to plant specialisation.[22]

Economies of scale are realised when average production cost decreases as the output increases.[23] Economies of scale are probably the type of efficiencies most commonly asserted by merging parties and they may be easier to quantify than any other type of efficiencies. However, economies of scale raise a number of issues.

First, certain economists and antitrust practitioners have questioned whether antitrust agencies should consider economies of scale, primarily on the grounds that firms can generally reach their efficient production scale by other measures that do not

19 See ABA, *Mergers and Acquisitions, Understanding Antitrust Issues* (2000), pp 143-144.

20 See W J Kolasky, Conglomerate Mergers and Range Effects: It's a long way from Chicago to Brussels, address before the George Mason University Symposium, Washington, DC, 9 November 2001, at p 5, available at www.usdoj.gov/atr/speeches; ABA, Mergers and Acquisitions, Understanding Antitrust Issues (2000), pp 143-144; and D Balto, 'The Efficiency Defense in Merger Review: Progress or Stagnation', *Antitrust* (Fall 2001), p 74.

21 See L-H Röller *et al*, n 14 above, at p 43.

22 See D Balto, n 20 above, at 75.

23 Economies of scale can be short term or long term. Short-term economies of scale can be realised through a merger by the elimination of duplicative fixed costs. This relates in particular to fixed costs that each firm pre-merger is obliged to incur to remain operational, regardless of output size (eg costs associated with administrative functions such as purchasing, billing, etc). As a result of the merger, these fixed costs are distributed over the larger combined output of the merged firm and duplication is eliminated. Long-term economies of scale occur when a doubling of all inputs leads to more than a doubling of total output. See L-H Röller *et al*, n 14 above, at pp 44-45. See also W J Kolasky and A R Dick, n 7 above, at p 52.

result in the elimination of a competitor from the relevant market.[24] It has been noted, however, that there may be economic or strategic reasons why realising economies of scale other than by a merger may not be attractive or would be significantly more expensive.[25] Secondly, economies of scale realised from the combination of the operations of two firms with mixed product offerings could result in the elimination of some products from the merged firm's portfolio and thus reduce consumer choice. It has been argued that this potential loss to consumers should be included in the assessment of the economies of scale.[26] Last, economies of scale vary on an industry-by-industry basis and thus a case-by-case analysis of the claimed efficiencies will be required to determine whether the efficiencies are likely to be realised, although this is equally true of other kinds of efficiencies.

Economies of scope arise when it is cheaper to produce two or more products together than separately. Economies of scope can be derived, eg from the common use of raw materials or input products in the manufacture of several products, the sharing of technology and knowledge in the manufacture and sale of several products, or complementary distribution channels and sales forces).[27] Economies of scope may be more difficult to measure than economies of scale, but may nonetheless be valuable for consumers' welfare.

Synergies are cost-savings or quality improvements that result from the integration of specific assets that would not be shared or exchanged absent a merger (*e.g.*, synergies can result from the sharing of complementary skills or the improvement of interoperability between complementary products).[28]

3.1.2 Dynamic or innovative efficiencies

'Innovative efficiencies are cost savings or product enhancement gains from the innovation, development or diffusion of new technology.'[29] These efficiencies can be realised from the diffusion of know-how between the parties,[30] or from changes to the R&D incentives between the parties.[31] Dynamic efficiencies can result in medium to long-term cost reductions (eg as a result of process innovation) or quality improve-

24 It has been noted, for example, that large firms have mostly been able to achieve scale economies internally and therefore scale economies would not frequently justify a horizontal merger between large firms. Scale economies could, however, justify a vertical merger or a horizontal merger between smaller firms, or a product line expansion joint venture. See J F Brodley, Proof of Efficiencies in Mergers and Joint Ventures: Testing ex ante claims against ex post evidence, 7 November 1995, available at www.ftc.gov/opp/global/brodley.htm. Scale economies may also be regarded with suspicion since they may involve reducing rival firms' share.

25 See W J Kolasky, 'Lessons from Baby Food: The Role of Efficiencies in Merger Review', *Antitrust*, (Fall 2001), p 16.

26 See L-H Röller *et al*, n 14 above, at p 45.

27 See, eg W J Kolasky and A R Dick, n 7 above, at pp 53-55; and L-H Röller *et al*, n 14 above, at pp 43-45.

28 See W J Kolasky and A R Dick, n 7 above, at pp 55-56; and J Farrell and C Shapiro, 'Scale Economies and Synergies in Horizontal Merger Analysis' (2001) 68 Antitrust LJ 685.

29 See J F Brodley, 'Proof of Efficiencies in Mergers and Joint Ventures' (1996) 64 Antitrust LJ 575, at p 579.

30 This can occur for example when one of the merging parties has clearly superior know-how and the merger allows the other party to learn and potentially adopt the better know-how, or when both parties will exchange know-how and improve their technological and administrative capabilities, or the merger leads to specialisation between the two parties in the production of intermediate products used in the making of the final products. See L-H Röller *et al*, n 14 above, at pp 45-46.

31 A merger can create an increased incentive for R&D (by internalising the benefits from R&D between the parties). See L-H Röller *et al*, n 14 above, at p 46.

ments (eg as a result of product innovation). The importance and value of innovative efficiencies is recognised, in particular in high-tech industries.[32] Dynamic/innovative efficiencies may be empirically more difficult to measure than productive efficiencies,[33] but in the long run, they may be more important for the continued vitality of competition in a relevant market.[34] There is thus a strong argument that dynamic efficiencies should be recognised in merger analysis.[35]

3.1.3 Transactional efficiencies

Transactional efficiencies are said to facilitate firms' achievement of productive and dynamic efficiencies. Transactional efficiencies generally result from the elimination of double-marginalisation (ie the costs of doing business with third parties, for example, for the purchase of inputs or raw materials, distribution or other services). A merger may bring about transactional efficiencies by enabling the merged firm to integrate some activities vertically while leaving other activities to market-based transactions.[36] Transactional efficiencies may benefit consumers by lowering the costs of goods and services or by increasing their value.[37]

3.1.4 Distribution and promotion efficiencies

Distribution and promotion efficiencies that can be generated by a merger include rationalisation of warehousing, closing of overlapping distribution centres and reduction in transport, distribution, advertising and promotion costs (better rates for larger accounts).

3.1.5 Increased buying power

Another type of efficiency that may result from a merger is the creation of greater purchasing power. Firms can obtain lower prices for their purchases of goods or services by simply increasing the volume of their purchases. Savings can also be realised by eliminating duplicative purchasing operations or adopting a more efficient purchasing process.[38] Unanimity does not exist on the appropriate treatment of purchasing efficiencies. Some commentators take the position that procurement efficiencies should be disregarded, eg because they merely amount to a wealth transfer from suppliers to the merging parties (ie similar to the wealth transfer from customers to the merging parties caused by an anti-competitive price increase).[39] Others argue

32 See D Balto, n 20 above, at p 76; J F Brodley, n 29 above; and W J Kolasky, Comparative Merger Control Analysis: Six Guiding Principles for Antitrust Agencies – New and Old, Remarks before the IBA Conference on Competition Law and Policy in a Global Context, Cape Town, South Africa (18 March 2002), available at www.usdoj.gov/atr/public/speeches.

33 For example, it may be difficult to measure and evaluate the likelihood of success and the timing of the delivery or implementation of innovation. As stated by Professor Brodley, 'the antitrust decision maker faces the heroic task of predicting whether a new combination of inputs will produce knowledge that does not yet exist': see J F Brodley, n 24 above.

34 See W J Kolasky and A R Dick, n 7 above, at pp 57-58; and J F Brodley, n 24 above.

35 See F Ilzkovitz and R Meiklejohn, n 15 above, at p 24; and L-H Röller *et al*, n 14 above, at pp 45-6.

36 See W J Kolasky and A R Dick, n 7 above, at pp 58-61.

37 See W J Kolasky, n 20 above, at p 22.

38 See L-H Röller *et al*, n 14 above, at pp 46-47.

39 The same would be true of other pecuniary savings such as tax reduction savings, which are a wealth transfer from society/government to the merging parties. See J F Brodley, n 24 above.

that procurement efficiencies should be recognised.[40] This would seem true in particular where the purchasing power of the parties is otherwise used by the agency in its evaluation of the transaction.[41] The DG ECO-FIN Study suggests that the positive or negative effects of increased buying power should be assessed in relation to the power of the suppliers.[42] Against this background, it would seem that, except in the rare monopsony cases, procurement efficiencies should be recognised.

3.1.6 Capital and management savings

By *reducing slack*, a merger can improve the internal efficiency (management and administrative practices) of the merged firm.[43] A merger can also increase competition between the merged firm and other participants in the market thereby forcing all competitors to improve internal efficiency and reduce slack. However, some economists note that the issue of whether mergers, through the impact on market competition, can improve the internal efficiency of firms is still an open question.[44] The value of managerial efficiencies is disputed and they are difficult to measure. As a result, some commentators dispute their relevance as non-merger specific.[45]

A merger may also generate *capital cost savings* by giving the merged firm (as a result of its larger size) access to financing at more favourable rates and opening new possibilities to raise capital.[46] One supporter of the recognition of these efficiencies has stated that 'extending access to cheap capital to a broader range of business activities is just as much an efficiency as extending access to any other valuable asset that is currently under-utilized'.[47]

3.1.7 Pecuniary savings

Only true cost savings, resulting from a saving of resources, should be accepted in an efficiency defence. It has been argued that other types of cost savings resulting from a transfer of wealth to the benefit of the merged firm (*e.g.*, tax avoidance gains) should not be counted as social efficiencies.[48]

3.1.8 Externalities

A distinction can be made between efficiencies that occur at the level of the merging parties (internal efficiencies) or at the industry level (externalities). Many of the

40 See D Balto, n 20 above, at p 77.

41 For example in the *Staples/Office Depot* case, discussed below (see page 239), the FTC defined a relevant product market limited to office supplies 'super-stores', considering among other factors, that the size of these stores and the resulting purchasing power singled them out from other office supplies stores. Yet, the FTC (and the Court) rejected purchasing savings claimed by the parties as efficiencies.

42 For example, the study finds that the increased buying power of the merged entity can bring about social benefits (as opposed to purely private gains) if it balances the pre-existing power of the suppliers. See L-H Röller et al, n 14 above, at p 46.

43 Internal management inefficiency is sometimes referred to as 'x-inefficiency'. See L-H Röller et al, n 14 above, at p 47.

44 See L-H Röller *et al*, n 14 above, at pp 48-49.

45 See J F Brodley, n 24 above (arguing, during the debate on the revision of the US Horizontal Merger Guidelines, that managerial economies should be recognised only in extra-ordinary cases since their existence assumes a shortage of available managerial talent or experience, which appears unlikely in most developed markets).

46 See L-H Röller *et al*, n 14 above, at pp 46-47.

47 See W J Kolasky, n 20 above.

48 See L-H Röller *et al*, n 14 above, at pp 43, 91 and 114.

efficiencies identified above can occur at firm-level and industry-level.[49] For example, industry-level cost savings can result from the reallocation of production from the merging firms to their competitors; or the merger may change the R&D incentives for competitors.[50]

The DG ECO-FIN Study mentions the theory of external impact developed by Farrell and Shapiro. Under that theory, if the externality[51] of a merger is positive then the merger must be found to increase total welfare since the proposed merger may be assumed to also be profitable (otherwise the parties would not undertake the merger).[52]

The DG ECO-FIN Study notes that only firm-level efficiencies are considered in most jurisdictions and attributes this situation to the fact that industry-level efficiencies are more difficult to verify and evaluate.[53] Nevertheless it would appear that external efficiencies should be taken into account as part of a dynamic analysis.

3.2 The United States' approach

The efficiency defence in the United States is not incorporated in the merger legislation. Section 7 of the Clayton Act prohibits transactions that may 'substantially lessen competition' or tend to create a monopoly and does not address the possibility of an efficiency defence. After years of development,[54] in 1997, the DOJ and the FTC incorporated efficiencies considerations in their joint Horizontal Merger Guidelines.

The Revised Guidelines provide that in applying the efficiencies defence, the agencies will examine only 'cognisable efficiencies'. Cognisable efficiencies are: (1) merger specific[55]; (2) verifiable[56]; and (3) not the result of anti-competitive output

49 This is true in particular for production rationalisation, economies of scale and scope, development of technical progress, purchasing economies and managerial efficiencies. See L-H Röller *et al*, n 14 above, at pp 43 and 56-57.

50 *Id.*

51 Externality is defined as the sum of the merger's effects on consumers and on competitors who did not participate in the merger.

52 See L-H Röller *et al*, n 14 above, at pp 56-57.

53 Parties can probably not be expected to provide detailed industry-wide information for the purpose of measuring the externality of a transaction and parties can also probably not be presumed to have more information than the competition authorities on externalities. See L-H Röller *et al*, n 14 above, at p 114.

54 For a summary of the historical developments that led to the adoption of the 1997 Revised Merger Guidelines, see ABA, Mergers and Acquisitions: Understanding Antitrust Issues (2000), at pp 143-165; W J Kolasky and A R Dick, n 7 above; and T J Muris, Statement to the Federal Trade Commission Hearings on Global and Innovation-Based Competition, 7 November 1995, available at www.ftc/gov/opp/global/muris.htm.

55 Merger-specific efficiencies are 'efficiencies likely to be accomplished with the proposed merger and unlikely to be accomplished in the absence of either the merger or another means having comparable anticompetitive effects'. To assess merger-specificity, the agencies will evaluate the claimed efficiencies only against alternative methods (to the merger) of achieving the same efficiencies that are 'practical in the business situation faced by the merging firms. ... The agency will not insist upon a less restrictive alternative that is merely theoretical'. Some commentators have noted that this wording recognises the fact that firms may decide for legitimate reasons not to pursue efficiencies internally. See W J Kolasky and A R Dick, n 7 above, at pp 27-8; R Pitofsky, n 9 above, at p 2.

56 The Guidelines provide that the parties 'must substantiate efficiency claims so that the Agency can verify by reasonable means the likelihood and magnitude of each asserted efficiency, how and when each would

reductions.[57] The Revised Guidelines do not include an express requirement that efficiencies be 'passed on' to consumers, but do provide that efficiencies that are directly passed on to consumers are given greater weight.[58]

The Guidelines list examples of acceptable types of efficiencies – including marginal cost reductions, improved quality, enhanced service, new products, efficiencies resulting from production reallocation among facilities, R&D efficiencies, procurement savings, management savings and capital cost efficiencies – and identify categories that are more or less likely to be 'cognisable'. The Guidelines do not mention distribution or promotional efficiencies.[59] The Guidelines' 'preference' seems to be for productive efficiencies,[60] although dynamic efficiencies (R&D) and transactional efficiencies are not excluded outright.[61] Recently, FTC Chairman Timothy Muris has advocated abandonment of the 'disparaging treatment' of promotional, capital and managerial efficiencies; however, his statement did not include procurement efficiencies.[62]

The Guidelines establish a sliding scale according to which greater anti-competitive effects will require the proof of greater efficiencies and state that efficiencies will almost never justify a merger to monopoly or near monopoly.[63]

The antitrust agencies have applied the efficiency defence in exercising their prosecutorial discretion (eg in support of decisions not to challenge transactions or not

be achieved (and any costs of doing so), how each would enhance the merged firm's ability and incentive to compete and why each would be merger-specific. Efficiency claims will not be considered if they are vague or speculative or otherwise cannot be verified by reasonable means'. Commentators have noted that this language does not necessarily require that each efficiency be precisely quantified. Some important efficiencies (in particular dynamic efficiencies) that are more difficult to measure are not excluded outright (although the Guidelines do mention that R&D efficiencies 'are generally less susceptible to verification'). See W J Kolasky and A R Dick, n 7 above, at p 29; and W J Kolasky, n 32 above.

57 The Guidelines do not elaborate on the statement that efficiencies that arise from anti-competitive reductions in output or service will not be considered. The Guidelines do, however, note that efficiencies resulting from production reallocation 'are less likely to result from anti-competitive reductions in output' whereas R&D efficiencies 'may be the result of anti-competitive output reductions'.

58 See 'Application in the United States, European Union and Canada' below.

59 Timothy Muris, before his appointment as FTC Chairman in 2001, commented that these efficiencies should be recognised and observed that in 'some industries, economies in product promotion are as important as economies of large scale production and distribution in providing cost advantage for market leaders. In consumer goods for example, promotional economies are substantial and may require larger market shares to achieve minimum efficient scale than would be suggested by only production and distributional efficiencies'. See T J Muris, 'The Government and Merger Efficiencies: Still Hostile After All These Years' (1999) 7 Geo Mason L Rev 729, 734. After his appointment as FTC Chairman, Mr Muris maintained his support for the recognition of distribution and promotional efficiencies to the extent that there are real cost savings. See T J Muris, 'Interview with FTC Chairman', Antitrust (Fall 2001), p 52.

60 Productive efficiencies are stated to be more likely to be susceptible to verification, merger-specific, substantial and less likely to result from anti-competitive output reductions.

61 R&D efficiencies are stated to be potentially substantial, but generally less susceptible to verification and may be the result of anti-competitive output reductions. Procurement, management and capital cost efficiencies are stated to be less likely to be merger specific or substantial.

62 Chairman Muris stated that to 'the extent, there are real cost savings, there is no reason to disparage them'. See T J Muris, n 59 above, at 52.

63 The one conceivable exception would be where the merger to monopoly (or near monopoly) both reduces marginal cost and increases output.

to issue a second request).[64] However, the US courts have not to date authorised a transaction (rejecting the FTC or DOJ action to enjoin the transaction) on the basis of claimed efficiencies after having found that a transaction substantially lessened competition.[65] The courts, however, have increasingly examined efficiencies claims as opposed to rejecting them outright as irrelevant under the Supreme Court's *Procter & Gamble* judgment.[66] This trend is illustrated by the three cases summarised below,[67] which involved heavily litigated and detailed efficiencies analysis.

In the *Staples/Office Depot* case,[68] Staples, the second-largest office supply superstore chain in the United States, proposed to acquire Office Depot, the largest chain. The FTC brought an action before the DC District Court to enjoin the transaction arguing essentially that the acquisition would substantially lessen competition on the market for office supplies superstores. The District Court did not dispute the FTC's market definition or substantive analysis and turned to the parties' efficiency claims. The parties claimed that the merged firm would save between $4.9 billion and $6.5 billion over five years, essentially from savings resulting from the increased bargaining power of the merged firm and its ability to obtain better prices from suppliers (estimated at 40 per cent of the total claimed efficiencies). The Court examined closely and rejected the efficiencies as largely overstated (when compared to projected savings claimed in internal company documents pre-dating the litigation) and not merger-specific because both parties were rapidly expanding on their own and the merger was thus not necessary to increase bargaining buying power.[69] The Court also found insufficient evidence that savings would be passed on to consumers.[70]

64 See R Pitofsky, n 9 above (citing the Tosco/Unocal and Chrysler/Daimler Benz transactions).

65 The former Chairman of the FTC indicated that he believes that it is just a matter of time until a court accepts an efficiency defence. See R Pitofsky, EU and US Approaches to International Mergers – View from the US Federal Trade Commission, EC Merger Control 10th Anniversary Conference, Brussels, 14-15 September 2000, available at www.ftc.gov/speeches.

66 In *FTC v Procter & Gamble Co*, the Supreme Court stated that 'possible economies cannot be used as a defense to illegality. Congress [in drafting section 7 of the Clayton Act] was aware that some mergers which lessen competition may also result in economies but it struck the balance in favor of protecting competition': 386 US 568, 580 (1967). In its earlier Philadelphia National Bank judgment, the Supreme Court had already stated that 'a merger the effect of which may be substantially to lessen competition is not saved because on some ultimate reckoning of social or economics debits and credits it may be deemed beneficial': *United States v Philadelphia National Bank*, 374 US 321, 371 (1963).

67 Efficiencies have been examined in numerous other cases, including sometimes with success to rebut in court the Government's prima facie showing of anti-competitive effects. See, eg *FTC v Butterworth Health Corp*, 121 F 3d 708 (6th Cir 1997); *FTC v Tenet Health Care Corp*, 186 F 3d 1045 (8th Cir 1999); *US v Long Island Jewish Medical Center*, 983 F Supp 121 (EDNY 1997); and *US v Country Lakes Foods, Inc*, 754 F Supp 669 (D Minn 1990).

68 *Federal Trade Commission v Staples Inc*, 970 F Supp 1066 (DDC 1997) (Hogan J). For a commentary of the case see, eg J Baker, Econometric Analysis in FTC v Staples, Remarks before the ABA Antitrust Section, Economics Committee, Willard Hotel (18 July 1997), available at www.ftc.gov/speeches/other/stspch.htm; and D. Balto, n 20 above, at pp 77-8.

69 The FTC estimated that 43 per cent of the purchasing savings would have been realised even without the merger.

70 The parties alleged that two-thirds of the savings would be passed on to consumers. The Court found that this fact was not sufficiently established given that Staples had a history of passing on only significantly smaller percentages of its savings to customers (15 to 17 per cent).

In the *Cardinal Health/McKesson* case,[71] the FTC sued to enjoin two related transactions, the proposed mergers between Cardinal Health and Bergen and between McKesson and Amerisource, the four largest drug wholesalers in the United States.[72] The parties argued that the transactions would generate substantial efficiencies (ranging from $146 million to $307 million), in three years after the merger and that at least 50 per cent of the gains would be passed on to consumers.[73] The FTC did not dispute the parties' claim that there would be some significant efficiencies, or that some savings would be passed on to consumers. The FTC did, however, argue that (1) the alleged savings were overstated; (2) some of the efficiencies were not merger specific; and (3) passing along 50 per cent of the gains to consumers was not sufficient where it had been demonstrated in prior cases that in a competitive environment, a firm can pass on as much as 80 per cent of cost savings to its powerful customers. The Court agreed with the FTC and found that the parties failed to prove extraordinary efficiencies in a case that was essentially a merger to monopoly.[74]

In the *Baby Food* case,[75] the parties also claimed efficiencies to attempt to avoid a prohibition and both the District Court and the Circuit Court examined the claims in detail.

The FTC opposed the proposed merger between the No 2 (Heinz) and No 3 (Beech-Nut) baby food producers in the United States on the grounds that: (1) the market was highly concentrated, with an HHI of over 5,300, out of a possible 10,000, rendering the merger presumptively unlawful; and (2) the transaction would have anti-competitive unilateral[76] and coordinated effects.[77]

To rebut the Government's *prima facie* case against the merger, the parties advanced an efficiencies defence. Heinz argued that the merger would enable the merged firm to achieve significant cost savings (and thus compete more effectively with Gerber)[78] by: (1) transitioning all baby food products to the Beech-Nut label; (2)

71 *FTC v Cardinal Health Inc*, 1998-2 Trade Cas (CCH) ¶ 72,226 (DDC 1998).

72 After the two mergers, the largest US drug wholesalers would have been reduced from four to two and the combined market share of the two merged firms would have ranged between 63 to 80 per cent of the pharmaceutical wholesale market.

73 Efficiencies included consolidation of distribution centres, increased discounts from suppliers resulting from the increased buying power, reductions in corporate overhead and inventory and reductions in capital cost.

74 Note, however, that three years later, the FTC permitted the merger between Bergen and Amerisource (the third and fourth largest wholesalers), inter alia, on the basis that there were significant efficiencies that met the Guidelines test, including distribution and promotion efficiencies. Statement of the Federal Trade Commission, Amerisource Health Corp/Bergen Brunswick Co (24 August 2001), available at www.ftc.gov/os/2001/08/amerisourcestatement.

75 See *Federal Trade Commission v H J Heinz Co*, United States District Court for the District of Columbia (18 October 2002), 116 F Supp 2d 190; *Federal Trade Commission v H J Heinz Co*, United States Court of Appeals for the District of Columbia Circuit (17 April 2001), 345 US App DC 364.

76 With regard to unilateral effects, the FTC argued that by eliminating substantial head-to-head competition between Heinz and Beech-Nut – which compete for the No 2 slot on retailers' shelves, the merger would have enabled the merged entity to increase its prices unilaterally.

77 With regard to coordinated effects, the FTC found that the transaction would create a duopoly, thereby significantly increasing the likelihood that the merged firm and Gerber would engage in coordinated behaviour.

78 The merged firm's market share on the US baby foods market would have been approximately 33 per cent, facing an entrenched market leader, Gerber, with a 65 per cent share of US sales.

producing all products in Heinz's state-of-the-art production facility[79]; (3) increasing innovation[80]; and (4) using Heinz's six regional distribution centres to distribute both firms' products and thereby achieve scale and scope economies of distribution. Heinz estimated the savings resulting from the transaction between $9.4 million and $12 million, the majority of which were expected to result from production efficiencies.

The FTC argued that the efficiency claims: (1) were not demonstrated, were overstated and were not merger-specific; (2) would lead to the loss of the Heinz brand and thus reduce customers' choice; and (3) were insufficient to outweigh the anti-competitive effects of the merger.

The District Court did not dispute the FTC's finding that the merger would be likely to have anti-competitive effects, but the court found that the parties had rebutted the presumption created by the high and increasing market concentration *inter alia*, by proving extraordinary efficiencies. In support of its conclusion that efficiencies would indeed outweigh the anti-competitive effects, the District Court recognised: (1) the substantial cost savings in salaries and operating costs resulting from the consolidation of the food production at Heinz plant; (2) substantial savings from reorganising distribution networks; (3) the improved quality as a result of recipe consolidation; and (4) increased incentives to innovation as a result of the merged firm's increased geographical distribution scope. The FTC appealed to the Circuit Court.

The Circuit Court found that the parties failed to produce sufficient evidence of the 'extraordinary efficiencies' required to rebut the presumption of anti-competitive effects (given the very high market concentration) and remanded. The parties abandoned the transaction before the District Court issued its judgment on remand.

With regard to efficiencies, the Circuit Court found that: (1) the District Court in its evaluation of the production efficiencies wrongly considered the reduction in variable costs of manufacturing rather than the reduction in total variable costs; (2) the District Court should have compared the cost reductions with the merged firm's total output rather than with Beech-Nut's output alone; and (3) the District Court failed to explain why the efficiencies (including distribution and innovation efficiencies) could not be achieved through reasonable, practical and less restrictive alternatives to the merger.[81]

Commentators have singled out the *Heinz/Beech-Nut* saga as an example of the continued difficulties faced by parties in their attempt to convince the agencies and the courts that efficiencies are sufficient to rebut the presumption of anti-competitive effects in highly concentrated markets.[82]

3.3 The European Union's approach

Article 2(1)(b) of the ECMR states that the Commission should take into account, in its substantive analysis of a notified concentration, 'the development of technical and

79 Beech-Nut's facility was old and outdated and could not be expanded or upgraded cost-effectively, whereas Heinz's plant was modern but operated only at 40 per cent of its dedicated baby food capacity.

80 Heinz argued that each of Beech-Nut and Heinz alone did not have a sufficient distribution volume to finance innovation.

81 For commentaries on the case, see W J Kolasky, 'Lessons from Baby Food: The Role of Efficiencies in Merger Review', *Antitrust*, (Fall 2001), p 82; T B Leary, 'An Inside Look at the Heinz Case', Antitrust, Spring 2002, p 32; and D Balto, n 20 above, at 74.

82 See W J Kolasky, n 81 above, at 82.

economic progress provided that it is to consumers' advantage and does not form an obstacle to competition'.

In the explanatory notes to the ECMR, the Commission indicated that 'the concept of technical and economic progress must be understood in light of the principles enshrined in Article 8(1)(3) of the Treaty, as interpreted by the case law of the Court of Justice'.[83] As noted in the DG ECO-FIN Study, there are, however, significant differences between the wording of Article 81(3) of the EC Treaty and Article 2(1)(b) of the ECMR. First, under Article 81(3) the Commission can only authorise agreements if they contribute 'to improving the production or distribution of goods or to promoting technical or economic progress, while allowing consumers a fair share of the resulting benefit'. Thus, under Article 81, efficiencies are not a defence, but a requirement for exemption, and that requirement includes some (undefined) form of consumer pass-through.[84] Secondly, in contrast to Article 81, the ECMR does not refer to improvements in production and distribution, which could be read to suggest that the only relevant efficiencies are those that result from or lead to innovation (as Article 2(1)(b) refers only to 'progress').[85] Thirdly, whereas Article 81 requires that a 'fair share' of benefits flow to consumers, the ECMR is silent on the way consumers must benefit.[86] Last, the ECMR's separate condition that technical and economic progress does not form an obstacle to competition raises the question of whether an efficiency defence could be accepted for a dominant firm since any improvement to the merged firm's efficiency may enhance its market power, and thus form an obstacle to competition.[87]

The potential that Article 2(1)(b) of the ECMR be used as the basis for efficiency considerations was, however, implicitly recognised by the Court of First Instance in its *Vittel* judgment.[88] The Court stated that 'Article 2(1)(b) of Regulation 4064/89 requires the Commission *to draw up an economic balance* for the concentration in question' (emphasis added).[89] Arguably, this invites an efficiency analysis.[90]

The few Commission merger decisions that have explicitly dealt with efficiency claims show some inconsistency.[91] In its assessment of efficiencies, the Commission appears to have informally followed the principles of the US Merger Guidelines. For example, decisions indicate that the Commission has examined whether the alleged efficiencies were substantial, merger-specific and to the benefit of consumers – all conditions mentioned in the US Guidelines. Some decisions appear to require

83 Notes on Council Regulation (EEC) 4064/89, published in *Merger control law in the European Union Situation in March 1998* (European Commission, Brussels-Luxembourg, 1998), p 53.

84 See F Ilzkovitz and R Meiklejohn, n 15 above, at p 13.

85 *Id* at p 14. This interpretation may, however, be too narrow, and it can be plausibly argued that the reference to 'economic' in addition to 'technical' progress sweeps in categories of efficiencies other than those associated with innovation.

86 See F Ilzkovitz and R Meiklejohn, n 15 above, at p 14.

87 *Id.*

88 *Comité Central d'Entreprise de la Société Anonyme Vittel et al v Commision*, Case T-12/93; Judgment of the Court of First Instance of 27 April 1995, [1995] ECR II-1247.

89 *Id*, at ¶ 39.

90 In the case in question, the issue related to the social dimension of merger control and in particular the impact of a concentration on employees.

91 All Commission merger decisions discussed below and for which no cite to the Official Journal of the European Communities is provided are available at www.europa.eu.int/comm./competition/mergers/ cases.

specifically that the benefit resulting from the efficiencies be passed on to consumers – a condition that is not expressly stated in the US Guidelines, but whose inclusion may echo the approach under Article 81(3). The Commission has also examined efficiencies as part of its dominance analysis and not as a separate defence once dominance has been found. In fact, several decisions have expressly rejected the notion of an efficiency defence by stating that as soon as dominance is found, efficiency arguments cannot be taken into account. It appears that efficiencies may nevertheless have played a role in the Commission's decision to clear some transactions (as efficiencies were among the factors leading to a no-dominance conclusion). It further appears that efficiencies (as factors in the dominance analysis) may have played a role in the Commission's decision not to clear certain transactions. Last, and most recently, despite initial statements that the ECMR does not allow for an efficiency defence, Commissioner Monti has now publicly stated that he supports the introduction of an efficiency defence in EC merger control and that Guidelines will be issued.[92]

The Commission addressed efficiency arguments as early as in its first prohibition decision.[93] In *Aerospatiale-Alenia/de Havilland*,[94] the parties submitted that cost savings were one of the primary objectives of the transaction. Savings were expected to result from rationalisation of parts procurement, marketing and product support and were estimated at ECU5 million/year. The parties also argued that savings would be realised by establishing a manufacture base in a dollar area, reducing the currency fluctuation risk. The Commission rejected these arguments finding that: (1) the savings were not substantial (they amounted to only 0.5 per cent of the combined turnover of the parties); (2) the savings were not merger-specific (they resulted (at least in part) from claims of better management of certain aspects of de Havilland's internal operations and could be achieved by the current owner or by any other potential buyer); (3) there were no alleged savings in R&D; (4) the advantages derived from a dollar manufacturing base were doubtful; and (5) the savings would not benefit consumers (the Commission found a high risk that the merged entity's dominant position would translate into a monopoly able to raise prices). In essence, the Commission found that the alleged efficiencies were not substantial, not merger-specific and would only enhance the merged firm's ability to behave independently from its competitors. Of course, the latter finding smacks of an efficiency offence as does the Commission's condemnation of the merged firm's ability to offer a full range of regional aircraft.

92 See the contribution of the Commission to OECD, n 4 above, at p 53.

93 Efficiencies were examined in a case preceding *de Havilland*. In *AT&T/NCR*, the Commission rejected the parties' claims of synergies (the parties argued that the exchange of know-how would enable the merged firm to develop new communication technologies at lower costs). The Commission found that such synergies could potentially create or strengthen a dominant position. The Commission's analysis suggests that it might not have cleared the transaction without remedies if it had believed there would have been efficiency gains. Case No IV/M.50 (Commission decision of 18 January 1991), OJ 1991 C 16/00, at ¶ 30.

94 *Aérospatiale-Alenia/de Havilland*, Case No IV/M.53 (Commission decision of 2 October 1991), OJ 1991 L334/42, at ¶ 65-71.

In subsequent cases, efficiencies explicitly raised by the parties were rejected because they were not merger-specific,[95] they were not substantial,[96] they were not proven,[97] they were unlikely to be passed on to consumers, [98] and/or because once it was found that the transaction had anti-competitive effects, efficiencies no longer counted.[99]

Efficiencies have, however, apparently played a role in the EU Commission's decisions to clear a merger in some cases where efficiency considerations were among the factors leading to a no-dominance finding.[100]

95 In *Nordic Satellite Distribution*, the Commission prohibited the transaction despite claimed efficiencies. The parties argued that the transaction would contribute to economic and technical progress and benefit consumers in the short, medium and long term. The Commission recognised that the proposed infrastructure could be highly efficient, but found that with the participation of the region's strongest broadcaster and the associated risk of foreclosure, there was a risk that the transaction could lead to less variety on offer to households in the future. The Commission found that the restrictions of competition were not necessary for the achievement of the claimed efficiencies. Case No IV/M.490 (Commission decision of 19 July 1995), OJ 1996 L 53/20, at ¶ 145-152.

96 In *Bertelsmann/Kirch/Premiere*, the parties claimed that it was only by pooling the resources of Bertelsmann and Kirch that the infrastructure necessary for the breakthrough of digital television could be established (because of the very high costs of building up a decoder base, setting up the digital transmission center and investing in programs). The Commission rejected the parties' efficiency arguments and prohibited the transaction. The Commission found that the costs could not possibly be of the magnitude indicated by the parties and that the parties' claim that only Bertelsmann and Kirch together were capable of supplying the attractive programmes necessary for the breakthrough of digital television was not substantiated. Case No IV/M.993 (Commission decision of 27 May 1998), at ¶¶ 119-122.

97 In *Gencor/Lonrho*, the parties argued that considerable synergies and cost reductions could be achieved by the merger particularly through productivity improvements resulting from the exchange of know-how and savings derived from closing certain processing and refining facilities. The Commission prohibited the transaction and rejected these arguments finding that the parties' claims of synergies were vague and that synergies could turn out to be negative due to the very different organisation cultures of the two companies which will make integration difficult and probably costly. The Commission further found that if there were any synergies, they would not be to the benefit of consumers since the operation would create a jointly dominant position in the platinum and rhodium markets and form an obstacle to competition in these markets. Case No IV/M.619 (Commission decision of 24 April 1996), at ¶ 212-214.

98 In *Accor/Wagons-Lits*, the Commission rejected the parties' claimed economies of scale finding that the savings were not merger specific, were unlikely to be passed on to consumers and that the concentration formed a significant obstacle to competition. The Commission cleared the transaction subject to remedies). Case No IV/M.126 (Commission decision of 28 April 1992), OJ 1992 L 204/1, at ¶ 26.

99 In *MSG/Media Service*, the Commission rejected the parties' claims under Article 2(1)(b) of the ECMR. The parties argued that the rapid acceptance of digital television would be promoted by the services offered by MSG and that therefore the operation contributed to economic and technical progress. The Commission noted that the reference to promoting economic and technical progress in Article 2(1)(b) of the ECMR is subject to the reservation that no obstacle be formed to competition. Per the Commission, the foreseeable effects of the concentration suggested that it would lead to the early creation of a dominant position on the future market for technical and administrative services and to a substantial hindering of competition on the future market for pay-TV. These restrictive effects of the concentration also led the Commission to question whether the progress claimed by the parties would be achieved . The Commission thus found that the conditions for the application of Article 2 were not met. Case No IV/M.469 (Commission decision of 9 November 1994), OJ 1993 L 364/1, at ¶ 100-1.

100 See *Alcatel/Telettra*, Case No IV/M.42 (Commission decision of 12 April 1991), OJ 1991 L 122/148; *Mercedes-Benz/Kassbohrer*, Case No IV/M.477 (Commission decision of 14 February 1995), OJ 1995 L 211/1; *ABB/Daimler-Benz*, Case No IV/M.580 (Commission decision of 18 October 1995), OJ L 11/29; *Mannesmann/Valourec/Ilva*, Case No IV/M.315 (Commission decision of 31 January 1994), OJ 1994 L

The frequently cited *Danish Crown/Vestjyske Slagterier* decision provides a detailed articulation of the Commission's treatment of the efficiency defence when raised by the parties to a merger that would result in 'dominance'.[101] In this decision the Commission stated that it may take into account efficiencies '*only to the extent that* it is to consumers' advantage and does not form an obstacle to competition'. Because it had been concluded that the transaction would lead to the creation of a dominant position, the Commission considered that the efficiency arguments presented by the parties could not be taken into account. However, it is interesting to note that the Commission nevertheless examined the claimed efficiencies – that the merger would permit substantial cost savings, enable the merged entity to supply customers with a full range of products, and enable the parties to maintain their market position in the Japanese market in the face of strong US competition – and declared them insufficient and not merger-specific. The Commission concluded that the majority of the cost savings listed by the parties would seem to be at least partly achievable without the merger so that the synergy-related costs reductions directly attributable to the merger were very small. The Commission also stated that it was not clear why it would not be possible for each of the parties to envisage merger with other partners, whereby benefits similar to the current merger could be achieved, with less restrictive consequences.

Most recently, efficiencies issues were raised again in the *GE/Honeywell* merger which was prohibited by the Commission in July 2001.[102] Numerous commentators have criticised the Commission decision for its application of questionable theories of competitive harm and for its treatment of efficiencies. Indeed, it has been said that the Commission prohibited the transaction on the ground that it would make the merged firm so efficient that its competitors would not be able to keep up and would be forced to exit the marketplace.[103]

Commission officials have denied that the Commission prohibited the merger because of the efficiencies it would have generated.[104] According to the Director of the

102/15; *Agfa-Gevaert/DuPont*, Case No COMP/M.986 (Commission decision of 11 February 1998), OJ 1998 L 211/22. Cases cited by P Camesasca, n 16 above, and R van den Berch and P D Camesasca, *European Competition Law and Economics, A comparative perspective* (Erasmus University Rotterdam), at pp 347-9.

101 *Danish Crown/Vestjyske Slagterier*, Case No COMP/M.1313 (Commission decision of 9 March 1999), OJ 2000 L 20/1, at para 198.

102 *General Electric/Honeywell*, Case No COMP/M. 2220 (Commission decision of 3 July 2001).

103 See W Bishop and Cristina Caffara, Economic Aspects of Recent Merger Cases, IBC: Advanced EC Competition Law Conference, 15/16 November 2001; Lexecon, The Economics of GE/Honeywell – Part 1: Mixed Bundling, 31 August 2001, available at www.lexecon.co.uk/publications; Lexecon, The Econonomics of GE/Honeywell – Part 2: Foreclosure via 'Share Shifting', 31 October 2001, available at www.lexecon.co.uk/publications; RBB Economics, A Bridge Too Far? – Complements, Substitutes and Theories of Exclusion in EC Merger Control, May 2002, available at www.rbbecon.com; Donna E Patterson and Carl Shapiro, 'Transatlantic Divergence in GE/Honeywell: Causes and Lessons', Antitrust, Fall 2001, p 18; A Lofara and Derek Ridyard, Beyond Bork: New Economic Theories of Exclusion in Merger Cases [2002] ECLR Issue 3, at p 151; and W J Kolasky, n 20 above, at p 22, available at www.usdoj.gov/atr/speeches.

104 Defending the Commission's analysis, see, eg G Drauz, *Unbundling GE/Honeywell: the Assessment of Conglomerate Mergers under EC Competition Law*, Fordham Corp L Inst International L Institute (B Hawk, ed, 2001); D Giotakos, L Petit, G Garnier and P De Luyck, 'General Electric/Honeywell – An insight into the Commission's Investigation and Decision', Competition Policy Newsletter, 2001 –

Merger Task Force, the parties did not argue that the transaction would lead to a long-term and structural reduction in the marginal cost of production and distribution, which would come as a direct and immediate result of the merger, which could not be achieved by less restrictive means and which would reasonably be passed on to the consumer on a permanent basis in terms of lower prices or increased quality. Rather, the parties argued that the merger would create cost savings which could be naturally expected from any merger as a result of the elimination of duplication. In the Commission's view, these cost savings could not automatically be equated to efficiencies because they did not automatically lead to sustainable and structural price reductions; rather they resulted in increased profit margins for the merged entity, which could not automatically be expected to be passed on to the consumers.[105] Similarly, Commissioner Monti stated that the Commission 'distinguish[es] clearly between – on the one hand – mergers leading to price reductions that are the result of strategic behaviour on the part of a dominant firm, the purpose of which is to eliminate or marginalise competitors with a view to exploiting consumers in the medium term, and – on the other – mergers which will objectively lead to significant and durable efficiency gains that are likely to be passed on to the consumer'.[106] Commissioner Monti concluded:

> 'when the merging parties do not provide a clearly articulated and quantified defense in terms of efficiencies as they did not, for instance, in the *GE/Honeywell* case – it is much harder for an antitrust authority to clear a transaction that is likely to lead to foreclosure effects, because if foreclosure takes place and competitors are marginalized, there is no guarantee that prices are going to be maintained, at least over the medium and longer term, at the low level that the merged entity might strategically set them at in order to foreclose competition.'[107]

This short review of the Commission's practice shows that while an efficiency defence as such has not been applied to save a transaction after a finding of dominance was made, efficiencies have sometimes been taken into account to support a finding of no dominance and, in cases where dominance was deemed to be created, have been rejected as a defence on the grounds both that the defence is not available but also on the basis that its conditions were not met.

As noted, Commissioner Monti has recently affirmed his support for the introduction of an efficiency defence in EU merger control and has stated that the upcoming market power Guidelines will also address the question of efficiencies.[108]

Number 3, October, p 5; and M Monti, n 5 above, at ¶ 26, available at www.europa.eu.int/comm/competition/speeches (where Commissioner Monti stated: 'the Commission does not rely on the fact that efficiencies resulting from a merger are likely to have the effect of reducing or eliminating competition in the relevant market (for example by enabling lower prices to be charged to customers) as a ground for opposing a proposed transaction . . . too bad if competitors do go out of business. ... That's okay if the monopolist is more efficient.').

105 See G Drauz, *European Union Law: Unbundling GE/Honeywell: The Assessment of Conglomerate Merger under EC Competition Law*, 2001 Fordham Corp L Inst (B Hawk, ed).

106 See M Monti Antitrust in the US and Europe: a History of Convergence, speech to the American Bar Association, Washington, DC (14 November 2001), available at www.europa.eu.int/comm./competition/speeches.

107 *Id.*

108 See M Monti, n 5 above, at ¶ 26; and M Monti, n 13 above.

3.4 The Canadian approach

In Canada, the efficiency defence is set forth in section 96 of the Competition Act which provides that the Competition Tribunal shall not prohibit a merger 'if it finds that the merger or proposed merger ... has brought about or is likely to bring about gains in efficiency that will be greater than, and will offset, the effects of any prevention or lessening of competition that will result or is likely to result from the merger or proposed merger and that the gains in efficiency would not likely be attained [in the absence of the merger] ...'.

The Canadian Merger Enforcement Guidelines detail the conditions for the application of the efficiency defence and recognise two broad categories of efficiencies: (1) production efficiencies; and (2) dynamic efficiencies.[109]

'Production efficiencies include: (i) product-level, plant-level and multi-plant level operating and fixed cost efficiencies; (ii) savings associated with integrating new activities within the firm; and (iii) savings attributable to the transfer of superior production techniques and know-how from one of the merging parties to the other.'[110] Examples of specific savings include economies of scale, economies of scope, mechanisation, specialisation, the elimination of duplication, reduced downtime, a smaller base of spare parts, smaller inventory requirements, the avoidance of capital expenditures that would otherwise be required, the rationalisation of administrative and management functions. The Guidelines also recognise: (1) transactional efficiencies (such as savings resulting from the integration of activities previously performed by third parties (eg input purchases, contracts for distribution and services)); and (2) efficiencies related to distribution, advertising and capital raising. The Guidelines do not mention procurement savings among the legitimate efficiencies. In fact, gains attributable to 'increased bargaining leverage' are generally found not to be 'brought about by a saving in resources' and are thus generally not considered in the trade-off analysis.[111] The Guidelines are also fairly sceptical of managerial efficiencies which, although not rejected outright, are found to be 'generally difficult to establish objectively'.[112]

Dynamic efficiencies include gains resulting from the optimal introduction of new products, the development of a new or more efficient production process and the improvement of product quality and service.

The Guidelines impose two conditions for efficiencies to be considered in the trade-off but do not contain a consumer pass-on requirement. First, efficiencies must be

109 See Appendix II of the Guidelines. The Guidelines are available at http://strategis.ic.gc.ca/SSG/ct01032e.html.

110 Appendix II of the Merger Guidelines.

111 Section 5.3 of the Merger Guidelines (the same rejection applies to other pecuniary savings). Not all types of procurement savings are automatically excluded however. Savings resulting from the rationalisation of purchasing functions can be accepted (Appendix II of the Guidelines). Also if it can be demonstrated that the source of the gains to the merged entity is also a legitimate saving for the supplier (for example, if because of larger orders, the supplier is able to reduce transport costs or to realise economies of scale), purchasing economies could be considered (Section 5.3 of the Merger Guidelines).

112 Appendix II of the Merger Guidelines.

merger specific, ie would not be realised in the absence of the merger and cannot be attained through less competitive means.[113]

Secondly, efficiencies must not be merely redistributive in nature. This condition seeks to exclude efficiencies that do not represent a true saving in resources. Examples of rejected efficiencies include pecuniary savings (such as tax-related gains), gains resulting from wage concessions or supplier discounts that can be obtained as a result of increased bargaining power,[114] or savings that flow from a reduction in output, service, quality or variety of products.[115]

The Guidelines do not establish a sliding-scale US-style approach, nor do they state that efficiencies cannot justify a merger to monopoly or near-monopoly.[116] Rather, the Guidelines provide that the efficiency gains must be 'greater than' and 'offset' the competitive harm. According to the Guidelines, the 'words "greater than" are considered to signify that the efficiency gains must be more weighty than, more extensive than, or of larger magnitude than the anticompetitive effects .... By comparison the term "offset" is considered to suggest that the efficiency gains must neutralize, counterbalance or compensate for the likely anticompetitive effects of the merger'.[117] The Guidelines further provide that there is a qualitative and quantitative element to the trade-off analysis.[118]

The *Superior Propane* case[119] involved a detailed discussion of the efficiency defence and its application.[120]

113 Examples of alternative means include internal growth, a merger with another party, a joint venture, specialisation agreement, licensing/lease arrangement or other contractual arrangement. To be relevant, the alternative means must be existing, be a common industry practice and not merely a theoretical possibility. See Section 5.2 of the Merger Guidelines. See also L-H Röller *et al*, n 14 above, at p 79.

114 Subject to exceptions, see above.

115 See Section 5.3 of the Merger Guidelines.

116 In fact, the *Superior Propane* case discussed below is an example of a near-monopoly merger saved by efficiencies.

117 See Section 5.4 of the Merger Guidelines.

118 *Id.*

119 The case relates to the proposed acquisition by Superior Propane Inc of ICG Propane Inc (announced on 16 July 1998). The Competition Tribunal dismissed the Commissioner's initial application to enjoin the transaction and the deal was closed. On 22 December 1998, the Commissioner applied to the Tribunal seeking a post-closing order to Superior to divest its shares in ICG. On 30 August 2000, the Tribunal rejected the Commissioner's application on the basis of the parties' efficiency arguments ('the Propane Tribunal Initial Decision'). On appeal by the Commissioner, the Federal Court of Appeal on 4 April 2001 reversed the Tribunal's decision ('the Propane Appeal Decision') and remanded the case to the Canadian Tribunal for a rehearing on the adverse economic effects of the merger. On 4 April 2002, the Tribunal issued its decision after re-examination of the case and found again that the transaction should be authorised on the ground that efficiencies far outweighed the alleged anticompetitive harm ('the Propane Tribunal Redetermination Decision'). The Commissioner has again appealed that decision to the Federal Appeal Court and the appeal is still pending. The judgments in the matter of *The Commissioner of Competition v Superior Propane and ICG Propane Inc* are available as follows: (1) for the Propane Tribunal Initial Decision (30 August 2000), available at www.ct-tc.gc.ca/English/cases/propane/192b.pdf); (2) for the Propane Appeal Decision (4 April 2001), available at http:/reports.fja.gc.ca; and (3) for the 'Propane Tribunal Redetermination Decision' (4 April 2002), available at www.ct-tc.gc.ca/English/cases/propane/0238a.pdf.

120 The discussion of the *Superior Propane* case in this section is limited to the type of efficiencies accepted. In the third section below, the case is discussed with regard to the type of welfare standard applied in the evaluation of efficiencies.

In its *Initial Decision,* the Canadian Tribunal addressed the types of efficiencies claimed by the parties. The Tribunal approved, despite the strong objections of the Competition Commissioner, the merger between the two leading Canadian suppliers of propane based on the parties' successful assertion of an efficiencies defence, despite very serious substantive concerns.[121]

The Tribunal found that the merger would generate approximately $29 million in efficiencies per year.[122] The Tribunal accepted the claimed efficiencies with regard to the parties' corporate centres,[123] customer support[124] and field operations.[125] The Tribunal denied the claimed efficiencies with regard to procurement costs,[126] public company costs[127] and propane supply and transport costs.[128]

3.5 Considerations for possible Commission guidelines

In formulating its guidelines, the Commission will have to consider whether the types of acceptable efficiencies should be limited. In particular, the Commission will need to consider whether the efficiencies defence should be considered only in the case of production and allocative efficiencies that are merger-specific and directly passed on to consumers.

121 The anti-competitive effects of the transaction and the resulting lessening of competition in Canada and many local markets across Canada were not disputed. The Canadian Tribunal agreed with the Commissioner's assessment that (1) the merged entity would have a combined market share of at least 70 per cent on a national basis and near monopoly in a number of local markets, and (2) there was a high level of concentration in the relevant market, high barriers to entry, no effective remaining competition in Canada and no foreign competition into Canada.

122 *Propane Tribunal Initial Decision,* at paras 380-383.

123 Savings were anticipated from headcount reductions at head offices, a decline of the office rent and a reduction of public company costs, legal and marketing expenditures. The Tribunal did, however, reduce the amounts claimed by the parties. Propane Tribunal Initial Decision, at paras 320 and 330-345. The Tribunal also reduced the parties' claimed efficiencies with regard to property tax savings and integration costs. *Propane Tribunal Initial Decision,* at paras 374-379.

124 Savings were expected from the closing of duplicative facilities, lay-off of redundant personnel and a restructuring of the regional operations. *Propane Tribunal Initial Decision,* at para 321.

125 Savings were expected due to redundancies in the overlapping geographical territories of the parties and from a reduction in supply, storage, inventory and transport costs. The Tribunal did however, reduce the amounts claimed by the parties in fleet and driver reductions. *Propane Tribunal Initial Decision,* at paras 322 and 353-363.

126 The Tribunal found that claimed savings to suppliers of the merging parties resulting from the combination of the purchasing activities of the merging parties in one company were largely pecuniary and unsubstantiated. *Propane Tribunal Initial Decision,* at paras 346-348.

127 The Tribunal rejected claimed savings that would be realised by avoiding expenditures that would have been incurred if ICG had gone public (stock exchange listing fees, costs of outside board directors, etc) because Superior failed to establish that it would likely take ICG public if it were ordered to divest its ownership. *Propane Tribunal Initial Decision,* at paras 349-352.

128 The Tribunal rejected claimed savings from the replacement of independent transport contracts by parties' own operations as largely pecuniary and unsubstantiated. *Propane Tribunal Initial Decision,* at paras 364-366.

3.5.1 The merger specificity requirement

The Commission's current position (as reflected in decisions and recent statements by Commissioner Monti and MTF Director Drauz)[129] seems to indicate that the announced Guidelines, in line with the US and Canadian approach, will most likely require that efficiencies be merger-specific.

Despite its apparent general acceptance, the merger specificity requirement raises several issues. First, requiring parties to prove that the claimed efficiencies could not be achieved in the absence of the merger may impose an obligation to prove a negative proposition, always a difficult task. Secondly, while alternative means to achieve the claimed efficiencies may in theory exist (eg internal growth, other contractual arrangements, etc), there may be valid economic reasons why these alternatives – even though they may well be less restrictive of competition – are not attractive to the parties.[130] Thirdly, predicting whether an alternative means is likely to be pursued in the absence of the merger and whether such an alternative is as effective in terms of realising the projected savings is a highly speculative exercise.[131]

It may be possible to reduce these problems by clarifying the merger-specificity requirement. One approach, advocated by certain US commentators, would be to focus not on whether similar cost savings could be achieved by other means but rather on whether any available alternative method to obtain the savings is less costly than, and can be implemented as rapidly as, the merger.[132] Under this definition of the merger-specificity requirement, it could be possible to provide that once the parties have proven that efficiencies are reasonably likely, the burden should shift to the Commission to demonstrate that the same efficiencies would likely be achieved in a similar time frame and at a similar cost, in the absence of the merger, by other means that are less restrictive of competition. In assessing alternatives, the Commission would arguably want to consider only alternatives that are practical in the particular situation faced by the merging parties and would not insist on merely theoretical albeit less restrictive alternatives.

3.5.2 The consumer pass-on requirement

The Commission's case law and statements of Commission officials suggest that the Guidelines are likely to require that efficiencies be 'reasonably passed on to the consumer on a permanent basis in terms of lower prices or increased quality'.[133]

129 These recent statements indicate that efficiencies must 'come as a direct and immediate result of the merger' and 'cannot be achieved by less restrictive means'.

130 For example, a firm may not wish to add capacity to achieve economies of scale if the added capacity has the effect of depressing prices. Similarly, the transaction costs of combining the complementary assets of two parties by contract could be higher than the integration costs of the merger. See W J Kolasky and A R Dick, n 7 above, at p 28.

131 See J Farrell and C Shapiro, n 28 above, at 691.

132 See T J Muris, n 54 above. This also appears to be the approach recommended in the study commissioned by the Commission on efficiencies. See F Ilzkovitz and R Meiklejohn, n 15 above, at p 24 (stating that the efficiencies need to be merger specific in that 'they would not materialize without the merger').

133 See above page 246. Mr Drauz stated that 'efficiencies in the form of cost savings that will not be passed on to the merging firms' customers are irrelevant for the assessment'. See G Drauz, Recent Developments in the Assessment of Dominance, Speech delivered to the EC Merger Control 10th Anniversary Conference, Brussels (14-15 September 2000), available at www.europa.eu.int/comm/competition/speeches.

As a matter of theory it would appear that the necessity for the pass-on requirement most likely turns on the welfare standard selected by the Commission for the evaluation of efficiencies, although it would appear that room can also be found for the consideration of such factors as externalities under a modified or flexible consumer welfare standard (see below). It can be debated whether the Commission's approach to the welfare standard and consumer pass-on requirement is limited by the current wording of Article 2(1)(b) which allows the Commission to consider technical and economic progress only to the extent that it is 'to consumers' advantage'. While the reference to 'consumers' advantage' would appear to require some degree of transfer of the efficiency gains to consumers, it does not in itself limit the nature of those gains to price, require that they be immediate or fully offset the anti-competitive effects of the merger and the reference to technical an economic progress could support a broader welfare standard.

It would appear from the foregoing that the Commission may, at the least, have the discretion to determine whether: (1) the gains resulting from the efficiencies must be passed on *directly and immediately* to consumers; (2) the gains must be passed on to consumers in the *same market* where the competitive harm is suffered; and (3) gain and harm to different groups of consumers can be weighed against each other.

These considerations are important. Certain efficiencies may have long-term effects, not evident in the short term, that will outweigh the anti-competitive effects on a net present value basis.[134] Requiring an immediate transfer of gains to consumers would require the Commission to ignore these efficiencies. The US Merger Guidelines have sought to preserve the agencies' flexibility with respect to this trade-off by allowing them to consider efficiencies that do not immediately and directly affect prices to consumers, but have delayed effects to the benefit of consumers.[135] The Canadian Guidelines (although there is no consumer pass-on requirement in Canada) also address the issue of a time delay between realisation of the efficiencies and the anti-competitive effects brought about by a merger,[136] thereby recognising that efficiencies that may not occur at the same time as the anti-competitive harm are not necessarily automatically disregarded.

Intuitively, it would seem fair that anti-competitive harm and efficiencies should be assessed on the same relevant market. Under this approach, it would be expected that efficiencies outweigh anti-competitive effects on every market on which a lessening of competition is found.

However, the Canadian Merger Guidelines take the view that all efficiencies should be counted, regardless of the product markets where they are realised.[137] As stated by the Competition Tribunal in its *Propane Redetermination Decision*, '... section 96 of the

134 These include in particular R&D and innovation efficiencies.

135 The Guidelines do not explicitly provide that to be cognisable efficiencies must be passed on directly and immediately to consumers. Furthermore, the Guidelines reserve the possibility for the agencies to 'also consider the effects of cognizable efficiencies with no short-term, direct effect on prices in the relevant market', although these 'delayed benefits from efficiencies (due to delay in the achievement of, or the realization of consumer benefits from efficiencies) will be given less weight because they are less proximate and more difficult to predict' (footnote 37).

136 Section 5.7.1 of the Guidelines provide that timing differences between the anticipated efficiencies and the anti-competitive effects must be addressed by discounting both to present constant dollar values according to a set methodology.

137 See Merger Guidelines, Section 5.1.

Act applies to the transaction in its entirety. There is no requirement that gains in efficiency in one market or area exceed or offset the effects in that market or area. Rather, the tests of "greater than" and "offset" in section 96 require a comparison of the aggregate gains in efficiency with the aggregate of the effects of lessening or prevention of competition across all markets and areas. Accordingly, the Act clearly contemplates that some markets or areas may experience gains in efficiency that exceed the effects therein, while other may not'.[138] The Guidelines only make an exception where a prohibition order is sought for part of a merger. In such a case, efficiencies that would be attained in markets that are not the focus of the Tribunal's prohibition order would normally not be considered in the trade-off analysis, except when they are inextricably linked to efficiencies that the Tribunal's order would prevent in the relevant markets.[139]

The US approach is different. Efficiencies and anti-competitive effects are assessed and traded off on each relevant product market and it is normally expected that there be a positive net result on each market. The Guidelines state that 'Section 7 of the Clayton Act prohibits mergers that may substantially lessen competition "in any line of commerce ... in any section of the country". Accordingly, the Agency normally assesses competition in each relevant market affected by a merger independently and normally will challenge the merger if it is likely to be anticompetitive in any relevant market'.[140] The US Merger Guidelines do, however, provide for a limited exception. The agencies may consider efficiencies not strictly in the relevant market if these efficiencies are 'inextricably linked' to the anti-competitive harm (ie the competitive harm in one market cannot be eliminated without also sacrificing the efficiencies in the other market) and the harm is small and the efficiencies are large.[141]

The Canadian Competition Tribunal has commented that under the US approach, 'the insufficiency of [efficiency] gains in even one relevant market can lead the enforcement agencies to disregard efficiency gains produced by the merger entirely'.[142]

Former FTC Chairman Robert Pitofsky has identified two problems with the assessment of competitive harm and efficiencies across markets as is done in Canada.[143] First, there is a measurement problem. How can one measure the trade-off between an increase of market shares in one market and a price decrease in another market?[144] Secondly, there is a fairness problem. Why should the welfare of consumers on one market be sacrificed to the betterment of consumers on another?

138 *Propane Tribunal Redetermination decision*, at para 140.

139 The Guidelines give the example of economies of scope between products in different markets. See Merger Guidelines, Section 5.2.

140 Footnote 36 of the Merger Guidelines.

141 Footnote 36 of the Merger Guidelines provides: '[i]n some cases, however, the Agency in its prosecutorial discretion will consider efficiencies not strictly in the relevant market, but so inextricably linked with it that a partial divestiture or other remedy could not feasibly eliminate the anticompetitive effect in the relevant market without sacrificing the efficiencies in other markets. Inextricably linked efficiencies rarely are a significant factor in the Agency's determination not to challenge a merger. They are most likely to make a difference when they are great and the likely effect on the relevant market(s) is small.'

142 *Propane Tribunal Redetermination decision*, at para 138.

143 See R Pitofsky, n 9 above.

144 See also L-H Röller *et al*, n 14 above, at p 91.

Yet, Mr Pitofsky notes that the narrow possibility preserved by the US Merger Guidelines to consider efficiencies across markets captures the rare cases, for example where the same consumers buy products on both markets, or where the efficiencies are huge and the competitive harm small.[145] A third problem has been identified that would be particularly relevant to the European Commission given the tight deadline for review under the ECMR. If cost savings in markets other than the affected markets (where the competitive analysis is detailed) are to be considered, the Commission would in effect be required to assess the effects of the transaction on these other markets. This would make the analysis more complex and would likely increase the information burden on the notifying parties.[146]

Another dimension to this issue is geographical. For example, should a transaction be approved if it has anti-competitive effects in the European Union but improves the competitiveness of the Community industry outside the European Union? In the United States, this would most likely not be accepted.[147] The Canadian Competition Act expressly mandates the Tribunal to consider whether increased exports or import substitution will result from any efficiency gains (section 96(2)).[148] However, the Guidelines clarify that section 96(2) does not expand the class of efficiency gains that may be considered in the trade-off analysis to include gains outside Canada.[149] This is confirmed by the Tribunal's interpretation in the *Superior Propane* case. There the Tribunal found that both efficiencies and deadweight loss in foreign markets resulting from a merger in Canada should be excluded from the application of the trade-off equation under the efficiency defence available under the Canadian Act. The Tribunal based its view in part on the fact that the Purpose Clause of the Act refers to promoting the efficiency of 'the Canadian economy'.[150] The ECMR similarly mandates the Commission to protect effective competition 'in the common market'. It is thus unclear whether efficiencies achieved outside the Common Market could be considered against anti-competitive effects within the Community.[151]

3.5.3 Exclusive focus on productive and allocative efficiencies

The ECMR, the Commission's case law and statements of Commission officials appear to indicate an intent to limit the acceptable efficiencies to 'long-term and structural reductions in the marginal cost of production and distribution' and to reject those 'cost savings which can be naturally expected from any merger as a result of the elimination of duplication'.[152]

145 See R Pitofsky, n 9 above.
146 See L-H Röller *et al*, n 14 above, at pp 91 and 114.
147 See R Pitofsky, 'Proposals for Revised United States Merger Enforcement in a Global Economy' (1992) 81 Geo LJ 195, 245; and L-H Röller *et al*, n 14 above, at p 75.
148 Section 96(2) requires that account be taken of whether gains in efficiency will result in '(i) a significant increase in the real value of exports; or (ii) a significant substitution of domestic products for imported products'.
149 Rather, it simply means to clarify that the output that will likely displace imports and any increased output that is sold abroad have to be counted in the calculation of the merged firm's output for the purpose of arriving at the sum of unit and other saving brought about by the merger. Section 5.6 of the Merger Guidelines.
150 *Propane Tribunal Redetermination Decision*, at para 196.
151 This issue also directly ties in with considerations of international trade and obligations that may exist under WTO and other multilateral or bilateral commercial treaties.
152 See above page 246.

Some US commentators have argued that there is no valid reason for limiting the acceptable categories of efficiencies to only production and allocative efficiencies.[153] The economists involved in the DG ECO-FIN study tend to favour efficiencies that result in variable cost savings over those that result in fixed cost savings, because the former are more likely to be passed on to consumers.[154] The argument that other efficiencies are more difficult to establish, verify and quantify does not, however, mean that they should be excluded; rather it leads to the conclusion that the merging parties will have to provide stronger evidence to support their claims and that the authority will be stricter in its evaluation.[155] This is the approach followed by the US Merger Guidelines which identify efficiencies that are 'more likely', 'generally less likely' or 'less likely' to be susceptible to verification, merger-specific or substantial, without rejecting outright certain types of efficiencies. The same approach is adopted by the Canadian Guidelines, subject to one exception (purely redistributive efficiencies, such as procurement savings from increased buying power, are excluded).

The Commission already appears willing to recognise production and distribution efficiencies. However, it would appear that consideration should also be given to expanding the list of relevant efficiencies to include dynamic or innovation efficiencies,[156] promotional and advertising efficiencies, capital-raising efficiencies and procurement efficiencies.[157] One approach (as is done in the United States and Canada) that merits some consideration would be for the Commission to detail the conditions that all efficiencies must satisfy (eg merger-specific, verifiable), without excluding from the outset certain categories of efficiencies, but providing that certain less verifiable efficiencies will require a higher level of proof or be given less weight.

Some commentators have questioned whether the types of acceptable efficiencies under the ECMR, if the efficiency analysis is to be based on the un-amended Article 2(1)(b), could go beyond purely dynamic efficiencies. The DG ECO-FIN Study points out that the wording of Article 2(1)(b) refers only to 'the development' of technical and economic progress and could therefore be interpreted to cover only dynamic, innovative efficiencies as opposed to static efficiencies.[158] With a view to ensuring that

153 See, eg T J Muris, n 54 above; and W J Kolasky, *United States and European Competition Policy: Are there more differences than we care to admit*, Address before the European Policy Centre, Brussels (10 April 2002), available at www.usdoj.gov/atr/public/speeches/10999.htm (where the stated that '[the view of the US DOJ] is that anything that serves to bring price down closer to marginal cost enhances allocative efficiency and thereby benefits consumers. We don't buy the notion, therefore, that some efficiencies are better than others.').

154 See L-H Röller *et al*, n 14 above, at p 114.

155 See T J Muris, n 54 above.

156 Certain innovation efficiencies may already be included in the statements of Messrs Drauz and Monti to the extent that they would result in lowering marginal production costs (process innovation).

157 This also appears to be the approach recommended in the study commissioned by the Commission on efficiencies. See F Ilzkovitz and R Meiklejohn, n 15 above, at p 24 (stating that the types of efficiencies should include static and dynamic efficiencies and that efficiencies that do not necessarily result in price reductions should be counted).

158 The authors compare Article 2(1)(b) of the ECMR with the wording of Article 81(3) of the EC Treaty which provides for the consideration of 'the improvement of production and distribution of goods and the promotion of technical or economic progress'. See L-H Röller et al, n 14 above, at pp 82-3; and F Ilzkovitz and R Meiklejohn, n 15 above, at pp 13-14. This interpretation may, however, be too narrow, and it can be plausibly argued that the reference to 'economic' in addition to 'technical' progress sweeps in categories of efficiencies other than those associated with innovation.

the proposed Guidelines provide maximum guidance to businesses and practitioners and eliminate as much as possible the uncertainty inherent in a change of the Commission's practice, it would be helpful for the Guidelines to reflect the Commission's position on the specific issues raised above, and in particular with regard to the categories of efficiencies that will be deemed most beneficial, the treatment of externalities, delayed efficiencies and efficiencies occurring in a different product or geographical market than the competitive harm.

4. Efficiencies and welfare standards

Conceptually, the main issue that the Commission faces in defining the role of efficiencies in EC merger control is the choice of the welfare standard under which efficiencies will be evaluated. The selection of the welfare standard will determine critical aspects of the efficiency analysis such as the calculation of the consumer loss that efficiencies must outweigh, whether gains must be passed on to consumers and the types of efficiencies likely to be deemed most beneficial.

The two welfare models supporting antitrust laws are the consumer welfare and the total welfare models. Under each model, there are several possible standards that can be used to measure efficiencies in relation to the anti-competitive effects arising from a transaction. In this section, we first define each model,[159] then we examine the approach in the United States, Canada and the European Union before discussing some of the advantages and disadvantages of each.

4.1 The competing standards

4.1.1 Consumer welfare model

In a consumer welfare model, the primary objective of the competition law is to prevent the unfair transfers of wealth from consumers to firms with market power.[160] The US[161] and the EU[162] competition laws are generally said to be based on a

159 Different commentators may use different terms to define the standards. We follow here the terminology and the definitions of the various tests presented by the Canadian Competition Tribunal in its Redetermination Decision in the Superior Propane case.

160 *Mergers and Acquisitions, Understanding Antitrust Issues* (2000), ABA, at p 145.

161 The Department of Justice states that the antitrust laws 'prohibit business practices that unreasonably deprive consumers of the benefits of competition, resulting in higher prices for inferior products and services'. US Department of Justice, *Antitrust enforcement and the consumer,* at www.usdoj.gov/atr/public. The Federal Trade Commission similarly states that the goal of antitrust laws is to make sure that 'competition benefits consumers by keeping prices low and the quality of goods and services high'. Federal Trade Commission, Promoting Competition, protecting consumers, at www.ftc.gov/bc/compguide.

162 See R Van den Bergh and P D Camesasca, *European Competition Law and Economics, A comparative perspective* (Erasmus Rotterdam University), at 62-69 (explaining that the EU competition laws predominantly reflect a consumer welfare model, although some isolated elements indicative of total welfare considerations can be found). See also M Monti, *Analytical Framework of Merger Review,* Speech delivered at the International Competition Network Inaugural Conference, Naples (28-29 September 2002), available at www.europa.eu.int/comm./competition/speeches (where Commissioner Monti stated that 'the ultimate policy goal [of the EU competition policy] is the promotion of economic performance and in particular the protection of consumer welfare').

consumer welfare model. Three possible standards have been presented to evaluate efficiencies.

The pure price standard. Under a pure price standard, 'a merger can be approved only if it does not lead to an increase in market power. No consideration of efficiencies is allowed, even if efficiencies can be shown to lead to a price decrease'.[163]

The modified price standard. Under the modified price standard, a transaction that leads to an increase in market power can be approved if it generates efficiency gains that are so large that despite the increase in market power, the post-merger prices will decrease.[164]

Under this standard, both the deadweight loss and the wealth transfer effects of an anti-competitive price increase are treated as consumer loss that must be outweighed by proven efficiencies. In order to offset the consumer loss, at least some of the cost savings must be passed on to consumers (in the form of lower prices) rather than retained by the merging parties.[165]

The consumer surplus standard. Under the consumer surplus standard, a transaction that results in a post-merger higher price to consumers can be approved if it generates other efficiencies that outweigh the negative effects of the price increase.[166] The Canadian Tribunal has phrased this test (somewhat confusingly) as being met '[i]f the gains in efficiency exceed the total loss of consumer surplus ...'.[167] The 'total loss of consumer surplus' is defined as the deadweight loss plus the consumer surplus that is redistributed from consumers to shareholders as excess profits,[168] but what is meant is that, on balance, there is no overall loss to consumer welfare.

In other words, this standard, like the modified price standard, counts deadweight loss and wealth transfer effects as part of the total consumer loss that must be outweighed by efficiencies. As with the modified price standard it also requires that the proven efficiencies be passed on to consumers. However, it differs from the modified price standard in that there is no requirement that post-merger prices decrease. Rather, the standard appears to recognise the countervailing consumer benefits of other kinds such as higher quality, better information, increased services or innovation.

4.1.2 The total welfare model

Under the total welfare model (also referred to as the social welfare model), the primary objective of competition law is to increase total social welfare by allocating resources to those users who value them most.[169] Canada's competition laws are based on the total welfare model. Under the total welfare model, it is irrelevant that producers rather than consumers capture the surplus resulting from the merger efficiencies as the overall social welfare benefits. It is not expected that efficiencies be passed on to consumers because the aggregate social welfare is already increased by

163 *Propane Tribunal Redetermination Decision,* at para 86.

164 A transaction that would result in post-merger higher prices would not be approved. *Propane Tribunal Redetermination Decision,* at paras 87-89.

165 *Id,* at para 88.

166 *Propane Tribunal Redetermination Decision* at para 91.

167 *Propane Tribunal Redetermination Decision,* at para 90.

168 *Id.*

169 See R Van den Bergh and P Camesasca, n 162 above, at pp 64-5.

Table 1

	Total Surplus	Balancing Weights	Consumer Surplus	Modified Price Standard
Deadweight Loss	Consumer Loss	Consumer Loss	Consumer Loss	Consumer Loss
Wealth Transfers	Neutral (consumer loss offset by producer gain)	Presumptively Neutral, but can be re-weighted case by case to reflect 'social values'	Consumer Loss	Consumer Loss
Cost Savings or other advantages	Producer Gain (regardless of whether passed on to consumers)	Producer Gain (regardless of whether passed on to consumers)	Producer Gain only if passed on to consumers	Producer Gain only if passed on to consumers in the form of lower prices

the fact that manufacturers are achieving efficiencies.[170] Two possible standards have been presented to evaluate efficiencies under the social welfare model.

The total surplus standard. Under this standard, a transaction that results in higher post-merger prices to consumers can be approved if it generates other efficiencies. Only the deadweight loss is counted as consumer loss that must be offset by the efficiencies; the wealth transfers from consumers to shareholders are deemed neutral,[171] and there is *no* requirement that efficiencies be passed on to consumers.[172] Efficiencies must only exceed the deadweight loss for a merger that results in increased market power and higher prices to consumers to be approved.[173] This was the standard applied by the courts and agencies in Canada until the *Superior Propane* case.

The balancing weight method. The balancing weight method is similar to the total surplus standard in that deadweight loss is always counted as consumer loss that must be offset by efficiencies and there is *no* requirement that efficiencies be passed on to consumers. The main difference is in the treatment of the wealth transfers from consumers to the merging parties. Such transfers are presumptively neutral (as in the

170 See R Van den Bergh and P Camesasca, n 162 above, at pp 64-5.

171 Total surplus is the sum of consumer surplus and producer surplus. Producer surplus is defined as the difference between a firm's revenues and its economic costs. See, eg G Allen, The Treatment of Efficiencies in Merger Analysis, speech to the Conference 'Meet the Competition Bureau' (3 May 1999), available at www.strategis.ic.gc.ca/SSG/ct01548e.html.

172 Under the total surplus standard, consumers and producers are treated equally (gains to producers are considered to be as valuable for society as gains to consumers).

173 *Propane Tribunal Redetermination Decision*, at paras 95-101.

total surplus standard), but they may be 're-weighed' on a case-by-case basis in order to reflect 'social values'.[174]

Table 1 shows how the various standards balance the different elements of the welfare equation.

4.2 Application in the United States, European Union and Canada[175]

4.2.1 United States

On balance, it can probably be said that the United States applies a modified price standard, although there may be signs of evolution towards a consumer surplus standard.

The 1997 Revised Merger Guidelines maintain language referring to the impact of efficiencies on lowering prices to consumers,[176] and the US practice (agencies and courts) also reveals that deadweight loss and wealth transfers from consumers to the merging parties are included in the consumer loss. However, the 1997 Guidelines may depart slightly from a modified price standard in two ways: (1) the Guidelines do not require that efficiencies *must* prevent price increases to outweigh competitive harm[177]; and (2) the Guidelines do not require that efficiencies be passed on to consumers to be cognisable. Whether the Guidelines should expressly provide for a consumer pass-on requirement was heavily debated during the 1997 revision of the Merger Guidelines.[178] The Guidelines ultimately did not include the express requirement but provide that efficiencies directly passed on to consumers are given greater weight.[179]

Despite the apparently more liberal language of the Guidelines, courts continue in their review of efficiencies to suggest that pass-on should be a requirement, showing that the modified price standard is holding its ground.[180] Antitrust agencies, when litigating a case in court, and in particular the FTC, also seem to require that

174 *Propane Tribunal Redetermination Decision*, at paras 102-109.

175 For the sake of consistency, we use in the discussion below the terminology used by the Canadian Tribunal in the *Superior Propane* case.

176 The Guidelines provide that 'the Agency considers whether cognizable efficiencies likely would be sufficient to reverse the merger's potential to harm consumers in the relevant market, eg by preventing price increases in that market'.

177 As noted by the Competition Tribunal in its *Propane Redetermination Decision*, the Guidelines as written 'appear to regard preventing a price increase as sufficient but not necessary to reverse the harm to consumers'. At para 123. Indeed the Guidelines refer to preventing price increase as an example of the ways in which efficiencies can outweigh competitive harm.

178 See J F Brodley, n 24 above (advocating that an efficiency defence should not be conditioned on an immediate pass-on of the cost savings to consumers); R Pitofsky, 'Proposals for Revised United States Merger Enforcement in a Global Economy' (1992) 81 Georgetown LJ 195; and T J Muris, n 54 above.

179 The Guidelines provide that greater weight is given to efficiencies that are passed on immediately to consumers, but the Guidelines also preserve the possibility for the agencies to consider efficiencies that have no direct short-term effect on prices, but will ultimately benefit consumers. These 'delayed-effect efficiencies', although recognised, are given less weight. See footnote 37 of the Revised Horizontal Merger Guidelines. See also W J Kolasky and A R Dick, n 7 above.

180 See the discussion of the *Staples/Office Depot* case above; and cases cited by D Balto, n 20 above, at footnote 31.

efficiencies be passed on.[181] For example, in the *Heinz/Beech-Nut* case, the FTC stated that 'even if an efficiencies defense can be entertained, defendants must show that the "proven" efficiencies will be passed on and that they overwhelm any possible anticompetitive effects of the merger'.[182] However, the FTC position may change in the future if its Chairman maintains his past views on the issue. Mr. Muris (before his appointment as FTC Chairman) criticized the pass-on requirement observing that it 'appears to be based on the belief that efficiencies will be passed on to consumers only where there is intense competition. According to economists, this belief is a fundamental misconception'.[183]

4.2.2 Canada

The standard applied in Canada under the total welfare model appears to be currently in flux between the total surplus standard and the balancing weight method. There is no requirement under either standard that efficiencies be passed on to consumers.

The standard traditionally applied in Canadian practice was the total surplus standard. In the *Superior Propane* case, however, the Competition Commissioner advocated the application of the balancing weight method.[184]

The Tribunal in its *Initial Decision* adopted the total surplus standard to assess the parties' claimed efficiencies and authorised the transaction, finding that the efficiencies dwarfed the estimated deadweight loss.[185]

On appeal from the Commissioner,[186] the Federal Appeal Court accepted the Commissioner's argument that the Tribunal had erred by adopting the total surplus standard, but appeared to give only qualified support to the balancing weight method[187] and provided no guidance on how to apply this alternative standard.[188]

On remand, the Tribunal applied the balancing weight method and, again, cleared the merger, finding that the projected efficiencies arising from the merger outweighed the deadweight loss and 'any reasonable' re-weighting of the wealth transfer effects

181 Note, however, that it is less clear that the agencies apply a strict pass-on requirement when they examine efficiencies outside court as part of the discretionary decision not to challenge a merger. See R Pitofsky, n 9 above.

182 See *FTC v H J Heinz & Co et al*, Reply Brief for the Plaintiff-Appellant FTC, No 00-5362 (29 November 2000), at 43 (citing *Cardinal Health* and *Staples*), cited in the *Propane Tribunal Redetermination Decision*, at para 127.

183 T J Muris, n 59 above, at 733.

184 The Competition Commissioner argued that the total surplus standard was too easily met and should be replaced.

185 The efficiencies were estimated at $29.2 million per year, compared to a deadweight loss estimated to be unlikely to exceed $3 million per year. *Propane Tribunal Initial Decision*, at paras 383 and 447.

186 See K von Finckenstein, Speech to the Canadian Bar Association, Competition Section, Annual Meeting (21 September 2000) (for a discussion of the objectives pursued by the Commissioner in his appeal), available at www.strategis.ic.gc.ca.

187 The Court stated that prescribing 'the "correct" methodology for determining the extent of the anti-competitive effects of a merger ... [is] a task beyond the limits of the Court's competence. Whatever standard is selected ... must be more reflective than the total surplus standard of the different objectives of the Competition Act [which per the Court does not intend to limit the possible negative effects of a merger to the deadweight loss]. ... It seems that the Balancing Weight Method ... adopted by the Commissioner meets these broad requirements'. *Propane Appeal Decision*, at paras 139-141.

188 At para 141.

arising from the merger.[189] The Commissioner's appeal of this second Tribunal decision is still pending.

4.2.3 European Union

Based on the current limited precedents in the European Union, it would seem that the Commission has applied a modified price standard. That is, in its limited assessment of efficiency claims to date, the Commission appears to require the two essential elements of the modified price standard: that (1) efficiencies be passed on to consumers, (2) in the form of lower prices. Current thinking also seems to include wealth transfers from consumers to the merging parties in the consumer loss that must be outweighed by the efficiencies and shows a preference for efficiencies that result in marginal cost reduction, two other elements pointing to a modified price standard.[190]

4.3 Advantages and disadvantages of the different standards

4.3.1 Modified price standard

The modified price standard is said to have a strong foundation in welfare economics because it is based on the 'Pareto Improvement Criterion'.[191]

However, the modified price standard has been criticised for (1) not recognising the value of gains to the merging firms[192]; and (2) creating a risk that mergers that are potentially welfare enhancing would be blocked.[193] Under the Pareto Improvement Criterion and the modified price standard, a transaction that would generate large cost savings and only a small price increase could potentially be prohibited.[194] The modified price standard has also been criticised for various issues associated with the consumer pass-on requirement, including: (1) the consumer pass-on requirement to be effective requires a nearly perfectly competitive market, in which case the transaction would raise no issues in the first place and efficiencies would not need to be

189 The Tribunal thus estimated the adverse redistributive effects of the transaction and attempted to 're-weigh' these effects. The Tribunal found that it was unable to determine the proper relative weight to assign to the adverse redistributive effects in the absence of a statutory basis in the Competition Act and due to lack of data. The Tribunal could only conclude that it was clear that the re-distributive effects were small and would under any reasonable weighing scheme be far exceeded by the undisputed $29.2 million of claimed efficiencies. *Propane Tribunal Redetermination Decision*, at para 371.

190 According to the Director of the Merger Task Force, valid efficiencies will lead to 'structural reduction in the marginal cost of production and distribution', 'reasonably will be passed on to the consumer on a permanent basis in terms of lower prices or increased quality' and do not 'result in increased profit margins for the merged entity, which cannot automatically be expected to be passed on to the consumers'. See G Drauz, *European Union Law: Unbundling GE/Honeywell: The Assessment of Conglomerate Merger under EC Competition Law*, 2001 Fordham Corp L Inst (B Hawk, ed).

191 This criterion is satisfied if an economic situation improves the situation of at least one economic agent and no agent is made worse off. See *Propane Tribunal Redetermination Decision*, at para 89 (referring to P Townley's critique of the standard).

192 Under this standard, only the direct welfare of purchasers in the market count. See *Propane Tribunal Redetermination Decision*, at para 89 (summarising the critique of Professor P Townley).

193 *Id.*

194 *Id.*

considered[195]; (2) it is unclear how much of the efficiency gains must be passed on[196]; and (3) the economic foundation of the consumer pass-on requirement has been questioned.[197]

4.3.2 Consumer surplus standard

The consumer surplus standard has been subject to various criticisms. It has been said that this standard 'will allow mergers that hurt consumers as consumers and forbid mergers that benefit the economy as a whole. It does not distinguish between the transfer of wealth and the destruction of wealth'.[198] The consumer surplus standard is stated to have no basis in welfare economics.[199] The consumer surplus standard is also criticised for (1) not recognising the value of gains to the merging firms that can be socially positive; and (2) treating all consumers alike and protecting all consumers when some consumers may be better off than others and some consumers may be better off than the merging parties' shareholders.[200]

4.3.3 Total surplus standard

The total surplus standard is preferred by many economists.[201] These economists take the position that competition policy should strive to achieve the maximisation of the total social surplus, ie the sum of consumer surplus and producer surplus.[202] These economists consider that there is no economic reason for favouring a dollar in the hands of the consumers of the products of the merged entity over a dollar in the hands of the producers or its shareholders.[203] The total surplus standard is said to follow most closely the economic concept of allocative efficiency.[204]

195 This is what Robert Pitofsky referred to as the 'killer standard', ie the pass-on requirement prevents efficiency considerations where efficiencies would be relevant. See R Pitofsky, 'Proposals for Revised United States Merger Enforcement in a Global Economy' (1992) 81 Geo LJ 195, 207-208.

196 L-H Röller, J Stennek and F Verboven indicate that the degree of pass-on depends on price elasticity, cost structure and industry structure. In their view, the focus should be on firm-specific pass-on. L-H Röller *et al*, n 14 above, at pp 161-163 and 184.

197 See T J Muris, n 59 above, at 733 (stating that the belief underlying the requirement was based on an economic misconception).

198 See D G McFetridge, 'Efficiencies Standards: Take Your Pick' (2002) 21(1) Canadian Competition Record 54.

199 See *Propane Tribunal Redetermination Decision*, at para 93 (referring to P Townley's critique).

200 *Propane Tribunal Redetermination Decision*, at paras 93-94 (summarising the critique of Professor P Townley).

201 As stated by the Canadian Court of Appeals, 'an impressive array of economists, and law and economic specialists, both in Canada and the United States, have argued that the total surplus standard is the appropriate basis for determining whether an anti-competitive merger that produces efficiency gains should be permitted'. *Propane Appeal Decision*, at para 134.

202 See, eg L-H Röller *et al*, n 14 above, at pp 50-57.

203 See *Propane Appeal Decision*, at para 47. See also, eg M Sanderson, Efficiency Analysis in Canadian Merger Cases, Washington, DC (2 November 1995), available at www.ftc.gov/opp/global/sandersn.htm.

204 The total surplus standard 'looks at the overall loss to the economy as a result of the fall in demand for the merged entity's products following a post-merger increase in price, and the inefficient allocation of resources that occurs when, as prices rise, consumers purchase a less suitable substitute. The resulting loss of resources to the economy constitutes deadweight loss'. *Propane Appeal Decision*, at para 45. However, consideration of producer welfare raises difficult political issues and it is notable that the Canadian statute makes express reference to the impact of the merger on Canadian exports and domestic consumption of imports which can be taken as a shorthand for the competitiveness of Canadian industry. For a review of some of the political considerations in the European context, see F Ilzkovitz and R Meiklejohn, n 15 above, at pp 18-19.

Proponents of the total surplus standard have developed theories to assess the industry-wide impact of a merger or the effect of the efficiency gains over competitors that did not participate in the merger.[205] Farrell and Shapiro, in particular, have developed a theory to evaluate the externality effects of a merger. The externality of a merger consists of the sum of the effects on consumers and on the competitors who did not participate in the merger. They conclude that if the externality is positive, then the merger must also increase total welfare since the proposed merger may also be expected to be profitable for the parties (otherwise it would not be proposed in the first place).[206] Farrell and Shapiro have identified conditions under which a price-increasing/output reducing merger can nevertheless have a positive externality, eg the market share of the two merging firms should be sufficiently small and the merging firms should operate at relatively higher marginal costs than their competitors. Farrell and Shapiro demonstrate that such a merger may be beneficial even where there are no internal efficiencies (or when internal efficiencies cannot be proven) by virtue of its effects on the reallocation of output to competitors.[207]

The total surplus standard has been criticised by some economists for (1) regarding the gains in shareholder profit and consumer losses of income as completely offsetting and thus, treating alike consumers and shareholders of the merged firm when they may be in different situations[208]; and (2) making assumptions about the neutrality of the transfer of wealth between consumers and shareholders.[209]

4.3.4 Balancing weight method

One key problem relating to the balancing weight method was identified by the Canadian Competition Tribunal in its initial rejection of the method. It is a subjective method that may lack the required degree of predictability expected in merger control. Specifically, this method appears to involve a high degree of prosecutorial and judicial discretion. It can result in decisions that will vary from case to case depending on the individual views of the members of the agency (or the Tribunal) on the 'weight' to be given to the groups affected by the merger.[210] How and when is it appropriate to divide or weigh presumptively neutral wealth transfers into negative or positive factors? What interests should be given greater weight? How much weight?[211] The questions are numerous and the answers likely to be subjective.

205 This relates in effect to the distinction between firm-level efficiencies and market-level efficiencies. See L-H Röller *et al*, n 14 above, at pp 43, 56-57 and 114.

206 See, eg L-H Röller *et al*, n 14 above, at pp 56-7.

207 *Id.*

208 See *Propane Tribunal Redetermination Decision*, at paras 97-101.

209 See G Allen, The Treatment of Efficiencies in Merger Analysis, speech to the Conference 'Meet the Competition Bureau' (3 May 1999) available at www.strategis.ic.gc.ca/SSG/ct01548e.html. See also G Allen, The Enforcement of the Efficiency Exception in Canadian Merger Cases, speech before Stikeman Elliott, Competition Law Group (25 June 1999), available at www.strategis.ic.gc.ca/SSG/ct01566e.html (arguing that neutral treatment disregards the impact of factors such as sales tax).

210 *Propane Tribunal Initial Decision*, at para 433.

211 The Tribunal in its Redetermination Decision stated that the 'correct weight [to the harm suffered by various consumer groups] should be established by society or should reflect social attitudes toward equity among different income classes. There may be several sources from which the proper weighting can be inferred, one such being the tax system, which is explicitly, although not solely, concerned with equity'. The Tribunal notes that it would expect to benefit from expert opinions on these issues. *Propane Tribunal Redetermination Decision*, at paras 110-112.

4.4 Considerations for possible Commission guidelines

It is not clear whether Article 2(1)(b) mandates a consumer or a broader welfare standard. As noted above, while Article 2(1)(b) provides that the Commission consider technical and economic progress only to the extent that it is to consumers' advantage, the precise nature of that advantage – long or short term, exclusively price-based, etc – is not defined. Thus there is scope for argument that the ECMR does not mandate a narrow consumer-based welfare standard.

If, on the other hand, the view that the Commission is required by Article 2(1)(b) to adopt a consumer welfare standard prevails, then the Commission's choice may be limited to the modified price standard and the consumer surplus standard.[212] The internal Commission economists who participated in the DG ECO-FIN Study recommend selection of a consumer welfare standard with a requirement that the 'positive welfare effects a merger may entail are transmitted to the consumers'.[213]

5. A FRAMEWORK FOR EFFICIENCY ANALYSIS: PROCEDURAL AND METHODOLOGICAL ISSUES

In devising an efficiency policy, the Commission will need to determine how efficiencies will be factored into the substantive analysis of notified transactions. This involves numerous procedural, methodological, and conceptual issues. We discuss two of these issues below.[214] First, the Commission will need to decide whether efficiency considerations should be taken into account in all mergers, or whether they should be excluded as a matter of law for certain categories of mergers. Secondly, the Commission will need to select a procedure for the incorporation of efficiencies into the framework for the analysis of concentrations and the calculation of the trade-off between the anti-competitive effects of the merger and the efficiencies it produces.

5.1 Should efficiencies be considered in all merger situations?

The question before the Commission is twofold. First, should the efficiency defence be limited to mergers raising coordinated effects issues or should it also be available for mergers involving unilateral effects? Secondly, should the consideration of efficiencies be allowed only in those mergers not rising to the level of monopoly or near-monopoly market power, or should they be considered in all mergers, recognising that they are most likely to make a difference when the likely adverse competitive effects are not

212 This may be the view expressed by the Economic and Social Committee in its recently released opinion on the Commission's Green Paper. The Committee supports the introduction of an explicit efficiency defence under the ECMR stating that '[w]hen [efficiencies] further the consumer interest and promote the objective of overall economic efficiency, the Committee fails to see why they should not be taken into account' (emphasis added). See Opinion of the Economic and Social Committee on the 'Green Paper on the Review of Council Regulation (EEC) No 4064/89', COM (2001) 745 final, OJ 2002 C 241/130, at para 3.2.

213 See F Ilzkovitz and R Meiklejohn, n 15 above, at p 24.

214 Other issues that the Commission will most likely need to address in the Guidelines include: (1) the allocation of the burden of proof between the parties and the Commission, the acceptable forms of evidence, whether there is a hierarchy between acceptable evidence and the standard of proof ('clear and convincing evidence', 'credible', 'clearly demonstrated'); and (2) the verification of the alleged efficiencies post-merger and actions that can be taken if the efficiencies were not realised. For a discussion of these issues, see, eg L-H Röller *et al*, n 14 above, at pp 94 and 115-117.

great, and that efficiency claims will rarely justify a merger to monopoly or near-monopoly.

The first question arises because Commission precedents[215] have been interpreted by some commentators as precluding the consideration of efficiencies in cases raising single-firm dominance issues.[216] We find that this statement may be too general. Its validity depends on what is meant by an efficiency 'defence' and it does not necessarily result from Commission precedents that there is no legal room for an 'efficiency justification' under the ECMR, even for single-firm dominance cases.

The Canadian and US systems, although they both refer to an 'efficiency defence' have adopted two different approaches to the concept.

The US Merger Guidelines provide that the:

> 'Agency will not challenge a merger if cognizable efficiencies are of a character and magnitude such that the merger is *not likely to be anticompetitive* in any relevant market. To make the requisite determination, the Agency considers whether cognizable efficiencies likely would be *sufficient to reverse* the merger's potential harm to consumers .... The greater the potential adverse competitive effect of a merger ... the greater must be cognizable efficiencies in order for the Agency to conclude that the merger *will not have an anticompetitive effect* ...' (Emphasis added.)

Under this approach, efficiencies must eliminate the potential anti-competitive effects and 'reverse' the merger's harmful effects. The analysis of efficiencies is directly tied to the analysis of the merger's competitive effects on consumers and it is only when the agencies are convinced that the negative effects have been eliminated that they will decide not to challenge the merger.[217] The two steps involved in the analysis are thus: (1) identify potential anti-competitive effects; and (2) examine whether efficiencies eliminate these potential effects. Thus, efficiencies are not a defence to a conclusion that there was a substantial lessening of competition; efficiencies are part of a two-step analysis leading to the conclusion that there is no substantial lessening of competition. In effect, efficiencies are only a defence to a *prima facie* presumption of competitive harm.[218] Rather than a 'defence', it may then be more accurate to speak of a 'rebuttal' or refutation of a finding of competitive harm: 'because of the efficiencies, the merger does not lessen competition and should be allowed'.[219]

Conversely, in Canada, the Competition Act and the Guidelines do not appear to require that efficiencies fully eliminate, prevent or reverse all the potential anti-competitive effects for a merger to be authorised. Section 96 provides that efficiencies must be 'greater than and offset' the effects of the lessening of competition. However,

215 See in particular *Danish Crown/Vestjyske Slagterier*, Case No COMP/M.1313 (Commission decision of 9 March 1999), OJ 2000 L 20/1. See above page 245.

216 See F Ilzkovitz and R Meiklejohn, n 15 above, at p 15 ('[t]he Commission and most commentators therefore concur in interpreting Article 2.1(b) [of the ECMR] as allowing no practical scope for an efficiency defence, once it has been determined that a dominant position will be created or strengthened. Cases of joint dominance by two or more firms constitute a possible exception. ....'); and L-H Röller *et al*, n 14 above, at p 80.

217 See *Propane Appeal Decision*, at para 134.

218 See *Propane Appeal Decision*, at para 135 (citing P Areeda *et al*, *Antitrust Law*, Vol IVA (revised edition) (Aspen Publishers, 1998), at p 28.

219 See L-H Röller *et al*, n 14 above, at p 95.

it appears that the anti-competitive effects can remain and do not need to be 'cleansed' or fully eliminated by the efficiencies for a merger to be approved. The two steps involved in the Canadian analysis are thus: (1) identify anti-competitive effects, and (2) examine whether efficiencies generated by the transaction as a whole are greater than and in effect, compensate the Canadian economy for these anti-competitive effects. At the end of the analysis, efficiencies are thus a real defence: the merger may well lessen competition on certain markets but due to the aggregate efficiencies it generates, it is nevertheless desirable and should be allowed.[220]

While this conceptual difference between the US and Canadian approach to efficiency defences is rarely noted by US commentators (subject to one remarkable exception),[221] it has been made by Canadian commentators[222] and has been endorsed by the Canadian Competition Tribunal.[223]

It can be argued that the wording of the ECMR precludes a defence *à la Canadienne,* but not necessarily a US-style analysis, although as will be seen below this is not altogether clear. Article 2 of the ECMR mandates that the Commission prohibit a transaction once it has found that there is a creation or strengthening of dominance and a resulting significant impediment to effective competition in the Common Market. According to one line of argument, there is no statutory exception with the result that an efficiency defence cannot be introduced to 'save' a merger once dominance has been found.[224] However, it can also be argued that the prohibition test involves two elements – a finding of dominance and a finding that, as a result of that dominance, there will be a sufficient impediment to competition. Under this approach, it might be possible to work an efficiencies defence into the analysis of whether dominance will in effect have negative consequences for consumer (or overall) welfare.

220 *Id.*

221 Professor Areeda wrote: '[a]lthough we [in the US] have, to be sure, spoken of an ... [efficiencies] "defense", it is not as a defense to a final conclusion that a merger "lessens competition" or is "illegal". Rather the "defense" terminology refers to the rebuttal of a first order inference from a portion of the evidence (such as market shares) that a merger presumptively lessens competition and violates the statute. That is, it is a defense to a prima facie case ....' See P Areeda *et al,* n 218 above, at p 28.

222 See G Allen, The Treatment of Efficiencies in Merger Analysis, Speech to the Conference 'Meet the Competition Bureau', Toronto (3 May 1999), available at http://strategis.ic.gc.ca/SSG/ct01548e.html (stating that '[i]n the US efficiencies are incorporated into the analysis of competitive effects resulting from the merger. Therefore, if after the consideration of efficiencies, the merger is still believed to raise price, the merger would not be approved. This approach is of course a big departure from the one used in Canada since the Bureau evokes a trade-off when a merger creates efficiencies along with a price increase.').

223 In its *Propane Redetermination Decision,* the Tribunal states that '[t]he requirement that proven efficiencies must "cleanse" the anticompetitive merger arises in the US from the absence of a specific affirmative statutory defense that would permit an anticompetitive merger to proceed'. At para 135. The Tribunal goes on to contrast the US approach with the Canadian approach. It states: 'the approach to efficiencies under subsection 96(1) of the Act is very different. There is no requirement for efficiency gains to prevent the [anti-competitive] effects ... from occurring. .... It is plainly Parliament's intent that, in merger review, efficiencies are to be considered only under section 96 and not under section 92. As a result, the consideration of efficiency gains is not to be tied into the analysis of competitive effects of the merger. Section 96 is worded accordingly by requiring that gains in efficiency be "greater than" and "offset" the effects of lessening or prevention of competition, rather than prevent those effects from occurring. Accordingly, "cleansing" of those effects is not required under the Act and indeed, effects of lessening or prevention of competition may remain even when the test under section 96 is met.' *Propane Tribunal Redetermination Decision* at paras 136-137.

224 See *Danish Crown/Vestjyske Slagterier, supra* page 245.

There are, of course, formal and linguistic problems with this latter interpretation. For example, it can be argued that the establishment of dominance must perforce include a finding that there is an impediment to competition or that the significant impediment to effective competition language cannot be stretched to include a consumer (or other) welfare test, although arguments to the contrary appear equally valid. At the end of the day, these word games may not be significant and should not be outcome determinative: from an economic perspective it should not make any difference if efficiencies are one of the factors that the Commission examines to determine whether a merger gives rise to (or strengthens) dominance or whether efficiencies are a defence to a finding of dominance because the significant impediment to effective competition language is deemed to provide scope for an efficiency defence. However, there would appear to be a real difference between an analysis that requires that *all* the anti-competitive effects be reversed for consumers and one that, under a more flexible approach, either does not require that prices decrease if there are other significant consumer benefits, or allows the regulator to balance the benefit and harm to different groups of consumers or permits a merger because the efficiencies realised by the merging firms are deemed to outweigh the anti-competitive effects on consumers.

Using efficiencies to *outweigh* a finding of dominance (or in connection with the significant impediment to effective competition test) has some obvious but limited parallels to the application of Article 81(3) to determine whether a derogation is possible from the prohibition imposed by Article 81(1). As in the case of the analysis under Article 81, merger analysis would require a second step: after the evaluation of market shares and other competitive factors leading to a *prima facie* presumption of dominance, the Commission would be required to examine whether efficiencies can outweigh the negative effects of dominance (or a finding that the merger would significantly impede effective competition). To a limited extent, the analogy with Article 81 can be used to suggest that an efficiency defence that would not require that all the anti-competitive effects of a merger be reversed may not be alien to EU law since in the Article 81 analysis exemption arguably does not *reverse* the finding that there has been a restriction of competition; rather, it establishes that, on balance, the agreement is more beneficial than harmful even though it is restrictive. However, the limitation comes from the incorporation in Article 81(3) of the requirement that competition must not be substantially eliminated – a condition which can be broadly identified as a no-dominance requirement.

Using efficiencies to *rebut* a *prima facie* finding of dominance would bear some similarities to US practice and may also be consistent with Commission precedents. The US Guidelines tie efficiency considerations directly into the competitive analysis of the transaction. Thus, the Guidelines recognise that (1) in a case raising coordinated effects issues, marginal cost reductions may make coordination less likely or effective by enhancing the incentive of a maverick to lower price or by creating a new maverick firm; and (2) in a case raising unilateral effects concerns, marginal cost reductions may reduce the merged firm's incentive to raise price. The Commission has already incorporated elements of this approach. For example, in *Airtours/First Choice*[225] (a coordinated effects case), the Commission examined whether efficiencies generated by

225 *Airtours/First Choice*, Case No COMP/M.1524 (Commission decision of 22 September 1999).

the merger could increase competition between Airtours and the remaining two large tour operators. However, the Commission found the alleged cost savings (synergies) insufficient to constitute a material change in the parties' overall cost structure and therefore insufficient to increase the incentives to compete.[226]

We turn now to the question of the possible exclusion of the consideration of efficiencies in mergers that raise very significant merit issues (monopoly or near-monopoly mergers).

The US and Canadian experiences provide some insight.

The 1997 Efficiencies Revision in the US Horizontal Merger Guidelines provides that 'efficiencies are most likely to make a difference in merger analysis when the likely adverse competitive effects, absent the efficiencies, are not great. Efficiencies almost never justify a merger to monopoly or near-monopoly'.

The US Guidelines adopt a sliding scale approach according to which the agencies do not simply mathematically compare the size of the anti-competitive effects and of the alleged efficiencies. The greater the harm, the greater the efficiencies will have to be to save the transaction. 'Extraordinarily great' efficiencies may even be required when the potential adverse competitive effect is likely to be particularly large. There are no bright-line thresholds of what constitutes a 'great harm' and what constitute 'extraordinarily great efficiencies'. This is where the agencies and the courts exercise discretion. It appears, however, that the potential for 'particularly large' anti-competitive effects is assessed, *inter alia* based on the degree of market concentration. As shown in the *Staples/Office Depot, Cardinal Health* and *Heinz/Beech-Nut* cases, it is very difficult to meet the burden of proving 'extraordinary efficiencies' where the market is highly concentrated.[227] In addition, under the US system, there is a degree of competitive harm at which point efficiencies (almost) never count – near-monopoly mergers, but again there are no bright-line thresholds of what combined firm market share is a near-monopoly.

As already noted, the Canadian Competition Act and Merger Enforcement Guidelines do not provide for a sliding scale,[228] nor do they exclude an efficiencies defence beyond a certain degree of anti-competitive effects, or a certain degree of market concentration. In theory (and in reality as was seen in the *Superior Propane* case), the Canadian system could allow for a merger to monopoly to be saved by efficiencies.

In its challenge of the *Superior Propane* merger, the Competition Commissioner argued that 'as a matter of law' a merger to monopoly could never be saved by an efficiency defence, stating that in such case there is no 'merger' under the Competition

226 The Commission noted that the transaction was only expected to lead to overall synergies of less than one per cent of the overall costs of the merged firm and that the cost savings mostly related to overhead and other fixed costs. 'Therefore, changes to the cost structure would not increase the incentives to compete.' At para 146. The Court of First Instance did not reverse the Commission on this point in its judgment annulling the Commission decision. *Airtours v Commission*, Case T-342/99, judgment of 6 June 2002 (not yet reported), at para 292.

227 See above page 239.

228 The very logic of the Canadian system does, however, recognise that the larger the competitive harm, the larger the efficiencies must be to meet the 'greater than' and 'offset' test. The Canadian Guidelines also provide that the comparison of efficiencies and harm is not done on a purely mathematic basis, but that there is a qualitative aspect to the comparison as well.

Act to which sections 92 and 96 can be applied.[229] This argument was rejected by the Tribunal and the transaction was approved (twice) on the basis of its efficiencies despite the fact that it resulted in a combined-firm Canadian market share of 70 per cent and near-monopoly shares on several local markets.[230] Therefore, after the Tribunal Redetermination Decision in the *Superior Propane* case,[231] under the current law and case law in Canada, a horizontal merger can be approved even if it leads to a substantial lessening of competition and very high market shares (even near monopoly) on the basis of efficiency considerations.[232]

Conceptually, practitioners would probably prefer that no category of mergers be excluded outright from the efficiency defence. They are therefore likely to prefer an approach under which the Guidelines provide that efficiencies may in principle be taken into account in all mergers, recognising that the merger is more likely to be saved when the likely anticipated adverse competitive effects are not great, and that efficiency claims will be less frequently successful in a merger to monopoly or near-monopoly.

We turn now to procedural issues.

5.2 Framework for merger analysis

The DG ECO-FIN Study suggests that three different approaches can be used to incorporate efficiency considerations in merger analysis and balance cost savings with loss of allocative efficiency: the case-by-case approach, the general presumptions approach and the sequential approach.

5.2.1 Case-by-case approach

The case-by-case approach involves a detailed analysis of anti-competitive effects and efficiency gains to determine the net welfare effect in each individual transaction that is reviewed. This approach recognises that every single merger can generate efficiencies,[233] and would seem the 'fairest' way to proceed as every transaction is given a chance to show its good side.

A case-by-case approach, however, can impose a significant burden on the parties and the enforcement agency and raises methodological issues. The burden on the parties and the agency to gather the required information to measure and analyse both the anti-competitive effects and the efficiencies is very important. This would be burdensome enough if information were readily available and reliable, but the issue is

229 *Propane Tribunal Initial Decision,* at para 414-417.

230 The Tribunal in its Redetermination Decision expressly disagreed with one of the judges of the Federal Appeal Court, rejecting his claim that section 96 was not meant to authorise the creation of monopolies. At para 277.

231 Subject to the pending appeal (the Commissioner appealed the Tribunal Redetermination Decision).

232 The Tribunal stated in its Redetermination Decision that '... in terms of the Section 96 inquiry, the finding of a monopoly according to any particular definition thereof is irrelevant. If the creation of a so-called monopoly is not per se sufficient to justify a conclusion of substantial lessening of competition under Section 92 of the Act, then its creation cannot be a bar to the application of Section 96'. At para 280.

233 See F Ilzkovitz and R Meiklejohn, n 15 above, at pp 22-3; and L-H Röller *et al*, n 14 above, at pp 94 and 99.

complicated by the fact there are many methodological issues associated with the quantification of market power and efficiency gains and the required trade-off analysis.[234]

5.2.2 General presumptions approach

An alternative approach is to use general presumptions on the likely effects of mergers and efficiencies. Under this approach, structural indicators are used as proxies to measure the likely average net effects of mergers.[235] For example, if set thresholds (eg maximum merged firm market share or maximum concentration ratio) are not exceeded, efficiency gains will be deemed always sufficient to outweigh the anti-competitive effects of the mergers. Mergers below these thresholds cannot be challenged. This is based on an implicit recognition of efficiencies and the assumption that below the set thresholds mergers are efficiency-enhancing or at a minimum neutral.[236] Only the mergers exceeding the set thresholds will require a detailed efficiency analysis.

This approach eliminates the high information cost associated with the case-by-case analysis, but has several problems of its own. It assumes that the structural indicators selected adequately measure the anti-competitive effects and efficiencies of the mergers. This is not necessarily so, as there is an inherent degree of imperfection and arbitrariness in any indicator.[237] For example, general indicators will not be adequate for every industry and each merger differs in the actual efficiencies that it realises.[238]

5.2.3 Sequential approach

The sequential approach is an intermediary approach that aims at combining the best aspects of the case-by-case and the general presumptions approaches.[239]

A sequential approach involves a two-step analysis. During the first step, structural criteria are used to screen mergers and separate them into three categories. During the second step, only those mergers that fall into the middle category are subject to a detailed efficiency and cost-benefit analysis.

The screening step is carried out on the basis of two thresholds based on the selected structural criteria. For mergers that fall below a *low threshold*, efficiency gains are presumed to be higher than the potential anti-competitive effects and the transaction is automatically approved without a case-by-case analysis of the efficiencies. For mergers that fall above a set *high threshold*, anti-competitive effects are presumed to be greater than efficiencies and a case-by-case analysis of efficiencies is also not undertaken.[240] Thus, the authority is required to engage in a detailed efficiency cost-benefit analysis only for those mergers that fall above the low threshold

234 See F Ilzkovitz and R Meiklejohn, *ibid*, at 22-3; and L-H Röller *et al*, n 14 above, at pp 94, 97 and 99.

235 See L-H Röller *et al*, n 14 above, at p 99.

236 See F Ilzkovitz and R. Meiklejohn, n 15 above, at p 22.

237 See L-H Röller *et al*, n 14 above, at pp 94 and 97.

238 See F Ilzkovitz and R Meiklejohn, n 15 above, at p 22; and L-H Röller *et al*, n 14 above, at p 99.

239 See L-H Röller *et al*, n 14 above, at p 97.

240 See F Ilzkovitz and R Meiklejohn, n 15 above, at pp 22-3; and L-H Röller *et al*, n 14 above, at p 94. According to that study, these transactions are, however, not necessarily automatically prohibited. The parties can still attempt to establish an efficiencies defence, but they will have the difficult burden of

but remain below the high threshold,[241] ie those cases where the likely anti-competitive effects are neither negligible nor very strong.[242]

The main advantage of this approach is that it limits the number of cases in which a detailed efficiencies analysis is required, thereby limiting the burden on the authority. The main problem is the difficulty of defining the structural criteria and the thresholds used in the screening process.[243] In particular, it will be necessary to find a balance between the risk of setting the high threshold too high and therefore potentially prohibiting welfare-enhancing transactions (Type 2 error) and setting the low threshold too low and therefore potentially authorising welfare-reducing transactions (Type 1 error).[244]

The economists, in the DG ECO-FIN Study, find that the current ECMR framework follows the general presumptions approach,[245] and recommend that the efficiency defence be incorporated in the ECMR under a sequential approach.[246] They note that the transition from a general presumptions approach to a sequential approach will require a revision of the currently used threshold criteria. Rather than a single dominance threshold level (distinguishing between acceptable and unacceptable mergers), two thresholds would be required. A first (low) threshold will separate automatically acceptable mergers from those that may be subject to an efficiency defense and a second (high) threshold will separate the mergers that may be subject to an efficiency defense from those that are deemed highly unlikely to benefit from such a defence. The first threshold would lie below the current dominance threshold level and the second threshold would lie above that dominance level.[247]

5.3 Implementation of an efficiency defence

Assuming that a consumer welfare standard is retained, ie that consumer loss includes deadweight loss and wealth transfers from consumers to producers,[248] the size of the

rebutting the presumption that efficiencies are insufficient to outweigh the anti-competitive effects. See, eg F Ilzkovitz and R Meiklejohn, n 15 above, at pp 22-3. It is not always clear whether Röller, Stennek and Verboven accept this possible rebuttal or whether they would exclude it automatically for mergers giving rise to shares above certain market share thresholds. For the purposes of the following discussion, we have considered the position to be that there will be a strong but not irrebuttable presumption that mergers above the upper market share threshold would be prohibited but that this prohibition would not be automatic (ie to the exclusion of an efficiencies defence if sufficient evidence could be mustered). If one accepts this possibility (and also adds to that the possibility that mergers within the 'safe harbour' thresholds may, in rare cases, prove to be anti-competitive), the sequential approach would begin to resemble the 'sliding scale' analysis used by the US agencies.

241 See F Ilzkovitz and R Meiklejohn, n 15 above, at p 23.

242 See L-H Röller *et al*, n 14 above, at p 94.

243 See F Ilzkovitz and R Meiklejohn, n 15 above, at p 23.

244 See L-H Röller *et al*, n 14 above, at p 98.

245 There is no explicit recognition of an efficiency defence, but there is a presumption that mergers below a selected structural threshold (25 per cent combined firm market share per Recital 15 of the ECMR) do not restrict competition and are thus welfare enhancing. See F Ilzkovitz and R Meiklejohn, n 15 above, at pp 22-23; and L-H Röller *et al*, n 14 above, at p 93 (indicating that the Commission itself finds that it using the general presumption method).

246 See F Ilzkovitz and R Meiklejohn, n 15 above, at p 23; and L-H Röller *et al*, n 14 above, at pp 94 and 97.

247 See F Ilzkovitz and R Meiklejohn, n 15 above, at p 23; and L-H Röller *et al*, n 14 above, at pp 99-100.

248 This is the case under both the modified price standard and the consumer surplus standard.

efficiency gains needed to justify a merger which is likely to have anti-competitive effects depends on the size of the anti-competitive effects. This leaves the antitrust authority with the difficult task of measuring anti-competitive effects and efficiencies. If a sequential approach has been selected for the incorporation of efficiencies in the merger evaluation, a third question is raised: how to select the structural indicators and fix the thresholds for the first screening step.

In the discussion below, we examine the methodologies proposed by economists in the DG ECO-FIN Study.

5.3.1 Sequential approach's screening test

The proposed sequential approach raises two issues: (1) what indicators should be selected; and (2) how should the thresholds be selected.

Market shares and concentration indices are the structural indicators most commonly used as proxies for the measurement of market power (which is what the screening indicators aim to measure). Some economists note that these two indicators alone may not provide a reliable measurement of market power.[249] These economists find that ideally, other market characteristics should be taken into account in order to reduce the risk of rejecting mergers that may generate efficiencies, such as entry barriers, high sunk costs, inelasticity of demand, the degree of product differentiation, large economies of scale, substantial excess capacity, important tangible assets and rapid technological developments.[250] From a practical standpoint though, it would seem that expanding the screening indicators beyond those that are most easily measurable would defeat the purpose of simplification that the first step of the sequential approach is meant to achieve. The economists in the DG ECO-FIN Study suggest that the most practical way to establish this screening step could be to resort to the same structural indicators that the authority is already using in the merits analysis as a measure of the expected net benefits from a merger, ie the indicator that is predominant in establishing a presumption of adverse effect. In the United States, that would be a concentration index (by reference to the Herfindahl-Hirschman Index) and in the European Union, it would have to be the market share of the merged entity and concentration ratio for the leading post-merger oligopolists.[251]

At what levels then should the low and high thresholds be set to minimise the risks of Type 1 and Type 2 errors?

As explained above, the low threshold (whether of market share or market concentration) separates the mergers that are presumptively always authorised, whereas the high threshold separates the mergers that are presumptively always prohibited. The cases that fall between the low and the high thresholds are those in which efficiencies can be evaluated carefully. The economists in the DG ECO-FIN Study do not propose numerical figures for the indicators,[252] nor do they expressly adopt a position on the type of structural indicator that the Commission should

249 See F Ilzkovitz and R Meiklejohn, n 15 above, at p 24.

250 *Ibid* at p 24.

251 See L-H Röller *et al*, n 14 above, at p 100.

252 Assuming a range from zero to one for the structural indicator (where zero raises no competitive issues and one is at monopoly level), they propose three possible approaches to set the levels of the thresholds. If the high threshold is set at one and the low threshold somewhere below that, this would allow

consider.[253] They recommend that the Commission adopt the following approach: (1) replace the current dominance threshold by a split low-high threshold; (2) fix the low threshold below the current dominance level – so that fewer mergers would be automatically accepted; and (3) fix the high threshold above the current dominance level – so that fewer mergers are classified in the category for which the efficiency defense is likely to be precluded.[254] It would appear that such an approach, if adopted, could result in a considerable tightening of EU merger review in that the proposed sequential approach would lower the threshold at which prohibition may occur *and* would also appear to incorporate a review of efficiencies *and perhaps efficiency requirement* for any concentration above this lower threshold.[255]

The economists advocating the adoption of the sequential approach in incorporating the efficiency defence under the ECMR have focused on the information costs to the parties and the Commission of adopting a case-by-case approach. However, given the potential rigidity of the sequential approach, it may be questioned whether a sliding scale case-by-case approach would not be preferable. The US experience suggests that the case-by-case approach does not necessarily result in a detailed efficiencies analysis in every notified transaction. There is a self-selection process that in practice is not far from the concept of a screening test although it may be less rigid because of its ad hoc character. By definition, parties will only bring efficiencies claims if they feel they are losing the 'no-anti-competitive effects' argument. In the European Union, a low threshold is already effectively embedded in the ECMR.[256] Rather than devising a high threshold, it may be easier to apply a case-by-case approach for cases

efficiency considerations for mergers that exceed the low threshold and would reflect the authorities' belief that low structural indicators predict net benefits reasonably accurately (because all mergers below the low indicator are automatically approved) whereas high structural indicators are perceived as less accurate in measuring net benefits. If the low threshold is set at zero and the high threshold somewhere above that, this would allow efficiency considerations for mergers that are below the high threshold and would reflect the authorities' belief that a high structural indicator predicts net harmful effects reasonably accurately (because all mergers above the high threshold are automatically prohibited) whereas low structural indicators would be deemed less reliable. Finally, if the low and high thresholds are set anywhere in the range (and not at the extremes), this would allow efficiency considerations for mergers that are above the low threshold and below the high threshold and would reflect the authorities' belief that structural indicators are accurate, except in borderline cases. Under each proposed approach, the closer the thresholds are set together, the narrower the room for an efficiency defence will be. See L-H Röller *et al*, n 14 above, at pp 100-102.

253 They refer implicitly to the combined firm's market share. It would be conceivable, however, for the Commission to construct a multifaceted structural indicator for the screening process. For example, the indicator could be a combination of the merged firm's market share and the market concentration. This combination of factors would in particular be useful for collective dominance cases. A mixed indicator would not be a novelty in merger review. For example, the Australian Merger Guidelines provide that the Authority may investigate a merger if the combined-firm share as a result of the transaction exceeds 15 per cent in a relevant Australian product market and the combined market share of the four largest firms in that market exceeds 75 per cent, or the combined-firm share exceeds 40 per cent. See The ACCC Merger Guidelines, available at www.accc.gov.au/merger.

254 See F Ilzkovitz and R Meiklejohn, n 15 above, at p 23; and L-H Röller *et al*, n 14 above, at pp 99-102.

255 This observation suggests that the introduction of an efficiency defence may well be part of the larger current debate on the appropriate substantive test under the ECMR.

256 Recital 15 of the ECMR provides that where the parties' combined market share does not exceed 25 per cent, the concentration may be presumed to be compatible with the Common Market.

where the merged firm will have a market share over 25 per cent and the parties argue efficiencies to rebut a presumption of dominance.

Analysis of efficiencies – measurement of market power and efficiencies. Whether the Commission adopts a sequential approach or a case-by-case approach, the analysis of efficiencies will involve two essential components: the calculation of the minimum required efficiencies and the measurement and verification of the actual efficiencies. An efficiency investigation should explicitly balance both components as transparently as possible.

Calculation of minimum required efficiencies (MREs). The calculation of MREs starts from the effect of a merger on price. The price effect can be divided into three separate components: (1) the price increase stemming from an increase in market power (holding the merging firms' costs constant); (2) the possible marginal cost savings resulting from the merger; and (3) the degree of pass-on of the savings into the consumer price.[257]

The calculation of MREs requires an assessment of the likely expected market power before and after the transaction, which may be a very difficult task given the various possible models (Cournot competition, Bertrand competition, collusive competition, etc). Different methods can be used to calculate the MREs. They are either based on assumptions or on simulation analysis with models of competition.

Röller, Stennek and Verboven propose an assumption-based method. They suggest using a 'worst-case scenario' to calculate minimum required efficiencies.[258]

Under the proposed analysis, the worst-case scenario would be that all firms in the market increase their price by five to ten per cent (assuming no changes in efficiencies). The next step in their analysis is to determine by how much marginal cost must decrease in order to compensate for the expected worst-case scenario price increase.[259] This will depend on the degree of pass-on of costs into consumer prices. For example if the pass-on is 50 per cent, a marginal cost decrease of ten per cent would be required for the price to the consumer to be reduced by five per cent. The minimum required efficiency (ie the required drop in marginal cost to compensate for the price increase) is then calculated by dividing the worst-case scenario price increase (ie five to ten per cent) by the pass-on rate. With a pass-on rate of 50 per cent, the minimum required cost reduction to compensate for the price increase will be in the range of 10-20 per cent.

Röller, Stennek and Verboven find that using the worst-case scenario and the estimated pass-on rate to calculate MREs greatly simplifies the analysis because there is ample empirical economic literature on the calculation of the pass-on rate.[260] They also note that if, with practice, the authority finds that it is possible to develop estimates of the pass-on rate that seem to apply across sectors of the economy, it may

257 See F Ilzkovitz and R Meiklejohn, n 15 above, at p 25.

258 In their view, the use of assumptions will avoid the need to assess the pre-merger and post-merger intensity of competition on the relevant markets which is required for the calculation of the price increase. See L-H Röller *et al*, n 14 above, at p 103.

259 We note that the method focuses on the reduction in marginal cost whereas as indicated above, not all the types of efficiencies that can be considered lead to reductions in marginal cost. It is unclear how the method would apply to these other efficiencies.

260 See L-H Röller *et al*, n 14 above, at pp 103-104.

be possible to use a general presumptions approach to calculate MREs.[261] Conversely, if it seems that pass-on rates vary significantly across industries and it is difficult to generalise an estimated pass-on accurately, the authority may need to do a case-by-case analysis of the individual facts to estimate the pass-on rate.[262]

Röller, Stennek and Verboven recognise some limitations of their proposed method. First, they admit that when they construct the worst-case scenario they assume that the merger authority used correct information in the market definition step (ie with regard to likely reactions of firms inside the market as well as firms outside the market). Should there be mistakes in the market definition step, the methodology may have to be adjusted. Secondly, they note that the five to ten per cent price increase is only a lower boundary for a maximum profitable joint price increase.[263] Thirdly, they note that the Commission's Market Definition Notice defines the relevant market by reference to a maximum profitable joint price increase, whereas other jurisdictions refer to optimal joint price increases. However, they find that a worst-case scenario can work under either approach subject to a different assumption about the rationale for the firm's behaviour.[264] They also recognise that the worst-case scenario may impose MREs that are too high and lead to the rejection of mergers with potential net benefits.[265]

Last, Röller, Stennek and Verboven consider some specific models of competition to derive more explicit and more accurate economic formulae to calculate the MREs.[266] They examine in particular industries with homogeneous products and Cournot competition, and industries with differentiated products and Bertrand competition. An analysis of these economic theories exceeds the scope of this paper.[267]

The proposed worst-case scenario method has been criticised on the grounds that: (1) it contains arbitrarily selected elements that would influence the analysis; and (2) it is too demanding.

The worst-case scenario is based on the assumption that all the firms in the market will increase their price by five to ten per cent. The price increase level is selected by reference to the Commission Notice on Market Definition, but remains an arbitrary selection.[268] Similarly, the proposed approach is said to simplify the analysis only if an average (or minimum) pass-on rate is assumed. The introduction of this additional assumption brings an additional element of arbitrariness to the proposed test.[269]

261 For example, if it seems empirically safe to assume that the pass-on rate is 50 per cent, then it would be easy to calculate the MREs by simply doubling the hypothetical price increase that was used when defining the relevant product market.

262 See L-H Röller *et al*, n 14 above, at pp 104-105.

263 Specifically they identify situations where a price increase substantially larger than five to ten per cent could be profitably implemented by the parties. See L-H Röller *et al*, n 14 above, at p 106.

264 Under the maximum joint increase approach, the worst that can happen is that firms increase their price up to the point where it is no longer profitable compared to the pre-merger situation. Under the optimal price increase approach, the worst that can happen is that the firms set their price in a joint optimal way. See L-H Röller *et al*, n 14 above, at p 106.

265 See L-H Röller *et al*, n 14 above, at p 106.

266 The idea is that if a particular model of competition can be shown to apply relatively well to the industry in which the merger takes place, then the MREs calculated on the basis of the pre-set formulae for that competition model would be more accurate than under the worst-case scenario method.

267 See L-H Röller *et al*, n 14 above, at pp 107-109.

268 See F Ilzkovitz and R Meiklejohn, n 15 above, at p 19.

269 See F Ilzkovitz and R Meiklejohn, *ibid*.

Furthermore, an assumed passed-on rate is economically inaccurate. The extent of a firm's pass-on depends on several factors, including capacity constraints, the price elasticity of demand, the degree of market power, and the market share of the merging firms.[270] In addition, the pass-on rate must be consistent with the assumed or estimated price increase in the absence of efficiencies. If the actual pass-on rate is to be calculated – which would be required for the analysis to be accurate – then, there is very little simplification of the analysis.

Critics of the proposed worst-case scenario advocate the use of a simulation analysis involving the simultaneous estimate of the price increase in the absence of the efficiencies and the degree of pass-on.[271]

A simulation analysis makes it possible to specify the nature of competitive interaction in the industry (pre- and post-merger) without using simplifying assumptions.[272] A simulation analysis typically involves three steps. First, one needs to develop a model of competitive interaction on the relevant market.[273] Second, the model needs to be calibrated to retrieve firm-specific parameter values for marginal cost and demand.[274] The third and final step involves the simulation of the post-merger equilibrium, including the calculation of the MREs.[275]

A thorough simulation analysis requires detailed data permitting the estimation of all the relevant elasticities (own and cross elasticities). Such data is however, rarely available. In most cases, therefore, even proponents of the simulation analysis recognize that it will be necessary to rely on some rough and ready quantitative procedures.[276]

5.3.2 Measurement of Actual Efficiencies

The Minimum Required Efficiencies must, in the final stage of the analysis, be compared with the actual efficiencies resulting from the merger. This raises issues relating to the merger-specificity requirement of efficiencies that we have examined above,[277] the allocation of the burden of proof and the type of acceptable evidence, the standard of proof, the verification of the claimed information and post-merger review.[278] These issues will most likely be addressed by the Commission in its Guidelines, but they are beyond the scope of this paper.

270 Röller, Stennek and Verboven recognise the impact of these factors on the pass-on rate. But in their method, these considerations would only come into play if the actual pass-on rate is calculated on a case-by-case basis. L-H Röller *et al*, n 14 above, at pp 104-105.

271 See F Ilzkovitz and R Meiklejohn, n 15 above, p 20.

272 Simulation analysis is increasingly used in the United States and Canada, primarily in response to the criticism that assumption-based methods do not apply to the industry under investigation. Röller, Stennek and Verboven note that as computer programs become more sophisticated and more available, simulation analysis may be used more frequently. L-H Röller *et al*, n 14 above, at p 110.

273 Certain economic models exist already (eg the logit and nested logit models of product differentiation). See L-H Röller *et al*, n 14 above, at p 110.

274 This is done on the basis of data provided by the parties on current prices, market shares and price elasticity of market demand. *Id.*

275 This implies factoring into the model the changes brought about by the merger and having the model calculate the new prices and new market shares. The model can be used to calculate the efficiency standards for price to decrease or total surplus to increase. *Id*, at p 111.

276 See F Ilzkovitz and R Meiklejohn, n 15 above, at p 20.

277 See pages 250.

278 For a discussion of these issues, see L-H Röller *et al*, n 14 above, at pp 114-116.

6. Conclusions

The Commission's consideration of the role of efficiencies in merger analysis is certainly timely and welcome since the absence of a systematic analysis (and the confusion over the availability of an efficiency defence in the European Union) has been one of the major differences between the EU, on the one hand, and the US and Canadian competition authorities on the other. Clarification of these issues will therefore be welcome.

However, as is clear from the foregoing discussion, incorporation of efficiencies into EU merger analysis raises a number of complex economic (and in some cases political) questions including, *inter alia*, the appropriate welfare standard to be adopted, the types of efficiencies that should be recognised and how, and with what presumptions, the efficiency analysis should be incorporated into the overall merits analysis. Some of these questions appear related to the broader debate over the appropriate substantive test and, ultimately, the role of econometrics and merger simulation as a standard feature of merger review.

Analysis of efficiencies is arguably indispensable in a coherent system of merger review. However, little is likely to be gained from the introduction of a narrow defence that is so limited and strict that it can never effectively be utilised. It is therefore desirable that, when considering the appropriate role of efficiencies in merger analysis, the Commission adopt a broad, dynamic approach that provides sufficient scope for their consideration.

7. Appendix 1: Overview Table

		United States	Canada	Current EU	Proposals or EU Guidelines per DG ECO-FIN Study
Source of the Defence		Enforcement Guidelines	Statute and Enforcement Guidelines	Article 2(1)(b) of the ECMR	Enforcement Guidelines
Type of Defence		Rebuttal defence	Real defence	No articulated defence efficiency considerations are possible	Rebuttal defence
Types of Efficiencies	Production rationalization	Yes	Yes	Yes	Yes
	Economies of scope	Yes	Yes	Yes	Yes
	Economies of scale	Yes	Yes	Yes	Yes
	Synergies	Yes	Yes	Not accepted if only elimination of duplication	Yes
	R&D/dynamic	Yes	Yes	No	Yes
	Transactional	Yes	Yes	No	Yes
	Distribution	Yes[279]	Yes	Yes	Yes
	Promotion	Yes[280]	Yes	No	Yes
	Procurement	Yes	Not accepted if only redistributive	No	Yes
	Capital savings	Yes	Yes	No	Yes
	Managerial savings	Yes	Yes	No	Yes
	Pecuniary savings	No	No	No	No
Merger specificity requirement		Yes	Yes	Yes	Yes
Welfare Standard	Type	Modified price standard	Balancing weight method (per current tribunal decision)	Unclear probably, modified price standard	Policy decision
	Consumer loss	Deadweight loss plus wealth transfers from consumer to producers	Deadweight loss. Wealth transfers from consumers to producers are presumptively neutral, but can be re-weighted case-by-case to reflect 'social values'	Deadweight loss plus wealth transfers from consumers to producers	Policy decision (but suggest a consumer welfare standard given difficulties involved in a total surplus standard)
	Consumer pass-on requirement	Yes	No	Yes	Policy decision (but suggest a consumer pass-on requirement)
Incorporation method		Case by case	Case by case	General presumptions	Sequential approach

279 Not mentioned in the Guidelines, but implicitly recognised by the courts (eg in *Staples/Office Depot*) and endorsed by current FTC Chairman, Timothy Muris.

280 *Id.*

Session 5

Assessment of Dominance: Unilateral and Coordinated Effects – Draft Commission Notice

20
Opening Remarks on the Assessment of Dominance

John Kay

Economist and author, London

1. Assessment of dominance

The purpose of this session is to consider the assessment of dominance in European merger control. We have speakers who will address these issues as a matter of law and from the perspective of economic analysis. My objective in this introduction is to set out the central questions which our panel will wish to review. The background is set by the decisions of the Court of First Instance in the summer.

I will invite the participants in the panel to address five principal questions:

1. the limitations of collective dominance;
2. the definition of collective dominance under an expansive interpretation;
3. the scope of the Merger Regulation under a narrow definition of collective dominance;
4. the evidence required to support a finding of collective dominance; and
5. the level of probative standard required.

2. The limitations of collective dominance

The Commission has relied extensively on a concept of collective dominance in recent implementation of merger control. As a matter of economics, prices in concentrated market structures may be above competitive levels for one or both of two reasons:

- Tacit or explicitly coordinated action by oligopolistic firms. Such coordination is more easily achieved if the number of such firms is small.
- Self-interested actions by firms large enough to recognise that their own actions have effects on the overall market. The larger the share of any firm, the greater the likelihood that there will be such an effect and that the firm will recognise it.

Unilateral effects will arise even if all firms behave in a self-interested manner, aiming to maximise their own profits given the actions of others. Tacit or explicit coordination, by contrast, requires other firms to exercise some restraint: to refrain from actions by which they would benefit in return for similar behaviour on the part of others. While perfectly successful coordinated action will have a larger impact on price than unilateral actions, unilateral effects may prove more profitable for all firms than coordination which is imperfect. This is, of course, the principal reason why attempts at coordination, whether tacit or explicit, frequently break down.

This distinction between unilateral and coordinated effects emerges clearly from the stylised formalisations of economic models. It is not as clear-cut in the business world itself. An industry such as the package holiday business considered in Airtours has experienced periods of aggressive price competition, punctuated by interludes of stability. Firms will have learned by experience that some actions have destructive consequences, while other forms of behaviour lead to a more profitable business environment. The distinction between coordinated and unilateral effects is not necessarily one on which business people themselves focus, important though it may be for purposes of economic analysis and jurisprudence.

It has appeared to some that the effect of the decision of the Court of First Instance in *Airtours* is to confine the doctrine of collective dominance to cases of tacit or explicit coordination. While the original decision of the Commission appeared to envisage that both unilateral and coordinated effects might give rise to collective dominance, that assertion does not appear to have been carried through to the Commission's argument before the Court. Nor was it accepted in the judgment of the Court. But the Commission appears still to take the view that the concept of collective dominance remains relevant to the analysis of unilateral effects. My first question for the panel is therefore: what is the current meaning of collective dominance, as a legal and an economic concept?

3. The definition of collective dominance under an expansive interpretation

Different subsequent questions arise depending on the definition of collective dominance. If the answer to my first question is that collective dominance should be defined widely, those who take that view must explain what exactly the criteria and definition of collective dominance are, and which unilateral effects should be treated as instances of collective dominance.

The problem here is that *any* horizontal merger will create additional scope for price increases through unilateral action. Presumably some threshold would need to be attained. An expansive view of collective dominance would seem to require the establishment of market share criteria definitive, or at least presumptive, of the existence of collective dominance. My second question, therefore, for those on the panel who believe the expansive definition of collective dominance remains valid: what is the relevant definition and how is it to be implemented?

4. The scope of the merger regulation under a narrow definition of collective dominance

The alternative view is that collective dominance is to be interpreted narrowly, as referring only to cases in which tacit or explicit coordination is possible as a result of a concentrated market structure. Is there then a 'gap'? Are there concentrations which would have adverse effects on competition and on the interests of European consumers but which would not meet the tests required to establish collective dominance?

Most economists, basing their judgment on the analysis and history of unilateral effects, might conclude that the answer to that question was yes. Indeed my own view is that *Airtours* itself is probably an example of such a case. The merger should have been blocked because of the negative consequences for competition, and consumer choice even if, in the judgment of the Court of First Instance, there was inadequate legal ground for doing so.

Alternatively, one might take the view that while the 'gap' is a theoretical possibility, cases which fall within it are not sufficiently frequent or significant in practice as to require any modification to the current state of the law or practice of merger control. It will be interesting to hear empirical evidence on each side of this debate. My third question to the panel is: 'is there a "gap" in European merger control following the *Airtours* judgment?'

In reviewing this question, I am conscious that it is very similar to the question 'is there a difference between the tests for collective dominance (which have become the basis of European competition law) and the test of substantial lessening of competition (which is used in the United States and in many other jurisdictions and is to be the basis of UK law)'. Since this issue was the subject of an earlier panel discussion, I ask the panel to refer to that discussion and not to spend too much time replaying it.

5. The evidence required to support a finding of collective dominance

If question (1) is to be answered in an expansive manner – collective dominance covers cases of both coordinated and unilateral effects – then it may be that, as I have suggested under (2), a simple market share test would be sufficient to identify collective dominance. If a narrow definition of collective dominance is to be adopted, however, along the lines indicated by the Court of First Instance, then the evidential burden becomes much greater.

Two cases need to be distinguished. If collective dominance already exists, and would potentially be strengthened by the concentration, then evidence should be available from current market behaviour to demonstrate that claim. This is not quite as easy as it might sound because, as I have emphasised, firms themselves do not distinguish sharply between coordinated and unilateral effects. Moreover, both coordinated and unilateral effects may be expected to have similar consequences for prices, profits, and capacity.

Where collective dominance does not currently exist, but would potentially be created by the concentration, the case is harder still. Indeed it was on this point that the Commission encountered particular difficulties before the Court of First Instance. Of necessity, such evidence can only take the form of speculation as to what would happen if the concentration took effect. In *Airtours*, evidence which was presented there both for and against the proposition that collective dominance would be created took the form of describing the conditions which would, in certain theoretical economic models, be conducive to the achievement of tacit coordination, or not.

Collective dominance thus defined depends fundamentally on the expectations of firms about the expectations and behaviour of other firms. The difficulty of reaching firm conclusions on such a question is obvious. This is a problem both for those who would assert collective dominance and for those who would dispute it. My fourth question for the panel, therefore, is this: what evidence could be brought to bear to demonstrate or refute the existence of collective dominance, under a narrow definition which relies on assumptions about expectations and motives to identify its presence?

This leads directly to my fifth question.

6.1 The level of probative standard required

The recent judgments of the Court of First Instance make frequent references to 'the required probative standard'. Although the implication of the context of this phrase appears to be that the required probative standard is high, at no point does it seem to be explicit at what level the required probative standard is to be set.

Statistical hypothesis testing provides the most widely accepted framework for setting probative standards. Any adjudication process is vulnerable to what statisticians recognise as Type I and Type II errors. A Type I error is the rejection of a true hypothesis, a Type II error the acceptance of a false hypothesis. In general, the probability of a Type I error can be reduced only at the expense of increasing the probability of a Type II error, and vice versa.

Common law jurisdictions have different probative standards for criminal and civil proceedings. In English and American judicial proceedings, these are expressed as 'beyond reasonable doubt' or 'the preponderance of the evidence' and 'the balance of probabilities'. For a statistician, the 'balance of probabilities' implies a likelihood in excess of 50 per cent – it is more probable that the hypothesis is true than it is not. 'Beyond reasonable doubt' implies a much higher standard.

The rationale for the existence of these different hurdles is the different assessment of the costs of Type I and Type II errors. If the hypothesis is 'the defendant is guilty', than a Type I error is convicting an innocent person while a Type II error involves letting a guilty individual go free. Most civilised societies take the view that the consequences of Type I errors in criminal cases are so serious that many Type II errors should be accepted in order to reduce their likelihood: 'better x guilty men go free than that one innocent man go to prison', where x is some large number. In civil proceedings, however, the social and individual costs of Type I and Type II errors are more evenly balanced.

My fifth and final question to the panel is: what should be and what is the probative standard appropriate to the merger regulation? What it should be will properly depend on an assessment of the costs associated with Type I and Type II errors. Would more damage be done to the European economy by the rejection of some desirable mergers than by the acceptance of some undesirable ones? In answering this question, we must recognise that the overwhelming majority of mergers referred to the Commission are approved, so that the ones which receive a stage two evaluation are already those where the potential for adverse effects on competition appear to be the largest.

There is one, rather particular, indication that the burden of proof in a merger case should reflect the civil (50 per cent) standard rather than the higher criminal standard. The Merger Regulation is symmetrical. A concentration which strengthens a dominant position must be declared incompatible with the Common Market: one which does not must be declared compatible with the Common Market. It is hard to argue that the probative standard applicable to one leg of the regulation is higher than that applicable to the other.

But if that is so, it seems the criterion must be the balance of probabilities. Otherwise, there would be a substantial class of mergers which could be declared neither compatible nor incompatible with the Common Market. While this is not a logical impossibility, it would create a preposterous situation: presumably such mergers could not go ahead (not being compatible with the Common Market) but could not be prohibited either (not being incompatible with the Common Market). On this paradoxical note, I throw the discussion open to the panel.

21

Airtours v Commission: Collective Dominance Contained?

Malcolm Nicholson and Sarah Cardell*

Slaughter and May, London

1. Introduction

It is by now a familiar and accepted feature of the European merger control system that the European Commission (the 'Commission') may, in cases involving oligopolistic industries, consider whether the proposed merger will lead to the creation or strengthening of a collective dominant position. However, the precise meaning of 'collective dominance' and its implications for the scope and development of European merger control have, at least until the European Court of First Instance (CFI) delivered its judgment in *Airtours plc v Commission,*[1] been shrouded in uncertainty. Following the Commission's reversal in that case, debate over whether the law needs to be changed to a 'substantial lessening of competition' test has intensified.

2. Summary of paper

We start by a reminder that 'collective dominance' is a creation of Community law, before going on to describe the 'coordinated effects' test of the US Merger Guidelines and the established economic model of 'tacit collusion'. The law as is developed in the *Kali und Salz* and *Gencor* cases is described. The *Airtours/First Choice* decision of the Commission is then analysed, and shown to depart both from economic orthodoxy and legal precedent. The pleadings in *Airtours* before the CFI are analysed, and it is demonstrated how the Commission was forced to re-cast its case in terms of an orthodox three-part theory of 'tacit collusion'. The CFI's judgment, with its emphasis on discharge of the burden of proof and identification of the manifest errors of assessment committed in the Commission decision, is described. Looking to the present, the authors conclude that following *Airtours,* the concept of collective dominance is to be limited to and equated with coordinated effects and tacit collusion. If that means there is a *lacuna* in the power to control mergers (and in particular mergers producing unilateral effects but not susceptible to single or collective dominance analysis under the current EC Merger Regulation) then the remedy is to change the law to a substantial lessening of competition test, not to torture the meaning of 'dominance' under the EC Merger Regulation.

* Malcolm Nicholson is a partner and Sarah Cardell is an associate at Slaughter and May. Slaughter and May acted as counsel to MyTravel Group plc (previously Airtours plc) throughout the administrative and judicial proceedings on the *Airtours/First Choice* merger. Views expressed are personal to the authors and should not be attributed to MyTravel Group or Slaughter and May.

1 *Airtours plc v Commission,* Case T-342/99 (judgment of the CFI dated 6 June 2002).

3. Background

EU antitrust legislation contains no express reference to 'collective dominance'. Article 82 of the EC Treaty prohibits an abuse 'by one or more undertakings of a dominant position' while the EC Merger Regulation (the 'Merger Regulation') simply provides that a merger will be prohibited if it 'creates or strengthens a dominant position as a result of which effective competition would be significantly impeded in the common market or in a substantial part of it ...'.[2]

Despite the absence of any express reference to collective dominance in either of these provisions, the European Court of Justice (ECJ) and CFI (together the 'European Court') have confirmed that the Commission can apply the concept of collective dominance both when investigating a potential abuse under Article 82 and when evaluating the consequences of a merger under the Merger Regulation. The remainder of this paper focuses on the application of the concept of collective dominance in merger control cases. However, it is important to bear in mind that the concept of collective dominance has also been developed and applied by the Commission and the European Court in Article 82 cases (albeit some may argue in a manner not always entirely consistent with the development and application of the concept under the Merger Regulation).

The legal concept of collective dominance has been developed independently by the Commission and is not a concept which has simply been imported from the United States. The approach adopted by the US antitrust authorities when assessing the potential adverse competitive effects of mergers is summarised in the DOJ/FTC 1992 Horizontal Merger Guidelines (revised 1997) (the 'US Merger Guidelines') and is closely aligned with economic theory. The US Merger Guidelines distinguish two ways in which competition may be reduced as a result of a merger: unilateral and coordinated effects. An acquisition may give rise to anti-competitive unilateral effects where merging firms 'find it profitable to alter their behaviour unilaterally following the acquisition by elevating price and suppressing output'.[3] This broadly corresponds to the model of 'single firm dominance' applied by the Commission (albeit possibly with a lower threshold for regulatory intervention than applies in the case of single firm dominance). Alternatively, the merger may result in a lessening of competition through coordinated effects where it enables the firms selling into the relevant market 'to engage in co-ordinated interaction that harms consumers'.[4]

Underpinning the concept of 'coordinated effects' as described in the US Merger Guidelines are the economic models of express and tacit collusion which are discussed in more detail below. On the face of it, one could reasonably expect that the Commission's theory of 'collective dominance' would be aligned with the US model of 'coordinated effects' and the economic theory on which the latter is based. However, it is clear from the way in which the Commission has sought to develop and interpret the collective dominance concept that this has not always been the case, although the CFI judgment in *Airtours v Commission* has provided a powerful corrective to move the law closer to the US model and standard economic theory.

2 Article 2(3) of Council Regulation of 21 December 1989 on the control of concentrations between undertakings (4064/89/EEC), as amended.

3 US Merger Guidelines, section 2.2.

4 US Merger Guidelines, section 2.1.

Thus the concept of collective dominance is not clearly defined in any EC legislation. Nor has it been imported 'wholesale' from the United States. Rather it is a legal concept, which has been developed by the Commission and refined by the European Court to justify regulatory intervention in certain oligopolistic markets. It is important to bear these background facts in mind when considering the way in which the Commission has applied this concept in the past and how it might seek to do so in the future.

4. Economic theory

Standard economic theory recognises the possibility that, in certain circumstances, the characteristics and structure of the market and the competitive interaction between the major players may be such that they are able collectively (and including in the absence of any express agreement) to act in effect as if they are a single undertaking with significant market power. This outcome may result from express coordination of activities, in other words a cartel. Alternatively it may be achieved through tacit coordination or collusion whereby the firms involved are able to coordinate their activities *as if* there is an agreement to that effect but where in fact no express agreement has been entered into. Clearly, the greater the number of firms in an industry, the more difficult it is to achieve and sustain coordinated behaviour (whether tacit or express). Hence the possibility of coordinated behaviour is most likely to arise in oligopolies, that is industries characterised by the presence of a small number of major players.

However, it is by no means the case that all oligopolies should automatically be regarded by regulators as anti-competitive. On the contrary it is essential to distinguish between 'benign' and 'anti-competitive' oligopolies. Even in the case of benign oligopolies the main players will, because of the degree of interdependence which characterises all concentrated industries, take into account the anticipated actions and reactions of their competitors when determining their commercial strategies. However, all decisions are taken unilaterally and there is no tacit coordination of strategic behaviour in such cases. The ability of the key players to reach a coordinated outcome (whether tacit or express) will depend on the characteristics of the market in which they operate and the nature of their competitive interaction. Clearly coordination will be even more difficult to achieve and sustain in the absence of express agreement. Consequently, a regulator seeking to prohibit a merger on the grounds that it would enable the major players in the industry to engage in tacit collusion post-merger must first carry out a detailed analysis of the facts of the particular case and apply a reasonably complex economic model to those facts. The difficult nature of this task is expressly recognised in the US Merger Guidelines.[5]

The standard economic model used to establish whether an oligopoly is conducive to tacit collusion (and thus anti-competitive) rests on a three-part test which requires the ability of the undertakings involved (1) to reach a tacit agreement; (2) to detect breaches; and (3) to punish any deviation from the tacit agreement reached. In other words the regulator must be able to show both that the parties involved are able to

5 US Merger Guidelines, section 2.1. For a topical example of just how difficult it is, consider the FTC decision (by a 3/2 majority) not to challenge the *Royal Caribbean/P&O Princess and Carnival/P&O Princess* Mergers: see the FTC Press Release and Statement of Reasons published on 4 October 2002.

identify and implement a tacitly coordinated outcome and that they are able to sustain that coordinated outcome over time. The risk is that once a coordinated outcome is in place, it may be rational for any individual firm to 'cheat' on that outcome, for example by reducing prices and thus winning market share, in pursuit of short-term profit maximisation. To avoid this each player must have an incentive to stick with the coordinated outcome. Put simply, economic theory suggests that this requires the consequences of 'deviation' to be made sufficiently unappealing, for example by the threat of a price war. However, this will only be effective if the threat of so-called 'punishment' is credible. Hence economic theory requires that each undertaking is able both to detect 'deviation' from the coordinated outcome and credibly threaten 'punishment' in the event of such deviation. If this is not the case, the incentive to deviate is likely to be too strong and tacit collusion will break down. Indeed, in these circumstances, it may be impossible for the parties involved to reach a coordinated outcome in the first place.

This three-part economic test underlies the approach taken by the US authorities to determine whether a merger will result in anti-competitive coordinated effects, as set out in the US Merger Guidelines. As previously noted, an assessment of whether a merger is likely to result in sustainable tacit collusion based on the economic model set out above requires an analysis of the structure and characteristics of the market in question post-merger. Typically this involves consideration of a number of features such as product homogeneity, cost structures, demand growth, market transparency and barriers to entry (often referred to as the 'checklist'). However, it is important to note that the only purpose of using the checklist is to identify market conditions in which tacit collusion is likely to be achievable and sustainable.

5. The European approach – collective dominance before Airtours

There is a view that the concept of collective dominance, as used in European Community law, ought to be equated with the concept of tacit collusion (and therefore also with the US model of coordinated effects). However, the development and application of the concept of collective dominance by the Commission has not always been in line with standard economic theory.

5.1 France v Commission

In *France v Commission*[6] the ECJ confirmed in principle the application of the Merger Regulation to collective dominance, although it annulled the Commission's finding of collective dominance on the facts of the case. The ECJ stated that, in the case of an alleged collective dominant position, the Commission was obliged to assess, using a prospective analysis of the reference market, whether the undertakings involved in the concentration and one or more other undertakings together 'in particular because of [factors giving rise to a connection between them,] are able to adopt a common policy on the market and act to a considerable extent independently of their competitors, their customers, and also of consumers'.[7] The ECJ added, 'such an approach warrants

6 *France and Others v Commission*, Joined Cases C-68/94 and C-30/95 (judgment of the ECJ dated 31 March 1998).

7 *Ibid*, para 221.

close examination in particular of the circumstances which, in each individual case, are relevant for assessing the effects of the concentration on competition in the reference market'.[8]

The analytical framework for collective dominance cases described by the ECJ in *France v Commission* would appear to accord with the economic approach to establishing tacit collusion discussed above. In particular the reference to a 'common policy' indicates that an element of coordination or cooperation is required on the part of the undertakings concerned (albeit tacit). This economic approach is also reflected in the analysis of both the Commission and the CFI in *Gencor*.

5.2 Gencor v Commission

The Commission's decision in *Gencor/Lonrho*[9] represented the first occasion on which the Commission had prohibited a merger based on a finding of collective dominance. It is clear from both the context and content of the Commission's decision in that case that the Commission's inquiry followed the traditional economic approach to establishing tacit collusion. The Commission made reference to various features of the market (including moderate demand growth, inelastic demand, insignificant countervailing buyer power, the small number of major suppliers, high market transparency, product homogeneity, high entry barriers, lack of effective competition from smaller suppliers outside the oligopoly and multi-market contacts) in support of its conclusion that the merger would lead to the creation of a collective dominant position in the platinum and rhodium markets. Drawing a clear parallel between collective dominance and tacit collusion, the Commission stated that 'active collusion would therefore not be required for the members of the oligopoly to become dominant'.[10] In the preceding sentence the Commission observed that a situation of collective dominance 'can occur where a mere adaptation by members of the oligopoly to market conditions causes anti-competitive parallel behaviour whereby the oligopoly becomes dominant'. This later became a critical statement on which the Commission sought to hang its more extended theory of collective dominance in *Airtours* but it seems clear from both its factual and textual context that the Commission was at the time simply contrasting active and tacit collusion.

In *Gencor v Commission*[11] the CFI upheld the Commission's decision to prohibit the merger on the grounds that it would lead to the creation of a collective dominant position. In reviewing and upholding the Commission's detailed analysis of market characteristics in this case, the CFI mirrored the approach taken by the Commission in equating collective dominance with tacit collusion. The parallel drawn between collective dominance and tacit collusion is clear from the CFI's statement that the objective of the Merger Regulation is to prevent the creation or strengthening of anti-competitive market structures including 'market structures of an oligopolistic kind where each undertaking may become aware of common interests and, in particular, cause prices to increase without having to enter into an agreement or resort to a

8 *France and Others v Commission*, Joined Cases C-68/94 and C-30/95, para 222.
9 *Gencor/Lonrho*, Commission Decision of 24 April 1996 (Case No IV/M.619).
10 *Ibid*, para 140.
11 *Gencor v Commission*, Case T-102/96 (judgment of the CFI dated 25 March 1999).

concerted practice'.[12] The reference to 'common interests' suggests more than simply a purely independent reaction to a competitor's unilateral behaviour; rather it appears to imply an unspoken meeting of minds and tacit coordination of behaviour.

In the preceding paragraph of the judgment, the CFI referred to 'the relationship of interdependence existing between the parties to a tight oligopoly within which, in a market with the appropriate characteristics, in particular in terms of market concentration, transparency and product homogeneity, those parties are in a position to anticipate one another's behaviour and are therefore strongly encouraged to align their conduct in the market, in particular in such a way as to maximise their joint profits by restricting production with a view to increasing prices'. The CFI further noted that in 'such a context, each trader is aware that highly competitive action on its part designed to increase its market share (for example a price cut) would provoke identical action by the others, so that it would derive no benefit from its initiative'.[13] Again, it is clear from the context of these statements that what the CFI is describing here is the standard economic model of tacit collusion (note the reference to alignment of conduct as opposed to mere unilateral behaviour), complete with the need for an effective retaliatory mechanism.

That the standard economic theory of tacit collusion underlies the CFI's approach in this case is clear from a full reading of the judgment. For example, when discussing the importance of price transparency the CFI described how 'members of the oligopoly can, in particular, immediately discern the decisions of other members of the oligopoly to alter the status quo by increasing their market share and they may take such retaliatory measures as may be necessary in order to frustrate actions of that kind'.[14] This statement clearly encapsulates the second and third elements of the standard economic model of tacit collusion.

Therefore at this stage, both the decisional practice of the Commission and the jurisprudence of the European Court regarding the assessment of collective dominance in merger cases appeared to be broadly in line with standard economic theory centred on tacit collusion.

6. The European approach – Airtours/First Choice

Buoyed by the CFI's judgment in *Gencor v Commission* in early 1999, the Commission later that year sought to expand the application of the collective dominance concept in merger cases. Its target was Airtours' proposed acquisition of First Choice. The Commission prohibited the proposed acquisition on the grounds that that it would lead to the creation of a collective dominant position in the market for short-haul foreign package holidays in the United Kingdom on the part of the three remaining major UK tour operators (Airtours/First Choice, Thomson and Thomas Cook).[15] This was the first case in which the Commission had relied on collective dominance to block a merger which would have reduced the number of major players in a market from four to three (*Gencor/Lonrho* would have led to the creation of a duopoly). However, it was not the use of collective dominance in a 'four to three' case *per se*

12 *Gencor v Commission*, Case T-102/96, para 277.

13 *Ibid*, para 276.

14 *Ibid*, para 227.

15 *Airtours/First Choice*, Commission Decision of 22 September 1999 (Case No IV/M.1524).

which caused the Commission's decision in *Airtours/First Choice* to arouse so much interest. Rather it was the fact that the decision raised serious questions about the appropriate legal test to be applied by the Commission in collective dominance cases and the apparent divergence between the Commission's analysis and standard economic theory which focuses on the concept of tacit collusion. These concerns were also at the heart of Airtours' application for annulment of the Commission's decision under Article 230 of the EC Treaty.

The Commission appears to have used this case as an opportunity to explore the boundaries for establishing collective dominance under the Merger Regulation. In doing so it moved away – whether deliberately or inadvertently – from the economic theory of tacit collusion and the legal framework established by previous Commission decisions and European Court jurisprudence and instead adopted an approach which comprised a misapplication of certain elements of the previously established test combined with some 'new thinking' on the part of the Commission. In particular, the Commission appeared to lower the necessary threshold to establish collective dominance, departing from the traditional three-part test to establish tacit collusion and instead applying a test which, while not clearly articulated, appeared to be based only on oligopolistic interdependence, rational behaviour and incentives. The result was a blurring of the distinction between benign and anti-competitive oligopolies with the potential consequence that, in future, almost any merger in an oligopolistic industry might be blocked on collective dominance grounds.

In addition, the Commission's departure from the tacit collusion model and its focus instead on rational individual oligopolistic behaviour appeared to confuse unilateral and coordinated effects (as defined in the US Merger Guidelines). Previously it had been clear that, under the European merger control system, the possibility that a merger might give rise to anti-competitive unilateral effects would justify regulatory intervention where a position of single firm dominance would be created or strengthened. Likewise a merger might be prohibited on collective dominance grounds where it would result in anti-competitive coordinated effects (effectively tacit collusion). However, in the *Airtours/First Choice* decision the Commission sought to apply the collective dominance concept outside the tacit coordination framework by prohibiting a merger on the grounds that the key players might face an incentive to constrain capacity but without requiring any element of coordination (while at the same time acknowledging that the merger did not give rise to any single firm dominance issues).

6.1 Analysis of the Commission's reasoning in Airtours/First Choice

It was clear from an early stage in the Phase II investigation that the Commission was seeking to explore the boundaries of the collective dominance concept and was thus prepared to depart from standard economic theory. What to those directly involved was striking about the Statement of Objections (SO) issued by the Commission during the course of that investigation was the lack of any coherent economic theory that was being applied, and in particular the absence of any detailed economic analysis of the mechanisms necessary to achieve and sustain tacit collusion. Instead, the Commission merely observed that 'a number of characteristics which make the market conducive to oligopolistic dominance are and will be present in the tour operating market after the merger'. Thereafter the Commission proceeded to carry out a whistle-stop tour of the 'checklist' of market characteristics, which may indicate that a market is conducive to collective dominance. However, the Commission largely failed to explain why or how particular market characteristics would make it easier to achieve or sustain collective dominance in the market in question. The Commission made no express mention of the standard three-part test for tacit collusion but simply applied the checklist in isolation. The only real explanation offered was that the market characteristics were such that the main players 'have an incentive to be cautious in their capacity setting decisions'. Likewise, although the SO contained some references to 'retaliation', there was no explanation of why retaliation is necessary to support collective dominance and limited discussion of how retaliation would work in this market.

These criticisms of the incoherence of the Commission's position during the course of the administrative procedure, led it to try and articulate more clearly the economic theory it was seeking to apply in its Decision. The new reasoning is at paragraphs 51 to 56 of the Decision which (as expanded by later factual findings) represents the economic theory the Commission was relying on to block the *Airtours/First Choice* merger.

The theory has been widely criticised,[16] and appears to have been flawed in a number of respects.

First, the Commission's analysis suggests a severing of the link between the legal concept of collective dominance and the economic theory of tacit collusion. Thus, in an apparent rejection of the tacit collusion model the Commission stated 'it is not a necessary condition of collective dominance for the oligopolists always to behave *as if* there were one or more explicit agreements ... It is sufficient that the merger makes it rational for the oligopolists, in adapting themselves to market conditions, to act, individually, in ways which will substantially reduce competition between them...'.[17] Crucially, the Commission's analysis in the *Airtours/First Choice* decision suggests that it is not necessary to establish that market conditions would support a mechanism through which tacit collusion could be achieved and sustained. According to the Commission's approach it appears to be sufficient to establish that the oligopolists would have incentives unilaterally to decide to reduce competition by constraining capacity.

Secondly, what is missing from the Commission's approach in the prohibition decision is the need for a mechanism through which the oligopolists can appreciate and act on their incentives. In particular, the Commission appeared to deny the need for a credible punishment mechanism to deter deviation stating that 'where, as here, there are strong incentives to reduce competitive action, coercion may be unnecessary'.[18] Again this suggests a failure to distinguish between a benign oligopoly (where players may in principle face an incentive to reduce competition but are unable, because of the absence of an appropriate mechanism, to achieve this ideal such that, in

16 See, among the papers for the 'Conference on EC Merger Control: 10 years on', the papers contributed by Jenny, 'Oligopoly Theory, Collective Dominance and EU Merger Control: the Airtours/First Choice Decision in Perspective', and Chappatte and Jewell, 'Collective Dominance: The Commission's Decision on Airtours/First Choice'. See also Lofaro and Ridyard, 'The Economic Analysis of Joint Dominance under the EC Merger Regulation' (2000) I *European Business Organisation Law Review* 539.

17 *Airtours/First Choice*, Commission Decision, para 54 (see also para 150).

18 *Ibid*, para 55.

practice, all competitive interaction in the market is based purely on unilateral non-cooperative decision-making) and an anti-competitive oligopoly (where market characteristics are such as to support a mechanism through which players can tacitly coordinate their strategic interaction resulting in a lessening of competition).

Thirdly, by detaching collective dominance from the economic theory of tacit collusion and thus relying simply on oligopolistic interdependence, rational behaviour and incentives (in this case to take individual action to restrict capacity) as the determinants of a collective dominant position, the Commission appeared to be seeking to run a 'unilateral effects' argument (falling short of single firm dominance) in a collective dominance case.[19] This approach was fundamentally at odds with previous Commission and European Court decisions as well as standard economic theory regarding tacit collusion. As such it created a high degree of uncertainty and unpredictability as regards the application of European merger control in collective dominance cases with the potential implication that the Commission could rely on the collective dominance concept as applied in the *Airtours/First Choice* decision to prohibit any merger in an oligopolistic industry.

Finally, although in the *Airtours/First Choice* decision the Commission departed from the concept of collective dominance based on the economic theory of tacit collusion, it nonetheless sought to utilise certain elements of the traditional tests in isolation. This resulted in an approach to collective dominance, which lacked sound legal and economic foundations. For example, as in the SO, the Commission's prohibition decision contains a review of the 'checklist' of market characteristics typically considered to be indicators of whether a market is conducive to collective dominance. However, the purpose of the checklist is to assist in identifying whether tacit collusion is likely to be achievable and sustainable. The Commission utilised the checklist while detaching it from the theory of tacit collusion to which it relates. A further example is the Commission's analysis of the scope for retaliatory action in the tour operating market. As noted above, the Commission appeared to reject the need for a credible retaliatory mechanism as an essential element of the test to establish collective dominance, while still arguing that there was 'considerable scope for retaliation' in the market in question.[20] The result, as the CFI itself wryly observed, was a 'somewhat ambiguous approach'[21] to the subject of retaliation.

6.2 Analysis of the Commission's pleadings in Airtours v Commission

These criticisms lay at the heart of Airtours' pleadings on the appeal. It was supported by a detailed catalogue of what were alleged to be numerous defects in terms of the Commission's factual assessment of whether the market characteristics in this case were conducive to creating and sustaining a collective dominant position post-merger.

That the Commission in the *Airtours/First Choice* decision sought to extend the scope of the concept of collective dominance beyond the traditional theory of tacit collusion is further evidenced by the Commission's subsequent retreat to a more conventional position during the course of the written pleadings on the appeal to the CFI.

19 See commentary to that effect in Whish, *Competition Law* (4th edn, 2001), p 491.
20 *Airtours/First Choice*, Commission Decision, para 55.
21 *Airtours plc v Commission*, Case T-342/99, para 191.

In its defence the Commission appeared in part to revise its approach to collective dominance, seeking to align its reasoning more closely with the traditional analysis of collective dominance based on tacit collusion. Thus the Commission in its defence accepted in principle the distinction between unilateral and coordinated effects and acknowledged that the *Airtours/First Choice* decision could not be justified in terms of unilateral effects. In addition the Commission appeared to recognise the need to tie its approach more closely to the three-part test for tacit collusion, stating that the following three conditions are required to establish collective dominance: (1) common recognition of advantage; (2) possibility of monitoring conduct; and (3) long-run negative consequences of deviation from parallel conduct. This attempt to put a more orthodox spin on the Commission's approach in the *Airtours/First Choice* decision appears to be a recognition that the Commission's original analysis lacked sound economic and legal foundations.

However, despite moving some way towards a more orthodox approach, the Commission's defence nonetheless contained statements which reflected a continued blurring of the distinction between benign and anti-competitive oligopolies. Thus although the three-part test set out by the Commission in its defence and referred to above only makes sense in the context of an analysis based on tacit collusion, the Commission continued to refer in its defence simply to oligopolistic interdependence and the fact that it was rational for one oligopolist to base its strategic decisions in part on the expected reactions of others. For example the Commission equated 'coordinated effects' with 'anti-competitive parallel behaviour or interdependent market conduct'. While the first comparison may be interpreted as referring to tacit collusion, the second clearly extends to include all cases of oligopolistic interaction.

Likewise the Commission in its defence continued to focus on the incentives facing the oligopolists rather than the existence of mechanisms through which a tacitly coordinated outcome could be both achieved and sustained. Thus it argued 'the essential question for the Commission in a case of potential oligopolistic dominance is whether or not the proposed concentration would result in a market structure in which each of the main players *had an incentive to adjust its market conduct*, having regard to the likely response of the others, so as to reach an outcome more profitable for all of them than the normal competitive equilibrium' (emphasis added). The critical factor which the Commission's approach therefore failed to recognise with any consistency even in the defence was that collective dominance goes one step further than oligopolistic interdependence and incentives and involves the coordination (albeit tacit) of the oligopolists' strategic interaction.

The defence therefore reflected a more traditional analysis of collective dominance but still retained some elements of the 'new' approach articulated in the *Airtours/First Choice* decision. The most striking example of the shift in the Commission's position concerns the need for a retaliation mechanism. In contrast to the bold assertion in the prohibition decision that no punishment mechanism was required, the Commission acknowledged in the defence 'that a situation of oligopolistic dominance requires that there should be a real risk of retaliation or long-run negative consequences for an operator that departs from the parallel conduct of the members of the oligopoly'. However, the Commission still failed to articulate clearly what kind of retaliatory action would be required to support collective dominance in practice (oscillating between 'the possibility of a capacity war with potentially devastating consequences' and simply 'the return to competitive conduct by all members of the oligopoly').

In its reply, Airtours characterised the theory relied on by the Commission in its defence as a hybrid – or mutant – drawing on elements of the theories of each of unilateral and coordinated effects, while accepting the disciplines of neither.

The Commission in its rejoinder sought to bring its approach even more closely in line with a traditional analysis of collective dominance based on tacit collusion, stating that 'collective dominance may arise where there is (i) recognition by the oligopolists that reduced competition can be beneficial for all of them, so that they act in a parallel manner, (ii) a means for them to observe each other's behaviour and (iii) a set of incentives which can be expected to deter any deviation from the parallel conduct, or what may be called a tacitly co-ordinated position'.

To which the proper answer is: too little and much too late. Airtours' reply had focused on the fact that while the Commission in the defence (and rejoinder) had moved towards economic orthodoxy in its approach to collective dominance, it (1) had not fully embraced the requirements of the tacit collusion test, (2) could not save a flawed Commission decision by restating the law to be applied (or 'legal revisionism') once on appeal, and (3) could not sustain its case on the factual evidence in front of the CFI.

6.3 CFI's judgment in Airtours v Commission

The shift in the Commission's approach during the course of the pleadings would also appear to have been recognised by the CFI. When articulating the test to be applied to determine whether a merger will lead to the creation of a collective dominant position the CFI observed 'as the applicant has argued *and as the Commission has accepted in its pleadings*, three conditions are necessary for a finding of collective dominance'[22] (emphasis added).

The CFI's judgment in *Airtours v Commission* provides a clear and comprehensive formulation of the legal test to be applied by the Commission in order to establish collective dominance. The key issue is whether, in the light of the market characteristics and in particular the alteration in market structure that the transaction would entail, each of the dominant oligopolists would 'consider it possible, economically rational, and hence preferable, to adopt on a lasting basis a common policy on the market with the aim of selling at above competitive prices, without having to enter into an agreement or resort to a concerted practice within the meaning of Article 81'.[23] The CFI continued at paragraph 62 that this will only be the case where the following three conditions, which are essential for a finding of collective dominance, are satisfied:

1. each member of the dominant oligopoly must have the ability to know how the other members are behaving in order to monitor whether or not they are adopting the common policy – sufficient market transparency is therefore critical to enable the dominant oligopolists to adopt and sustain a tacitly coordinated 'common policy';

22 *Airtours plc v Commission,* Case T-342/99, para 62.
23 *Ibid,* para 61.

2. the situation of tacit coordination must be sustainable over time, that is there must be an incentive not to depart from the common policy on the market – the notion of retaliation and adequate deterrents is inherent in this condition;
3. the Commission must also establish that the foreseeable reaction of current and future competitors, as well as of consumers, would not jeopardise the results expected from the common policy.

This analytical framework for assessing potential collective dominance (and in particular the first two limbs) broadly accords with the three conditions which standard economic theory would suggest are necessary for tacit collusion to be both achievable and sustainable. It also corresponds closely with the 'coordinated effects' analysis familiar in US merger control. The third limb is implicit in any analysis of oligopolistic markets: where entry barriers are low and countervailing force is effective, there is no cause for antitrust concern.

6.4 Methodology of the CFI

Having determined the key point, namely that the CFI has reaffirmed the conventional approach to collective dominance as equating to tacit collusion or 'coordinated effects', a brief legal diversion is in order.

The grounds of appeal against Commission decisions set out in Article 230 of the Treaty include 'infringement of the Treaty or of any rule relating to its application'. This is most commonly pleaded to include manifest error of assessment leading to error of law (as indeed it was in the *Airtours* case). This is for good reason. As the matter is succinctly described in a leading textbook on competition law: 'The Court has on occasion annulled decisions of the Commission on the ground that the Commission's analysis of the substantive law was incorrect. More frequently, the Court has annulled decisions of the Commission on the ground that the facts as established did not support the application of a particular rule of substantive law.'[24] One consideration flowing from this insofar as the CFI is concerned is that an appeal to the ECJ lies only on a point of law.[25]

Here, there lies a potential problem. It is, and has long been, conventional wisdom that the European Court will be reluctant to second-guess the exercise by the Commission of its discretion in economic matters: as put in *Consten and Grundig* as long ago as 1966: 'The exercise of the Commission's powers necessarily implies complex evaluations on economic matters. A judicial review of these evaluations must take account of their nature by confining itself to an examination of the relevance of the facts and the legal consequences which the Commission deduces therefrom.'[26] Although initially articulated in the context of what is now Article 81 (and especially in relation to the economic balance sheet exercise comprised in Article 83(3)), the same attitude of judicial self-restraint is expressed to apply in regard to its review of cases under the Merger Regulation.[27]

24 Bellamy and Child, *European Community Law of Competition* (5th edn, 2001), para 12-139.
25 Article 225(1) EC and Article 51 of the Statute establishing the CFI.
26 *Consten and Grundig v Commission*, Joined Cases 56 and 58/64.
27 *France v Commission*, Joined Cases C-68/94 and C-30/95, para 223; *Gencor v Commission*, Case T-102/96, paras 164 and 165.

That on its face makes for considerable difficulty for individual parties seeking to challenge decisions under the Merger Regulation, which, after all, are based very largely on an economic assessment made by the Commission. In doing so, litigants have two weapons at their disposal. First, the European Court's acknowledged role to evaluate the relevance of facts, and the legal consequences drawn therefrom, opens the door to a rigorous judicial scrutiny of the facts and the conclusions drawn therefrom, if this appears merited. As the former Judge Bellamy has said (speaking extrajudicially), the European Court works to the parameters of: 'are the facts established; is the economic appreciation supported by the evidence; have the important arguments been answered in a credible way.'[28] Secondly, and supplementing the previous point, the burden of proof in cases under the Merger Regulation is on the Commission (mergers are presumptively lawful unless the grounds for prohibition are established) and is substantial: see the judgment in *Airtours* at paragraph 63.[29] The burden of proof is of particular importance in cases where tacit collusion is alleged: the charge is that the oligopolists will act as if a single monopolist, but without any evidence of covert agreement, leaving all to be proven from the surrounding circumstances.

The *Airtours* judgment is a clear example of the preparedness of the CFI to intervene where circumstances merit and in particular where it concludes that a manifest error on the facts by the Commission has wrongly influenced its analysis of the economic effects of the merger. The judicial technique employed by the CFI in *Airtours* was to decline to answer the second plea (argument in principle that the decision involved the application of an incorrect definition of collective dominance) on grounds that it should look at how the law has been applied to the facts of the case. Having said that, the CFI then immediately answered the issue of principle by setting out at paragraphs 61 and 62 the analytical framework for establishing collective dominance, described above. Thereafter the CFI proceeded to a systematic demolition of the Commission's decision on the facts. Thus, the CFI found: 'the Commission made errors of assessment in its analysis of competition obtaining in the relevant market prior to the notification'[30]; 'the Commission's examination of competition obtaining between the main tour operators at the time of the notification was inadequate, and ... the Commission made errors of assessment concerning the development and predictability of demand, demand volatility and degree of market transparency'[31]; the Commission 'erred in finding that the factors mentioned would ... . be a sufficient

28 In Hawk (ed), Fordham Corporate Law Institute International Antitrust Law and Policy 1998 (Juris, 1999), p 392.

29 It is surprisingly difficult to find a clear and unambiguous judicial statement of the applicable burden of proof in merger cases. In oral argument before the CFI, counsel for Airtours referred (with apparent judicial recognition) to the test applied in UK merger control proceedings. In *Berisford/British Sugar* (1981) at para 9.40 the then UK Monopolies and Mergers Commission put the test as follows: 'The question we have to consider is not merely whether there is a possibility that the merger will operate against the public interest. If only a possibility were required, hardly any mergers would ever be allowed to proceed, for it is very rarely that such a possibility can be quite excluded. The question is whether the evidence creates the expectation that the merger will operate against the public interest. To put the matter colloquially, the required conclusion is not "This may happen", but "We expect that this will happen".'

30 *Airtours plc v Commission,* Case T-342/99, para 120.

31 *Ibid,* para 181.

incentive for a member of the dominant oligopoly not to depart from the common policy'[32]; 'the Commission's assessment of the foreseeable reaction of smaller tour operators, potential competitors, consumers and hotel operators was incorrect'[33]; 'the Commission has failed to prove that the result of the transaction would be to alter the structure of the relevant market in such a way that the leading operators would no longer act as they have in the past and that a collective dominant position would be created.'[34] In conclusion, the CFI found[35]: 'In light of all the foregoing, the Court concludes that the Decision, far from basing its prospective analysis on cogent evidence, is vitiated by a series of errors of assessment as to matters fundamental to any assessment of whether a collective dominant position might be created.'

Thus, under the guise of identifying manifest errors of assessment, the CFI picked up and dealt with all those key criticisms of the Commission's economic theory and its application to the facts of the case, described above. Future potential litigants should rightly derive a degree of comfort from the CFI's robust approach to those matters.

6.5 Merger control of oligopolies following Airtours

That leaves open the wider question of the control of oligopolies following *Airtours*. It seems clear that, buoyed with its success in *Gencor v Commission*, the Commission had been determined to use *Airtours/First Choice* as an opportunity to extend the concept of collective dominance beyond the bounds of the traditional framework of tacit collusion: that framework had been presented to the Commission in the course of the administrative proceedings, and the Commission refused in its decision to allow itself to be constrained by the three-part test.

In an article published shortly thereafter,[36] Massimo Motta, an economist viewed by many as close to the Merger Task Force, discussed the *Airtours/First Choice* decision. He noted that it pushed the boundaries of collective dominance as traditionally understood, but suggested that in economic terms, it was justifiable on the basis of its unilateral effects: 'an approach inspired by economic thinking would not require the Commission to prove a high likelihood of dominance, but would control the assessment on the extent to which the merger would lead to price increases.' With considerable prescience, Motta suggested that to attack such cases as involving collective dominance created the risk of a lack of transparency and of very uncertain outcomes in the courts. The answer, he concluded, was to amend the Merger Regulation to deal with mergers producing unilateral effects in the absence of a dominant position.

However, the policy line of the Commission remained that the *Airtours/First Choice* decision provided a bridge enabling the Commission under the existing Merger Regulation to control mergers in oligopolistic industries without recourse to showing tacit collusion. Speaking at the EC Merger Control 10th Anniversary Conference in September 2000, Götz Drauz, head of the Merger Task Force, said: 'we have recently

32 *Airtours plc v Commission*, Case T-342/99, para 207.
33 *Ibid*, para 273.
34 *Ibid*, para 293.
35 *Ibid*, para 294.
36 Motta, 'EC Merger Policy and the Airtours Case' [2000] ECLR 199.

realised that the traditional distinction between unilateral (ie single dominance) and co-ordinated (ie oligopolistic dominance) appears to be blurred.' He continued:

> 'I believe that oligopoly assessment is and will continue to be a stimulating challenge for antitrust regulators. It is so fast-moving that, looking back to the beginnings of the EC Merger Regulation in 1990, one could see that it has gone through three distinct conceptual stages: from the first generation of more active collusion theories, oligopoly assessment moved on to tacit collusion and the use of game theory models, while *we are now entering the third generation of what I would call non-co-operative co-ordination models*' (emphasis added).

Only very much later, as the pleadings in *Airtours* before the CFI unfolded and the Commission retreated to try and defend its position on grounds equating collective dominance with tacit collusion, did the public stance soften. Thus Christiensen and Rabassa, Merger Task Force officials writing in a private capacity, sought to justify *Airtours* on traditional grounds of coordinated effects and tacit collusion, while noting 'the question of whether collective dominance should only result from co-ordinated effects or also unilateral effects has never been decided'[37].

What is, however, observable is that as the proceedings in the *Airtours* case unfolded, and the CFI's likely position became clearer (notably following the oral hearing in autumn 2001), the Commission adopted a more rigorous and conventional approach to defining and then applying a test of collective dominance based on coordinated effects. The joined *UPM-Kymmene/Haindl* and *Norske Skog/Parenco/Walsum* cases provide an example.[38] These cases were examined together and concerned the markets for newsprint and wood-containing magazine paper. The Commission investigated whether the proposed concentrations would result in the creation of a collective dominant position in these two markets. In its decision the Commission (at paragraph 74) expressly stated that 'collective dominance is usually associated with the joint exercise of market power through the tacit co-ordination of market behaviour of a group of firms' reflecting a more traditional approach to collective dominance. This was further reflected in the analytical framework set out by the Commission as a guide to establishing collective dominance in the cases, which included consideration of whether the characteristics of the market made the market conducive to tacit coordination as well as the sustainability of the coordination, notably the ability and incentive to deviate from the coordinated outcome and the ability and incentives of non-deviators to retaliate. Following that line of analysis, the Commission concluded that the merger should be allowed to proceed. A similar analytical approach and outcome occurred in a case involving a four to three merger in the iron ore industry.[39]

In the aftermath of the *Airtours* judgment, and in a reversion to the 'spin' that followed the original *Airtours/First Choice* decision, some commentators have suggested that the CFI did not rule out the possibility that the concept of collective dominance extended to cover situations other than those involving coordinated

37 Christiensen and Rabassa, 'The Airtours decision: Is there a new approach to collective dominance?' [2001] ECLR 227.

38 *UPM-Kymmene/Handl* and *Norske Skog/Parenco/Walsum*, Commission Decisions of 21 November 2001 (Case No COMP/M.2498 and COMP/M.2499).

39 *Mitsui/CVRD/Caemi*, Commission Decision of 30 October 2001 (Case No COMP/M.2420).

effects; and even that the failure of the CFI to answer the second question (the definition of collective dominance as a matter of principle) was designed to pave the way to that conclusion.

This calls for three comments in response. First, it is wholly apparent from the record, described above, that by the time the pleadings had closed, the Commission had abandoned all pretence of trying to justify its decision on any grounds other than traditional tacit coordination. Secondly, the fact that the CFI did not answer the second question before it is indicative only of a judicial technique it frequently employs and it was employing in this case. Thirdly, the CFI did (at paragraphs 61 and 62) define collective dominance in terms exclusively consistent with tacit collusion and coordinated effects. Given the concessions made by the Commission in the pleadings, the CFI was not required to state the principle more widely. But it had the opportunity to do so, was familiar with the arguments, and did not do so. Indeed, given the terms in which it ruled it is hard to see how the term 'collective dominance' can henceforth be interpreted otherwise than synonymously with 'tacit collusion' and 'coordinated effects'.

So the question is whether there is some other form of dominance ('non-cooperative coordinated', 'non-collusive oligopolistic' or whatever other sobriquet is chosen) that exists and might fall to be prohibited under the Merger Regulation, and indeed whether there exists a 'gap' that needs to be filled. Three observations occur.

The first is that if such a 'gap' exists, then it is only a very small gap. The hypothetical examples cited in discussions revolve almost entirely round variations on the *HJ Heinz/Beech-Nut* 'next nearest competitor' case.[40] But the evidence to date is that the Commission has not identified a problem of real scale here. The question was raised in the Commission's Green Paper on the Review of the Merger Regulation which contained the following comment:

> 'One of the more specific hypothetical questions that has occasionally been raised about the reach of the dominance test in the Merger Regulation is the extent to which it would allow for effective control in some specific situations where firms unilaterally may be able to raise price and thus exercise market power. The type of example that tends to be cited is of a merger between the second and third largest players in a market, where these firms are the closest substitutes. In such a scenario the merging firms may remain smaller than the existing market leader. The argument goes that the SLC test would be better adapted to addressing such a situation, in particular if the market characteristics would not be conducive to a finding of collective dominance. While interesting as a hypothetical discussion, the Commission has so far not encountered a situation of this kind.'

Secondly, we would argue that any such *lacuna* should not in policy terms, and cannot in legal terms, be closed by torturing further the meaning of 'dominance' for purposes of the Merger Regulation. As to policy, no one suggests that merger policy should be put into a straitjacket, so there is no flexibility for further development. But predictability in merger control is a major objective in itself: three theories of oligopoly in a decade are cause for concern, not congratulation. Simply to turn round now and to say that the *Airtours* judgment can be set on one side and ignored while new theories of multi-firm dominance are explored would be deeply unsatisfactory.

40 *FTC v HJ Heinz Co*, 246 F 3d 708 (DC Cir 27 April 2001).

Consultation on Merger Regulation reform and publication of guidelines on the approach to dominance and market power may be of some assistance. But even then, for the Commission simply to take decisions as it wishes and to wait for the law to be clarified by the European Court at a later stage, always assuming the merger parties are prepared to appeal, is not the correct way to develop the law.

It also appears to the authors, as lawyers, that there is no scope for bringing further situations under the 'dominance' heading. Single firm dominance, with its link to unilateral effects, can be understood. Situations of collective dominance can be encompassed where circumstances exist which 'allow oligopolists to behave as one single monopolist'[41]. As put by Fennelly AG in his Opinion in *Compagnie Maritime Belge*[42] (an Article 82 case) 'a single dominant position has to be established, ie that several undertakings act as a single entity and thus unilaterally on the market', a test interpreted by the ECJ in the same case as 'whether the undertakings concerned together constitute a collective entity vis-à-vis their competitors, their trading partners and consumers'. Collective dominance as characterised by tacit collusion meets the criterion: unilateral effects in cases where there is no single firm dominance clearly does not. We thus think there is no legal scope to extend further the meaning of 'dominance' for the purposes of the Merger Regulation.

Thirdly, if the outcome of the analysis is that the *lacuna* is big enough to require filling (and on the evidence the case is 'not proven'), that would thus involve amendment of the Merger Regulation for the purpose. But we would be hugely reluctant to see any change the practical effect of which was simply to enable the Commission take a more cavalier approach to mergers to be prohibited on grounds of a substantial lessening of competition, without any longer being required to observe the twin disciplines of discharging the burden of proof and ensuring that its case was established against a robust economic theory on the facts without any material error of assessment. The temptation to change the law simply to make convictions easier must be resisted. Otherwise, the lessons of *Airtours* are also lost. That would be a risk to which everyone involved in the area must be alert: the price of fairness under the Merger Regulation, like that of freedom, is eternal vigilance.

41 Briones, 'Economic Assessment of Oligopolies under the Community Merger Regulation' [1993] ECLR 118.

42 *Compagnie Maritime Belge Transports SA, Compagnie Maritime Belge SA and Dafra-Lines A/S v Commission,* Joined Cases C-395/96 and C-396/96.

22
Merger Control and Oligopolistic Dominance in the Wake of the Airtours Judgment

Francisco Enrique González-Díaz*

Head of Unit, Merger Task Force, European Commission, Brussels

1. Introduction

Competition policy has adopted a nuanced and multifaceted approach to the problems posed by oligopolies. Article 81 has been applied, *inter alia*, to instances of anti-competitive parallel behaviour attributable to concerted practices[1] and certain facilitating practices.[2] Article 82 has been applied to abusive conduct carried out by a group of undertakings occupying a collective dominant position[3] as well as on the part of an individual member of such a group.[4] The European Merger Regulation (ECMR) constitutes a third and integral prong of the assessment of oligopolistic markets under EC competition law.

Mergers between rivals in markets with only a few large suppliers may have two main negative effects on competition. First, they may result in (anti-competitive) coordination between the merged firm and the remaining suppliers (collusive oligopoly). Secondly, the merger may significantly reduce the degree of competition prevailing in the relevant market and lead to a price increase regardless of whether there is coordination between firms (non-collusive oligopoly). The question arises whether the notion of dominance can be applied to these situations.

This paper is structured as follows. The next section will outline the common features of oligopolies; the problem of oligopoly for competition policy; how mergers may affect such markets and the implications for merger analysis. The third section will then consider the legal issues raised by oligopolies in the context of merger control. In particular, it will consider whether Article 2 of the ECMR can and should be applied to non-collusive oligopolies. Furthermore, it will examine whether *Airtours v Commission* can and should be the last word on oligopolistic dominance. The fourth section discusses the background to the Draft Guidelines on Horizontal Mergers. The fifth section will conclude.

* The author would like to thank the substantial contributions and comments made by David Bailey, Vincent Verouden, Guillaume Loriot and Claes Bengtsson on previous drafts. Errors are obviously exclusively the author's.

1 See, eg Case 48/69, *ICI v Commission* [1972] ECR 619 ('*Dyestuffs*').

2 See, eg Cases C-8/95 P, *New Holland Ford v Commission* [1998] ECR I-3175.

3 See, eg Case C-396/96, *Compagnie Maritime Belge Transports v Commission* [2000] ECR I-1365.

4 See, eg Case T-228/97, *Irish Sugar v Commission* [1999] ECR II-2969.

2. Mergers and oligopolistic markets

2.1 The 'oligopoly problem'

Oligopoly comes from the Greek words *oligos* meaning few and *polein* referring to the ability to sell. An oligopolistic market refers to a market structure characterised by a small number of suppliers.

In contrast to monopolists or firms competing in a perfectly competitive market, oligopolists cannot ignore how their commercial actions affect other firms in the market. By definition, a monopolist has no rivals and consequently its profit maximising price is essentially a function of its marginal cost and the elasticity of market demand.[5] In contrast, the individual firms in a perfectly competitive market are too small to affect the market price. Each firm can thus ignore the consequences of its actions on any other firm. In an oligopoly, given the limited number of firms present in the market, each firm knows that its price/output decisions can affect the market price and hence its rivals' behaviour (eg their likely reaction to a price increase). Thus, the key difference between oligopolistic markets and both monopolistic and perfectly competitive markets is that in the former a firm must consider its rivals' behaviour in deciding its own commercial policy. The behaviour of firms in oligopolistic markets is thus interrelated and strategic. This interrelation or interdependence of oligopolistic behaviour must not be interpreted as meaning that oligopolistic firms act together as in a cartel in order to determine their commercial policy in the marketplace. Indeed, both economic theory and experience show that the behaviour of the members of a given oligopoly is a function of a number of variables and can yield results approximating those of perfectly competitive markets or those of monopoly. The interesting thing about oligopolistic interaction is that even in the absence of *explicit* agreements/contracts firms may, depending on a number of structural and/or institutional/behavioural factors, charge prices substantially above competitive levels and in some cases, in particular in cases where the oligopolists are able *tacitly* to collude, charge prices approximating those of a monopoly. Against this background, specifically in the wake of the *Airtours* judgment of the European Court of First Instance (CFI) and of the debate on the reform of the substantive test of the ECMR, the question arises how supra-competitive pricing in oligopolistic markets, even in the absence of tacit collusion among the members of the oligopoly, should be dealt with.

2.2 Explaining non-collusive oligopoly

But, how is it that oligopolistic firms can charge supra-competitive prices in the absence of explicit or tacit collusion? The most recent explanation of this economic phenomenon has been provided and systematised by the so-called 'single-period' (or 'one-shot') game theoretical models of oligopolistic behaviour, a subset of the general category of non-

5 Marginal cost is the increase in total costs of production resulting from increasing output by one extra unit; the elasticity of demand measures the responsiveness of demand for a product to alterations in its price.

cooperative oligopoly models developed by modern industrial organisation theory.[6] However, the basic mechanisms behind oligopolistic pricing had already been identified by Augustin Cournot, as long ago as 1838, and by Joseph Bertrand.

The basic intuition behind the Cournot model is that, under certain structural conditions,[7] the commercial strategy of the oligopolists (in the original model the duopolists) would depend on their expectations about the behaviour of their rivals. If Firm 1 expects that Firm 2 will sell a given quantity, Firm 1 can determine the quantity it has to sell itself to maximise its profits. It can do this by, first, deducting from the total market demand the quantity supplied by Firm 2, ie by identifying its residual demand and, secondly, by maximising profits as if it were a monopolist over its residual demand (ie by setting quantity at the point of intersection between its marginal revenue curve and its marginal cost curve; that is, its profit-maximising output). The function that relates Firm 1's profit-maximising quantity to Firm 2's hypothesised quantity level is known as its 'best-response function' (or 'reaction function'). The best-response function is the optimal action Firm 1 can take given its expectations about the way its rival will behave. Firm 2's best response function is derived in a similar way. The market price equilibrium will be the point at which these two reaction functions intersect. This equilibrium means no firm can obtain a higher profit by choosing a different strategy (that is, a different level of output). This equilibrium is an example of a so-called 'Nash equilibrium': once achieved, no firm has an incentive to change its strategy because each is selling the quantity that maximises its profits given its (correct) expectations about the other firm's choice of output. In equilibrium, therefore, each firm sets its output as the best response to its rival's expected output.[8]

The basic Cournot model yields two important results:

1. prices in this market situation are higher than those prevailing in a perfectly competitive market but lower than the monopoly level; and
2. the exact price level is contingent on the number of firms – the larger the number of firms, the smaller is output per firm, the larger is industry output and hence the lower is the market price.

Paradoxically, if rather than fixing output/capacity the oligopolists choose prices as their main strategic variable then, as pointed out by Bertrand in 1883, the market equilibrium price will actually converge to the level where price will equal (marginal)

6 For a general discussion of these models see Carlton and Perloff, *Modern Industrial Organisation* (Longman, 3rd edn, 1999). Church and Ware, *Industrial Organisation: A Strategic Approach* (McGraw-Hill/Irwin, 2000). Scherer and Ross, *Industry Market Structure and Economic Performance* (Boston Houghton Mifflin, 3rd edn, 1990). Cabral, *Introduction to Industrial Organization* (MIT, Cambridge, Massachusetts, 2000). Tirole, *The Theory of Industrial Organization* (MIT Press, Cambridge, Massachusetts, 1988).

7 Firms act independently of each other – ie they do not collude – choose output, are protected by high barriers to entry, sell homogeneous products, compete in a single period, have the same and constant marginal costs and no fixed costs, face no capacity constraints and a linear demand curve.

8 As to the formation of these expectations, or 'beliefs' as they are technically referred to, Daughety (1985) describes the process as follows: Firm 1's manager thinks about what Firm 2's manager is thinking 'I think that Firm 2's manager thinks that I think that Firms 2's manager thinks that I think ...' Firm 2's manager thinks about Firm 1's manager's model similarly. Based on this type of reasoning, each firm chooses an output level. Daughety shows that the Cournot equilibrium is the only possible result of this type of reasoning.

costs. However, this result may not obtain when the oligopolists are either capacity constrained and/or sell differentiated products. In such market conditions, firms may be in a position to set prices at a supra-competitive level.[9] This outcome depends on the number of players. Indeed, the larger the number of firms in the market the lower the market price will tend to be.

In sum, economic theory shows that even in the absence of tacit or explicit collusion, oligopolistic interaction may lead to supra-competitive pricing and thus to potentially significant losses of both allocative efficiency[10] and consumer welfare. Merger control has thus a significant role to play in this type of market settings if its aims are to be properly fulfilled.[11]

2.3 Impact of a merger on an oligopolistic market

In oligopolistic markets, a horizontal merger is likely to increase the market power of both the merging firms, and possibly their competitors. To assess the implications of this increase in market power for effective competition in the relevant market, and possibly for barriers to entry, one needs to compare the increase in market power against any benefit the merger may bring about in terms of cost-related efficiency gains, improved quality of the relevant product and so forth.

The impact of the same merger on the scope for tacit coordination is a more delicate task because some mergers may facilitate coordination while others may make it more difficult to achieve. Thus, it is important to remember that an increase in market concentration caused by a merger need not always be associated with an increase in the ability of the members of an oligopoly to earn supra-competitive profits through collusion.

Whether firms primarily compete in terms of prices or quantities (or capacities) and in the absence of any offsetting efficiency gains, a merger between competitors is likely to increase the resulting firms' market power (ie that of the merged firm and its competitors), thereby leading to higher prices and lower output.[12] This is so because the merged entity is likely to act in a less competitive way than the two independent firms would have done prior to the merger. The exact nature of this increase in market power depends, in particular, on whether firms compete in prices or quantities. To understand the overall effect of a merger it is useful to distinguish the impact of the merger on the merging parties and on the remaining firms.

9 The decision how to model a specific industry (Cournot versus Bertrand) very much depends on the timing of the main strategic decision (output/price). If capacity and output can be easily adjusted, then the Bertrand model is a better approximation of the way in which firms are likely to interact in that particular oligopolistic market. If output and capacity are difficult to adjust, then the Cournot model would be a better approximation to oligopolistic interaction.

10 Allocative efficiency, also known as 'Pareto efficiency', is obtained when resources are allocated in such a way that it is impossible for a different allocation to improve the position of one firm without worsening the position of another firm.

11 On the aims of the ECMR, see the CFI in Case T-102/96, *Gencor v Commission* [1999] ECR II-743, at para 106 ('...while the elimination of the risk of future abuses may be a legitimate concern of any competent competition authority, the main objective in exercising control over concentrations at Community level is to ensure that the restructuring of undertakings does not result in the creation of positions of economic power which may significantly impede effective competition in the common market...').

12 Assuming there are no factors constraining the exercise of market power such as, for example, countervailing buyer power, see Case No IV/M.1225, *Enso/Stora*, OJ 1999 L 254/9.

2.3.1 Impact of the merger on the parties

The impact of a merger on the parties themselves is qualitatively the same regardless of whether or not firms compete on prices or quantities/capacity. For example, in a merger involving two firms that produce two imperfect substitutes, the new firm gains a monopoly position on the residual demand for these two products, ie the demand accruing to the firm given its rival's decisions, whereas before the transaction the two merging firms were not only reacting to the other rival's decisions but also competing among themselves.

To put the matter differently, a merger between two competitors allows them to 'coordinate' the prices of their products perfectly. If the two goods are (even imperfect) substitutes, raising the price of one firm's product induces some consumers to buy more of the other firm's product.[13] Prior to the merger, each party would have considered the potential loss of business to its rival whenever it decided to change its price. Following the merger, this is no longer a consideration. The effect of a change in price of one of the merging party's products on the demand for the other party's product is 'internalised'. As a result, the merging firms will have an incentive to raise their price-cost margins and/or reduce the output of each product.

The extent to which the merging firms will increase their prices or reduce output will, however, depend *inter alia* on the degree of substitution between their products and those offered by the remaining competitors, and on the nature of competition (prices versus quantities). A merger between firms that produce close substitutes is more likely to lead to price increases than a merger between firms that produce imperfect substitutes. The reason for this is that a merger involving close substitutes is likely to remove significant competitive constraints on the behaviour of the merging parties that previously existed between them. Similarly, a merged firm is likely to raise prices to a lesser extent if other competitors produce close substitutes than if they produce imperfect substitutes. And this latter effect is likely to be more important in the case of price competition, since the elimination of competition between substitutes will matter more in that case.

2.3.2 Impact of the merger on other competitors

The effect of a merger on the remaining competitors mostly depends on whether firms primarily compete on prices or on quantities/capacity. While in both cases an increase in the merging firms' prices or a reduction in their output limits the competitive pressure on the other firms and thus allows them to achieve higher profits, the precise reaction of rivals to such a change of behaviour post-merger may differ according to the nature of competition in the relevant market.

When firms compete on price, their pricing strategies may be said to be 'strategic complements': an increase in the price of one product will typically lead competing firms to increase their own prices, although probably to a lesser extent. An increase in the merging firms' prices is likely to trigger a positive response from the other firms – and this expectation will further encourage the merging firms to raise their own prices in the first place. The direct impact of the merger on the behaviour of the new firm is

13 Similarly, reducing the output of one firm's product will increase the demand for and price of the other firm's product (if the other firm's output remains constant).

thus exacerbated by the way in which all firms are likely to adapt to the new market structure.

When firms compete on the quantity produced, on the other hand, quantity decisions are often 'strategic substitutes': a reduction in the output of one firm typically leads competing firms to expand their own output, although not necessarily to the extent of fully compensating the initial output reduction. Thus, a reduction in the merging firms' output triggers an opposite response from the other firms – which contributes to discouraging the merging firms from reducing their output. The strategic substitutability of quantities means that the direct impact of the merger on the behaviour of the new firm is somewhat attenuated by the firms' adaptation to the new industry structure.

2.4 Implications for merger analysis

Merger analysis, therefore, needs to consider the impact of the merger not only on the structure of the market but also on the incentives of the merging parties and their rivals. In an industry where firms compete on price, not taking the reaction of rivals into account would lead to an underestimation of the likely price increase. The opposite result would be true in an industry where firms compete on quantities.

The strategic nature (complementarity or substitutability) of prices and quantities also has some bearing on the firms' incentives to merge. In the case of price competition, a merger is likely to be profitable even in the absence of any efficiency gain: this is because the merging firms both eliminate competition between them and induce their competitors to raise their own prices. Put differently, a merger allows the firms to gain a monopoly position over the residual demand for their products, and they benefit from the induced increase in competitors' prices. In contrast, in the case of quantity competition, a merger may well be unprofitable in the absence of significant efficiency gains. Indeed, despite the fact that the merger eliminates competition between the merging firms, it also triggers a more aggressive response from the rival firms, which may suffice to reduce the profits of the merging firms (even if it does not lower the equilibrium prices).

Evaluating the impact of the merger thus requires a detailed assessment of the nature of competition (in prices, quantities, capacities), of the degree of substitution between competing products and, if established by the merging parties, of the expected efficiency gains generated by the merger.

However, the oligopoly problem transcends the boundaries of the static models of strategic behaviour described above since, as acknowledged by modern industrial organisation theory, the potential welfare losses identified above, in the context of non-collusive oligopolies, may be compounded by the prospect of tacit coordination in situations where oligopolistic firms interact with each other over time (ie over more than one period – the so-called 'multi-period' oligopoly game-theoretic models). In multi-period games, firms may change their behaviour in one period depending on the behaviour of rivals in previous periods. As such, firms may seek to influence their rival's behaviour, by making their own behaviour dependent on the behaviour of the latter. A firm can, for example, 'signal' to another firm that it does not want to compete aggressively by lowering its output for a few periods. If the other firm responds by lowering its output, both behave in a less competitive way *de facto* without the need for an explicit agreement between them. If either firm increases its output, the other may be able to retaliate by raising its output to punish the cheating firm. This ability to signal and punish in multi-period games may allow firms to restrict output beyond the competitive level and most importantly beyond the Cournot or Bertrand price levels referred to above. However, all repeated games do not necessarily result in collusion. The equilibrium reached in such category of games is particularly sensitive to the oligopolists' ability to threaten and potentially punish one another.[14]

Successful coordination between oligopolists, therefore, requires a mechanism for coordinating the firm's interdependent decision-making, a means of detecting deviation from such coordination and a way of disciplining those firms that choose to deviate.[15]

It is important, however, to avoid over-categorising the problems associated with collusive and non-collusive oligopoly. Both as a theoretical and as a practical matter, the problems of collusive and non-collusive oligopoly are not mutually exclusive and merger control may consider both problems in relation to one and the same merger.[16]

In the case of a collusive oligopoly, it is the merger's impact on the strategic interaction between oligopolists that is important. For example, a merger may change the nature of competition in an oligopolistic market. It may make coordination more likely or even accentuate the anti-competitive effects of pre-existing coordination. This impact has been recognised and addressed by the case law of the Community courts and the decisional practice of the Commission.[17]

2.5 Summary

By definition, a horizontal merger reduces the degree of competition existing between the merging parties beforehand. Where the products of the merging parties are close substitutes for one another, the parties may have a greater incentive to raise their prices after the merger. Indeed, in this case one source of competitive constraint on the parties' pricing and output decisions would have been removed. The relevant question is thus whether, post-merger, the merged entity would be in a position to increase prices or otherwise act anti-competitively without facing sufficient competitive constraints. Whether the merger has a significant negative effect on competition or not will depend *inter alia* on the ability of actual and potential competitors or customers to counterbalance this ability and incentive of the merged entity to exercise market power. For example, potential competitors may enter the market and actual competitors may increase their output in order to benefit from the customers' incentive to switch their purchases away from the more expensive product of the

14 The effectiveness of the threat depends in turn on the importance of the future relative to the present, the length of the game and the credibility of the threat.

15 See, to that effect, the CFI in Case T-342/99, *Airtours v Commission* [2002] ECR II-2585, at para 62.

16 See *Mergers: substantive assessment, A consultation paper*, October 2002, OFT 506, at para 4.7, and *Europe Economics, Study on Assessment Criteria for Distinguishing between Competitive and Dominant Oligopolies in Merger Control – Final Report for the European Commission Enterprise DG* (London, 2001), at para 3.5.

17 See, eg Commission decisions on collective dominance range one of the earliest in Case No IV/M.190, *Nestlé/Perrier* to one of the most recent in Case No COMP/2816, *Ernst & Young France/Andersen France* and the jurisprudence of the Community courts has evolved in Case C-68/94, *France v Commission* [1998] ECR I-1375, at paras 169-178; Case T-102/96, *Gencor v Commission* [1999] ECR II-743; and Case T-342/99, *Airtours v Commission* [2002] ECR II-2585.

merged firm. Overall, it is therefore imperative to ascertain whether the change in market structure induced by the merger will create or enhance significant market power and significantly impede effective competition.

3. The ECMR and the oligopoly problem

3.1 Introduction

This section will address two legal issues relating to the application of the ECMR to oligopolistic behaviour. First, it will examine whether the competition concerns arising from non-collusive oligopolies may be legitimately tackled under Article 2 of the ECMR. In particular, it will consider whether the judgment of the CFI in *Airtours v Commission* has excluded the possibility of applying the notion of dominance to such concerns. Secondly, it will address whether the *Airtours* judgment has definitively determined how a collusive oligopoly is to be appraised under the ECMR.

3.1.1 Literal interpretation

The wording of Article 2 of the ECMR does not exclude the possibility of applying it to situations of non-collusive oligopoly. Under Article 2, a merger must create or strengthen dominance within the Common Market. This wording does not distinguish between dominant positions held individually or collectively[18] nor does it distinguish between the different effects on competition.[19] This interpretation does not deny the complexities inherent in defining and understanding oligopolistic dominance but recognises that Article 2 is not necessarily limited by textual considerations. The recognition of a failing firm defence under the ECMR[20] or the fact that the concept of collective dominance can be applied not only to duopolies but also to the strengthening of an oligopoly[21] tend to confirm this understanding of the substantive test.

3.1.2 Teleological interpretation

The European Court of Justice (ECJ) has held that the ECMR should 'apply to all concentrations with a Community dimension in so far as they are likely, because of their effect on the structure of competition within the Community, to prove incompatible with the system of undistorted competition envisaged by the Treaty'.[22] Moreover, the CFI stressed in *Gencor* that the application of the ECMR is based on 'the need to avoid the establishment of market structures which may create or strengthen a dominant position, and not on the need to control directly possible abuses of a dominant position'.[23] In other words, the ECMR is designed to prevent anti-competitive market structures from arising in the first place and thereby pre-empt the opportunity for abuses of a dominant position from occurring. This underlines the foundational principle on which the ECMR is premised, ie the need to prevent

18 Case C-68/94, *France v Commission* [1998] ECR I-1375, at para 166.

19 *Ibid*, at para 146; the same point was made by the CFI in Case T-5/02, *Tetra Laval v Commission* [2002] 5 CMLR 1182, at para 146; this case is on appeal to the ECJ in Case C-12/03 P, *Commission v Tetra Laval* (judgment pending).

20 *Ibid*, at paras 109-124.

21 See Case T-342/99, *Airtours v Commission* [2002] ECR II-2585.

22 *Ibid*, at para 170.

23 Case T-102/96, *Gencor v Commission* [1999] ECR II-743, at para 106.

dominant positions from being created or reinforced and thereby prevent the corollary opportunity for firms to commit abuses.

3.1.3 Effectiveness of merger control

The Community courts have consistently delineated the scope of the ECMR by reference to its underlying purpose and its place within the wider scheme of competition rules under the EC Treaty.[24] Dominance under Article 2 ECMR has always been understood and applied with the purpose of merger control in mind. For instance, in *France v Commission*, the fact that collective dominance was not expressly mentioned in Article 2 was not decisive[25] since the ECMR was intended to apply to *all* concentrations with a Community dimension which may impair undistorted competition. To hold otherwise would deprive the ECMR 'of a not insignificant aspect of its effectiveness'.[26]

This supports the view that non-collusive oligopolies may legitimately be tackled under the ECMR. This is also coherent with the general view taken by the Community courts that 'in view of the consequences which the oligopolistic structure of the markets may have, it is all the more necessary to protect residual competition'.[27]

3.1.4 Evolution of the jurisprudence on collective dominance

The substantive test under Article 2 of the ECMR has historically been given a broad, dynamic interpretation. This development may be briefly summarised as follows.

In *Hoffman-La Roche*, the ECJ seemed to distinguish between a dominant position under Article 82 and parallel conduct between firms, which is typical of oligopolies.[28] This view was eschewed by the CFI in *Italian Flat Glass*.[29] In that case, the CFI recognised, in principle, the possibility for two or more undertakings, when united by economic links, jointly to hold a dominant position.[30] This judgment was subsequently clarified by the CFI in *Gencor*, holding that such economic links may actually be based on the strategic interdependence of the oligopolists.[31] Subsequently, the CFI has even identified collective dominance in a vertical commercial relationship in *Irish Sugar*.[32] More recently, the CFI has further refined and clarified the meaning of collective dominance in *Airtours v Commission*.

In *Airtours*, the Court laid down three necessary conditions for a finding of collective dominance as discussed further below. In broad terms, these conditions relate to transparency, adequate deterrent mechanisms and the absence of sufficient constraints from competitors or customers. These conditions relate to the possibility, effectiveness and sustainability of tacit coordination. For present purposes, the case

24 See Case C-68/94, *France v Commission* [1998] ECR I-1375, at paras 169-178; Case T-102/96, *Gencor v Commission* [1999] ECR II-743, at paras 148-158.
25 Case C-68/94, *France v Commission* [1998] ECR I-1375, at para 168. See also Case T-102/96, *Gencor v Commission* [1999] ECR II-743, at para 148.
26 Case C-68/94, *France v Commission* [1998] ECR I-1375, at para 171; Case T-102/96, *Gencor v Commission* [1999] ECR II-743, at para 150.
27 Case T-141/94, *Thyssen/Commission* [1999] ECR II-347, at para 302.
28 Case 85/76, *Hoffman-La Roche v Commission* [1979] ECR 461, para 39.
29 Case T-68/89 etc, *Società Italiano Vetro SpA v Commission* [1992] ECR II-1403.
30 *Ibid*, at para 358.
31 Case T-102/96, *Gencor v Commission* [1999] ECR II-743, at paras 273-277. See also Case C-396/96, *Compagnie Maritime Belge Transports v Commission* [2000] ECR I-1365, para 36.
32 Case T-228/97, *Irish Sugar v Commission* [1999] ECR II-2969, para 63.

raises the following question: did the Court's judgment rule out the possibility of applying collective dominance and, thereby the ECMR, to the problem of the non-collusive oligopoly? Put differently, is tacit coordination a prerequisite for a finding of oligopolistic dominance?

A careful reading of the judgment in *Airtours* reveals that the problem of non-collusive oligopoly was sidestepped by the Court. The salient part of the Commission's decision addressing this problem was paragraph 54 which stated:

> '[I]t is not a necessary condition of collective dominance for the oligopolists always to behave as if there were one or more explicit agreements (eg to fix prices or capacity, or share the market) between them. It is sufficient that the merger makes it rational for the oligopolists, in adapting themselves to market conditions, to act, individually, in ways which will substantially reduce competition between them, and as a result of which they may act, to an appreciable extent, independently of competitors, customers and consumers.'[33]

However, the Court considered that paragraphs 51 to 56 of the Commission's decision were merely preliminary observations which summarised the Commission's conclusions on the likely negative effects of the merger.[34] The Court thus confined its review to the remaining paragraphs of the decision. It then proceeded to examine the way in which the law had been applied to the facts and adjudicated on the merits of the Commission's findings concerning the effects of the concentration on competition.[35]

Therefore the Court did not have to rule on whether or not the ECMR can be applied to non-collusive oligopolies. It thus remains to be seen how the Community courts will interpret and apply the ECMR to such situations. However, the likely judicial approach on the issue may be gleaned from the way the ECMR has been interpreted to date. As described above, this has centred on a teleological interpretation of the ECMR and the need, so far as is possible, to avoid any lacuna in its application.[36]

The fact that the emphasis in the case law on collective dominance up to and including *Airtours* was on the coordination between the parties to the merger and third parties is partly historical, for this was the first situation in which the question of collective dominance arose, and partly reflects the fact that theory and practice in merger control evolve with experience. This evolution is also to be found in the development of the US Horizontal Merger Guidelines. Nevertheless, this emphasis has tended to obscure the fact that it is really the outcome resulting from the interaction between oligopolies which should determine the application of the ECMR. The case law of the Community courts and the decisional practice of the Commission tends to confirm that the meaning of dominance is not fixed, but has rather responded to developments in economic thinking and the surrounding market circumstances. Therefore, both the unilateral exercise of market power by oligopolists, as well as the latter's tacit coordination, could support a finding of dominance under the ECMR.

33 Case No IV/M.1524, *Airtours/First Choice*, OJ 2000 L 93/1, at para 54.
34 Case T-102/96, *Gencor v Commission* [1999] ECR II-743, at paras 51-52.
35 *Ibid*, at para 53.
36 See, by analogy, the ECJ's teleological approach to Article 82 in Case 6/72, *Continental Can v Commission* [1973] ECR 215, at para 22.

3.1.5 Summary

Once it is recognised that it is the effects of the merger and not the means by which these effects are brought about that should determine the substantive application of the ECMR, there appears to be no reason to exclude non-collusive oligopolies from the scope of application of the ECMR.

3.2 Is Airtours the last word on tacit coordination and, if so, should it be?

The judgment in *Airtours v Commission* is a welcome development. It helpfully clarified the meaning of collective dominance with respect to tacit coordination. However, it is not possible to speak of this judgment as if it were the last word either on tacit coordination or, as discussed above, on oligopolistic dominance generally.

The CFI held that three conditions are necessary for a finding of coordination[37]:

1 market transparency;
2 adequate deterrent mechanisms; and
3 competitors or customers must not put in jeopardy the coordinated strategy.

Once these conditions are satisfied, the prospect of coordination becomes a realistic competition concern. These conditions will be analysed in greater detail in the section outlining the background to the draft Guidelines on Horizontal Mergers. What is important to bear in mind at this stage is that the judgment did not prescribe rigid rules for the establishment of anti-competitive parallel behaviour. As is typical of all judicial decisions, *Airtours* was decided on the individual circumstances of the case.

For example, the CFI did not hold that, as a matter of law, coordination is impossible whenever market conditions are volatile. While volatility may indeed constitute a factor militating against a finding of collective dominance, it does not rule out such a finding. On the facts, the CFI found that fluctuating market shares and changing conditions of demand in the relevant package holiday market rendered the creation of a dominant oligopoly more difficult.[38] It does not follow, however, that volatile market conditions preclude coordination in all market situations. Provided there is sufficient transparency in the market, fluctuating market conditions may not necessarily prevent tacit coordination. Indeed, transparency may allow the members of a dominant oligopoly to observe and distinguish between changes in market conditions and deviation from coordination.

The retaliatory measures in *Airtours* were found to provide an insufficient incentive to adhere to the terms of coordination due, partly, to the potential economic loss likely to be incurred by the retaliating firms.[39] However, it should be emphasised that an approach to retaliation based on economic loss must be applied carefully. In some market situations, firms may be willing to incur substantial costs to punish deviating firms. Retaliation will depend on the balancing of the short-term losses incurred during the punishment phase and the longer-term recoupment of supra-competitive profits. It is thus not an 'all-or-nothing' question based exclusively on the magnitude of the loss.

37 Case T-342/99 [2002] ECR II-2585 at para 62.
38 Case T-342/99, *Airtours v Commission* [2002] ECR II-2585, at paras 109-147.
39 *Ibid*, at para 206.

In addition to what the CFI has said, it is important to point out that in many cases the loss of profit which ensues from the unravelling of coordination may suffice to prevent deviation. Indeed, as mentioned above, the incentive to sustain tacit coordination depends not only on the losses inflicted by the punishment mechanisms but also on the difference between the long-term benefits of anti-competitive behaviour compared to the short-term gains of competition on the merits.[40] Although the opportunities for anti-competitive parallel behaviour are necessarily complex, the motivation of firms to coordinate will also be influenced by simple but important considerations such as the benefits which may be derived from coordination.

It is clear that the notion of collective dominance has been greatly elaborated since the CFI's recognition of the concept in *Italian Flat Glass*.[41] As part of this process, *Airtours v Commission* has shed much light on the concept of collective dominance. However, it is critical to bear in mind that the CFI's judgment does not answer every question in relation to tacit coordination or the oligopoly problem. To date, an integral feature of collective dominance has been its application to the problem of collusion. This has been developed on a case-by-case basis and should continue to be so developed.

4. Background to the Draft Guidelines on Horizontal Mergers

As part of the recent review of the ECMR[42] and in the interests of transparency and legal certainty, the Commission has published a Draft Notice on the appraisal of horizontal mergers under the ECMR (the 'Guidelines').[43] The Guidelines aim at providing detailed guidance on how Article 2 of the ECMR should be interpreted and, more specifically, how it applies to both non-collusive and collusive oligopolies.

The Draft Guidelines are broadly structured as follows. The background to the substantive test under the ECMR is described at the outset. This is then followed by the analysis of horizontal mergers creating or strengthening a position of single dominance. The Draft Guidelines also outline the approach that the Commission may be expected to apply in the course of assessing the competitive effects of non-collusive and collusive oligopolies. Standards on entry conditions, countervailing buyer power, possible efficiencies claims and the failing firm defence are also set forth in the Draft Guidelines.

The Guidelines will, of course, be without prejudice to the jurisprudence of the Community courts.[44] They are based on the Commission's diverse experience in enforcing the ECMR over the last 12 years. However, the Guidelines do not replace the guidance provided by the Commission's previous or future merger decisions. Instead,

40 See Commission Guidelines on Market Analysis and the Assessment of Significant Market Power under the Community Regulatory Framework for Electronic Communications Networks and Services, OJ 2002 C 165/6, at para 99.

41 Case T-68/89 etc, *Società Italiano Vetro SpA v Commission* [1992] ECR II-1403.

42 See *Green Paper on the Review of Council Regulation (EEC) No 4064/89* COM (2001)745/6 final, 11 December 2001.

43 OJ 2002 C 331/18.

44 This point was clearly demonstrated by the CFI's judgment in Case T-251/00, *Lagardère/Canal+ v Commission*, judgment of 20 November 2002, at para 109 (rejecting the interpretation of the Commission's Notice on Ancillary restraints on whether the Commission was obliged to assess whether an obligation is ancillary or not).

they seek to distil the principles developed in those decisions. In other words, they complement and reinforce the Commission's decisional practice. Overall, the Guidelines should provide a dual benefit: to give greater legal certainty to would-be merging parties and to eliminate any lingering doubts as to the meaning of dominance under the ECMR.

The following sections of this paper will concentrate on the principles and past decisional practice animating the draft Guidelines' approach to oligopolistic dominance, starting with the concerns raised by non-collusive oligopolies and following with the negative effects of collusive oligopoly. It does not purport to analyse in detail the draft Guidelines themselves.

4.1 Non-collusive oligopolies

As explained above, a merger may diminish the degree of competition in an oligopolistic market and thereby increase the market power of one or more firms. As a result, the merged firm, and its rivals, may find it profitable to increase their prices.[45] This consequence is not dependent on coordination between the members of the oligopoly.

It is, therefore, necessary to consider the way in which a merger will affect the dynamics of strategic interaction between the merged entity and its rivals. What is important in this context, however, is how the individual members of the oligopoly are likely to react to the change in market structure brought about by the merger. The relative shift in market behaviour of the merged entity and its competitors will determine the extent to which effective competition will be impaired.

4.1.1 Differentiated product markets[46]

In differentiated product markets the products involved are imperfect alternatives to each other and thus vary in their degree of substitutability for one another.[47] Some are close substitutes, others are not. Products may be distinguished in various ways by virtue of, *inter alia*, their product characteristics, their end uses or level of quality. Such product differentiation has two main consequences. First, the degree of competitive pressure on such a market depends not only on the merging parties' share of the market but also on the relative market position of competing products. In this type of market, it is vitally important to determine the closeness of substitution both as between the merging parties' products and as between them and competing products.[48] This will determine the significance of the competitive constraint faced by a merged firm's line of products. Secondly, in these markets, all firms have a varying degree of autonomy in determining their prices. This autonomy will, however, be restrained and influenced by the commercial decisions made by their competitors, especially those selling the next-best alternative products.[49]

45 *Europe Economics, Study on Assessment Criteria for Distinguishing between Competitive and Dominant Oligopolies in Merger Control – Final Report for the European Commission Enterprise DG* (London, 2001), at para 3.2.
46 See, eg Case No IV/M.776, *Saint-Gobain/Wacker Chemie/NOM*, at paras 175-179.
47 See, eg Case No COMP/M.2650, *Haniel/Cementbouw/JV (CVK)*, at para 98.
48 See, eg Case No COMP/M.2658, *Haniel/Ytong*, at paras 110 and 115.
49 See, eg Case No M.1227 *Nestle/Dagerty*, at paras 28-31.

A horizontal merger involving product lines considered to be close substitutes by a substantial proportion of consumers may give rise to negative effects on competition.[50] For example, the loss of direct competition between close substitutes may generate an incentive for the merged entity to raise prices. The Commission's decision in *Haniel/Ytong* illustrates this effect. This case concerned a concentration in the market for Dutch wall-building materials. The merger brought together materials used for the same building purpose, namely small-scale construction projects. The Commission found that the merger would strengthen the dominant position of the merged entity because it combined the supply of two of the most popular building materials for smaller constructions. As a result, the merged entity may have been expected to raises prices above the competitive level.[51] The case was cleared subject to structural commitments.

A merger between suppliers of close substitutes may thus remove important competitive constraints and lead to a change in pricing incentives. In this context it is particularly important to determine the proportion of lost sales that, following a likely price increase, would be recaptured in the form of higher sales by the other brands offered by the merged firm.[52] The strength of this incentive to increase prices will also depend on the availability of competing close substitutes and on the foreseeable repositioning of currently not closely competing products by actual and potential competitors with a view to becoming closer substitutes for the products of the merged entity.[53] This analysis will normally help in determining whether effective competition is significantly impeded in the reference market.

Therefore, it is of paramount importance to analyse mergers in such markets by reference to the relative substitutability of competing products before and after the merger.

4.1.2 Homogeneous product markets[54]

Non-collusive oligopolies may also arise in markets for homogenous products. Since the product in question is virtually identical, there may be little scope for charging different prices. Where firms produce homogeneous products and compete on capacities and/or on output, prices are decided by the total amount of output produced in the market.

When two producers of homogeneous products merge, the resulting increase in market share may encourage the merged entity to restrict its output in order to charge supra-competitive prices. Whether or not this is feasible depends on the extent to which the merged entity is constrained by the reactions of its current and future competitors and customers. Hence, a merger analysis must consider, *inter alia*, the capacity utilisation of existing competitors and their ability to expand output, as well as the existence of significant barriers to entry. Overall, whether the merger has a

50 See, eg Case No IV/M.623, *Kimberly-Clark/Scott*, at paras 166-177 and Case No COMP/M.2817, *Barilla/BPL/Kamps*, at paras 34-38.

51 See, eg Case No COMP/M.2658, *Haniel/Ytong*, at paras 126.

52 The proportion of lost sales following a price rise recaptured in the form of higher sales of other branded products manufactured by the merging firms is known as the 'diversion ratio'.

53 The analysis would be analogous to assessing the likelihood and effectiveness of entry conditions.

54 The Cournot model of oligopolistic competition is, as outlined above, particularly suitable to markets in homogeneous product market where capacity or output decisions are the most important strategic decisions.

negative effect on competition will depend on the extent to which competitors and customers may counteract the restriction of output likely to be effected by the merged entity.

In bidding markets, the conditions of competition may be determined, in particular, by the presence of credible alternative suppliers.[55] The credibility of suppliers depends, *inter alia*, on their ability to serve specific groups of customers. A merger between two firms serving the same group or groups of customers may give rise to competition concerns. This may be the case where the merging firms have been competing against one another to supply the same customer prior to the merger.

Typically, in a public auction, each firm faces the risk that competing bidders will undercut its offer. The winning bidder will supply the product that satisfies the customer's specifications at the lowest possible price considering the likely offers of competing bidders. As a result of the ever-present risk of prices being undercut, the most efficient firm will tend to bid marginally below the price of its closest rival. If, for example, the most efficient firm merges with its closest rival, then the vigour of competition is likely to be diminished because in future bidding rounds the merged entity is likely to fix its price against that of the next lowest-cost bidder, ie at a higher price.

The effect of a merger on a bidding-like market was analysed in *Alcoa/Reynolds*, a decision concerning a merger involving two aluminium producers.[56] In assessing the effects of the merger on the smelter-grade alumina market, the Commission considered whether the merger would enable the merged firm to raise its prices. Since the operation concerned the lowest-cost bidder – Reynolds – the Commission found that, following the merger, the average bidding price was likely to increase because in the future the merged entity would be likely to set its price close to the next lowest-cost bidder, ie at a higher level. The case was cleared with commitments.

4.2 Collusive oligopoly

4.2.1 Overview

Tacit coordination, sometimes referred to as 'tacit collusion' or 'conscious parallelism', describes the process by which a few firms may collectively exercise market power: setting their prices at a supra-competitive level by recognising their mutual commercial interests in so doing.[57] To explain why this outcome is likely, the interaction of oligopolists over time must be considered in more detail.

4.2.2 Coordination between oligopolists

> 'A satisfactory theory of oligopoly cannot begin with assumptions concerning the way in which each firm views its interdependence with its rivals.'[58]

In an oligopolistic market, every firm is aware that highly competitive action on its part, such as a reduction in its prices designed to increase its market share, may elicit

55 See, eg Case COMP/M.1879, *Boeing/Hughes*, at para 42.

56 See, eg Case COMP/M.1693, *Alcoa/Reynolds*, at para 53.

57 See Scherer and Ross, *Industry Market Structure and Economic Performance* (Boston Houghton Mifflin, 3rd edn, 1990) at pp 199-208.

58 G Stigler, 'A Theory of Oligopoly' (1962) 72 *Journal of Political Economy* 44-61.

identical action by its rivals. No benefit may result from such an initiative since the net outcome may be a general lowering in prices.[59] This reflects the interdependence between oligopolists, ie that they do not act in isolation. A firm's decision affects and is affected by the decisions of its competitors. The question whether to change the status quo and raise prices will depend on how the other firms react. The *incentive* to raise prices above the competitive level thus depends on whether rivals are likely to act similarly. The question then is how this parallel behaviour can be achieved. The answer is coordination.

The Commission's decision in *MCIWorldCom/Sprint* put forward four fundamental questions to be answered in relation to tacit coordination under the ECMR[60]:

1 Are there incentives for the market players to engage in parallel behaviour?
2 Is it easy for market players to monitor the competitive behaviour of the other market players?
3 Are there disincentives for the market players to deviate from the parallel behaviour?
4 Is it possible for the demand to constrain the parallel behaviour?

In applying this analytical framework, a viable coordination mechanism must thus be identified. For example, in *MAN/Auwärter*, the concentration resulted in a duopolistic market structure with each firm supplying nearly 50 per cent of the German city-bus market. However, the Commission concluded that there was no risk of collective dominance by tacitly sharing the market due to the absence of any practicable means of coordinating their behaviour.

In addition to a viable coordination mechanism, such coordination must also be achievable and sustainable. Whether coordination is likely to take place or not depends on various well-established factors. For example, the number of market participants is significant because it is easier to form a common understanding on a market strategy the fewer firms there are. Moreover, the more firms participate in the coordination, the lower the share of the coordinated profit each firm receives. This has two consequences: first, it makes deviations from the terms of the coordination more likely and, secondly, it reduces the effectiveness of retaliation since the short-term gains from deviating may well outweigh the long-term benefit of sustaining coordination.[61]

A further problem likely to be encountered by would-be collusive oligopolists is that of how to monitor and enforce the 'agreed on' terms of coordination. It has been suggested that the ability to sustain coordination over time depends on four factors[62]:

1 the potential benefit from seeking to enhance market share by undercutting existing competitors;
2 the potential loss in the event of retaliatory measures by competitors;
3 the probability of undercutting triggering retaliation;
4 the relative importance of short-term versus long-term profits.

59 See Case T-102/96, *Gencor v Commission* [1999] ECR II-743, at para 276.
60 See Case No COMP/M.1741, *MCIWorldCom/Sprint*, at para 259.
61 P Rey, 'Collective dominance and the telecommunications industry', 7 September 2002, at pp 8-9; accessible at http://europa.eu.int/comm/competition/antitrust/others.
62 Rey, *ibid*, at pp 4-6.

In weighing the relative gains from 'cheating' and the effectiveness of retaliation it is of critical importance to determine, in particular, how often firms will interact with one another. The relative gains from deviations will diminish if they may be promptly punished and the effectiveness of retaliation is enhanced by swift implementation.

These principles must be borne in mind when analysing whether coordination is likely, sustainable and effective. They are based on the predictions of economic theory and, in particular, on the conclusions drawn from 'game theoretical' explanations of oligopolistic behaviour.[63] Game theory can be insightful in two ways. First, it helps to determine the conditions under which coordination is likely to be sustainable. Game theory shows that there may be various market features that support the occurrence of coordination. A competitive assessment thus calls for an economically realistic and dynamic assessment of the relevance and significance of each such market feature.[64] Secondly, it helps to identify which market characteristics will influence whether the oligopolists choose to cooperate or compete.

The usefulness of game theory is limited by its inability to predict whether firms will actually coordinate in different market situations. However, notwithstanding the difficulties involved in ascertaining whether collusion exists or will actually occur, the key question for the purposes of merger control is whether such coordination is *likely* to occur in the foreseeable future. Although the possibility for and the likelihood of coordination may be influenced by an array of factors,[65] each of the necessary conditions enumerated by the CFI in *Airtours* will be addressed in turn.

4.2.3 Market transparency

As the Commission stated in *Exxon/Mobil*, 'Market transparency is ... one of the basic conditions characterising markets conducive to [anti-competitive] oligopoly'.[66] The insights of game theory may be used to illustrate how and why market transparency is an essential condition for an oligopoly to result in negative effects on competition. A 'game' repeatedly played by the relevant oligopolists will be more likely to end in coordination, in conditions of market transparency. As the CFI recognised in *Airtours*, the following reasons are at play.[67]

First, market transparency influences what firms may infer from changing and often equivocal actions taken by other firms. Indeed, market behaviour is often open to misinterpretation. A finding of coordination is thus more likely if market conditions are sufficiently simple and transparent to allow the firms to 'signal' to one another and tacitly establish the terms of coordination.[68] Furthermore, securing ongoing coordination is easier when it is possible for firms to track how one another is behaving. It enhances the feasibility of such coordination because firms can infer and

63 See Scherer and Ross, n 57 above, at pp 208-215 and Church and Ware, n 6 above.

64 See Commission Guidelines on Market Analysis and the Assessment of Significant Market Power under the Community Regulatory Framework for Electronic Communications Networks and Services, OJ 2002 C 165/6, at para 98.

65 See, eg Case No IV/M.619, *Gencor/Lonrho*, at paras 141-159 and Case No COMP/M.1741, *MCIWorldCom/ Sprint*, at para 258.

66 Case No IV/M.1383, *Exxon/Mobil*, at para 474.

67 Case T-342/99, *Airtours v Commission* [2002] ECR II-2585, at paras 62 and 159.

68 Other factors which help establish the terms of coordination include the stability of market conditions, the number of suppliers, the structural links between them, and the homogeneity of the product lines concerned.

rationally adapt to a mutually acceptable market outcome by observing each others' price and output decisions. Conversely, where suppliers negotiate prices with individual customers and refrain from publishing standardised price lists, for example, price levels may be obscured and the likelihood of coordinated behaviour reduced.[69]

Consequently, sustainable coordination may be impaired if firms are unable to monitor each other's behaviour. In transparent market conditions, such coordination will be more likely to endure since possible deviations can be monitored, detected and swiftly punished.[70] Thus, transparency determines how likely it is or will be that instances of deviation will be detected. In this way, transparency also affects the incentive to uphold tacit coordination. The converse is normally true in respect of markets characterised by volatile conditions of competition, whereupon coordination becomes more difficult, but not necessarily impossible.

4.2.4 Retaliatory mechanism

There may be an incentive for a member of a dominant oligopoly to diverge from the coordinated outcome and thereby increase its own profitability. Such divergence of interests jeopardises the resilience of coordination. Detecting and retaliating against deviations from the terms of coordination are intended to ensure that the short-term individual gains from deviation are outweighed by the prospective costs of reprisal. There must be cogent evidence that collective dominance is stable in the longer-term and that tacit coordination is sustainable. As pointed out in the second section of this paper, a plausible retaliatory mechanism is crucial for coordination between oligopolists to stand the test of time. Indeed, the CFI specifically noted in *Airtours* that the substantive analysis of an alleged collective dominant position called for an assessment of:

> 'that position statically at a fixed point in time – the point when the transaction takes place and the structure of competition is altered – but must also assess it dynamically, with regard in particular to its internal equilibrium, stability, and the question as to whether any parallel anti-competitive conduct to which it might give rise is sustainable over time.'[71]

The Commission is not required to prove 'a specific retaliation mechanism involving a degree of severity'; it must show that these are adequate deterrents to deviate from the coordinated behaviour.[72] This means that it is not necessary for the Commission to show that the precise quantum and duration of a punishment mechanism, ie predicting price discounting by 45 per cent from list prices for 12 weeks. However, the prospect of retaliatory measures will only be plausible if, first, they sufficiently punish firms which choose to deviate from the terms of coordination and, secondly, they may be swiftly implemented in response to such deviation.[73] In this way, the temptation for members of the dominant oligopoly to cheat will be adequately deterred.

The absence of a credible retaliatory mechanism was an essential factor in the Commission's conclusion that tacit coordination on investments would be unsustain-

69 See, eg Case No IV/M.358, *Pilkinton-Technict/SIV*, at para 63.

70 See, eg Case No IV/M.190, *Nestlé/Perrier*, at para 122.

71 Case T-342/99, *Airtours v Commission* [2002] ECR II-2585, at para 192.

72 *Ibid*, at para 195.

73 *Ibid*, at paras 203-205.

able in the market for newsprint and wood-containing magazine paper in *Norske Skog* and *UPM-Kymmene/Haindl*.[74] Whether retaliatory measures are plausible depends on a range of factors. For present purposes, two examples help demonstrate the influence of such factors: the symmetry between firms and the existence of the so-called 'first-mover advantage'.

In relation to symmetry, coordination is obviously easier among equals. Where firms differ in their productive capacities, quality of output, market shares or their relative efficiency, two consequences are likely. First, the problem of coordinating in the first place is made even more difficult. Differences in firms' cost structure mean that more efficient firms would be inclined to charge lower prices than their less efficient counterparts. One way to mitigate this problem would be to allocate market shares in accordance with the relative efficiency of different firms. Still, this may be difficult to achieve in the absence of express collusion. The second consequence would be that retaliation might be less effective. Punishment inflicted by a less efficient firm is less likely to discipline a more efficient firm which is 'cheating' on the coordinated outcome since the latter, by definition, is more competitive than the former.[75]

Another way in which the utility of a punishment mechanism may be appraised is whether it is possible to resume coordination after taking retaliatory measures. This may be important in market situations which give rise to a so-called 'first mover advantage', also known as a strategic barrier to entry. In such situations, there may be a strong incentive to 'cheat' on the terms of coordination since it would give the firm an unassailable market share. This would hinder the effectiveness of prospective punishment and thereby undermine ongoing coordination. Such a 'first mover advantage' was identified in the market for top-level or universal internet interconnectivity for example.[76]

Overall, the success of tacit coordination depends on the incentives to cheat and the existence of a credible punishment mechanism to counteract those incentives. Retaliation should be both plausible and effective. However, retaliation need not occur on the same market as that where coordination is taking place in order to be an adequate deterrent. For example, where the oligopolists are present on a number of number of different markets, there are simply more possibilities for punishment. This was discussed in *MCIWorldCom/Sprint*.[77]

4.2.5 Absence of competitive constraints

The CFI stressed that whether coordination is sustainable or not is also contingent on the probable response of current and future competitors and customers.[78] Their ability to counteract coordination by the members of the dominant oligopoly relates to the classic definition of dominance: the ability to act independently of significant competitive constraints. To put the point in a different way, the question is whether

74 Case No COMP/M.2499, *Norske Skog/Parenco/Walsum* and Case No COMP/M.2498, *UPM-Kymmene/ Haindl*, both at para 135 (discussing the difficulties associated with detection and rapid punishment of deviation from coordinating investments and capacity decisions).

75 P Rey, n 61 above, at pp 9-10.

76 Case No IV/M.1069, *WorldCom/MCI*, at paras 130-131 (discussing the 'snowball' effect that might be induced by a merger between companies in the market for top-level internet interconnectivity.).

77 Case No COMP/M.1741, *MCIWorldCom/Sprint*, at para 289.

78 Case T-342/99, *Airtours v Commission* [2002] ECR II-2585, at paras 62 and 210.

existing and potential competitors are able to exploit the competitive opportunities offered by anti-competitive coordination.

The significance of this requirement has also been underlined by a number of Commission decisions. For example, in *Norske Skog* and *UPM-Kymmene/Haindl*, the Commission found that, notwithstanding a plausible coordination mechanism of output down times between suppliers in newsprint and wood-containing magazine paper, any such coordination would be likely to be undermined by the action of fringe players.[79] The Commission also found that the merger was unlikely to lead to anti-competitive parallel behaviour in global telecommunications services in *MCIWorldCom/Sprint* [80] because of the ability of actual competitors and customers to undermine it.

5. Conclusion

The approach of the Commission and the Community courts to the notion of collective dominance has been animated by the imperative to ensure the proper functioning of the Common Market. Four conclusions may be drawn. First, controlling anti-competitive oligopolistic behaviour will inherently call for difficult judgments to be made by administrative and judicial authorities. Secondly, the way collective dominance has been interpreted and applied does not exclude the possibility of applying it to other forms of oligopolistic interaction. Thirdly, the judgment of the Court in *Airtours v Commission* was an important decision in the area of collective dominance but did not resolve every issue relating to the problems posed by oligopolies. Finally, the interpretation of dominance under the ECMR should relate to what the Regulation is meant to achieve, ie maintaining competitive market structures within the Community.

79 Case No COMP/M.2499, *Norske Skog/Parenco/Walsum* and Case No COMP/M.2498, *UPM-Kymmene/Haindl*, both at paras 139-148.

80 Case No COMP/M.1741, *MCIWorldCom/Sprint*, at para 258.

23
Collective Dominance in Merger Cases after Airtours

Frank Montag and Andreas von Bonin*

Freshfields Bruckhaus Deringer, Brussels

1. Introduction

On 6 June 2002, the European Court of First Instance (CFI) handed down a long-awaited decision on the assessment of collective dominance in merger cases. *Airtours*[1] was expected to provide some answers, where previous analysis by the Commission and legal and economic commentators had produced a lot of questions.

This paper will put *Airtours'* statements on the nature of collective dominance into context and analyse the Commission's obligations when prohibiting a merger between firms. It will then look beyond *Airtours* and examine whether *Airtours* leaves the Commission with too little room for prohibiting mergers. In particular, it will ask whether there are cases involving anti-competitive 'unilateral effects' that cannot be caught under today's substantive 'dominance' test of the European Merger Regulation. The third section of the paper discusses whether it would make sense to replace this test with the 'substantial lessening of competition' (SLC) test. Finally, the paper will discuss some procedural aspects of the *Airtours* judgment, in particular the high burden of proof imposed by the CFI.

2. Judgment in the case Airtours plc v Commission

The appeal by *Airtours* against the Commission decision prohibiting its acquisition of a competitor, the UK-based package holiday operator *First Choice*, was decided on 6 June 2002. Almost two years and nine months after the decision and long after the companies had abandoned their merger project, the CFI annulled the prohibition and concluded that the Commission's oeuvre, 'far from basing its prospective analysis on cogent evidence, is vitiated by a series of errors of assessment as to factors fundamental to any assessment of whether a collective dominant position might be created'.[2]

* Dr Frank Montag is a partner and Dr Andreas von Bonin is an associate in the Brussels office of Freshfields Bruckhaus Deringer.

1 See judgment in Case T-342/99 of 6 June 2002, *Airtours v Commission.*

2 See *Airtours* judgment, *ibid*, para 294.

2.1 Main findings

The Court based its judgment on three main findings, which it paradigmatically set out in three paragraphs in the opening of the substantive part of the decision[3]:

> 'As the applicant has argued and as the Commission has accepted in its pleadings, three conditions are necessary for a finding of collective dominance as defined:
>
> - first, each member of the dominant oligopoly must have the ability to know how the other members are behaving in order to monitor whether or not they are adopting the common policy. ... There must, therefore, be *sufficient market transparency for all members of the dominant oligopoly* to be aware, sufficiently precisely and quickly, of the way in which the other members' market conduct is evolving;
> - second, the situation of tacit coordination must be sustainable over time, that is to say, there must be an incentive not to depart from the common policy on the market. ... *The notion of retaliation in respect of conduct deviating from the common policy is thus inherent in this condition.* ... which means that each member of the dominant oligopoly must be aware that highly competitive action on its part designed to increase its market share would provoke identical action by the others, so that it would derive no benefit from its initiative ...;
> - third, to prove the existence of a collective dominant position to the requisite legal standard, the Commission must also establish that the foreseeable *reaction of current and future competitors, as well as of consumers, would not jeopardise the results* expected from the common policy.
>
> The prospective analysis which the Commission has to carry out in its review of concentrations involving collective dominance calls for *close examination* in particular of the circumstances which, in each individual case, are relevant for assessing the effects *of the concentration on competition in the reference market.* ... where the Commission takes the view that a merger should be prohibited because it will create a situation of collective dominance, *it is incumbent upon it to produce convincing evidence thereof.* The evidence must concern, in particular, ... the lack of effective competition between the operators alleged to be members of the dominant oligopoly and the weakness of any competitive pressure that might be exerted by other operators.
>
> Furthermore, the basic provisions of Regulation No 4064/89, in particular Article 2 thereof, confer on the Commission a certain discretion, especially with respect to assessments of an economic nature, and, consequently, when the exercise of that discretion, which is essential for defining the rules on concentrations, is under review, *the Community judicature must take account of the discretionary margin implicit in the provisions of an economic nature* which form part of the rules on concentrations ... .'(Emphases added.)

2.2 Consequences for the concept of collective dominance

The rules for the treatment of mergers in concentrated markets are of paramount importance for firms that do business globally. This explains part of the considerable impatience with which the *Airtours* judgment was awaited. In particular, the

3 See *Airtours* judgment, n 1 above, paras 62-64.

Commission's decision in this case had confused undertakings, economists and lawyers alike as to the future of the Commission's merger control policy in an oligopoly context. However, part of this confusion had been cleared up already by subsequent decisions in the cases of *MAN/Auwärter*[4] and *UPM-Kymmene/Haindl*.[5] In these subsequent cases the Commission took a less expansive approach to the application of the notion of collective dominance than it had in the *Airtours* decision. Against this background, it may well be questionable whether the *Airtours* judgment is properly characterised as a 'landmark judgment [which] will change the face of EC merger review in a number of ways'.[6] The judgment's achievement is rather that it provides some necessary clarifications. It summarises the Courts' jurisprudence from the *Kali und Salz*[7] and *Gencor*[8] judgments and generally confirms the Commission's approach towards collective dominance as it had been taken in *MAN/Auwärter* and *UPM-Kymmene/Haindl*.

The three-prong test, which the Court introduces as the condition for a finding of collective dominance, is no revolution, either. It is distilled from previous case law,[9] well-known economic theory,[10] information given in the submission of the parties and the long-standing practice of Member State authorities, such as the Bundeskartellamt.[11]

On the procedural side, the Court confers an adequate burden of proof on the Commission when it intends to prohibit a merger, but does not limit the degree of discretion the Commission enjoys especially with respect to economic questions.[12]

2.2.1 Terminology and the meaning of 'collective dominance'

After the *Airtours* judgment, the meaning of collective dominance is somewhat clearer than it was after the *Airtours* decision. If the Commission intends to show that a merger leads to the creation of a collective dominant position, it needs to demonstrate and prove two assumptions: first, before the merger, the oligopoly firms have been in a state of competition or at least of a 'non-cooperative equilibrium',[13] ie notwithstanding the concentration of the market, coordination between the oligopolists was not feasible or competition from outside the oligopoly presented a sufficient constraint on

4 See Case No COMP/M.2201 of 20 June 2001, *MAN/Auwärter*.

5 See Case No COMP/M.2498 of 21 November 2001, *UPM-Kymmene/Haindl*.

6 Eric Mahr and Ylenia Ariano, 'European Court Annuls Airtours/First Choice Merger Prohibition' (2002) 30 *International Business Lawyer* 243; see also Enrico Adriano Raffaelli, European Union Competition Policy Subsequent to the Airtours Case, *Fordham Corporate Law Institute, The Twenty-Ninth Annual Conference on International Antitrust Law and Policy*, 31 October and 1 November 2002.

7 See judgment in Cases C-68/94 and C-30/95 of 31 March 1998, *France v Commission (Kali und Salz), SCPA v Commission*.

8 See judgment in Case T-102/96 of 25 March 1999, *Gencor Ltd v Commission*.

9 See *Kali und Salz* and *Gencor* judgments, nn 7 and 8 above.

10 Boris Etter, 'The Assessment of Mergers in the EC under the Concept of Collective Dominance: An Analysis of the Recent Decisions and Judgments by an Economic Approach' (2000) 23(3) *Journal of World Competition* 103; see also Frederic Jenny, Collective Dominance and the EC Merger Regulation, in *Annual Proceedings of the Fordham Corporate Law Institute-International Antitrust Law and Policy* (Juris Publishing, Inc, 2002), Chapter 13, p 361.

11 Bundeskartellamt, Diskussionspapier: Das Untersagungskriterium in der Fusionskontrolle-Marktbeherrschende Stellung versus Substantial Lessening of Competition?, 8/9 October 2001.

12 See *Airtours* judgment, n 1 above, paras 63-64; see below, 'Procedural and practical consequences of the *Airtours* judgment'.

13 See *Airtours* judgment, n 1 above, para 63.

their behaviour. Secondly, the oligopolists will be able to collectively behave independently from competitors, customers and consumers[14] *after* the merger, because of the non-explicit coordination between them enabled by it. The Commission thus needs to show that the merger produces *coordinated effects* as opposed to *unilateral effects*.[15] The language used in the *Airtours* decision suggests that the Commission was of the opinion that collective dominance could also be created by mergers, which brought about unilateral effects 'plus something'[16]:

> 'Furthermore – contrary to the apparent view of Airtours ... – it is not a necessary condition of collective dominance for the oligopolists always to behave as if there were one or more explicit agreements ... between them. It is sufficient that the merger makes it rational for the oligopolists, in adapting themselves to market conditions, to act – individually – in ways which will substantially reduce competition between them, and as a result of which they may act, to an appreciable extent, independently of competitors, customers and consumers.'

The Court did not agree with this proposition, but held that collective dominance required a 'cooperative equilibrium', in which prices are either uncompetitively high or capacity uncompetitively low, because each member of the oligopoly is aware that it would not benefit from any competitive action due to the fact that others could follow immediately. Thereby, the Court confirms that collective dominance is the legal terminology for the situation economists call 'tacit collusion'.[17]

However, some argue that the judgment also leaves questions open.[18] If collective dominance, *alias* tacit collusion, means the situation of a 'cooperative equilibrium'[19] and not the situation of a 'non-cooperative equilibrium', which is further away from a situation of full competition following the merger, it is hard to see where there should be room for a 'strengthening' of a collectively dominant position. Collective dominance is either present or not present, Jenny argues, but cannot be strengthened.[20] This may be true and logical from an economist's perspective. From a legal point of view, collective dominance – like single firm dominance – can be strengthened by factors, which lie outside the distinction between 'unilateral and coordinated effects'. A merger, which enhances the financial power of one or more oligopoly firms, increases their vertical integration or weakens the fringe, may strengthen a 'cooperative equilibrium' that already existed pre-merger.[21]

14 See judgment in Case C-85/76 of 13 February 1979, *Hoffmann-La Roche & Co AG v Commission* and judgment in Case C-27/76 of 14 February 1978, *United Brands Company and United Brands Continentaal BV v Commission.*

15 See *Airtours* judgment, n 1 above, para 62.

16 See Case No IV/M.1524 of 22 September 1999, *Airtours/First Choice*, para 54.

17 See *Airtours* judgment, n 1 above, paras 61-62.

18 See Frederic Jenny, n 10 above, p 366.

19 See Frederic Jenny, *ibid*, p 369.

20 *Ibid*, p 370, therefore also proposes to include non-cooperative oligopolies in the meaning of collective dominance.

21 In our view, the issue is not whether the merger will 'reinforce the oligopolistic interdependence on a market' (which in Jenny's view would mean that a merger could be prohibited because it will lessen the degree of competition on the market), but whether the merger will add other anti-competitive effects to an existing and unchanged situation of tacit collusion.

2.2.2 Conditions of the market

The CFI makes it clear that collective dominance can only occur on markets which show a sufficient transparency for all members of the dominant oligopoly. The reason for this pre-condition is that the oligopolists must be able to anticipate *sufficiently precisely and quickly* how the other members' behaviour *is evolving*. Such constant monitoring may be facilitated or inhibited by a number of factors. These include the homogeneity or heterogeneity of the oligopolists' products (leading to similar or different cost structures and pricing decisions), the stable or unstable development of demand (preventing or provoking ongoing capacity changes), a low or high rate of innovation (having an effect on cost structures and marketing), the presence or absence of countervailing buyer power and long-standing customer relations (having an effect on the predictability of the oligopolists' marketing efforts).

The Court's particular emphasis on 'market transparency' as an overall prerequisite for a finding of collective dominance underlines the continuing importance of the 'checklist' previously employed by the Commission.[22] The Court itself examines some items from this list.[23] Many other items may help firms and advisers to assess whether the market is transparent enough to enable constant monitoring within the oligopoly. However, the Commission must not use the list schematically. The various factors need thorough investigation and their presence or absence must be well reasoned.[24] Firms who want to use the checklist have to take into account the fact that the list is open and that the absence of certain factors does not preclude a finding of sufficient market transparency. There is also a 'checklist' of factors tending to disprove joint dominance, which deserves equally close attention by firms, the Commission and the courts.[25]

2.2.3 Competition within the oligopoly

In the *Airtours* judgment, the Court very simply ends the main controversy resulting from the Commission decision in this case: sustainable tacit coordination is a condition of a finding of collective dominance and the *notion of retaliation* is *inherent* in this condition.[26]

Collusion, not competition, must prevail within the oligopoly. The absence of internal competition within an oligopoly has long been recognised as a key factor for a finding of collective dominance by the competition laws in some Member States. For example, in Germany, section 19(2)(2) of the Act against Restraints of Competition states that 'two or more undertakings are dominant insofar as no substantial competition exists between them with respect to certain kinds of goods or commercial services ...'. Internally, the oligopoly must be characterised by its members' knowledge of their uniform interests and their mutual interdependence ('Group Awareness'/ '*Gruppenbewusstsein*').[27]

22 John Temple Lang, Oligopolies and Joint Dominance in Community Antitrust Law, in *Annual Proceedings of the Fordham Corporate Law Institute-International Antitrust Law and Policy* (Juris Publishing, Inc, 2002), Chapter 12, p 321; see also Annex II of the Framework Directive.

23 See *Airtours* judgment, n 1 above, para 121 et seq.

24 See *Airtours* judgment, n 1 above, para 148 et seq.

25 See John Temple Lang, n 22 above, p 334.

26 See *Airtours* judgment, n 1 above, para 62.

27 Bechtold, *GWB* (2nd edn), § 19, para 42.

It is precisely this last element which has led to some confusion. Game theorists and economists have explained that oligopolies can only maintain a cooperative equilibrium if there is a 'credible punishment mechanism'[28] which prevents oligopoly members from undertaking competitive action such as increasing output or reducing price unilaterally. The interdependence of the individual oligopolists' behaviours is precisely what makes the anti-competitive effects of this equilibrium 'coordinated'. In its *Airtours* decision, the Commission insists that no punishment mechanism is necessary to find collective dominance and quotes the CFI's *Gencor* judgment in support of this point.[29]

The confusion has been based partly on terminology, partly on substance. The Court has now eliminated it: what economists call 'credible punishment mechanism' is in fact nothing more than the actual possibility of oligopolists to react to a unilateral competitive action by one of their peers (ie capacity increase or price reduction) with a similar action, thereby rendering the unilateral move unprofitable. Profitable effects can thus only be achieved by (tacit) coordinated behaviour. The Court calls it a 'notion of retaliation' and agrees[30] (as it had already held in *Gencor*[31]) that it is an inherent condition for collective dominance.

So far, it was just a problem of terminology. But the Commission wanted more. It wanted a case on the books, which (even by way of *obiter dictum*) established collective dominance merely on the basis that an individual member of an oligopoly behaves rationally and unilaterally and thereby causes anti-competitive effects.[32] The Court – by insisting on a demonstration of tacit collusion – has excluded that possibility. It held that a prerequisite for collective dominance is tacit collusion, an inherent condition of which is the knowledge that there is a possibility of retaliation by the other oligopolists, ie 'coordinated effects'.

However, while the Commission seems to accept that 'collective dominance' requires 'tacit collusion', it insists that there must, nevertheless, be some other form of impermissible 'oligopolistic dominance' which can be created or strengthened by 'unilateral effects' occurring as a consequence of a merger. This raises the question of whether there are oligopoly cases which are not caught by the 'dominance' test of the European Merger Regulation (ECMR) as construed by the CFI in *Airtours*. These questions will be discussed below.[33] However, the *Airtours* court judgment does not permit the prohibition of mergers because of a finding of 'oligopolistic dominance' which does not involve tacit collusion.

In the *Airtours* judgment, the Court is not hostile to the Commission's idea that tacit collusion can work with respect to capacity. In the case in hand, however, the Commission has failed to show to the necessary standard of proof that capacity collusion was feasible.[34] However, it may be observed that – following its *Airtours*

28 See Boris Etter, n 10 above, pp 124, 136.

29 As an argument for this allegation, the Commission – correctly – refers to its decision in *Gencor/Lonrho*, where it did not discuss the necessity of a punishment mechanism, and to the judgment of the Court of First Instance in that case, which did not put any emphasis on that point.

30 See *Airtours* judgment, n 1 above, para 191 et seq.

31 See *Gencor* judgment, n 8 above, para 227.

32 See *Airtours* decision, n 16 above, paras 54 and 150 read together.

33 See below.

34 See *Airtours* judgment, n 1 above, para 156 et seq.

decision – the Commission itself took a more cautious approach towards capacity collusion in *UPM-Kymmene/Haindl*.[35]

2.2.4 Competition between the oligopoly and the fringe

The third prong of the Court's test for collective dominance in *Airtours* concerns external competition, ie the competition between the oligopoly as a whole and the other market players, the so-called 'fringe'. It is obvious that the strength of the actual and potential competitive pressure the fringe can develop, is decisive for the sustainability of the tacit collusion or the 'cooperative equilibrium'.[36]

The Court dedicates considerable discussion in its judgment to the role of the fringe.[37] It concludes that the Commission did not sufficiently demonstrate that the fringe was unable to exercise substantial competitive pressure on the oligopolists. It is likely that the Commission will – in the future – pay more attention to external competition when assessing collective dominance. In the case of *UPM-Kymmene/Haindl*, the Commission opened Phase II investigations and sent a statement of objections to the parties alleging that 'the fringe players could have little incentive to challenge the top-suppliers'.[38] However, subsequently the Commission was persuaded that the 'fringe players' in the paper industry have actually played and continue to play an important role. Norske Skog, a company which the Commission names among the 'top suppliers', had been a 'fringe player' itself some years ago.[39]

3. Does Airtours leave the Commission with too little room for prohibiting mergers?

The *Airtours* judgment for many observers has either demonstrated or confirmed that the Commission's weapons against mergers in oligopoly markets are too blunt.[40] However, in our view this observation cannot be based on this judgment. Nor does the concept of dominance within the ECMR framework overly restrict the Commission's ability to block anti-competitive mergers.

3.1 (Collective) dominance does not cause a 'gap' and is sufficiently flexible

If *Airtours* has to be read as preventing the Commission from blocking any merger in oligopoly markets, unless the parties tacitly coordinate (ie are in a cooperative equilibrium), the question becomes whether there are oligopoly cases involving non-cooperative equilibria, which are anti-competitive but cannot be prohibited.

Observers thus state that there is a 'gap' in the existing dominance test of Article 2(3) ECMR, which – in particular – inhibits the blocking of mergers leading to anti-

35 See *UPM-Kymmene/Haindl* decision, n 5 above, para 135.

36 The absence of substantial external competition is therefore also a condition for a finding of collective dominance under section 19(2)(2) of the German Act against Restraints of Competition.

37 See *Airtours* judgment, n 1 above, paras 208-259.

38 See *UPM-Kymmene/Haindl* decision, n 5 above, para 76.

39 See *UPM-Kymmene/Haindl* decision, n 5 above, para 141.

40 John Kay, 'Airtours' landmark victory against the European Competition Commission signals the need for a reform of the system', *Financial Times*, 18 June 2002; see also Richard Whish, 'Substantive Analysis under the EC Merger Regulation: Should the Dominance Test Be Replaced by "Substantial Lessening of Competition"?' in *International Merger Control: Prescriptions for Convergence* (IBA, 2002), and Frederic Jenny, n 10 above.

competitive 'unilateral effects'.[41] Many cases and (often purely hypothetical) constellations are quoted in this context, only some of which should be briefly reviewed here. We will show that – if necessary – those cases can either be caught under the notion of *collective* dominance as defined by the Court in *Airtours* or by the traditional *single* dominance test. This result can also be confirmed when looking at the alleged 'gap' from a more conceptual perspective.

3.1.1 Hypothetical and actual examples

Babyfood. The textbook case in this context is the US case of *H J Heinz/Beech-Nut*,[42] where Heinz and Beech-Nut, the second and third ranked producers of baby food, planned to merge. Heinz (17 per cent) and Beech-Nut (15 per cent) had similar market shares, they had regional brands and their retail activities had limited overlaps. Almost no supermarket carried both brands, but either Heinz or Beech-Nut together with the market leader, Gerber, who had a market share of 65 per cent. The Federal Trade Commission (FTC) concluded that the merger would substantially lessen competition in the market for jarred baby foods. The FTC was also concerned by the likely coordinated effects of the merger. It observed: 'No environment could be more conducive to coordinated interaction than a duopoly and because of the substantial entry barriers in this market, it is without doubt that this duopoly is forever.' The FTC had evidence that suggested the likelihood of tacit collusion in that both Gerber and Heinz had in the past signalled a wish to see less vigorous competition. The Court of Appeal, however, could see nothing in the conditions in the baby food market to suggest that the remaining two suppliers would be unable successfully to tacitly collude if the merger was permitted.[43]

From a European perspective, it is not apparent why this case could not have been caught under the market dominance test of the ECMR. Gerber and the merged entity would have had a combined market share of 97 per cent! If market characteristics were found to be conducive to tacit collusion and there was sufficient proof that the merger would change the market from a competitive equilibrium to a cooperative equilibrium, indicated by Gerber's and the merged entity's wish to see less vigorous competition, the *Airtours* requirements for a finding of collective dominance should be met. Also, a prohibition could have been issued on the ground that Gerber's pre-existing dominant position would have been strengthened by the decrease in competition for the second place in the market.[44] In any case, the practical relevance of this constellation for merger control policy seems to be limited. With respect to this

41 See recently John Fingleton, Does Collective Dominance Provide Suitable Housing for All Anticompetitive Oligopolistic Mergers? Paper submitted to the EC Merger Control Conference in Brussels, 7/8 November 2002, p 8 et seq; Nicholas Levy, Dominance vs SLC – A subtle distinction?, Paper submitted to the EC Merger Control Conference in Brussels, 7/8 November 2002, p 23 et seq.

42 See US Federal Trade Commission *In the Matter of H J Heinz Company; Milnot Holding Corporation; and Madison Dearborn Partners Capital, LP*, 28 November 2000, Docket No 9295.

43 After the District Court had not followed the FTC's request for a preliminary injunction blocking the merger, its decision (http://www.dcd.uscourts.gov/00-1688.pdf) was annulled on appeal. The Court of Appeals (http://www.pacer.cadc.uscourts.gov/common/opinions/200104/00-5362a.txt) ordered the District Court to issue the requested injunction. The merger was then abandoned.

44 See Bundeskartellamt, Diskussionspapier, n 11 above.

example, the Commission has itself stated that it had not 'so far encountered a situation of this kind.'[45]

UK Banking. In this case, Lloyds TSB, a UK bank, acquired a smaller 'maverick' type competitor, Abbey National. The merger took place in concentrated markets, *inter alia*, the personal current account market (PCA) and the market for banking services for small and medium-sized enterprises (SME), with C4 market shares of 72 per cent and 85 per cent respectively. Lloyds had market shares of 22 per cent in PCA and 19 per cent in SME, Abbey National had five per cent PCA and one per cent in SME. The UK Competition Commission has recommended the prohibition of the merger.[46] Looking at the case from the perspective of the dominance test, the possibility of the creation of a collectively dominant position by the elimination of a maverick comes to mind. Indeed, the Competition Commission has stated: 'we believe that the PCA market is vulnerable to tacit collusion in pricing.'[47] This being the case, it seems probable that removing the only or most important maverick, ie the only factor disturbing the development or the more seamless functioning of a coordinated equilibrium, creates or strengthens a collective dominant position. A 'unilateral effects story' would be unnecessary. There is nothing in the dominance test which would prevent the Commission from taking into account the potential competition from a maverick, whose elimination stabilises the coordinated oligopoly. The Commission often even perceives the proposed acquisition of a maverick as an indication of (the possibility of) tacit collusion.

A variation of this is the (hypothetical) case of a large, established firm buying a new, innovative competitor with the intention of preventing the innovations from being marketed.[48] In such a situation, however, the intention of the purchaser shows that he is able to behave independently from competitors, customers and consumers, because otherwise he would hardly be able to refrain from using the innovation to an economic advantage. The case could thus be caught under the concept of single firm dominance even in the absence of market shares of 40 or 50 per cent.[49]

The 'lachende Dritte'. A further example involves the creation or strengthening of a (collectively) dominant position of a firm or firms, which are not a party to the merger under review.[50] Both the Commission[51] as well as Member State authorities[52] operating under a market dominance test have investigated such situations. Therefore there is no reason to believe that those cases could not be caught by the existing substantive test.

45 European Commission, Green Paper on the Review of Council Regulation (EEC) No 4064/89 of 11 December 2001, COM (2001) 745/6.

46 See the UK Competition Commission Report on *Lloyds TSB Group plc and Abbey National plc*, July 2001, http://www.competition-commission.org.uk/reports/458lloyds.htm.

47 See UK Competition Commission, *ibid*, p 21. However, Fingleton, n 41 above, p 9 simply states that 'tacit collusion was not an issue because of consumer inertia'.

48 See UK Competition Commission, Mergers: Dominance v. Substantial Lessening of Competition cited in Bundeskartellamt, Diskussionspapier, n 11 above.

49 See below 3.1.2.

50 Examples include situations in which, for example, a customer acquires an oligopolistic supplier exclusively for its own demand. This might lead to the strengthening of the (collective) dominant position of the remaining supplier(s).

51 See Case No COMP/M.2353 of 19 March 2001, *RWE/Hidroeléctrica del Cantábrico*, para 10.

52 See Bundeskartellamt, Case *Hapag/TUI/Bavaria*, TB 1978, 78 et seq.

Earlier Commission cases. The Commission indicates that some of its earlier decisions may be understood to have already laid the groundwork for reasoning, according to which unilateral effects may be taken into account in merger analysis.[53] This, however, is questionable. The idea seems to be that anti-competitive effects may occur when, after a merger in a non-coordinated oligopolistic market, the non-merging oligopolists do not react to a unilateral price increase by the new merged entity because, eg they do not have the necessary capacity resources. In such a situation, customers could not switch to a competitor's product, but would have to stick to the merged entity's products and pay the increased prices.[54] Thus, the effect of the merger would be unilateral action, because its profitability does not depend on a reaction of the other market players. However, it is not clear why such a situation should only be discussed under a notion of 'oligopolistic dominance'. The fact that unilateral price increases may be more profitable in capacity-constrained markets does not depend on the presence of an oligopoly. In *Barilla/Kamps,*[55] often cited as a 'unilateral effects' case as well, the Commission's 'serious doubts' arose from a classical single-firm dominance problem: The merger brought together Wasa and LiekenUrkorn, the largest German brand of crisp bread and one of its closest substitutes. In this situation, customers would have lost an attractive substitute post-merger, which would have facilitated unilateral price increases by the merged entity.[56] Again, a price increase may be more attractive if there are no strong competitors,[57] but conceptually this is not an oligopoly problem. As explained above, the *Airtours* court case stressed that anti-competitive oligopolies are characterised by the fact that unilateral action is *not* profitable. It is within the context of single-firm dominance that factors like brand loyalty, marketing and capacity are relevant for the assessment of how profitable a unilateral price increase is in a given situation. After *Airtours,* it is very questionable whether the European courts would sustain a Commission decision, which viewed unilateral behaviour – in the absence of any other aggravating factors – more critically in non-cooperative oligopoly markets than in any other markets.

These examples already suggest that the 'gap' is in fact a chimera. This suggestion becomes even more plausible when one looks at the question of unilateral effects in a more conceptual way.

3.1.2 'Unilateral effects' cases are single-firm dominance cases

The understanding of unilateral effects is often based on the definition of this term in Section 2.2. of the US Horizontal Merger Guidelines (1992/1997)[58]: 'A merger may

53 In personal conversations, Commission officials pointed to Cases No COMP/M.2256 of 1 February 2001, *Philips/Agilent*; COMP/M.2537 of 14 September 2001, *Philips/Marconi*; COMP/M.2817 of 8 May 2002, *Barilla/BPL/Kamps*; and COMP/M.1693 of 18 November 1999, *Alcoa/Reynolds.*

54 In *Philips/Agilent,* para 36, the Commission has stressed that even the smallest player had sufficient resources to meet increased demand in case of a unilateral price increase by the market leader. This was a reason to clear the merger.

55 See *Barilla/BPL/Kamps,* n 53 above.

56 The commitment offered by the merging parties in phase 1 included the divestiture of Kamps' crisp bread business in Germany.

57 That was not the case in *Barilla/BPL/Kamps.* Barilla's Wasa brand was very strong, but there were at least two competitors with comparable market share to Kamps' LiekenUrkorn and a strong private label segment.

58 US Department of Justice and Federal Trade Commission, Horizontal Merger Guidelines, 4 Trade Reg Rep (CCH) 13, 104 (1992) as amended.

diminish competition even if it does not lead to increased likelihood of successful coordinated interaction, because merging firms may find it profitable to alter their behaviour unilaterally following the acquisition by elevating price and suppressing output.'

However, their formulation does not suggest anything else than a situation of single-firm dominance as defined by the Court of Justice: a firm can only find it profitable to raise price or suppress output unilaterally – ie without the profitability of the action being dependent on the reaction of its competitors and customers – if it is in 'a position of economic strength ..., which enables it to prevent effective competition being maintained on the relevant market by giving it the power to behave to an appreciable extent independently of its competitors, customers and ultimately of its consumers'.[59]

The ECJ's broad definition of 'dominance'. Such a finding will usually involve a firm with substantial market shares. But – different from what some commentators in the ongoing discussions seem to take for granted[60] – the European courts' jurisprudence does not indicate that only the market-leading firm can be dominant. It may be true that the Court defined the term 'dominant' different from its literal meaning (in particular in relation to the English language), which connotes 'dominant' with 'first'.[61] However, in a legal context it is not uncommon that words stand for more than what their literal meaning implies – this is why many people are in need of professional legal advice. The service of the learned lawyer is to know the 'legal' meaning of words, which in a European law context is often the meaning attributed to a word by the courts. In the ECJ's definition, there is nothing which would prevent the Commission from investigating whether a firm with a 30 per cent market share would be in a position to raise prices unilaterally or otherwise behave independently of customers and consumers post-merger.[62]

It may be a useful clarification to insert into Article 2 ECMR a clause which confirms that firms with a lower than the leading market share can also be dominant.[63]

The role of market definition. While it is possible under the ECMR to find firms with around 30 per cent market share 'dominant', one should always be alerted if it is alleged that such a firm will (be able to) engage in anti-competitive unilateral behaviour post-merger. If competition authorities are concerned that firms with a small market share may find it profitable to raise prices or restrict output unilaterally, this finding may be the result of a wrong market definition. A five to ten per cent price increase, which is *profitable* because the firm will only lose few customers to a competing product, is usually an indication that those competing products are actually in a different market. In the words of the Commission: 'If substitution were enough to make the price increase unprofitable because of the resulting loss of sales, additional

59 See *United Brands* judgment, n 14 above.

60 See comments made by J Fingleton and S Salop during the discussions of the 'Assessment of Dominance' panel at the IBA/Commission EC Merger Control Conference in Brussels on 8 November 2002.

61 See *The Concise Oxford Dictionary*: 'Dominant = dominating, prevailing, most influential.'

62 The Commission has already found firms dominant with market shares of under 30 per cent. See Case No COMP/M.1684 of 25 January 2000, *Carrefour/Promodes*.

63 Commissioner Monti has instead proposed to the Commission and the Council a 'clarification' in Art 2 ECMR to the effect that 'unilateral effects' are covered by the ECMR, see proposal for a new ECMR, OJ 2003 C 20/4.

substitutes and areas are included in the relevant market. This would be done until the set of products and geographical areas is such that small, permanent increases in relative prices would be profitable.'[64]

On a – correctly – more narrowly defined market, the firm in question may have a far larger market share or may even be the market leader. Then, nobody would find it odd to catch this firm's unilateral anti-competitive behaviour under the notion of single-firm dominance. There may also be cases in which customers will not switch to available substitute products (belonging to the same market) even in case of a small but significant, non-transitory price increase. Brand loyalty, image and other factors may be reasons for this. If the producer of a branded product with 30 per cent market share will be able to increase prices post-merger without losing its customers, he may be in a position to behave independently of competitors, customers and consumers.[65]

Article 82 EC. Enlarging the (potential) scope of 'dominant' firms by including firms with lower market shares and defining narrower markets does not cause grave problems in the application of Article 82 EC, either. Concerns that many large but non-leading firms would then have to live under the Damocles' Sword of Article 82 EC, or refrain from merger in the first place in order to avoid being labelled 'dominant', are overstated.

First, a dominance finding in a merger review process can possibly have an effect of precedent for a (hypothetical subsequent) Article 82 investigation only if the Merger Task Force finds that the merging parties have a dominant position, but clears the merger (because there is no strengthening)[66] or if a merger is prohibited because of the pre-existing dominant position of one merging party. These cases are rare exceptions.

Secondly, the courts' interpretation of dominance under Article 2(3) ECMR and Article 82 EC have already diverged to some extent, in particular with respect to collective dominance.[67] This can be explained by the different purposes of the provisions, the different time perspective they take and by the different ways in which both provisions are enforced. So far, this has not reduced the perception of legal certainty among the business community.

Finally, even if dominance in Article 2(3) ECMR and Article 82 EC had to have identical meanings and even if the suggested clarification in Article 2 (see above) should bring more firms than today under a 'dominance' label, that alone would not increase those firms' exposure to Article 82 risks. Article 82 holds no sanction for dominance, but only for its abuse.

3.1.3 Conclusion

Some fear that the market dominance test provides the Commission with too little flexibility in its assessment of mergers. A thorough analysis of the case law shows that the Commission has regularly been able to deal with particular cases in an appropriate way. Those particular cases do not only include mergers in oligopolistic markets, but

64 See Commission Notice on the Definition of Relevant Market for the Purposes of Community Competition Law, OJ 1997 C 372, p 5 *et seq*, para 17.

65 As explained above, this concern was mentioned in *Barilla/BPL/Kamps*, n 53 above. It is a concern which is conceptually unrelated with the problem of oligopoly.

66 See Cases T-125/97 and T-127/97 of 22 March 2000, *Coca Cola v Commission*, in which the Court has expressed that such an effect of precedent actually does not exist.

67 See Montag and von Bonin, Kollektive Marktbeherrschung nach Art 82 EG und der Fusionskontrollverordnung, Paper for the 9th St Galler Kartellrechtsforum, Neueste Entwicklungen im europäischen und internationalen Kartellrecht, 2002, p 335.

also mergers involving indirect effects,[68] vertical effects[69] and conglomerate (or portfolio) effects.[70] Insofar as these cases have raised serious competition concerns, the Commission was – under the market dominance test – able to either prohibit the merger or demand wide-ranging concessions from the merging parties.[71] If, on appeal, the European courts have annulled a prohibition decision, it was not because the Commission had applied Article 2(3) ECMR in a manner that was too flexible, but because there were significant flaws in the Commission's reasoning and its allegations were unproven.[72]

This result is confirmed by an analysis of the concept of dominance in comparison with the concept of unilateral effects. If the firm which will allegedly engage in anti-competitive unilateral behaviour has a non-leading market share, an important question to ask is if the applied market definition is correct or if the market actually has to be defined more narrowly. The European Court of Justice has defined dominance in a broader way than the literal meaning of the word. Also a firm with a lower than the leading market share can be in a dominant position. This should be clarified by way of an amendment of Article 2 ECMR.

At this point, we must observe that it is not so much the analysis of the case law which leads to different assumptions about the necessity to change the substantive test for mergers from a market dominance test to an SLC test. It is more the conclusions drawn from that analysis which make the difference. The Bundeskartellamt concludes that no change of test is necessary, because the existing market dominance test permits flexibility, as demonstrated in the various cases.[73] From essentially the same analysis, Whish concludes that the case law shows such flexibility only because the Commission has in fact been applying an SLC test for many years.[74]

3.2 'Substantial lessening of competition' – the ultimate remedy?

How to catch anti-competitive effects of oligopolistic dominance is the problem most frequently mentioned in the context of discussions about the efficiency of the various substantive tests in merger control.[75]

68 See, eg Case No COMP/M.1439 of 13 October 1999, *Telia/Telenor* and Case No COMP/M.1630 of 18 January 2000, *Air Liquide/BOC/Air Products.*

69 See, eg especially cases giving rise to foreclosure concerns: Case No IV/M.469 of 9 November 1994, *MSG Media Service*; Case No IV/M.993 of 27 May 1998, *Bertelsmann/Kirch/Premiere*; Case No IV/M.1027 of 27 May 1998, *Deutsche Telekom/Beta Research*; Case No COMP/M.2050 of 13 October 2000, *Vivendi/Canal+/Seagram.*

70 See Case No IV/M.938 of 15 October 1997, *Guinness/Grand Metropolitan*; see also Case No COMP/M.2220 of 3 July 2001, *GE/Honeywell.*

71 Insofar as cases involving oligopolistic markets have been finally cleared without undertakings, the parties have been able to persuade the Commission that the merger would in fact not create or strengthen an individual or joint dominant position. See *UPM-Kymmene/Haindl* decision, n 5 above, *MAN/Auwärter* decision, n 4 above, and Case No IV/M.1016 of 20 May 1998, *PriceWaterhouse/Coopers & Lybrand.*

72 See most recently judgment in Case T-310/01 of 22 October 2002, *Schneider v Commission* and judgment in Case T-5/02 of 25 October 2002, *Tetra Laval v Commission.*

73 See Bundeskartellamt, Diskussionspapier, n 11 above, p 35.

74 See Richard Whish, n 40 above.

75 See Bundeskartellamt, Diskussionspapier, n 11 above.

The Bundeskartellamt, which undertook a thorough review of the case practice in countries with an SLC test and those with a market dominance tests, has concluded:

> 'The actual case practice in Germany and in the European Union demonstrates that the application of a market dominance test allows an effective, comprehensive and flexible assessment of restrictions of competition related to problems of collective dominance. The basic criteria, which are used to assess oligopolies and the resulting probability of coordinated effects, seem to be the same in the practice of [most relevant] competition authorities and seem to be based on sound economic theory.' [76]

Commissioner Monti has repeatedly stated that in the view of the current jurisprudence of the European courts, he will not propose the introduction of SLC in the ECMR.[77] Commission officials have also made similar comments.[78] Indeed, it is hard to see why the substantive standard of merger review in Europe should be altered in the absence of a significant dysfunction of the current system.

If there is neither a harmful 'gap' nor a significant lack of flexibility when applying the market dominance test to merger cases, then the motivation of those who advocate an introduction of the SLC test into the ECMR may be to lower the thresholds for the intervention of the European Commission. However, this motivation should not be supported for a number of – in part very fundamental – reasons. First, even if one believed in the necessity to prohibit more mergers than are currently prohibited, it has so far not been demonstrated that the SLC test would actually make this possible. In fact, *GE/Honeywell*[79] seems to suggest the contrary. Secondly, any attempt to lower the threshold for the prohibition of mergers by way of introducing an SLC test would risk not being in line with Community law. Thirdly, the US model of the SLC test is embedded in a particular set of procedural rules. If taken in isolation, the substantive test could not be easily transferred into the procedural environment of the ECMR.

3.2.1 Not more prohibition decisions under SLC

The enforcement of the SLC test as applied by the US antitrust authorities does not seem to lead to more prohibition decisions than the enforcement of the market dominance test by the European Commission. A comparison of the data available for the year 2001 shows that in the United States the agencies issued second requests in 70 out of 2,376 transactions. Twenty-six cases ended by way of a consent decree and 29 transactions were abandoned, restructured or prohibited. Even if it were assumed that all of these 29 transactions would have been prohibited,[80] this would correspond to a prohibition rate of 1.22 per cent. In 2001, the Commission opened Phase II proceedings in 20 cases out of 335 notified transactions. Five mergers were declared incompatible with the Common Market, corresponding to a prohibition rate of 1.49 per cent. We admit that a sophisticated comparison would have to take into account

76 *Ibid*, p 24.

77 Internal note taken in Brussels, 25 October 2002.

78 See F Enrique González Díaz, 'Tenth Anniversary of the Merger Regulation: the Way Forward' in *EC Merger Control – Ten Years On* (London: International Bar Association/European Commission, 2000), p 405 *et seq* (409).

79 See *GE/Honeywell*, n 70 above.

80 That would certainly not have been the case. Many projects are abandoned because of the burdensome procedure, even if they would later have been cleared.

the special factual situation of each case. However, in our view, this general data shows that the outcome of the application of the two tests in the European Union and the United States is not widely different.

3.2.2 Considerations of law and public policy

Obviously, these statistical considerations cannot predict how a different authority, such as the European Commission, with different policy objectives and traditions would apply an SLC test in practice. It cannot be excluded that an interventionist Commission might use the inherent vagueness of the test to limit severely the freedom to merge.

Illegal vagueness of the SLC test. Before addressing legitimate competition policy concerns, it is appropriate to examine whether an incorporation of the SLC test into the ECMR would – generally – be permissible under Community law. The first concern arises with respect to the very characteristic of the test which its supporters like most: its vagueness. This vagueness is no surprise, as the SLC test has its origins and is predominantly used in common law systems (US, UK, Australia). As with many common law concepts, the test – although included in a statute – is primarily meant to support and guide the evolving case law, which in itself is the main source of the law. Consequently, the test only works properly when accompanied by or based on extensive case law.

Community law does not have such a common law tradition. Although the courts' case law plays an important role, one of the fundamental principles of EC law is the principle of legal certainty. As the Court has stated time and time again, 'Community legislation must be clear and its application foreseeable for all interested parties'.[81] More precisely, the Court requires a high standard of predictability of Community norms that immediately affect Community citizens and firms:

> 'As the Court has repeatedly held, the principle of legal certainty is a fundamental principle of Community law which requires in particular that rules imposing charges on a taxpayer be clear and precise so that he may be able to ascertain unequivocally what his rights and obligations are and take steps accordingly.'[82]

This jurisprudence is not limited to the area of tax law.[83] On the face of it, an SLC test seems too vague to meet these constitutional requirements.

Illegal change of concept: from the right to merge to a burden to justify mergers. A second aspect is even more important. Introducing an SLC test into the Merger Regulation would change the traditional notion of economic freedom as it is protected by the fundamental rights of the Community and its Member States.

81 See judgment in Case C-325/91 of 16 June 1993, *France v Commission*, para 26.

82 See judgment in Case C-354/95 of 17 July 1997, *Farmer's Union*, para 57; judgment in Case C-177/96 of 16 October 1997, *Banque Indosuez v Commission*, para 27; judgment in Case C-143/93 of 13 February 1996, *Gebroeders van Es Douane Agenten v Inspecteur der Invoerrechten en Accijnzen*, para 27.

83 See Opinion of Advocate General Léger in Case C-63/00 of 16 May 2002, para 34.

Conceptually, to merge is a *generally* permitted economic activity, protected not only by the constitutional rights of the European Union,[84] but also by the fundamental guarantees in various Member States.[85] It is only for legitimate public policy considerations that mergers have to be notified and cleared in advance. Like a building permit, a prior merger clearance is required only because the consequences are so difficult to undo once somebody has made use of his freedom in a manner that is incompatible with the existing regulations. These existing regulations, in turn, have to be proportionate and must not lead to a situation in which the protected activity becomes practically impossible.

In the absence of strict guidelines and long-standing case law, an SLC test could turn the freedom to merge into an obligation to justify a merger: Every merger in the regulatory sense is associated with a 'concentration'.[86] In all cases which give rise to antitrust concerns, a competitor is taken out of the market.[87] It does not seem too far-fetched to say that where the number of players on a given market is reduced by one, the consequence is a lessening of competition.[88] If the eliminated competitor had substantial activities in this market, one could well say that the lessening of competition is substantial. If thus every problematic merger – and especially every merger in an oligopoly situation – is susceptible to a substantial lessening of competition, the burden is on the merging parties to justify that their concentration does not actually have that effect.

This conceptual change has led commentators to emphasise that a robust efficiency defence must be introduced immediately, should the substantive test of merger review be changed to SLC.[89] However, that would turn the concept of the freedom to merge on its head.

Non-binding guidelines would not help. One can expect that the Commission would provide guidelines containing parameters as to how it would apply an eventual SLC test in practice. These parameters may be binding on the Commission. However, such guidelines could not heal the non-proportionate restriction of the basic right of undertakings to merge brought about by an overly vague SLC test, which would be part of the ECMR. First, those guidelines would not bind the Community courts, but only give informal guidance as to how the test is to be construed. Secondly, as mere administrative rules whose enactment has not followed the procedural requirements of the legislative process, those guidelines would not have the legal quality to ensure that basic rights are respected to the extent required by higher-ranking law.

3.2.3 Procedural differences – absence of effective judicial review

There are also practical reasons which speak against an introduction of SLC into the ECMR. It must not be forgotten that in the United States the SLC test is embedded in

84 See Constitutional Traditions Common to the Member States (eg see judgment in Case C-11/70 of 17 December 1970, *Internationale Handelsgesellschaft mbH v Einfuhr- und Vorratsstelle für Getreide und Futtermittel*); European Convention on Human Rights and Fundamental Freedoms, signed 4 November 1950, in Rome; European Union Charter of Fundamental Rights, signed at the European Council meeting in Nice, 7 December 2000.

85 See, eg Articles 14 and 2 German Grundgesetz.

86 See Art 1 of Council Regulation (EEC) No 4064/89.

87 In case of full function JVs – two actual (or potential) competitors unite their market activities.

88 See – very openly – Richard Whish, n 40 above, p 101 *et seq.*

89 See John Temple Lang, n 22 above, p 310.

an entire procedural framework, which differs substantively from the merger review procedure in the European Union.[90] Only the key aspects need to be recalled here.

The vagueness of the SLC text might be less of a concern in a procedural environment in which the antitrust agency must argue and prove its case in court when a prohibition of a merger is sought. In Europe, the Commission is in the dual role of prosecutor and judge. It would thus find it less difficult to use the vague wording of the test to block a merger on political grounds if it had an intention to do so. As effective judicial review within a time frame that allows for the commercial rescue of the merger is lacking in the European Union, the Commission would have wide-ranging *de facto* powers.[91] European commentators therefore stress the necessity of more effective judicial review, should SLC be introduced over here.[92]

The US proceedings before the administrative or governmental agencies in merger cases are more flexible and less formalised than their European counterparts. Also, they tend to be less transparent and less protective of the interests of the notifying parties and third party interveners. All this may be acceptable in a procedure in which the administration has to argue an attempt to prohibit the merger in court. With the European Commission having its dual role to play, any shortening of procedural rights would be impermissible. It does not seem completely inconceivable that a successful attempt by the Commission to cherry-pick the substantive test from a complex US merger control system might lead to attempts to continue to cherry-pick some procedural rules which are to its advantage. These points also speak in favour of keeping the substantive test as it is under the ECMR.

4. Procedural and practical consequences of the *Airtours* judgment

From a substantive perspective, the impact of the *Airtours* judgment on the interpretation of the concept of collective dominance is rather limited. It mainly restates that a credible punishment mechanism is required.

However, the impact of the judgment on the procedural and practical application of the concept of collective dominance in the Commission's case practice must not be underestimated. In this respect, the judgment is in line with the two later judgments of the Court of First Instance annulling Commission decisions prohibiting recent mergers, *Schneider v Commission*[93] and *Tetra Laval v Commission.*[94]

The Court essentially confirms the Commission's discretion as to the assessment of economic questions and generally upholds its freedom to employ and develop economic theories and models, such as portfolio and conglomerate theories. However, it imposes a strict burden of proof on the Commission. In all three cases, the Commission has been unable to meet this burden. This provokes questions about necessary reforms of the merger review procedure by the European Commission.

90 See James S Venit and William J Kolasky, 'Substantive Convergence and Procedural Dissonance' in *Antitrust Goes Global: What Future for Transatlantic Cooperation?* (Brookings Institution Press, 2000), p 79 *et seq.*

91 *Ibid*, p 96.

92 See John Temple Lang, 22 above, pp 358-359.

93 See *Schneider* judgment, n 72 above.

94 See judgment in *Tetra Laval*, n 72 above.

4.1 Commission's discretion remains untouched

Since its decision in the cases of *Consten* and *Grundig*, the European courts have vested the Commission with broad discretion when it comes to the assessment of economic facts and the application of competition law to these facts.[95] The *Airtours* Court does not change this, but re-emphasises that the Community judicature must take account of the discretionary margin implicit in the provisions of an economic nature which form part of the rules on concentrations.[96]

Nevertheless, the Commission must not exceed the margin of discretion. The conclusion it draws must flow from the assumptions made and the underlying facts. While the Commission enjoys a certain freedom as to which theory it applies, it must correctly base this application on the facts and come to the correct results.[97]

As a result it must be remembered that the Commission – even after *Airtours* – enjoys a significant degree of manoeuvring space, especially with respect to economic issues.

4.2 A strict burden of proof

The *Airtours* judgment will certainly be remembered as the end the Court of First Instance put to the – more or less obscured – attempts of the Commission to enlarge the meaning of collective dominance. However, taken together with the judgments in *Schneider*[98] and *Tetra Laval*,[99] *Airtours* also unveils the Court's structural concerns as to the quality of the Commission's merger review. In *Airtours*, in *Schneider* and in *Tetra Laval*, the Commission's economic and competition law analysis was found wanting and characterised by methodological errors, omissions, inconsistencies and contradictions. Consequently, the Court has held in all three cases that the Commission did not meet the standard of proof required under Article 2(3) ECMR.

Particularly with respect to the required standard of substantiation in collective dominance cases, the Court held in *Airtours* that the Commission, in examining a collective dominant position, must ascertain whether the creation or strengthening of a position of that kind is the *direct and immediate effect of the concentration.*[100] Whenever the Commission intends to prohibit a merger because of the creation or strengthening of a collective dominant position, the Court requests *convincing evidence* thereof.[101] In conformity with its judgment in *Kali und Salz*,[102] the Court seems to indicate here that the prospective assessment of competition leaves no scope for speculation and that the Commission has to give, in detail, the reasons why the existence of specific structural features of the market is likely to entail a future

95 See judgment in Joined Cases 56 and 58/64 of 13 July 1966, *Consten and Grundig v Commission*; see *Kali und Salz* judgment, n 7 above, paras 223 and 224, and *Gencor* judgment, n 8 above, paras 164 and 165.

96 See *Airtours* judgment, n 1 above, para 64.

97 An inconsistency of reasoning was found in, for example, the *Schneider* judgment, n 72 above, para 147 et seq.

98 See *Schneider* judgment, n 72 above.

99 See judgment in *Tetra Laval*, n 72 above.

100 See *Airtours* judgment, n 1 above, para 58.

101 See *Airtours* judgment, n 1 above, para 63.

102 See *Kali und Salz* judgment, n 7 above.

impairment of external and internal competition.[103] This strict standard is not limited to the analysis of collective dominance, but also applies, eg, to the assessment of conglomerate effects.[104]

However, the standard of *convincing evidence* in a situation in which the Commission enjoys a margin of discretion is very difficult to handle in practice and to review in Court, because the word *convincing* suggests a subjective evaluation of the evidence. Therefore, the *convincing evidence* holding needs clarification. In this context, the following considerations should be taken into account.

First, a high standard of proof is a direct consequence of the general freedom to merge which is protected by the basic freedom of economic behaviour in the constitutional order of the European Union and the Member States.[105] It is incumbent on the Commission to show that a merger creates or strengthens a dominant position and not on the parties to prove that that the merger is not harmful.

Secondly, a distinction has to be made between the various *factual* elements which the Commission needs to look at in the framework of the three-prong test of collective dominance (ie market transparency, concentration levels, other checklist items) and the elements of *prognosis* as to the effect of the merger on competition in the respective market. Regarding the first set of elements, the Commission simply has to prove that its assessment is correct. Only a full proof of these facts (ie 100 per cent certainty) would meet the *convincing evidence* standard. As to the second set of elements, the Commission cannot be charged with the burden of full proof or even with a *beyond reasonable doubt* standard (ie about 90 per cent certainty), because these assessments involve prognoses for the future. However, when requiring *convincing evidence,* the Court clearly goes beyond merely scrutinising 'manifest errors' in the Commission's assessment. Although the Commission may have doubts as to the exact burden of proof, which the Court imposes on it, it can be assumed that a mere *probability* test (more than 50 per cent probability), would not satisfy the Court's requirement of convincing evidence. This is demonstrated by a simple reflection: a demonstration by the Commission of 49 per cent or even 50 per cent probability would be no evidence at all. With 49 per cent, it is more probable than not that the Commission is wrong; a 50:50 situation cannot justify the prohibition of a merger, either, as that would actually place the burden of proof on the parties and would thus be incompatible with their constitutional right to merge.[106] If 51 per cent was already convincing evidence, then there would be no room for a degree of probability, which is evidence, but not yet convincing evidence. Therefore, it seems an appropriate interpretation of the standard of proof as required by the Court of First Instance to oblige the Commission to predict any alleged harmful effects on competition with at least a *high degree of probability.*

Thirdly, it is also in the Commission's interest to take these requirements set up by the court seriously. Having to meet a high standard of proof increases is not necessarily an onerous burden on the Commission, but can increase the quality, persuasiveness and thus acceptance of its decisions when prohibiting mergers.

103 Heiko Haupt, 'Collective Dominance under Article 82 EC and EC Merger Control in the Light of the *Airtours* Judgment' (2002) 23(9) *European Competition Law Review* 434 at 443.

104 See *Tetra Laval* judgment, n 72 above, para 155.

105 See discussion above 3.2.2.

106 See discussion above 3.2.2.

Moreover, if the Commission committed to a standard of a *high degree of probability*, it would be in line with the practice of other Member States' competition authorities. The Bundeskartellamt, for example, has to take future developments of competition into account, if 'it can be said on the basis of concrete facts and with a *high degree of probability*' (emphasis added) what changes in the conditions of competition will occur as a consequence of the merger.[107] Under the decision practice of the German Bundeskartellamt and the German courts, the competition authority is thus under an obligation to demonstrate elements of prognosis, on with it intends to base a prohibition of a merger, with a high degree of probability.

Such helpful clarification can be provided either by the European courts or, subject to judicial review in individual cases, by Commission guidelines. The forthcoming draft of Commission Guidelines for the Assessment of Horizontal Mergers would be a good place to include a commitment that the Commission will assume its responsibility to demonstrate the underlying facts of a case with absolute certainty and the legal implications of the merger with a 'high degree of probability'.

5. Conclusion

In conclusion, the *Airtours* judgment is a useful clarification of the scope of a possible finding of collective dominance in merger control cases. Even more importantly, *Airtours*, seen in the context with the more recent judgments in *Schneider* and *Tetra Laval*, raises the standards of methodological clarity and precision of assessment which must be met by the European Commission if it wants to prohibit a merger. The Court does not cut back on the discretion vested in the Commission's economic expertise, but it asks for a stringent and well-reasoned case. Thereby, the European Court strengthens the fundamental right of firms to merge subject to the requirements of the dominance test of the ECMR. A change of the substantive test employed by European merger control is unnecessary. The dominance test catches mergers, which bring about anti-competitive effects. This is also true for 'unilateral effects', which are in essence nothing else than effects brought about by the creation of single firm dominance. A change of the substantive test would also face grave legal concerns. A US-style SLC test, taken out of its procedural and traditional context and implemented into the ECMR, is too vague to be permissible under the fundamental rights of the European Union.

The *Airtours* judgment does not call for a change of the substantive test, but for an overhaul of various very practical elements of the Merger Task Force's day-to-day business. Commissioner Monti has now announced – and partly implemented – such an overhaul. It will include the appointment of a Chief Economist, but also extends to procedural reforms such as the introduction of 'devil's advocate' panels and the strengthening of the role of the Hearing Officer.

107 See Statement of Purpose (Gesetzesbegründung) for the (Second) Reform of the Act Against Restraints of Competition of 18 August 1971, p 29; Federal Supreme Court (BGH), judgment of 21 February 1978 – *Kfz-Kupplungen*, WuW/E BGH 1501 (1506 et seq); Federal Supreme Court (BGH), judgment of 15 July 1997 – *Stromversorgung Aggertal*, WuW/E DE-R 24 (28).

24

Does Collective Dominance Provide Suitable Housing for All Anti-Competitive Oligopolistic Mergers?

JOHN FINGLETON*

Chair, Irish Competition Authority, Dublin

This paper has also been published in the proceedings of the Twenty-Ninth Annual Conference on 'International Antitrust Law & Policy', organised by Fordham Corporate Law Institute

1. INTRODUCTION

Collective dominance is used to address 'oligopoly mergers', ie where the merged firm is not dominant. Such mergers may harm competition for two reasons: tacit collusion or multilateral effects. While it has become increasingly clear that collective dominance safely covers tacit collusion, no such clarity prevails in respect of multilateral effects. There is a policy lacuna.

As a result, the Commission, using collective dominance, may fail to prohibit some mergers that harm competition, both because some multilateral cases cannot be tackled at all and others will be tackled incorrectly or inefficiently.

The possible solutions to this problem within the dominance framework – single-firm dominance or a new concept of oligopolistic dominance – are unattractive, unlikely to work, and would increase legal uncertainty. Similarly, a market power test, while superior to a dominance test, also has drawbacks. In contrast, a competition-based test would address all of the problems identified with the collective dominance concept.

In the broader context of the reform of the Merger Regulation, most attention has been given to Type I error (blocking good mergers). However, the continued use of a dominance based merger test will (1) create legal uncertainty and (2) mean that EU policy will neglect Type II error (allowing bad mergers) and will be unable to block a set of seriously anti-competitive mergers.

2. ECONOMIC THEORY AND HARM TO COMPETITION

Where the merged firm is the largest with a post-merger share above 40 per cent, the case can generally be characterised as single-firm dominance. I put such cases aside[1] and use the term 'oligopoly merger' to describe remaining cases. Examples include:

* This paper has benefited from discussions with and comments from Eleanor Fox, Kirtikumar Mehta, Noreen Mackey, Dermot Nolan, Francis O'Toole and Andrew Rae. The author takes responsibility for any errors.

1 This also puts aside cases involving portfolio effects such as the *GE/Honeywell* case.

1. A merger between small players that makes the market more symmetric and in which the merged firm joins the 'big' players.[2] The *Airtours*[3] case with 27—20—21—11 is approximately in this class.
2. A merger between two small players in which a third firm is already dominant, as in the US Babyfoods[4] case where the figures were 65—17—15.
3. A merger in a stable oligopoly in which one firm buys a smaller rival or entrant. The UK *Lloyds/Abbey National* case is in this set.[5]

Market shares are used here to describe the classification of oligopoly mergers, and have no particular significance in terms of harm to competition. Whether competition is reduced will generally depend on the detailed facts of a particular case.

Two types of anti-competitive effect can arise: multilateral effects and tacit collusion.

2.1 Multilateral effects[6]

Multilateral effects are based on economic models of oligopoly. These models have a number of typical features:

- A small and stable number of firms.
- Each firm maximises its profit, taking account of each of the reactions of rivals (ie strategic interdependence). A best response (or reaction) function for each firm expresses how its optimal price[7] depends on the prices of its rivals.
- Equilibrium is a (generally) unique outcome in which no firm can do better, even in the short term, by changing price, given what others are doing. This is known as the 'static equilibrium'.

The effect of a merger can be described as happening in two stages.

1. The best reaction function of the merged firm (which replaces that of the two firms) shifts up as it sets a higher price than the separate firms did before. This is the first-order effect.
2. This price change by the merged firm induces a reaction in competitors. Their best response functions do not change, but they now respond to a different price by the merged firm, so they increase[8] their prices.

The effect on consumer welfare is the combined effect that takes account not just of the effect on the merged firm's price, but that also incorporates the reactions of rivals. The term 'unilateral' is used in the United States, but it could be taken (erroneously) to

2 For a 3 to 2 merger, shares might be 50—25—25 and for a 4 to 3, shares of 33—33—17—17, and for 5 to 4 mergers, 25—25—25—13—12, where the solid dash indicates the merging firms.

3 Taken from the Commission figures in which the significant players accounted for 79 per cent of the market: Case IV/M.524.

4 *FTC v Heinz*, 116 F Supp 2d 190 (DDC 2000), *rev'd* 246 F 3d 708 (DC Cir 2001).

5 See the UK Competition Commission Report on Lloyds TSB Group plc and Abby National plc, July 2001.

6 The term is suggested by John Vickers (see his speech *Competition Economics and Policy*, 3 October 2002, www.oft.gov.uk).

7 I use 'price' throughout to mean 'price or quantity' and an 'increase in price' for 'an increase in price or reduction in quantity', etc.

8 This is an important difference between models of price competition like Bertrand and output competition like Cournot. In Bertrand, the second order effect is in the same direction as the first, whereas in Cournot the reactions of rivals is in the opposite direction (but not as large as the first order).

suggest that we are only interested in the first step. The term 'multilateral effects' better describes the inclusion of the reactions of rivals.

The effect on welfare is not due solely to an increase in market power of the merged party, although this might play a large part in some (especially differentiated product) instances, but rather to how the merger alters the equilibrium. To the extent that the merger has significant 'externalities' on the other participants, as for example, when one oligopolist buys out a maverick that threatens all.[9] In that case, a focus on the market power of the merged firm does not fully capture the anti-competitive harm.

In fact, there appear to be two distinct arguments:

1. unilateral market power that is less than the level of market power associated with monopolisation (US) or dominance (EU) as, for example, if two close substitutes merge in a differentiated product market; and
2. multilateral effects whereby the emphasis is not on the market power of the merging parties but rather on the equilibrium outcome as, for example, if a maverick is bought out.

From the point of view of terminology, it is not clear whether we should use a single term (eg multilateral) to include both of these, or distinguish both multilateral and unilateral.

There is no collusion in models of this kind because firms set their prices or quantities in a rivalrous fashion and no change in their strategy would increase the profit in that period. Yet the outcome in terms of consumer welfare varies between fully competitive and monopoly depending on a host of market-specific factors.[10] For example, no harm might result from a 3 to 2 merger in the presence of strong price rivalry while considerable harm could result from a 6 to 5 merger that removed a maverick.

Oligopoly theory thus demonstrates that harm to competition can result from mergers in oligopolistic markets where there is neither tacit collusion nor single-firm dominance. It also provides a framework, and a list of important factors, for the case-by-case examination of such mergers. Where adequate data are available, it may even be possible to calibrate a model and simulate the effect of the merger on prices.[11]

2.1.1 Tacit collusion

Tacit collusion is based on the same theory of oligopoly in which a small and stable group of firms compete and take account of each other's reactions in setting prices (or quantities). What is different is that firms do not maximise their own profit in the current period, but instead set higher prices in the expectation that others do likewise. If all firms follow a similar strategy, an equilibrium results in which the market price is significantly above the static equilibrium price. The collusive equilibrium has a number of characteristics that distinguish it from the static equilibrium.

9 An example of this might be the British banks case (see n 5 above).

10 These include whether firms set prices or quantities, whether the product is homogenous or differentiated, consumer switching costs, the shape of cost curves (and especially capacity constraints), and the elasticity of demand.

11 This is most commonly undertaken in the United States (eg *Staples Office Depot*), but the European Commission has recently undertaken such analyses. In May 2002, economists from the US Department of Justice conducted a training programme in merger simulation methods for economists from the competition offices of EU countries, organised by the Swedish Konkurrensverket.

- firms do not set prices as instantaneous best responses in the sense that each firm could do much better this period by cutting price (known as cheating or defection);
- the collusive equilibrium is not unique: one possible outcome is the monopoly price; and
- the theory does not explain how the collusion works, and does not distinguish between an explicitly agreed cartel and collusion that arises without any communication between the parties.

A collusive equilibrium is potentially unstable because of the incentive to cheat. However, this is tempered by the fact that cheating, if detected, is likely to be punished by a period of intense competition (eg a price war). Each firm must thus weigh up the advantages of a short-run boost in profit from cheating with later loss arising from the breakdown of the collusive arrangement.

The theory of tacit collusion offers no predictions as to how a merger would affect the price in a market in which there is already collusion. However, by identifying market characteristics (known as 'plus factors') that make collusion more likely, it helps to understand whether a merger could tip a market from rivalry to tacit collusion. In essence, this relies on establishing that the market exhibits many of the plus characteristics and arguing that the reduction of one player, especially if that makes the market more symmetric or eliminates an 'asymmetric'[12] competitor, increases the likelihood of collusion.

The application of oligopoly theory to tacit collusion is less satisfactory than to multilateral effects for several reasons:

- The theory offers less insight into how a change in the number of firms affects the equilibrium outcome.
- It is based on a change in the *type* of equilibrium (static to collusive) as opposed to a change in the static equilibrium outcome (ie paradigm shift versus change within paradigm).
- The merger must be the straw that breaks the camel's back. Collusion does not happen before the merger, despite a preponderance of plus factors, yet is likely to happen afterwards.
- Experience of past cartels questions the reliability of plus factors.[13]

2.1.2 These differences matter

Oligopoly theory underlies both multilateral effects and tacit collusion explanations of harm to competition. Both assume a small number of firms in a stable setting with strategic interdependence (in the sense of taking account of each other's actions). What is different is that harm to competition from tacit collusion flows from a common policy by all firms that involves each forgoing short-run profit in expectation that others will do likewise and the market outcome will involve higher prices than would result from the static equilibrium that would otherwise prevail.[14]

In terms of applying these theories to mergers, it is clear that:

12 A firm that is small, or a price-cutting maverick or new entrant, or a firm that cares less about future profit.

13 See Section D of a recent speech by William J Kolasky, *Coordinated Effects in Merger Review: From Dead Frenchmen to Beautiful Minds and Mavericks*, http://www.usdoj.gov/atr/public/speeches/11050.htm.

14 Mergers with mavericks who undercut 'regular' firms can be anti-competitive under both theories.

1. Interdependence and the presence of a small number of suppliers are common to all oligopoly models. They are not useful in predicting outcomes, and simply tell us that we are talking about oligopoly. The legal interpretation of the term interdependence handed down through case law might appear to suggest that it is synonymous with tacit collusion,[15] suggesting economists and lawyers may be at cross purposes when they use the term.
2. The application of oligopoly theory to multilateral effects is inherently more sound and reliable than its application to tacit collusion.

Ironically, much greater stress in merger analysis appears to be put on tacit collusion (or coordinated effects) where the theory is complex and less conclusive than on multilateral effects where the theory is more straightforward and capable of prediction.[16]

3. Collective dominance

3.1 Covers tacit collusion[17]

The EU Merger Regulation[18] prohibits mergers that 'create or strengthen a dominant position as a result of which effective competition would be significantly impeded ...'.[19] This is based on the concept of dominance developed by Article 82 case law over the previous 30 years and as articulated by the European Court of Justice (ECJ) in *Michelin*[20] (and later in *Hoffmann-La Roche*[21]) as: 'A position of economic strength enjoyed by an undertaking which enables it to hinder the maintenance of effective competition on the relevant market by allowing it to behave to an appreciable extent independently of competitors and ultimately of consumers.' At the outset, there was an ambiguity about how the dominance test as stated above would apply to oligopoly mergers. The Commission first applied the concept of collective dominance[22] in merger control in 1992 in *Nestlé Perrier*,[23] but it was not until *Kali und Salz*[24] in 1998 that the ECJ confirmed collective dominance as where 'one or more undertakings which together, in particular because of factors giving rise to a connection between them, are able to adopt a common policy on the market and act to a considerable

15 See John Temple Lang in 'Oligopolies and Joint Dominance in Community Antitrust Law', 2001 *Fordham Corp L. Institute* (B Hawk, ed), pp 274 and 290. Part of the confusion may also lie in the fact that the law questions more the mechanics by which the collusion occurs (and thus distinguishes tacit from explicit collusion) whereas economists emphasise the welfare effects.

16 In policy analysis as in merger decisions. See for example, the report of the OECD Roundtable in May 1999 (See 'Oligopoly' in *OECD Journal of Competition Law and Policy*, Vol 3, No 3, 2001) and the Bundeskartellamt Discussion Paper on *Prohibition Criteria in Merger Control – Dominant Position versus Substantial Lessening of Competition?*, both of which focus almost exclusively on coordinated effects.

17 For a recent comprehensive account of the development of the law and policy on collective dominance, see Temple Lang, op cit.

18 Council Regulation (EC)4064/89.

19 The part that refers to competition is of little relevance other than qualifying the dominance concept.

20 [1983] ECR 3641, [1985] 1 CMLR 282.

21 Case 85/76 [1979] ECR 461.

22 Its approach was based on Article 81 case law (*Compagnie Maritime Belge* Case C-365 & 396/96P [2000] 4 CMLR 1076 and *Italian Flat Glass* Case T-68, 77 & 78/79 [1992] ECR I-1403) on joint dominance that stressed joint profit maximisation.

23 Case No IV/M.190.

24 Case 30/95 [1998] ECR I-1375.

extent independently of their competitors, their customers and also of consumers'. This illustrates that collective dominance is closely linked to dominance as defined in Article 82 and that it relies on a common policy, as is the case with tacit collusion.

The identification of collective dominance with tacit collusion was strengthened in *Gencor* [25] in 1999 where, in regard to collective dominance, the Court included:

> 'the relationship of interdependence existing between the parties to a tight oligopoly within which, in a market with the appropriate characteristics, in particular in terms of market concentration, transparency and product homogeneity, those parties are in a position to anticipate one another's behaviour and are therefore strongly encouraged to align their conduct on the market, in particular in such a way as to maximise their joint profits.... Each trader is aware that highly competitive action on its part to increase its market share (for example, a price cut) would provoke identical action by the others, so that it would derive no benefit from its initiative.'

It is clear from this that the Court had tacit collusion in mind, in terms of the reference to plus factors, joint profits being maximised and the incentive to cheat.

The correspondence between collective dominance and tacit collusion was strengthened considerably in *Airtours*[26] in 2002 where, at paragraph 62, the Court sets out three necessary conditions for a finding of collective dominance:

> 'first, each member of the dominant oligopoly must have the ability to know how the other members are behaving in order to monitor whether or not they are adopting the common policy...second, the situation of tacit coordination must be sustainable over time, that is to say, there must not be an incentive to depart from the common policy on the market...third...[it must be proven that] the foreseeable reaction of current and future competitors, as well of consumers, would not jeopardise the results expected from the common policy.'

These cases establish that collective dominance clearly includes tacit collusion, and that the Court understands tacit collusion in the sense outlined above as a situation where firms forgo short-run profit in expectation of the gain that arises if others also do so. *Airtours*, in spelling out a three-part test, has established a clear standard based more precisely on the underlying economic theory of tacit collusion. It also makes clear the correspondence between collective dominance and the US concept of coordinated effects.[27]

3.2 But does not cover multilateral effects

Collective dominance does not cover multilateral effects. Some say that because the Commission has not yet prohibited an oligopoly merger based on such a clearly articulated theory of non-collusive price raising and the Court has not had the opportunity to opine in the matter the question is moot.[28]

25 Case T-102/96 [1999] ECR II-753.

26 Case T-342/99.

27 See Kolasky *op cit* at p 21.

28 For example, see Eleanor Fox in 'Collective Dominance and the Message from Luxembourg' in *Antitrust* Fall 2002 (forthcoming).

Perhaps the Court has already spoken. Some read the *Airtours* decision of the Court as implicitly ruling out a multilateral effects approach (support for which is found in paragraphs 56 to 63 generally).[29] Others go further and argue that one leg of the Commission's case in *Airtours*[30] was a multilateral effects story,[31] and that the Court explicitly rejected it.

Even if the Court has not spoken definitively, existing judgments do little to suggest willingness to accept the extension of collective dominance to multilateral effects. The Court's definition of collective dominance is extremely closely linked to single-firm dominance, and a defining feature is the fact that the firms act as if they enjoyed a monopoly and that they adopt a common policy. There is a clear dividing line between the common policy underlying tacit collusion and the unilateral behaviour underlying multilateral effects.

The Commission has already set out such a position in its Notice on Access Agreements in the Telecommunications Sector[32] where it states: 'for two or more companies to be in a joint dominant position, they must together have substantially the same position vis-à-vis their customers and competitors as a single company has if it is in a dominant position.'

The Court might also be reluctant to extend the concept because it seriously stretches language to describe as 'collective' a situation in which firms compete to maximise individual profit at each point in time. It would suggest that any behaviour in an oligopoly, even if very rivalrous, could be termed 'collective' or 'joint' simply because there are few players. Again, the Commission's telecom Notice provides support for this view[33]: 'for two or more companies to be jointly dominant it is necessary, though not sufficient, for there to be no effective competition between [them].'

In summary, collective dominance clearly houses tacit collusion. It does not house multilateral effects and there are enormous doubts that it ever will.

4. This creates a policy problem

The fact that multilateral effects are not covered by collective dominance creates a serious policy problem with several elements.

4.1 A 'gap'

Certain multilateral cases, possibly where the post-merger market structure is asymmetric or plus factors are not present, are clearly not caught by collective dominance. The US Babyfoods case (type B on page 344 above) may be an example of the gap, but a clearer example is the UK Lloyds/Abbey National merger (type C on page 344 above). This was a merger between a maverick with a five per cent share and

29 See Malcolm Nicholson and Sara Cartell, 'Airtours v Commission: Collective Dominance Contained?', paper presented at the EC Merger Control Conference, November 2002.

30 Case No IV/M.1524 – *Airtours/First Choice*, Commission decision of 22 September 1999. The reasoning in paragraphs 54-56 of that decision certainly leaves room for ambiguity on this point.

31 That is, the Commission was using a Cournot model (or more precisely, a variant of the model developed by Kreps and Scheinkman) in which output would be reduced by the move from four to three significant players. See OXERA, 'Collective Dominance from an Economic Perspective', Competing Ideas, June 2002.

32 OJ 1998 C 265/2, para 78.

33 Commission Notice *op cit* at para 79.

a leading bank with 22 per cent, in a market where four leading banks had 72 per cent. Single-firm dominance could not apply at 27 per cent. Tacit collusion was not an issue because of consumer inertia. It appears that a merger such as this might not have been prohibited under a dominance standard.

Some believe that the gap is small and not likely to cover many cases: this elicits two responses. First, while the concern with the gap pre-dates[34] it, the decision of the CFI in *Airtours* has increased the gap by laying down a clear standard for applying collective dominance to tacit collusion. This makes it more difficult to masquerade a unilateral effects case as tacit collusion. Secondly, even a small gap may be a serious concern because so few mergers get prohibited anyhow.

4.2 Cases incorrectly characterised

Multilateral effects cases may get described incorrectly as tacit collusion. Many oligopoly mergers increase market symmetry. If the market additionally exhibits some plus factors, then it may be possible to argue tacit collusion, even if this has no fundamental validity.

In some cases, incorrect characterisation will give the right result (blocking a harmful multilateral effects merger) for the wrong reason (tacit collusion). This risks opening the door for the wrong result in a wider set of cases. Even with the right result, there is a danger that remedies may be inappropriate.

As noted above, *Airtours* makes it more difficult to characterise cases incorrectly, but any reduction in incorrect characterisation simply increases the 'gap'. Indeed, *Airtours* could possibly be an example of a case that got incorrectly characterised as tacit collusion instead of multilateral effects.[35]

4.3 Cases inefficiently characterised

Other cases may raise simultaneous concerns about tacit collusion and unilateral effects.[36] In other words, there is likely to be a price rise in a non-cooperative equilibrium, and there is some possibility that the market may switch towards tacit collusion.[37]

For many of these, characterisation as multilateral effects may be more efficient, because the anti-competitive effect can be predicted more precisely. If we can show that there will be a multilateral effect sufficient to block the merger, then it is hardly necessary to show that there may alternatively be a tacit collusion problem that would be worse. In addition, it is generally more plausible to focus on multilateral effects: this does not require an argument that the entire nature of interaction will change from non-cooperative to cooperative, but rather that non-cooperative rivalry will

34 The idea that a gap existed prompted the inclusion of the topic in the consultation process on the Merger Regulation and was announced at Fordham in October 2001. Ironically, it was presented as a reaction to the *GE/Honeywell* case, although that case is totally unrelated to the test.

35 See John Kay's article on this subject, *Financial Times*, 18 June 2002 or http://www.johnkay.com/regulation/250.

36 For example, in the *Babyfoods* case (see n 4), the Federal Trade Commission emphasised a unilateral effects story, but the Court appears to have both unilateral effects and tacit collusion in its reasoning.

37 This set may be small in the sense that, if there is going to be a multilateral non-cooperative price rise, the relative benefits of tacit collusion are reduced.

lessen. Or, to put it another way, when given a choice why not rely on the straightforward economic theory in place of the more complex stuff?

4.4 And these add up to a sizeable problem

The gap clearly raises type II error, because mergers that harm competition cannot be blocked. Inefficient characterisation has the same effect because it prevents the authority from choosing the most efficient and straightforward economic theory. Incorrect characterisation also raises type II error, because such cases may fail, but has the additional nuance that compensation in response to this could instead increase type I error.

5. This problem cannot be solved within the dominance framework

Can multilateral effects be housed elsewhere within the dominance framework?

5.1 ...not within single-firm dominance

Applying single-firm dominance to multilateral effects would focus directly on the market power of the merging parties, that is, on the first order effect outlined above. This creates problems:

- the omission of the rivals' responses would underestimate the damage to competition if price competition, and overestimate if quantity competition;[38]
- if it involved narrow market definition, it would create problems for subsequent mergers[39] or in Article 82 cases more generally; and[40]
- if it does not involve narrowing the market definition, there would be a serious doubt as to how the courts could find single-firm dominance where there is a similar or larger player in the market.

Eschewing market definition to focus on market power directly does not reduce these problems significantly. The fundamental problem is that the single firm dominance concept is aligned to monopoly-type market power, and is not associated with a change in the equilibrium in an oligopoly.

5.2 ...nor via a new approach like oligopolistic dominance

If it was possible to create the collective dominance notion for tacit collusion, why not develop a new concept of oligopolistic dominance for multilateral effects?

38 See n 8 above.

39 For example, suppose two firms with 17 per cent each merge where there are two rivals with 33 per cent each. If the market is defined narrowly, each party would have 50 per cent of the market and the merger could be blocked. But it would then be difficult to challenge a 17-33 merger because the parties could argue that they were not in the same market.

40 It might be argued that the recent *Tetra/Sidel* case, Case T-5/02 and Case T-80/02, illustrated this issue to some extent. In a previous Article 82 decision, the Commission had defined a market for aseptic cartons on which Tetra was dominant. This meant that the Tetra and Sidel were in different markets, even though their products exhibit a degree of substitutability. The fact that Sidel may not have in the past exerted sufficient competitive pressure to discipline Tetra's market power in aseptic cartons does not mean that a merger between the two would not reduce competition. Refer also to RBB Brief 01 May 2002, 'A Bridge Too Far? – Complements, Substitutes and Theories of Exclusion in EC Merger Control.'

There must be considerable doubt as to whether the Court would accept the use of the term oligopolistic dominance to describe a situation in which the members of an oligopoly are rivals. While the oligopoly element may be correct, the dominance part is not. Static oligopoly equilibrium cannot reasonably be described as a situation in which firms behave 'independently of competitors'. So the approach would risk failure.

Even if it succeeded and the Court were to accept an oligopolistic dominance concept, there is a danger that this would increase the burden on all merging firms in oligopolistic markets. It would not be clear from this structuralist legal terminology what distinguishes an oligopoly merger in which competition is unaffected (or increased) from one in which it is harmed.

In the meantime, there would be considerable legal uncertainty surrounding the standard for such oligopoly mergers. Even with a fast-track appeals procedure, it would take several years for the right case to clarify the situation (*Airtours* came more than ten years after the Merger Regulation).

It seems foolhardy to invite years of uncertainty, with a low probability of success, and further problems if one does succeed.

5.3 ...because the fundamental problem is with dominance

The fundamental problem is the use of the dominance concept for oligopoly mergers. This has several elements[41]:

- The dominance concept was developed under Article 82 for monopoly situations. It may be reasonable to describe colluding competitors as collectively acting as a monopolist (although theory suggests the outcome might differ). But it is much less reasonable to describe oligopolies generally as dominant.
- The dominance concept, when applied to oligopoly, risks being overly structural, and hints at the outmoded SCP[42] paradigm that, when applied to policy, condemned concentrated markets. A structural approach could have the effect of limiting oligopolistic mergers generally. This would be inefficient, especially as we know from the work of Sutton[43] and others that higher market concentration may be driven by rivalry and efficiency.
- The application of dominance to oligopoly mergers raises concerns about the possible re-importation into Article 82 case law. While the Court has qualified the linkage,[44] in practice it already has two related negative effects:
  1. Firms that are found to be dominant or collectively dominant as a result of attempting a merger face a higher defence burden in subsequent private or public actions under Article 82. It would be of particular concern if a concept of 'oligopolistic dominance' were to emerge in Article 82 case law as

41 This draws on Richard Whish, 'Substantive Analysis under the EC Merger Regulation: Should the Dominance Test Be Replaced by "Substantial Lessening of Competition"' in *International Merger Control: Prescriptions for Convergence* (Rowley ed, IBA, 2002).

42 SCP refers to economic paradigm whereby Structure causes Conduct which causes Performance. This idea, which underlay the heavily structuralist approach to US antitrust in the 1950s and 1960s, has been replaced by a more thorough approach that recognises that structure may also be caused by conduct.

43 John Sutton, *Sunk Costs and Market Structure* (MIT Press, 1991).

44 See Cases T-125/97 and T-127/97, *Coca Cola v Commission* [2002] ECR II-1733, para 87.

an import from *ex ante* merger regulation, especially as structural remedies are being introduced.[45] Even if Article 82 does not apply strictly, firms labelled as jointly dominant in a merger case may face a significantly higher burden in subsequent litigation, especially in the national courts, in disproving the link between the two types of dominances.

2. In anticipation of the first effect, firms may not go ahead with mergers for fear of attracting such a label. I am aware of one recent case in point. A related example is that General Electric's appeal of the Commission decision of July 2001 appears to be motivated by ridding itself of the dominance label rather than overturning the prohibition decision. This in turn raises a further point.

- A test based on dominance unnecessarily requires the competition authority to comment on the level of competition in the market, and not just on its change. Temple Lang expresses the same point:

  'It has been suggested that the *Airtours* decision was an effort by the Commission to extend the test of dominance in the Merger Regulation to mergers which substantially lessen competition. It is not easy to see how this would work, because the Regulation is based on the idea of creating or strengthening dominance, and at least in theory dominance either exists or it does not. The Regulation as it is now written would not easily apply to a merger merely by reference to the fact that it made the market substantially less competitive than it had previously been. The Regulation is based on the result (dominance or increased dominance), rather than the significance of the change resulting from the merger. Substantially reduced competition is not necessarily dominance: dominance is as a result of how much competition is left, not how big the change has been.'

- A related issue is the need to have an explicitly different standard for *ex ante* analysis of mergers as compared with *ex post* analysis in Article 82. There is a fundamental difference between firms winning market share directly by vying for customer business and from purchasing a competitor's customers on the stock market.

Overall, a solution within the dominance concept runs a very high risk of being unsuccessful and, even if it were to succeed, would result in an inability to block some anti-competitive mergers and undesirable legal uncertainty.

Not everybody agrees that there is a problem with dominance. Some consider that there is a difference between the dominance standard applied in Germany and that in the European Union.[46] Even still, the Bundeskartellamt states:

> 'In merger control, a mere reduction of the intensity of competition without the creation of a dominant position is not a condition that would give rise to concerns. In dynamic competitive processes imbalances and also fluctuations in the intensity of competition will constantly occur anyway. There is only reason for concern if

45 In the reform of Regulation 17/62 (known as modernisation), it is proposed that the Commission would have a break-up remedy in Article 82 cases. Such remedies may also exist in the laws of the Member States, as in section 14 of the Irish Competition Act 2002.

46 For example (unscripted) remarks by Judge Joachim Bornkamm at the Fordham conference on 1 November 2002.

the advantage one company gains over others by means of a merger reaches a level where the remaining competitive forces alone can no longer be expected to wear away the market power achieved.'[47]

5.4 Language matters

Some proponents of the dominance test argue that it produces identical outcomes as SLC, and that the formal language of the test is less important than how it is applied. While the application of law can often matter more than how the law is written, I strongly disagree.

First, we are about competition policy not anti-dominance policy. We refer to competition authorities (not anti-monopoly offices), (anti-) competitive effects, harm to competition, competitors, etc. Article 81 represents a whole body of competition policy that is mostly exclusive of the dominance concept. Dominance is one part of the flip side of the competition coin, but only one part.

Secondly, the approach seriously risks creating a mystical 'black box' approach to mergers, where it does not matter what words we use, as long as the outcomes are correct. What happens inside a box that has 'Dominance' on the front and 'Competition' on the back? Such an approach must necessarily risk enormous legal uncertainty, especially if the merger policy is of the 'I know it when I see it' type.

6. Alternatives to a dominance test

6.1 What criteria should a merger test satisfy?

In view of the problems just outlined, there are some general criteria that any desirable merger test should meet if it is properly to capture multilateral effects cases. These might include:

1. avoid a link with the language of Article 81/82 so that the *ex ante* and *ex post* standards are clearly separate;
2. focus on the change in competition resulting from the merger, not on the pre- or post-merger level of competition;
3. be firmly rooted in the consumer welfare standard;
4. avoid undue reference to market concentration or strategic interdependence, as these are common features of all oligopoly mergers, whether or not competition is harmed;
5. take account of the second order effect of the merger on rivals' reactions as well as on the merging parties; and
6. avoid substantial (unnecessary) legal uncertainty.

6.2 ...a test based on market power?

At the ICN meeting in Naples, Eleanor Fox proposed a 'significant increase in market power test'. This improves on dominance because it (1) breaks the link with Article 81,

47 See Bundeskartellamt, Contribution from the Bundeskartellamt, Germany submitted to the International Competition Network (ICN) Merger Control Working Group, Analytical Framework Sub-group available at www.internationalcompetitionnetwork.org/afsggermany.pdf. 2002, pp 13-14.

(2) focuses on market power directly, (3) is rooted in the consumer welfare standard, and (4) does not depend on concentration or interdependence.

However, it runs into problems on (5) because there is a danger that it focuses only on the market power of the merging parties. This is fine for single firm dominance and perhaps also for tacit collusion. But a focus on the market power of the merging parties is less suitable for oligopoly mergers with multilateral effects. Of course, it could be defined as market-wide market power, but this diminishes its original attraction as a simple test.

It may also run into problems on (6) because it is a new concept and it would take some time for the Court to interpret the concept.

Another problem is that it is not currently reflected in any Member States.

6.3 ...or a test based on competition?

A test based on lessening competition (1) avoids the Article 82 link, (2) focuses on the change in competition, (3) is firmly rooted in consumer welfare, (4) avoids reference to concentration or interdependence, and (5) enables account to be taken of the equilibrium effect rather than the first order effect on the merging parties.

Some might argue that moving from a dominance test to a competition test would increase legal uncertainty either because of novelty or because of the loss of existing jurisprudence. This need not be so. For one, the specific jurisprudence has only been developed in the past few years, and decisions in cases like *Airtours* would continue to be relevant. Also, case law on issues such as market definition would not be affected. Nor is novelty a problem, as the application of the SLC concept, complete with guidelines, in other jurisdictions, would serve to minimise such uncertainty. On this basis, I conclude that it meets criterion 6.

There are concerns that a competition test could be too broad. After all, it was under SLC that a merger to 5.2 per cent share of the market was prohibited in the United States.[48] This concern may be overstated. Ultimately, we need a test that prohibits mergers that reduce consumer welfare. The SLC test has, through its usage, and more importantly through explicit guidelines, come to be synonymous with a consumer welfare standard.

A competition test is used in several (and a growing number of) Member States.[49] It also offers an opportunity to send a clear and strong signal that economic analysis is at the core of European merger policy.

6.4 Must we choose?

It is not clear that we face a stark either/or choice. One possibility is to *add* a separate competition-based test such as SLC[50] to Article 2 of the ECMR in addition to the dominance test that is already there. This would have a number of clear benefits including:

1. it would provide a competition test to close the gap;

48 *Brown Shoe v United States*, 370 US 294 (1962).

49 France and Spain have such a test that is close to SLC, and Ireland and the UK are switching to it.

50 It need not be called SLC. There are other possibilities based on that part of the current test which refers to 'effective competition [being] significantly impeded'.

2. it would enable a flexible choice between the two tests so that cases could be characterised efficiently;
3. it would retain the dominance concept in the Merger Regulation, and consequently all of the existing case law would be relevant;
4. it would mean that the EU merger test encompassed the tests used in the various Member States; and
5. it would enable us to learn more about the benefits of each test over time.

So it may not be down to a stark choice between dominance and SLC: perhaps they can cohabit in balanced fashion.

7. Conclusion

Before concluding, I would like to place this issue in the wider context of the current debate about the reform of the Merger Regulation. Enormous attention focuses on type I error, ie a concern that the Commission may block harmless deals. This is clearly seen in the reaction to recent decisions[51] in which the Court has overturned Commission prohibitions.

The question as to whether collective dominance covers multilateral effects raises type II error, because the system may not be able to prohibit harmful mergers. We should be concerned with this for several reasons:

- removing legal uncertainty in this area would not only reduce type II error, but also indirectly reduce type I error;[52]
- recent CFI decisions do not automatically indicate type I error. The Commission may have lost cases, not because there was no harm to competition, but because it was unable to show that harm (under the existing collective dominance test); and[53]
- those concerned with type I error are generally more vocal, articulated and organised than the consumer interests more concerned with type II. Indeed, the arguments for changing to an SLC test come primarily from scholars (economists and lawyers) and those in public enforcement whose interest lies in having an effective system of merger control.[54] In particular, there is little evidence of business interests or those from outside the European Union, pushing on this question.

Multilateral effects can harm competition in oligopolistic markets. Reliance solely on collective dominance, or indeed any other dominance concept, to deal with such mergers risks higher ongoing and systematic type II error, greater legal uncertainty, and possible contagion effects on Article 81/2. Even if the dominance concept could be

51 In addition to *Airtours*, Case No IV/M.1524, there is *Schneider/Le Grand* Case T-310/01 and *Tetra/Sidel*, Case T-5/02 and Case T-80/02.

52 The Commission (or the courts) is likely to find multilateral cases that clearly lessen competition and, in order to get the right answer, find collective dominance. This will ultimately reduce legal predictability and possibly indirectly raise type I error.

53 Event studies, while requiring careful interpretation because of how they treat cases involving remedies, may suggest that type II error is greater than type I in EU merger control See Neven and Roller (2002), although their analysis suggests that Airtours is type I.

54 It is equally interesting to note that there are no authoritative US sources pressing for a change to SLC. Rather this is an internal EU debate.

stretched to include multilateral effects, it would be undesirable to seek to extend the concept in this manner.

In determining what type of test to have for merger control, several factors are important:

- Dominance is but one part of the flip side of the coin of competition; it shares the reverse side with tacit collusion and unilateral effects. Merger control should explicitly recognise the full complement of anti-competitive possibilities, rather than try to subsume several of them under the heading of one.
- Legal language that accords with economic theory reduces unnecessary uncertainty. Conversely, the 'black box' approach with dominance on the entrance and competition on the exit militates against such clarity.
- A merger test that examines whether consumer surplus would fall should focus on the size of the change in competition, rather than on its absolute level.
- Different standards should apply to *ex ante* merger control than to *ex post* questions. It is of particular concern if concepts or decisions used in merger regulation could walk, creep or seep into Article 82 cases.

European competition policy needs to find a home for multilateral effects, and the SLC test may satisfy this need. Providing a home for multilateral effects does not mean abandoning the dominance test that has served us well. In other words, we may not need to move house, but simply build a suitable extension. This could be done retaining the current dominance test and adding a competition or welfare based test in Article 2 of the Merger Regulation. In that way, neither dominance nor competition need dominate, but rather coexist peacefully, and efficiently.

Closing Address: Review of the EC Merger Regulation – Forging a Way Ahead

Philip Lowe

Director-General for Competition, European Commission, Brussels

1. Introduction

Commissioner, ladies and gentleman, you're enormously patient. I'm the 40th speaker in this Conference but I think you share with me some degree of gratitude to everyone who has organised it, in particular to the IBA but also within the Commission to my own services, to the Merger Task Force and other services who have provided us with two days of consistently stimulating debate and discussion. So stimulating that we virtually articulated almost all the issues in merger control worldwide. At the same time we have not resolved them all. So we can guarantee a series of major merger control conferences from now until the year 2010.

However, the major objective for our participation at this Conference and our contribution to it obviously was to conclude a review of the merger control regulation and our merger practice. And that task has in my view been significantly fulfilled by this Conference as the preparation for a package of measures which Commissioner Monti as he described yesterday will be proposing to the Commission at the beginning of December.

As you know, there are a number of metaphors which have been used throughout this Conference. We've referred to the baby, the bathwater, the gap and Humpty Dumpty, and also Malcolm Nicholson has kindly reminded us that there is also the danger that the combination of these things could lead to the slippery road to hell... I can reassure you all that the objective of our package is to ensure that the baby falls into the gap, lands on Humpty Dumpty who is then drowned in the bathwater.

The second thing I want, however, to emphasise to you in a serious way is that, naturally, one conference at the end of a process of a year of consultation does not end the dialogue between the legal and business community, national authorities and the Commission on the proposed changes.

What we are preparing is a package of proposals which includes a proposed revision of the Merger Regulation, which will have to be negotiated next year with the active decision-making role of the Member States and taking into account the opinions of both the European Parliament and national parliaments. So to a certain extent this is the beginning of a long process of discussion and debate both here in Brussels and at national level. Secondly, the other two major documents in the package which are draft horizontal merger guidelines (covering also efficiencies) as well as draft best practice guidelines for merger investigations will be put out for full consultation over the same time period. So any of you who had the impression that after this year of consultation and debate, the conclusions we have reached now are already cast in stone, I can reassure you we are only beginning this real phase of debate and negotiation on the changes to be put into practice. Naturally too there are a number of things we will be able to do straightaway. After all, legislative action and best practice guidelines in conjunction with all those affected have to be discussed and debated. But we also want to reorganise internally. We want to make our own machine run better. I'll be coming to that later on. We can do some of those changes straightaway for your benefit. But we will of course continue to discuss with you actively and deeply the proposals which Mr Monti outlined in a general way yesterday and which we will finalise in December.

2. A few preliminary remarks

Now if you look back at the discussions we have had over the last two days, there are some fundamental issues which seem to be at the centre of our deliberations. They go to the heart of the values which underpin our system of merger control in Europe. This system is the expression of one of the most fundamental tenets of the European Union – that is the principle of an open market economy with free and fair competition. As the guardian of the Treaty, the Commission obviously bears primary responsibility for ensuring that the Community's policies respect those principles. And in the area of mergers, this means striking the right balance between the public interest as expressed in a competition test aimed at protecting consumer welfare from anti-competitive harm has to be balanced against the necessary private interest of investors in getting their deals done.

As Commissioner Monti has pointed out, the current exercise is the first radical appraisal of the EU Merger Regulation since its adoption in 1989 so as to equip us with a framework capable of facing up to the challenges over the next decade. I would emphasise that the philosophy we started with in 1989 – an open and transparent system developed in dialogue with business – remains of course the cornerstone of our policy. As we have this unique opportunity for legislative change, you can understand that we are going very much into the detail of what we can clarify, and do now, to make sure that our practice has a solid legal base. This is better than leaving unanswered questions to decisions of judicial review.

I would now like to do something which is always very controversial. The Commission will now attempt to summarise the discussions we have had during the last 48 hours. I hope therefore that in making this summary of our investigations together, you will not accuse me of being jury as well as investigator on this point.

3. Jurisdictional issues

On jurisdictional issues, as you know, one of the main aims of the current review process was to work out how best to allocate merger cases between the Commission and national competition authorities, in line with the twin pillars of EU merger control: the one-stop shop and the principle of subsidiarity, that is answering the question 'who does what?' in a clear and sensible way. Yesterday, I think, we were given a reminder of the strong support for a clear system, based on the one-stop shop principle, while also recognising the need to address the issue of multiple filings.

Overall, the reforms which we plan aim to offer an early window of opportunity to address requests for referrals at pre-notification stage. Our objective has therefore been to respond to the multiple filings issue by offering a 'facility' to notifying parties so that they can request cases which would normally fall under the Commission's jurisdiction to be dealt with by national authorities and vice versa. We had concluded therefore on a preliminary basis that it would be better to keep the baby in the bath tub. A 'voluntary 3+ rule' would run the risk of forum shopping while a 'mandatory 3+ rule' would pull in too many outflanking canteens. However, we note the concerns about the possible length and complexity of jurisdictional issues discussed at the pre-notification and notification stage, and we will obviously pay close attention to those aspects before finalising our proposals.

Let me just underline again however that these proposals don't intend to base competence on geographical market definition. Rather the reforms on case allocation are directed by the principles of clarity, subsidiarity and proportionality.

4. Keynote Address from the European Parliament

We then moved on yesterday to the address from Mrs Randzio-Plath, Chair of the Economic and Monetary Committee of the European Parliament. I would like to say here how much the Commission welcomes the support of the Parliament in its endeavours to improve EU merger control. She raised a number of important issues which arise in the context of a merger investigation. The protection of consumer welfare is naturally central to the Commission's analysis of mergers. In our reform proposals we want to create a new Consumer Liaison function through which we can gather consumer views.

The substantive competition test however, whichever it is, will not be designed to address the issue of the social impact of mergers. In the Commission's view, these matters are best dealt with by specific tailor-made legislation for this purpose, such as the European Works Council Directive. We have however decided to ensure that firms are specifically reminded of their obligations to respect these employee-related legislative questions in the notification provisions in Form CO. In addition, in discharging its merger control function, the Commission will continue to respect the rights of employee representatives to be heard. One particular example is their right to receive information regarding proposed divestiture commitments and comments on them.

5. Role of the Commission and the Community courts

Yesterday afternoon, we heard a view from inside the Court of First Instance on the workings of the judicial system and how it might be improved. President Vesterdorf called our attention to the respective roles of the Commission and the Court. The Commission's job is to ensure that the correct legal framework is in place to maintain competitive markets, and to develop matters of competition policy accordingly. The Court on the other hand is entrusted with the task of ensuring that the decisions taken by the Commission, are lawful, both in terms of substance and procedure. He recalls, however, that in each case the matter is decided on the facts, not on issues of institutional balance.

He outlined in particular more clearly for us the Court's view as to the discretion that exists for the Commission in the competition assessment of a merger. As far as the existing facts are concerned, I heard him say that that discretion did not exist.

However, as to the future behaviour of firms, there is some scope for discretion, related precisely to the issue which we have just heard discussed, of the balance of probabilities. The quantitative expression of expectation and likelihood, if I remember rightly from some of my own courses on statistics, is a probability. Therefore the balance of probabilities as to the likely behaviour of firms in a specific market structure is necessarily central to the Commission's reasoning and central to the Court's assessment of the decision which we take.

Whatever the outcome of individual cases might be, I personally think that the impetus given through judicial review towards developing a body of European case law in the field of merger control has to be welcomed. The common concern expressed here was nevertheless that judicial review has to be timely. President Vesterdorf made it quite clear that this could be done only with more resources for the Court. There too, the precise nature of the instance which could review merger decisions on a fast-track procedure, remains to be defined after certainly more discussion between the Commission and the Court.

On interim measures as applied in merger cases, President Vesterdorf also recognised that such relief might be available in certain circumstances, but he expressed some reservations about its feasibility in practice, especially for prohibition decisions.

Another important question of the moment, which emerged in the afternoon session yesterday, is what happens after a judgment annuls the Commission's prohibition or clearance of a merger? Article 10(5) provides that the clock on the time available for a merger starts again. But the situation remains unclear. On the one hand, the Commission's decision in *Kali und Salz* suggests that we should start from the beginning of Phase I. On the other hand, views were expressed that Article 10(5) should be reviewed to provide a more flexible means for giving effect to the Court's judgments. Here, interestingly, the afternoon panel addressed the possibilities on successful challenges of prohibition or clearance decisions. But it did not discuss what to do when the Court's judgment partially vindicates a decision and partially annuls it. Clearly, we need in the Commission to look at Article 10(5) again in the context of the merger review.

6. Judicial review: a comparison of the EU and US systems

We then went on in the afternoon session to look at the obviously thought-provoking debate which was going to go on and on about the respective merits of the European Union's administrative system and the US prosecutorial system of merger control. In the United States, the parties' rights of due process are mainly protected within the context of the judicial proceedings. By contrast, the administrative process in the European Union is characterised by extensive checks and balances throughout the investigative procedure as well as during the judicial review if it comes to that.

We then had a lot of talk about the baby and bathwater again. All I can say is that those who have advocated that the Community should overhaul its current administrative system of merger control in favour of a prosecutorial system were given some food for thought on this issue. Unlike the United States, here in the European Union, the control of concentrations with a Community dimension is entrusted to a supra-national institution. Both in legal and political terms, this entails the transfer of national sovereignty to the Commission. The *quid pro quo* for such a system has so far been a relatively transparent and by and large predictable system of merger control in consultation with Member States. By contrast, a move over to a US-style system would remove the rationale for our current checks and balances, since the Commission would only be taking a preparatory step. The rights of all interested parties would have to be respected during the judicial proceedings, as is the case today in infringement proceedings brought by the Commission against Member States which Richard Wainwright referred to in the afternoon session. Far from removing power from the Commission, such a development could in fact concentrate even greater power in the hands of the 'prosecutor' without providing any obvious countervailing benefits in terms of due process or timeliness.

7. Procedure and due process

As to the due process itself, in the last few years it has had to face increased pressure, not only due to the growth in the number of merger notifications, but also to the greater economic complexity of the cases being reviewed. Higher levels of industrial concentration have also meant the need for greater sophistication in the economic analysis contained in our recent decisions. To paraphrase Bill Kovacic from yesterday, the Merger Task Force has had to fly more planes and more sophisticated planes more often – and it has not always had an immediately available operating manual to look at. In addition, an increasingly expert private bar operating at a European level has developed a dialogue with us on the interpretation of the Merger Regulation which has led to a much more incisive application of its provisions. I know that that dialogue has to continue and I know that my colleagues in the Merger Task Force very much share my view on this. Without that dialogue we will not be able to maintain the reputation which we have built up for so many years for the efficiency and the objectivity of our decision-making process on mergers.

The review exercise, however, has revealed a real need for greater respect for the rights of all parties, be they notifying parties or third parties, in the conduct of our investigations – and for alleviating the time squeeze put on all concerned at given key moments. Commissioner Monti outlined yesterday that we shall seek to introduce greater flexibility through 'stop-the-clock' provisions to allow for more time to be spent on the conduct of investigations or the negotiation of remedies in addition to the extension of parties' rights to which I have already referred. Obviously all these extensions of deadlines will be either at the initiative or with the agreement of the notifying parties.

We also heard yesterday afternoon from the Hearing Officers, their reaffirmation of their independence from DG Competition and their explanation of the ways in which they have discharged their recent mandates. Clearly, it is not for me to comment on the way they carry out their tasks, which they do independently from DG Competition. However, I would like to make two points. First, they play an essential role throughout the investigations and decision-making process in EU competition law. They help guarantee the right to be heard and the fairness of our procedures. Secondly, I would simply like to underline that the more resources that the Hearing Officers have at their disposal, the greater the likelihood is that they will be able to exercise their mandate in the truly independent way that their mandate implies. That is why the reference Mr Monti made yesterday to giving them extra resources is not an idle one. It is something which we will follow up by the end of this year.

We referred too to another external check on the work of the Commission in the merger field and that is the role of the Advisory Committee. Clearly every Member State is not in a position, either from a policy point of view or from a resource point of view, to follow every stage of every investigation carried out by an administration at European level. However, we do feel that it is necessary to increase the role of the named 'rapporteur' or 'discussant' of the Member State who is responsible for following the course of investigation in the second stage. We intend to involve that discussant right from the beginning of the second phase process to ensure that they can give an informed and independent view to other Member State authorities in the consultative committee. We feel too that in that light he will have to play a key role with the Commission in planning the organisation of a hearing and planning the organisation of the discussion the Consultative Committee which can draw out and concentrate on the key issues to be addressed at those meetings. That is a very important function too in the context of the growing and closer network of national competition authorities with the Commission. I would hope that we would also be involving those national competition authorities who have very in-depth knowledge of particular sectors due to recent cases and due to particular problems in their own countries. They too would play an active upstream role in the preparation of the Advisory Committee.

8. Substantive test

Having listened to three sessions on the substantive test, efficiencies and on forms of dominance today, I have to say that I might be recommending to Mario Monti that we do not just need a Chief Economist in DG Competition. We also probably need a Chief Behavioural Psychologist – and maybe a Chief Psychiatrist to help us in the period after we have actually heard from our economists what their analysis of a market is. However, I personally feel that the debate has been as good and incisive as any we have had so far throughout the world on this issue. My sense of the discussion today is that the focus is on what legal framework we put in place to cover the economic targets of our competition concerns. There now appears to be a growing consensus, if not on the actual scope of those competitive concerns, at least on the actual and potential objects of those concerns. We have heard a variety of vocabularies used to describe the effects to which we wish to pay attention, whether unilateral or multilateral, whether attached to a situation of single dominance or left somewhat in limbo waiting for them to be attached to the overall competition assessment of a case! Ironically, the more complex our market investigations become, the wider the scope of the tests which we may potentially want to apply if it was free for us to establish a new test each time we had a merger investigation. And naturally the more scenarios we want to cover, the greater the likelihood is that specific descriptions of market structures do not necessarily lead at the beginning to a presumption of pro-competitive or anti-competitive behaviour. We have to wait for our full analysis before we arrive at the situation of saying 'yes, this looks like a difficult case from the point of view of competition and the consumer'.

I would like to emphasise that this does present us with a problem as an authority, particularly as a supranational authority. The work of an antitrust authority is, after all, based on a mandate from democratic institutions which expect that authority to behave within the limits of the mandate given to it. Equally too, those who have allowed the legislation to be put in place and those who control the exercise of our application of that legislation wish to have the assurance that we are applying it in a predictable way and a transparent way. Hence our need and our conviction that we could never move forward at the present time without clear guidelines as well as a clear test. As to the clarity of the test, I think that Kevin O'Sullivan among others, was right to say, that before we move to a future test, we have to carry out to a certain extent a cost-benefit analysis of any change. As Commissioner Monti outlined yesterday, we want to change Article 2, we want to introduce new recitals to the article and we will produce new guidelines. Together these changes should, in our view, produce what John Vickers referred to as a somewhat bifurcated Article 2 where we, in addition to the existing dominance provision, also interpret dominance to cover the kinds of behaviour in non-collusive oligopolistic situations which we referred to earlier. That change will be limited to the Merger Regulation and should not affect Article 82. In the course of our final discussions on that proposal, we will not simply be looking at the substance of the question but also the process by which we arrive at a final and good result for merger control in the European Union.

We will of course be negotiating this change to Article 2 over the next year. In a wider political context in which the issue of the limits to the Commission's powers will have to be also a consideration, we believe the change we are proposing goes in the right direction with the greatest chance of obtaining legal coverage of the gap. In reply to those who believe that there is a simple way to cover the gap, our only cautious note is that we need to make a proposal which has the greatest chance of being accepted and has the greatest chance of getting to the result we want with the minimum degree of disturbance of the application of the existing law.

9. Efficiencies

I felt in the discussion on efficiencies that we were less on ground which could suddenly break out into gaps or bathwater! As my colleagues explained this morning, there are reasons why we did not have, at the beginning of the application of the Merger Control Regulation, an explicit role for efficiencies – in particular the history surrounding the adoption of the Merger Regulation and the subsequent commitment by the Commission to make it clear that merger policy was about maintaining competitive markets and not an instrument of industrial policy. We hope to clarify in the horizontal merger guidelines what our policy and practice will be. What is clear however is that efficiencies need to be reflected, if necessary, right from the outset of a merger investigation, in the initial competitive assessment, at least as far as static efficiencies are concerned. In the final assessment, the parties will have the ultimate burden of the proof, including presentation of more dynamic efficiencies which are less easy to quantify and less easy to prove.

10. Draft Commission Notice on the Assessment of Dominance

What do all these changes imply for the way we manage DG Competition? How do I see, under the authority of Commissioner Monti, my role as Director General for DG Competition and my role – hopefully not for too long – as Acting Deputy Director General for mergers. I think there are three major objectives:

First of all, I have to ensure that we have the maximum amount of internal debate of all the issues, legal and economic, before they leave No 70 Joseph II. The premium for me will be on giving a case-team informed and timely guidance and, through the panel system, allowing the team to test its own argumentation before it becomes public. This does not mean that we would adopt a 'timid' approach towards competition enforcement. On the contrary, I would expect that we would continue to define and redefine the enforcement boundaries of the Community's competition policy through cases based on a thorough and informed assessment of the factual underpinning and the strength of the legal argumentation. In this sense, we will be looking for the deference of the Court in the way in which it was referred to yesterday.

Secondly, as senior management of DG Competition, I and my colleagues have to engage in the strategic policy choices which are taken in individual decisions on cases. This engagement means giving policy guidance and support on the one hand and, finally and necessarily, taking personal responsibility for the proposals we make to the Commissioner and the rest of the Commission. I would emphasise that this means that no member of DG Competition – from the case handlers negotiating remedies with notifying parties in merger cases, to case managers steering the conduct of an investigation – no member is acting alone. It is impossible in my view for the head of an antitrust authority to make some artificial distinction between management of policy and management of administration. With scarce resources and competing priorities, our senior management decisions set the parameters for any case investigation. Policy determines resource management and resource management determines the success of policy.

My third objective is to represent and communicate the policy we have both in substantive and procedural terms. Obviously that is a clear and normal task but as we are also supposed to be ensuring fair competition, it is essential too that the Director General and the Deputy are an expression of the openness, fairness but firmness of our own attitude to any individual negotiation, especially in relation to what was referred to earlier as the neutral aspect of our approach to merger investigations. Our policy concerns have to be given a full airing and they also have to be given the full backing of the Director General when they are proposed by the case teams, ensuring that we deliver our views in as authoritative and as responsible a manner. But power has to be exercised with caution, even when we are in a situation of a need for firmness and speed. Shakespeare actually wrote a sonnet on this. I had to get in this reference because John Fingleton wanted me to make a literary reference! In sonnet 94 he wrote:

> 'They that have power to hurt, and will do none
> that do not do the thing they most do show,
> they rightly do inherit heavens graces,
> and husband nature's riches from expense,
> ...
> others but the stewards of their excellence!'

meaning that the exercise of our responsibility must reflect the high degree of financial and political engagement of all those involved in a merger transaction at European or global level.

In working to these three objectives, there are several important issues. Recent debates have understandably centred on the issue of checks and balances, especially in relation to the role of the Court *vis-à-vis* the Commission. But I want to emphasise it would be wrong to see what we envisage for our internal decision-making process as adding yet more bureaucratic checks. In my administrative experience, that is a system which simply does not work. A successful administration relies on the commitment and motivation of its corps of highly qualified officials. They have to be given guidance, attention and support. Any case handler or case-team is already working under the constraint of relatively complex administrative procedures and under tight deadlines. Increasing the breadth and rigour of internal debate on cases as well as policy issues must therefore take account of this.

That is why I will be putting forward proposals for further reorganisation of DG Competition later this year in agreement with Mario Monti. Two of the principal aims of this reorganisation will be to increase flexibility in the allocation of staff to merger and antitrust cases and to strengthen our in-house sectoral expertise. However, as the Commissioner has already said, we also want to create a unit devoted to what I call decision scrutiny and litigation. It would be directly attached to the Director General and built on the role which some of the services of our policy Directorate play today. This 'Scrutiny Office' would follow cases throughout their development and organise panels at key moments, for example before Statements of Objection are issued and on final decisions in the second phase of a merger investigation. Perhaps in these days of discussion of 'judicial panels', confusion over a new beast – the devil's advocate panel – was inevitable. I will do my best to clarify that as things go along.

It is clear that the organisation of a panel for each and every case will not be necessary. The Scrutiny Office should have in my opinion the authority to make that judgment under the guidance of the Director General having consulted, where necessary, the Commissioner. However, the panels themselves will not just consist of officials whose objective is to question, ie the devil's advocate role, but also to streamline our internal systems and remove procedures which are too formalistic. This will be in the interest not only of case teams but also of parties for whom timely decisions are crucial.

As to the involvement of third parties, there is no doubt that their rights must be protected. And as Mario Monti said yesterday, we are addressing this issue in relation to access to file, in relation to normal best practice of state of play meetings and by parties' capacity to ask for additional meetings where ideas can be confronted, especially prior to the Statement of Objections. All this is in addition to their formal rights of defence as protected by the Hearing Officer. But we nevertheless have to draw a line in the sand between participation in discussions which are essentially contradictory and discussions which are aimed at improving the quality of the Commission's decisions. I therefore believe that it would be appropriate that the Scrutiny Office might participate in meetings with the parties, and indeed that the Scrutiny Office would participate in hearings and other contradictory meetings. However, it would not be sensible, and it would be mixing up the roles, if we gave the impression that the panels existed for direct discussion with the parties. The parties will continue to work and negotiate with the case teams who work under our responsibility. The panels will be established to guide, educate, improve and contest – without threat – the ideas of the case teams. In that sense, they are also good for the parties.

There was discussion yesterday about the future role of a Chief Economist. I see him or her having three essential tasks. In the first place, he or she should provide us with guidance on methodological issues of economics and econometrics in terms of the manner in which established policy is applied. Secondly, he or she should be involved in providing general guidance in individual cases, upstream right at the beginning of the case and ongoing from that moment. And thirdly, in complex cases, there should be a possibility of secondment of a member of the Chief Economist's team to work in the case-teams.

As far as reporting lines are concerned, the Chief Economist would report directly to the Director General. In this way, should there be a divergence of views on any given issue, it will be picked up quickly and at a sufficiently senior level within the organisation so that decisions can be made in the proper way. His or her advice would also remain on the table and be documented independently of the final proposal to the Commissioner and thereafter to the College of Commissioners.

I have also heard the view expressed here that we should instead move to a system more directly based on US experience. At the present time, dividing the troops we have on the ground into the lawyer camp on the one hand and the economist camp on the other seems to be unrealistic.. There are doubtless many good things to say about it and sufficient numbers of those here today expressing that view. But I am convinced that multidisciplinary case teams is the way forward, supplemented by an in-house scrutiny and the independent view of a Chief Economist who is eminent in the academic field and on secondment to the Commission. He/she would provide a very important contribution to the rigour and objectivity of our economic analysis.

As far as the work of senior management directly is concerned on strategic issues and resources, I want to make it clear that the availability of the Director General and his Deputies for discussion with parties is not only useful but, in many cases, essential. One of my predecessors as Director of the Merger Task Force described his policy with regard to contacts with parties as 'come early, come often'. It is a view which I subscribed to then, as I do in my new role as Director General, subject to the hours of the day. However, the reason over the years why successive Directors of the Merger Task Force, and particularly Götz Drauz, have been able to develop effective and efficient management of the merger process is by giving the maximum amount of responsibility with the minimum amount of bureaucracy to case teams who are dealing with any particular case. I want to preserve that element, that philosophy inside the Merger Task Force and extend it to the rest of DG Competition. But of course that goes hand in hand with the need for senior management to give strategic direction, to set priorities, to test the rigour, objectiveness of the final decisions and exceptionally, where necessary, intervene directly.

Finally, the issue of resources is a vital one. We cannot: (1) bring in additional economic expertise; (2) enhance sectoral expertise; (3) extend the rights of the parties, with access to files and other changes, without making some choices about how we deploy our own scarce staff. And I do not rule out some overall increase in staff. But we will also need to manage our existing resources even more efficiently. Our internal reorganisation will have to address this issue. The 'first choice' (if I can use that expression in a slightly more pleasant context) is made for us by legislation: we have to deal with notified mergers, state aids and complaints in an effective and efficient way, to the standards set in our jurisprudence, but hopefully applied with some degree of proportionality and common sense. That may mean sometimes that we cannot deal with all the anti-competitive concerns which even one case throws up. I cannot personally see how we can avoid some degree of concentration on the issues in a case which solve the most important competition problems, and have a credible and preventive effect, while leaving others without further investigation.

The second even more difficult choice we have to make is how to couple our obligation to handle notifications in certain areas with the need to devote resources to our *ex officio* priorities: for example cartel investigations or abuse of market power in antitrust. To do this, as I have said, we need to develop a much more flexible use of resources across all our departments. And we also need to examine closely with national authorities how our enforcement priorities can be combined to maximum effect with theirs.

11. Conclusion

I hope by this last explanation of the seriousness with which we regard this merger review and the need for further changes in DG Competition, you have gained the sense of importance and urgency which we have attached to the results of this Conference and the importance and urgency which we attach to the implementation of the proposals which we finally decide on. I hope that in future conferences of this kind, including not just on merger control but hopefully one day I will be able to change the field of my own concentration to other aspects of competition policy rather than mergers. I look forward to that further debate with you, I thank you most sincerely for the contribution you have made and I thank you finally for your patience until this late hour on a Friday night.